FRAGILE STRUCTURES

Harper's
MAGAZINE PRESS

HARPER'S MAGAZINE PRESS
Published in Association with Harper & Row
New York

Peter Amory Bradford

FRAGILE STRUCTURES:

A Story of Oil Refineries, National Security, and the Coast of Maine

Grateful acknowledgment is made for permission to reprint the following:

Excerpts from *The Greening of America* by Charles A. Reich. Copyright © 1970 by Charles A. Reich. Reprinted by permission of Random House, Inc.

Excerpts from *Papers on the War* by Daniel Ellsberg reprinted by permission of Simon & Schuster, Inc.

Excerpts from *North Toward Home* by Willie Morris reprinted by permission of Houghton Mifflin Company.

John Cole's editorial which appeared in the April 4, 1969, and February 26, 1971, issues of the Maine *Times* reprinted by permission of the author.

Ted Brook's column *From the Oil Desk*—A Letter to Major Firms, which appeared in the June 25, 1969, issue of The Wichita *Eagle* reprinted by permission of The Wichita Eagle & Beacon, Knight-Ridder publications.

Excerpt from "Is the Oil Shortage Real?" by M. A. Adelman reprinted from *Foreign Policy* 9. Copyright 1972 by National Affairs, Inc.

Designed by Dorothy Schmiderer

Library of Congress Cataloging in Publication Data

Bradford, Peter.
  Fragile structures.
  Includes index.
    1. Petroleum industry and trade—Maine. 2. Free ports and zones—Maine. I. Title.
HD9567.M3B7 1975   338.4'7'6655309741   72-12096
ISBN 0-06-120450-1

75 76 77 78 79 10 9 8 7 6 5 4 3 2 1

Contents

praised in Wyoming—The King Resources oil terminal plan appears in Portland, sponsored by an Olympic sailor—The Machias Bay refinery is moved inland—Senator Russell Long forgets the Civil War—A dozen leading petroleum economists agree in vain

Some Approximate Numbers

A barrel of crude oil
—contains 42 gallons, weighs 1/7 of a ton
—can be refined into some 21 gallons of gasoline, 10.5 gallons of home heating oil, and 10.5 gallons of industrial oil. The exact product mix varies widely among types of crude and types of refineries.
—when spilled covers between .5 and 3 square miles of water and can poison perhaps 500 pounds of clams along with most lobsters, fin fish, seals, or birds who chance to come in contact with it
—contains enough energy to run a typical home furnace for four days of winter use in the Northeast
—gives off about one pound of particulate matter and 6.5 to 20 pounds of sulfur oxides. These wastes along with nitrogen and carbon monoxide contribute to lung cancer, heart trouble, respiratory diseases, eye discomfort, metal, stone, and paint corrosion
—would generate 500 kilowatt hours of electricity, assuming a 100 percent efficient generating and transmitting system. This is enough to run an average American home for a month, or an average Russian home for five months. Given the actual energy losses involved in power generation and distribution, a barrel of oil delivers about 150 kilowatt hours of electricity
—is the energy equivalent of 460 pounds of coal, 5600 cubic feet of natural gas, one third of a cord of wood
—is 1/16,700,000 of the amount used in the U.S. in a day in 1973
—is 1/9,000,000 of the amount produced in the U.S. in a day in 1973
—is 1/55,400,000 of the amount used in the world in a day in 1973
—is 1/100,000,000,000 of the oil produced in the U.S. to date
—is 1/350,000,000,000 of the known U.S. reserves and 1/1,000,000,-000,000 of the probable total U.S. reserves but is only 1/39,000,000,000 of the oil that can be produced from currently installed equipment at known U.S. fields and 1/80,000,000,000 of the amount recoverable from known U.S. fields with maximum applications of current technology

On each of these problems are we not sort of meeting ourselves going around the barn?

Senator Philip Hart (D.–Michigan),
Governmental Intervention in Market Mechanism,
Part I, p. 1760, Subcommittee on Antitrust and
Monopoly, March 26, 1970

The intent of the project is to examine the complex of problems troubling men of all nations: poverty in the midst of plenty; degradation of the environment; loss of faith in institutions; uncontrolled urban spread; insecurity of employment; alienation of youth; rejection of traditional values; and inflation and other economic disruptions. . . . It is the predicament of mankind that man can perceive the problematique, yet despite his considerable knowledge and skills, he does not understand the origins, significance, and interrelationships of its many components and is thus unable to devise an effective response. This failure occurs in large part because we continue to examine single items in the problematique without understanding that the whole is more than the sum of its parts, that change in one element means change in the other.

Dennis Meadows et al., *The Limits to Growth*

The Limits to Growth is best summarized not as a rediscovery of the laws of nature but as a rediscovery of the oldest maxim of computer science: garbage in, garbage out. . . . Critical to the model is the notion that growth creates stresses (on the environment, on mineral and agricultural resources) which multiply geometrically. . . . While the world model hypothesizes exponential growth for our future industrial and agricultural activities, it places arbitrary nonexponential limits on the technological progress that might accommodate them.

Peter Passell, Leonard Ross, and Marc Roberts,
The New York Times Book Review, April 9, 1972

. . . this most unhappy people, strong believers in arithmetic, never expected to be confronted with the algebra of their history.

James Baldwin,
The New York Review of Books, January 7, 1971

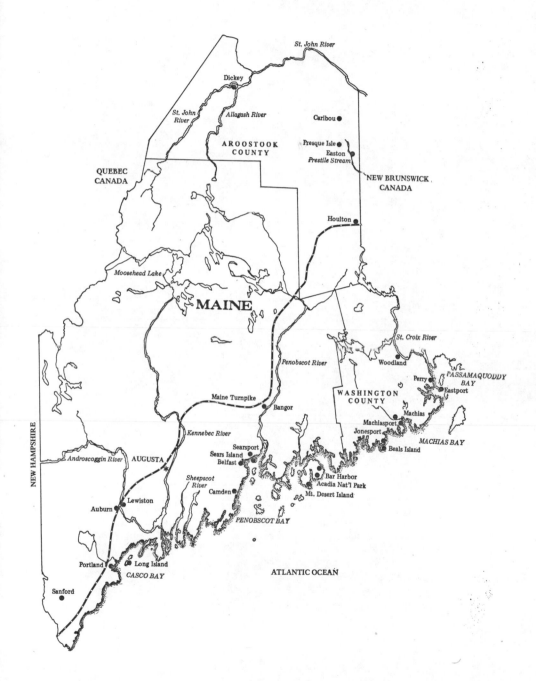

St. John River

Dickey

St. John
River

Allagash River

Caribou

AROOSTOOK
COUNTY

Presque Isle
Easton
Prestile Stream

QUEBEC
CANADA

NEW BRUNSWICK
CANADA

Houlton

Moosehead Lake

MAINE

St. Croix River

Penobscot River

Woodland

Perry

PASSAMAQUODDY
BAY

Eastport

WASHINGTON
COUNTY

Machias

Maine Turnpike

Bangor

Machiasport

Jonesport

NEW HAMPSHIRE

Kennebec River

Searsport

Sears Island

Belfast

Beals Island

MACHIAS BAY

Androscoggin River

AUGUSTA

Bar Harbor
Acadia Nat'l Park

Sheepscot
River

Camden

Mt. Desert Island

Auburn

Lewiston

Portland

Long Island

CASCO BAY

PENOBSCOT BAY

ATLANTIC OCEAN

Sanford

1: Headwaters

There rolls the deep where grew the tree,
  O earth, what changes hast thou seen!
  There, where the long street roars, hath been
The stillness of the central sea.

The hills are shadows, and they flow
  From form to form, and nothing stands;
  They melt like mist, the solid lands,
Like clouds they shape themselves and go.
                    Tennyson, *In Memoriam*

Roll on, Columbia, roll on.
Roll on, Columbia, roll on.
Your power is turning our darkness to dawn.
Roll on, Columbia, roll on.
                    Woody Guthrie,
                    for the Bonneville Power Administration, 1941

The alternatives that could have saved Glen Canyon are still unused. Fossil
fuels, for one . . .
                    David Brower, *The Place No One Knew*, 1963

THE ENERGY HAPPENINGS in any given year are predetermined during
the preceding decade, generally shaped during the most recent century,
geologically molded in eons. There can be no daredevil rescues, no
cathartic high noons. That is why it is so important that in October,
1968, the Foreign Trade Zones Board, a hybrid federal body consisting
of the Secretaries of Commerce, the Treasury, and the Army, sent the
late N. Norman Engleberg, a hearing examiner, to Maine to take testimony on the state's application for a foreign-trade zone in Portland
and a subzone containing the world's largest oil refinery 150 miles to
the east at Machiasport.
    The hearing lasted three days. Most of the testimony focused on
United States policies restricting the importing of foreign oil, a subject that Engleberg had ruled irrelevant at the outset. The prestige of

1

those who ignored the ruling persuaded him not to enforce it. On one side, governors and Congressmen from the six New England states wanted permission to import the oil necessary to run the refinery. In opposition, governors or their representatives from the Rocky Mountain and Southwestern states that produced or hoped to produce oil and natural gas wanted no inexpensive foreign competition. The opposition also included several dozen representatives of major oil companies, minor oil companies, oil producers' associations, and oil refiners' associations. Four residents of the Machiasport area testified, their testimony occupying 3 percent of the hearing record and taking a total of thirty minutes.

The most prestigious opponent was Louisiana Congressman Hale Boggs, then majority whip in the House of Representatives, later House majority leader. Congressman Boggs, like Lyndon Johnson, had come to terms with the oil industry in his home state in order to survive a relatively liberal record on civil rights and other domestic issues. His position and ability combined into one of the dozen most powerful oil-policy voices in American public life, a voice on this occasion so incoherent that it would be an injustice to his otherwise admirable career to assert that it was typical of him. He had had too much to drink.

After the hearings, the Foreign Trade Zones Board took the matter under advisement. The board never reached a decision, and it never will. The roots of that impasse, all ignored by the board, include Maine coastal history, national oil policy, environmentalism, economic growth, and supertankers. Their unrelated origins require that these elements initially be considered separately. They will converge after the 1968 hearings are described more fully. Before then the reader may think them unrelated, but that is the mistake that we all made at the time.

Within five years of the hearings, oil and energy shortages had engulfed industries then promoting endless consumption. Oil shortages threatened to mortgage the American economy to the very Arabs (and Venezuelans and Indonesians and Nigerians and Canadians) from whom the oil industry then claimed to have been protecting us. The specter of deepening energy scarcity was said to justify raising prices, forgiving taxes, curtailing recently achieved environmental protections, and tolerating noncompetitive behavior in the energy industries. A few incidents in the 1960–70 decade are signposts for any inquiry into what went wrong. The Machiasport oil refinery is one of them.

Machiasport is a small Maine fishing village, actually a confederation of the four smaller villages of Machiasport itself, Larrabee, Starboard, and Bucks Harbor. Its 800 people are mostly fishermen or their families. The largest employers are a small seasonal fish cannery and an Air Force radar station.

The town is a Florida-shaped peninsula running seven miles south from hill to valley to hill to a sea next interrupted by Venezuela. Though some of the peninsula was once extensively farmed, it has gone so far to forest that only 15 percent of the land is kept clear. Beyond the point where the last road falters at a stream bed traversable only at low tide, a few houses are strung out half a mile to the land's end. Some 200 yards east of them rises Starboard Island, a hilltop in the sea with a cleared western slope on which four locally owned summer homes rise away from the shore. At low tide, Starboard Island is connected to the mainland by a strip of rocky beach. The high tide severs it. Half a mile east of Starboard Island, Stone Island rises gently to its eastern edge and disappears over a cliff into waters 100 feet deep. The island is heavily forested and is fogbound part of most summer days. It has been owned by a series of men who have never lived there, and its only permanent residents have been ospreys.

To construct a tanker terminal on Stone Island—its pipelines running across a causeway to Starboard Island, then humpbacked over Starboard to massive silver storage tanks beside the pipes and towers of a refinery humming among the unpruned apple trees and aldered fields of a peninsula as distant as possible from large East Coast oil markets—would seem demented, but Stone Island is one of fewer than ten locations in the United States where the water next to shore is more than fifty feet deep.

This exceptional water depth is the product of some of the same geological processes that had buried oil deposits 300 million years before they created the coast of Maine. The Maine and Canadian maritime coasts, unlike those to the south, bore the full weight of the most recent icecap. In the last million years, the advancing glaciers forced the earth hundreds of feet down into itself. When the glaciers retreated, the seas of the Pleistocene epoch flooded the valleys of the Pliocene. At a rate averaging less than a foot per century, the former land has struggled back toward the surface, and the more than 2000 islands that punctuate the Maine coast are actually submerged hills and ledges, sculpted once by the rivers, again by the glaciers, and now by the sea.

Along a few Maine and Canadian fault lines where erosion resistance differed dramatically over short distances, the islands or the mainland have been sheared away to water depths of a hundred feet within a stone's throw of dry land. The ocean bottom south of Maine, spared the full weight of the Ice Age and with differently arrayed fault lines, offered no harbors more than seventy feet deep.

To imagine the trappings of fifty years of oil commerce laid over those valleys drowned unlamented for a thousand centuries is to comprehend the historical scale that a conservationist has in mind when he objects to defining progress in terms of industrial development. Pointing out that if time since the Creation were to be treated as six days, the two centuries since the Industrial Revolution would be one fortieth of a second and the life of an oil refinery one quarter of that, the conservationist argues that those who project inevitabilities from trends in the fortieth of a second "are considered normal, but they are stark raving mad."[1]* He is less likely to mention that the Maine coast as we know it has endured less than two minutes on this clock and is no older than man.

Maine's deep water, like any natural resource, was without monetary value until man found a use for it. That use emerged from a growing U.S. demand for foreign oil coupled with the construction of a new generation of oil tankers which, like floating Empire State buildings, were as long as four football fields and which needed water up to eighty feet deep. Because powerful groups preferred to see the United States rely on its (and their) own oil, coal, and natural gas, the development of an eastern Maine oil port needed two unnatural resources controlled by the U.S. government—permission to bring the oil in and a foreign-trade zone in which to refine it.

A foreign-trade zone is a small area of United States soil treated for customs purposes as another country. Foreign raw materials can be shipped in, blended with American goods and labor, and imported into the United States or exported into the world market. Customs duties are paid only on the finished product, not on the original materials. The goods produced from tariff-exempt raw materials are better able to

* Superior numbers refer to Source Notes beginning on p. 371.

compete in foreign markets, while the jobs and capital investment remain in the United States.

At the time of the Maine application, nine such zones existed in the
United States. No application had ever been denied, for Congress had
intended that zones be easily obtained. A mere showing that foreign
commerce would be generated was all that the law required. Maine
clearly contemplated considerable foreign commerce, for the Occidental Petroleum Company wanted to use the proposed Machiasport subzone to build an oil refinery that would have taken in 300,000 barrels
of oil every day and put out 100,000 barrels of home heating oil,
75,000 barrels of low-sulfur industrial oil, and 125,000 barrels of jet
fuel and naphtha, a product used in the manufacture of plastics, synthetic rubber, and other petrochemicals.

The oil would have come to Machiasport from Libya and Venezuela,
mostly in supertankers capable of carrying 300,000 tons. These vessels
could carry as much as 1500 *Mayflowers* or 20 *Queen Elizabeth IIs*.
Any one of them could carry 30 percent more than the entire 746-
vessel U.S. whaling fleet of 1846. They are ten times as large as the
largest tankers used during the 1940s, five times as large as those of
the 1950s, and almost three times as large as the 120,000-ton *Torrey
Canyon* (itself technically a supertanker, since the use of the word
begins at about 100,000 tons), which went aground on a British reef in
1967 and involved British and French beaches in the world's most
notorious oil spill.

To the international oil industry and to the oil consumer, the supertanker was benign. The 1956 Suez crisis had closed the Canal and
added 5000 miles to the distance from Arab oil fields to the United
States and Europe. To carry the same weekly amount of oil twice as far
required twice as much tanker capacity, which is why several tanker
owners are today among the richest men in the world. The only alternatives, higher prices and less dependence on oil, were unacceptable
in the United States and Western Europe. The resulting demand for
more and bigger tankers stimulated the construction of ships of 100,000,
then 200,000, then 300,000 deadweight tons.

The new (250,000 tons and up) supertankers made their first
voyages in 1968. They were able to move Middle Eastern oil around
Africa for as much as $1.20 per barrel less than their predecessors. To
an average individual consumer of oil, this meant a possible saving of
six cents per gallon or perhaps thirty-nine dollars per year. To a power
company like Consolidated Edison of New York, which burns 50

million barrels per year, the saving would have been $60 million. An oil company operating a 300,000 b/d (barrel per day) refinery could save $126 million per year. A nation concerned about its balance of payments and importing a million barrels per day by supertanker* might save $438 million annually.†

In 1968 the U.S. oil-producing states, the oil producers independent of the major oil companies, and the U.S. divisions of the major international oil companies regarded supertankers the way Carry Nation would have regarded improved whiskey bottles. To them, cheap oil was a menace and cheap foreign oil an abomination. As long as supertankers not only carried foreign oil but actually made it cheaper still, they had no place in the domestic oilman's America. Their possible encroachment at Machiasport was to inspire such oil-state Senators as Gordon Allott of Colorado and Clifford Hansen of Wyoming to defend the Maine coastal environment with more passion than they had ever expended on threatened terrain in their home states.

To conservationists of longer standing, 300,000-ton supertankers were to the *Torrey Canyon* what a nervous breakdown is to a nightmare, but in October, 1968, the environment was not of broad national concern. Earth Day was nineteen months away. As strong a conservationist as folksinger Pete Seeger had just reissued Woody Guthrie's "Roll on, Columbia," a celebration of the river-plugging dams of the Bonneville Power Administration, and David Brower's defenses of the Colorado River had barely saved the Sierra Club from further defeats like those sustained at Hetch Hetchy and Glen Canyon, two lovely valleys now damned and flooded deeper than the floor of Machias Bay. Hetch Hetchy was a smaller twin to Yosemite Valley itself and a part of what was even then Yosemite National Park. After a ten-year struggle that split the Sierra Club into preservationist and multiple-use factions, Congress decided in 1914 to dam it to provide both a recreational lake and low-cost water and power for San Francisco. The recreational hope died when the power and water demands caused the water level to fluctuate sharply; the cheap power did not survive the

* In 1968 the United States imported 2.5 million barrels per day, but 2 million came from Canada or Venezuela and would not have moved in supertankers.
† These figures are maximums. They are probably overstated in at least three significant ways. First, the $1.20-per-barrel savings are approximate and would be too high for Libyan, Nigerian, or Indonesian oil, which need not have gone around South Africa. Second, the full savings are not likely to have been passed on. Third, because some import costs would have been repatriated in any case (to American stockholders in tanker-owning companies, for example), the supertanker savings do not translate into a 100 percent balance-of-payments gain.

subsequent transfer of the water rights from governmental to private hands.

Glen Canyon was being visited by fewer than 500 people a year during the 1950s when Congress approved Bureau of Reclamation plans to make it a reservoir for Arizona and Southern California. More people have enjoyed it since its burial than ever saw it firsthand. This is in small part because its new tenant, Lake Powell, is now visited by thousands of motorboaters and water skiers who frolic above the vanished cascades of Cascade Canyon and the submerged roof of the former Cathedral in the Desert, almost within reach of the once majestically distant underarch of Rainbow Bridge. It is in larger part because a postmortem Sierra Club book entitled *The Place No One Knew* was to make of the Glen Canyon Dam a kind of environmental death camp, a birthplace of the "Never Again" determination that prevented construction of three other Colorado River dams and became a cornerstone of what is now called the ecological movement. Under the banners of that movement, many opposed the oil-burning "Four Corners" power plants in New Mexico, which others said were necessitated in part by the absence of power from the aborted Colorado River dams.

David Brower's factually dubious defenses of those three surviving Colorado River canyons succeeded, but his "Should we also flood the Sistine Chapel so tourists can get nearer the ceiling?" ads cost the Sierra Club its tax exemption, and, because the unavailing gentility of the Hetch Hetchy struggle still predominated in the club membership, Brower lost his job as well. In early 1969 he was to form Friends of the Earth (FOE) with the aid of a $40,000 contribution from the chairman of the board of Atlantic Richfield. FOE, unhampered by aspirations toward tax-exempt status, was to join in filing the suits that enjoined the Trans-Alaska Pipeline and increased the pressure to meet U.S. needs with oil imported in supertankers, whose construction in the United States was subsequently delayed by a suit brought by a newly emboldened Sierra Club.

Although visited more frequently than Hetch Hetchy or Glen Canyon, Machiasport is beyond Maine's tourist zone. It is deep in Washington County, remote by geography, climate and history. The nation's easternmost county, reduced in 1839 to a boot-shape half the size of Connecticut, is all trees and water. From the south the unbroken Atlantic, gray or blue with the weather, fragments into bays and passages among the forested islands and peninsulas that shield the coast. On the

east the St. Croix River and Passamaquoddy Bay, the latter named for
the Indian tribe whose 1500 surviving members live on two reservations
near its shores, separate the county from the Canadian province of
New Brunswick. The bay's nine-mile mouth is broken by more than
fifty islands, some hardly larger than the herring weirs they shelter.
The county's salt-water rim contains some twenty fishing harbors,
speckled with lobster boats and trawlers that together do not have the
carrying capacity of the *Torrey Canyon.*

The inland county is a blend of lakes, rivers, and forest. From a
small plane at moderate height, it seems a pine-green rug with water
patterns. There are only a dozen asphalt roads, a few cleared fields, and
occasional towns of no more than 500 people at former sawmill or
tannery sites. Moose and bear are common, the latter inevitable at
town dumps. Four of the rivers offer most of the Atlantic salmon fishing left in the United States. They drain a land that is gradual but
rarely flat. Approached slowly by road through clearings in which
peeling billboard sunrises proclaim entry to "The Sunrise County,"
Washington County's second-growth woods are still imposing enough
to seem, like the land itself when viewed from the open ocean, too
unbroken to permit passage.

Had the United States been settled from west to east, the interior of
Washington County would almost certainly be uninhabited today.
The county was not permanently settled until 1763, when some
twenty refugees from a season of drought and fire in southern Maine
arrived to cut fodder on the marshes and set up a sawmill. Machias
Bay's only previous water-borne commerce had been fishing and
piracy. The piracy provided the area's first link to Libya, for it was
the example of the North African and Madagascar pirate domains that
inspired an American pirate named Samuel Bellamy to seek remote
headquarters from which to harass North Atlantic shipping. At the
beginning of the eighteenth century he fortified a corner of Machias
Bay, only to be captured and hanged in Massachusetts during his first
search for women to cohabit his kingdom to be.

Machias Bay reverted to wilderness and visiting Indians. Fifty years
later, in 1763, the Treaty of Paris terminated French claims to the
area, and several sawmilling settlements took root in the decade before
the Revolutionary War. The pioneers, unlike those who settled the rest
of the East Coast, were American born. They were self-reliant, necessarily oriented toward their own families and communities rather than
the Massachusetts Bay Colony or the Crown. The closest colonial gov-

ernment was in Boston; the seat of the real authority was London. Both
were more nuisance than support. The King laid a frequently ignored
claim to the finest trees for ship masts, and the British gave so little
weight to local laws and land claims that secure homesteading was
difficult. The independent nature of the settlers magnified these
grievances and the others that vexed the rest of the colonies.

When the Revolution broke out, commercial and personal ties to
Massachusetts prevailed over proximity to Canada, and the eastern
Maine settlements (population under 2000) joined the rebellion.
Machias Bay was the scene of the first two naval engagements of the
war as the colonists surprised and captured a British frigate and four
smaller ships.

During the century after the Revolution, coastal Washington County
grew beyond a frontier economy and prospered.[2] New settlers arrived,
and the vast inland timber resources were harvested, floated down the
Machias River, milled, and exported. Shipyards and a rail line were
built on the Machiasport Peninsula. By 1880, there were three separate
yards in Machiasport alone, but although their combined years of
operation were more than a century, they turned out less than half the
carrying capacity of a single supertanker.

The only major interruptions to coastal prosperity came during the
War of 1812 and the Civil War, when traditional export markets were
cut off and New England's prosperity was temporarily sacrificed to the
security of the nation. Before and during the War of 1812, the Embargo and Nonintercourse policies of the federal government halted
virtually all shipbuilding and lumber sales. Eastern Maine responded
with a smuggling fervor unmatched in the United States until Prohibition.

After the Civil War, metal began to replace wood in ship construction, and promising rock formations replaced whales under the pointed
implements of men seeking oil. The Erie Canal network and then the
railroads drained New England ports and farms. As the demand for
Maine lumber declined, only the fishing industry continued to thrive.
Four fish canneries were built in the three Machiasport villages. The
neighboring towns of Jonesport and Beals Island became major fishing
communities, but fishing and fish processing alone could not sustain
the manufacturing economy, which had been based on lumber, and all
of Maine, particularly the coast, experienced a gradual decline. Paper
mills eventually took up some of the slack, but not on Machias Bay.

The shipyards are gone from the peninsula now, and so are the lumber mills. Intruding high into the eastern sky across the bay from Machiasport, the Navy's red-lighted Cutler radio towers blink in Tinkertoy communication with the nuclear submarine fleet, the bay's sole remaining link with international shipping. Three of the four canneries are closed; one still operates part time. Governments are the leading employers on Machias Bay—the normal town, county, state, and federal offices, plus the Bucks Harbor Air Force Station, the Machias campus of the University of Maine, and the Cutler installation.

Although not prosperous, the Machias Bay towns have stopped declining. The homes are not grand, but they are rarely tarpaper. Unlike the worst of Appalachia, with which the county economy has sometimes been compared, these towns have not been plundered. They are still clean, and they still have pride. But they do not have enough jobs. Unemployment in Washington County has exceeded 10 percent since the 1930s. More than 35 percent of the country's 20–29-year-olds leave in any decade. In Maine as in Harlem, some see this statistic as evidence of a commendable upward mobility, but it dismays the people left behind, the people to whom state government must respond. Promises to "do something for Washington County" have appeared in programs and platforms since the Depression first induced Maine people to expect such efforts from public officials. The problem is older than the promises, for in 1880 the population of the county was nearly 50,000, of whom 1531 lived in Machiasport. Today, both of these figures are 40 percent smaller, while Maine's population has increased by a half and the nation's has quadrupled.

During coastal Washington County's century as a commercial center of consequence, the Maine Yankee established a reputation for entrepreneurial prudence and agility. Maine sailors (sometimes entire captains' families) sailed, traded, and whaled throughout the world. As long as they dealt in familiar commodities like ships and boards, the coastal communities were as sophisticated as any in America, but there was and perhaps remains the disturbing potential inherent in Parson Paul Coffin's 1800 observation that "want of learning, religion, and love of order suffers the people to be imposed upon by quacks in divinity, politics, and physic."[3]

One hundred fifty-six Jonesporters lived down to Parson Coffin's worst fears of Yankee susceptibility sixty-six years later. They let George Washington Adams, a British actor turned Mormon but fallen afoul of Brigham Young, convince them that the Second Coming was imminent in Jerusalem and that their role, as members of his Church of the Messiah, was to be there "to commence the great work of restoration foretold by the old prophets, patriarchs, and apostles, as well as by our lord himself."[4]

Selling all they had to skeptical neighbors, the 156 sailed off to Jaffa, near present-day Tel Aviv. Before they arrived, Adams was deep in the bottle. The Lord did not come to them, but many, unaccustomed to desert climates after their fog-shrouded former home, went to Him. Many others went home, although they are said to have avoided Jonesport, but enough were stranded to attract the attention of a New York reporter, Moses S. Beach, who somehow raised the return fare for forty of them. They shared the ship back as far as Alexandria with Mark Twain, who told the story in *The Innocents Abroad* and may thereby have contributed to the hypersensitivity to outside journalistic comment that persists even more strongly in contemporary Washington County than in most of Maine.

In October, 1968, the energy shortages which were to manifest themselves in 1973 were predictable but not predicted. Government, industry, and independent projections all indicated that U.S. oil consumption (then 13.1 million barrels per day) must inevitably pull further away from the maximum possible domestic oil production sometime during the 1970s and that very large numbers, forces, and consequences would then be involved in what could only be increasing dependence on volatile Arab leaders.

People whose introduction to oil policymaking has come during the 1973–74 problems of high price and low supply must remember that the nightmare against which they have been carefully protected is the reverse—low price and superabundant supply. That emergency last occurred in the early 1930s, when the immense East Texas discoveries combined with Depression-depressed demand and the uniquely American rule of capture to create real market chaos.* The victims of

* The significance of the rule of capture in creating the chaos is hard to overstate. This rule permitted anyone to drain any oil pool that he could drill into, thereby forcing overdrilling and overproduction by producers who had to assume that the oil they left in the ground would be captured by their neighbors. The oil quickly produced had to be quickly sold. Prices collapsed. The pool was wastefully drained. Prices rose. Exploration was resumed by those left solvent. The wastes and risks inherent in this cycle ultimately led the industry to invite governmentally imposed stabilization. In most other nations the rule of capture does not apply and oil discoveries have generally, though not always, been developed more efficiently even if somewhat less colorfully.

that chaos persuaded Franklin Roosevelt that he had to marry the production rate to the government to have the price. That marriage lasted forty years, until, with the resource scarcer and dearer again, the enterprise got freer and braver again.

Since the Depression, U.S. oil policy had generally flowed toward two partially inconsistent goals: assuring adequate capital for oil exploration and production, and protecting domestic oil markets from oil that would depress prices or give other nations unacceptable leverage over American foreign policy. Since the 1920s the government had pursued the goal of adequate industry capital through a generous system of tax forgivings, of which the depletion allowance is the best known. The second goal, the protection of American oil consumers from price reductions not in their best interest, had been attained partly through import limitations and partly through state controls (called prorationing) of domestic production, controls which Texas and Louisiana enforced in fervent memory of the 1901 and 1931 Texas discoveries whose unfettered exploitation drove the price of crude oil down to ten gallons for a penny. These state controls, under which the price of crude oil rose during the 1960s to approximately $3.44 per barrel (8.2 cents per gallon), could be sustained only as long as foreign oil, which declined during the same period to about $2.25 per barrel,* was restricted from American markets.

Imports had been limited by tariff since 1932, and they were unimportant until the early 1950s, when U.S. prices began to rise. Foreign oil became more attractive, threatening not only to penetrate the rapidly growing U.S. market but also to upset the coordinated state prorationing systems. In 1954, a Cabinet task force consisting of an oilman, a gas man, a coal man, and a judge recommended firmer import restrictions. Firm limitations were finally achieved in 1959, when President Eisenhower, announcing that oil imports threatened "to impair national security," proclaimed the Mandatory Oil Import Program, limiting oil imports into the forty-three states east of the Rocky Mountains to 9 percent of their estimated oil demands. Eisenhower's

---

* These price figures are taken from *The Oil Import Question: A Report on the Relationship of Oil Imports to the National Security*, by the Cabinet Task Force on Oil Import Controls, February, 1970. The figures are for oil delivered to the Louisiana Gulf Coast, the point at which foreign and domestic prices would have been likely to equalize under free trade. The foreign-oil price in New England did not differ from the Gulf price, but domestic oil from the Gulf reached $3.90 per barrel in New England, so the actual cost of oil-import controls to New England by 1970 can be roughly estimated at $1.65 per barrel (nearly four cents a gallon).

action is often cited as the beginning of oil-import controls, but it actually did little more than shore up restraints that had already been achieved through an impromptu combination of tariffs, Congressional investigations of imports and importers, governmental legitimization of what would otherwise have been illegal collusion against imports, and finally a Voluntary Oil Import Control Program adopted in 1956.[5] As a result of these several restraints, American consumers were denied access to foreign oil, which was declining in price, and were forced instead to consume domestic oil, which was increasing in price because of the state production restrictions.

At the same time, the world oil market, separated from its potential outlet into the United States, moved toward surplus conditions at the prevailing prices. Several of the larger American independent companies had obtained exploration rights in the Middle East after World War II and had succeeded, in the words of one oil historian, "at finding oil beyond their wildest dreams."[6] In 1957 they tried to raise both the real prices and the "posted" prices used to compute the producing nations' taxes. Because of the abundance of oil, the real price increases were competed away, leaving only the higher taxes resulting from the higher posted prices. Consequently, the companies cut the posted prices in 1959 and again in 1960.

The income of the producing nations declined dramatically, and they resented both the loss and the manner in which it had occurred. To prevent further reductions, they formed the Organization of Petroleum Exporting Countries (OPEC). Weak at first, OPEC grew inconspicuously stronger through its first dozen years. When burgeoning domestic demand forced the United States into irrevocable reliance on foreign oil in the 1970s, this stepchild of the 1959 import controls was there to avenge its members a thousand times over for the revenue losses that had brought it into being.

In 1963, President Kennedy changed the import ceiling to 12.2 percent of the oil production in the eastern United States, an amount more restrictive in the long run than Eisenhower's 9 percent of demand. By 1966, Northeastern power companies and other large industries were unable to obtain enough industrial fuel at prevailing prices. Consequently, President Johnson liberalized the program by permitting unrestricted industrial oil imports on the East Coast.

Between 1966 and 1968 the oil-import restraints were further loosened by Secretary of the Interior Stewart Udall. Udall was given control over the administration of the quota system by President Johnson, who did not want his White House accused of favoring his former Texas constituents. Knowing that he could not scrap the system, Udall decided at least to try to keep it from impeding economic development in depressed areas and air-pollution control in Los Angeles. To these ends he devised an import-bonus system for refiners in California who made low-sulfur industrial oil, and he granted import permits to refiners in Puerto Rico and the Virgin Islands who promised to reinvest a percentage of their winnings in job-creating industries, training programs, and urban beautification.

Eastern Maine was a depressed area. New York and Boston needed low-sulfur oil. The oil industry was moving toward supertankers. Maine had the only deep-water harbors on the East Coast. New England felt unfairly burdened by oil-import restrictions. An imaginative and energetic man who knew all these things needed only oil and money to get rich.

2: 1961–1968

The only way you keep the oil moving is by treating the wildcatter like the prince that he really is.
"Duke" Redmond, a wildcatter, 1974

The greatest menace to the future of the Texas and other producers is their obsession that the world owes them a living. It is this loss of touch with reality that seems to mark a group as being ripe for destruction: "The Lord shall smite thee with madness and blindness, and astonishment of heart; and thou shalt grope at noonday, as the blind gropeth in darkness, and thou shalt not prosper in thy ways."
Maurice Adelman, a petroleum economist, 1964

PRESS ON
NOTHING IN THE WORLD CAN TAKE THE PLACE OF PERSISTENCE. TALENT WILL NOT. NOTHING IS MORE COMMON THAN UNSUCCESSFUL MEN WITH TALENT. GENIUS WILL NOT. UNREWARDED GENIUS IS ALMOST A PROVERB. EDUCATION WILL NOT. THE WORLD IS FULL OF EDUCATED DERELICTS. PERSISTENCE AND DETERMINATION ALONE ARE OMNIPOTENT.
Jack Evans's 1971 Christmas Card.
He's not sure who wrote it but thinks it
probably came from a magazine ad.

THE AMERICAN OIL INDUSTRY's self-portrait assigns considerable canvas to the wildcatter, the independent explorer who seeks oil where it has not been found before. Canvas is about all that ever went to Edwin Drake, Patillo Higgins, and Columbus "Dad" Joiner. Drake drilled the nation's first oil well in Pennsylvania in 1859. Higgins located the huge Spindletop pool in Texas that cracked the Standard Oil Trust's U.S. monopoly in 1901. Joiner discovered the 1931 Kilgore field, which was more responsible than any other for the Texas oil image and for precipitating government involvement in the production and pricing of oil in the United States.

The solo wildcatter looms smaller in the industry than in industry lore, and the massive expenditures required to drill in deep water or in the Arctic will continue to diminish the significance of the undercapitalized Gabby Hayes figure leading two laden burros across Death

Valley. On the other hand, some who began as wildcatters did prosper. H. L. Hunt's fortune, largely derived from the Joiner discovery, has been a basis for the Kansas City Chiefs football team, the World Championship Tennis League, the flamboyantly conservative "Facts Forum" and "Lifetime" radio programs, the 1960 preprimary circulation (on Lyndon Johnson's apparently unknowing behalf) of a sermon reprint arguing that "the election of a Catholic President would mean the end of religious liberty in America,"[1] and the Presidential candidacy of George Wallace.

Hugh Roy Cullen estimated that he gave more than $150 million to schools and hospitals with enough left over to buy the thirty-eight-state Liberty Network of radio stations, primarily to keep it out of the hands of "socialists."[2]

Clint Murchison endowed the Dallas Cowboys, bought a publishing house, and helped finance the campaign, subsequently described by a Senate investigating committee as "despicable" and "back street," that drove Millard Tydings from the Senate after the Maryland conservative had chaired a committee which found no substance to Joseph McCarthy's charges that the State Department was a center of Communism.[3]

Everette De Golyer went on to establish De Golyer & McNaughton, leading consultants in petroleum geology, and helped to revive the recurrently foundering *Saturday Review*.

Because wildcatters did not usually begin as rich men, they often had to sell a new piece of their percentage to finance each additional hundred feet of drilling. The contrast in postdiscovery prosperity between the Drakes, Higginses, and Joiners and the Hunts, Cullens, Murchisons, and De Golyers lay in the ability of the latter to acquire or associate with sufficient financial and political capital to complete the discovery without surrendering or being done out of the discoverer's right to a percentage of the eventual revenues. Those who struck oil while they still had a percentage got rich. Those who didn't, didn't.

Wildcatting isn't basically different from many other types of business ventures, including the building of oil refineries. Such ventures may be undertaken by well-financed coalitions or individuals, who can spread losses among many investors or offset them against other income or against taxes. They may also be undertaken by men without resources or partners, men whose inability to absorb sizable losses over long periods or to make big investments quickly will force them eventually to give up, to sell out, to take new partners, or to do something desperate. Those seeking to build refineries on the Maine coast have tried everything.

In early April, 1961, fifty-six Washington representatives of the oil and gas industry received an unusual fund-raising communication, unusual at least in that it was in writing. It read:

Dear Friend:

Secretary [of the Interior] Udall, who happens to be a friend of long standing, has asked me as a personal favor to him to solicit the oil and gas industry in Washington in an effort to help the Secretary to dispose of a "very sizeable quota of tickets to the Jefferson-Jackson day dinner."

The dinner will be held on President Kennedy's birthday on May 27.* Tickets are $100 per plate or $1000 per table of ten. It is being held at the National Guard Armory in Washington, D.C.

The procedure that the Secretary has asked me to follow is to have all checks made payable to the Democratic National Committee, and, if for some personal reason you do not wish to follow this system please contact me.

Send your check to me together with a note indicating to whom and where you wish the tickets to be mailed.

Thank you for your cooperation.

Sincerely,

Jack Evans

cc: The Honorable Stewart L. Udall

Any collection of fifty-six oilmen probably includes forty Republicans, and by May 3 the letter was on the front page of *The New York Times*. Udall ascribed the month's delay to Republican desire for a scandal timed to defeat his brother Morris's bid to fill his own former Congressional seat in a special election held in Arizona on May 4.

Jack Evans, an expansive sixty-year-old Welshman who had become one of Royal Dutch Shell's top Washington representatives after doing well enough in Canada's Red Lake gold rush to stake himself to night courses at Columbia and N.Y.U. during his Shell traineeship in the early 1930s, could not understand the furor. His only reported comment was: "I acted as a private citizen of our democracy with no thought of gaining personal favors. The fact that I put it in writing is

* Jefferson-Jackson Day is a uniquely floating commemoration. Its sole raison d'être is fund raising, and Democrats have probably somewhere celebrated it every day except Christmas and Easter.

testimony to my sincerity." He later added that the letter had been sent out without his clearance and that someone else had signed his name. An anonymous recipient of the letter told the *Times* that he had called Evans because "I knew it was a time bomb and tried to explain why. But he was astonished by my attitude and couldn't see anything wrong."

Congressman William Miller, later Barry Goldwater's choice for Vice-President, demanded that Udall cease "blackjacking the oil industry" and resign.

Udall said that he had been flabbergasted and embarrassed and had asked that the letter be considered withdrawn. He suggested that "Mr. Evans was attempting to impress some people in the oil business" and added that he could "take care of the Republicans, but who is going to protect me from my friends?"

Asked about the letter at his May 5 press conference, President Kennedy stammered on the specifics and came out for federally financed elections.

Evans's résumé notes that he took early retirement from Shell in 1961 to form and to lead the Independent Fuel Oil Marketers of America (IFOMA), which conducted a successful five-year campaign to persuade the Interior Department to relax import controls on industrial fuel oil.

The early retirement was Shell's and Evans's recognition that their relationship had outlived its usefulness, but the company had no desire to make his departure uncomfortable. He was a man of real flair and was well liked. Furthermore, very few oil companies are in any position to deal harshly with their top Washington staff. It is wiser to have the leverage of a continuing salary against the day the man might decide to write a book or have a few drinks with Jack Anderson, and this continuing salary was one reason for Evans's camel-like ability to survive strongly between distant water holes in his later life.

Evans's years with Royal Dutch Shell were fine background for the IFOMA campaign. Owned predominantly by Dutch and British interests, Shell had in 1913 taken advantage of proliferating U.S. oil discoveries and the Standard Oil Company's preoccupation with the antitrust laws,* the Archbold letters,† and a Shell-initiated kerosene

* In 1911 the Supreme Court ordered the dissolution of the Standard Oil Company of New Jersey. From that trust came Standard of New Jersey (Exxon), Standard of New York (Mobil), Standard of California (Chevron), Standard of Indiana (Amoco), Continental (Conoco), and Standard of Ohio (Sohio), among many others.

† These letters, written mostly in 1904 to and by Standard vice-president John D. Archbold, provide a record of Standard Oil Company bribes to a wide variety of

price war in China to obtain a position in the U.S. market.

The U.S. market itself was exploding in response to the needs of the automobile, and, by way of perspective, a generally growing energy demand that had in 1913 induced Congress to authorize the twelve-year process of damming Hetch Hetchy. Shell became the only foreign company to do a substantial oil business in the United States until British Petroleum was able to combine Alaskan discoveries with acquisition of Sinclair and Sohio retail outlets in 1969.

Shell's foreign ownership left it with an odd marketing structure that ran afoul of the import controls imposed by President Eisenhower in 1959. Those controls allowed importation of industrial fuel oil only by companies who had been importing their own before the controls were imposed. Shell had imported industrial oil through Asiatic Petroleum, a foreign subsidiary, barred by its charter from doing business in the United States. Asiatic sold the oil on an f.o.b.-foreign-port basis to other companies, which in turn often sold the oil to separately owned terminals. Consequently, many terminal operators supplied by Shell were technically not importers and did not qualify for import allocations when the controls went into effect.

With many substantial importers thus cut off, the remaining suppliers had a more stable market with higher prices, but the marooned former Shell distributors formed IFOMA. They were supported by power and paper companies, which are the largest users of industrial fuel oil. For an organizer, they turned to Jack Evans, a knowledgeable man, familiar with the Shell system, and obviously not without ties to the Interior Department.

Maine's largest industry was pulp and paper production. Electric power was among the significant runners-up. The Maine industrial oil market had very few suppliers, and the entire state east of the

Senators, Congressmen, and federal and state officials and legislators. Stolen by a Standard employee, they were sold to William Randolph Hearst, who unveiled them in a 1908 attempt to arouse the nation against both major parties on behalf of his Independence League candidate, Thomas Hisgen. The letters implicated Senators Thomas Platt and Chauncey Depew of New York, Boies Penrose and Matthew Quay of Pennsylvania, Joseph Foraker and Mark Hanna of Ohio, Anselm McLauren of South Carolina, and Joseph Bailey of Texas. Congressman Joseph Sibley of Pennsylvania was shown to have written to Archbold that he had "told the President [Theodore Roosevelt] some plain, if impalatable truths as to the situation politically, and that no man should win who depended upon the rabble rather than upon the conservative men of affairs."[4] Hisgen got less than 1 percent of the vote, finishing fifth behind the Socialist and Prohibition candidates.

Penobscot River was exclusively supplied by one dealer, the C. H. Sprague Company,* which was making five times more profit on industrial oil sales in eastern Maine than on sales in more competitive areas.

An organization seeking to lower the cost of industrial oil could expect considerable support from Maine's large consumers, so Evans, who had married a girl from the Maine paper-mill town of Millinocket, headed north. In Maine and throughout New England he found a business community slowly awakening to the impact of oil-import controls on the regional economy and even more slowly to the relative powerlessness of its men in Washington, Kennedys though some of them were, to do anything about it.

The 1954 legislation on which oil-import controls were based enabled the President to restrict imports. It did not require that he do so. President Kennedy could have abolished the restrictions as easily as President Eisenhower had promulgated them, and the petroleum study committee that he had formed upon taking office recommended that he at least liberalize them. The fact that he didn't was attributable to the maxim that within limits politicians, like godfathers, may act against the interests of friends more safely than against those of allies. Friends are more forgiving and would anyway prefer having their friend in office. Allies have their own friends. President Kennedy and the Southwest of Lyndon Johnson had been electoral allies, and that alliance was severely strained in the postelection Congress.

President Kennedy's New Frontier legislative program was being treated roughly by an alliance between Republicans and Southern and Southwestern Democrats. Vice-President Johnson, one of the most dominating figures in Congressional history and a midwife to oil-import controls,† was being counted on to help pass the legislative program. For additional help, Kennedy relied heavily on Senator Robert Kerr of Oklahoma, a 22 percent owner of the Kerr-McGee Company, which was itself a significant producer of domestic oil and

---

* The Sprague Company was itself 25 percent owned by Shell. However, because it owned or leased its own tankers, it had been an importing terminal operator prior to 1959 and was therefore given a quota allocation of the type denied to many pre-1959 Shell importers.

† A member of the staff of the 1954 task force that had recommended quotas to President Eisenhower describes being summoned with his chairman to a meeting in House Speaker Sam Rayburn's office. Rayburn was concise. "I'm speaking for myself and Lyndon Johnson," he said. "Either you people come up with a way to cut back imports, or we'll legislate restrictions that will curl your hair."

gas. Kerr was the oil industry's most outspoken and flamboyant agent
in the Senate, and he exchanged his cooperation on the New Frontier
for a specific promise from President Kennedy that oil would not be
one of the areas of freer trade resulting from the Kennedy Round of
tariff negotiations pursuant to the Trade Expansion Act of 1962.[5]

If Senator Kerr needed help regarding industrial oil imports, it was
available from such powerful coal-state Senators as Jennings Randolph
and Robert Byrd of West Virginia, Hugh Scott of Pennsylvania, and
John Sherman Cooper of Kentucky. Coal competed with industrial oil,
and the coal-state Senators arguments for higher coal prices were
enhanced by a sympathy for Appalachia that had been kindled in the
Kennedy White House by the shocking coal-town conditions encountered in the 1960 West Virginia primary. This sympathy was expanded by the 1962 publication of *Night Comes to the Cumberlands,*
Harry Caudill's compelling portrayal of destitution and exploitation in
an ignored region.

So demonstrative was Senator Byrd's defense of West Virginia's
coal industry that on one occasion it led to the Interior Department's
only recorded oil spill. Seeking to prove at an Interior hearing that industrial oil was just a form of inelegant glop, Senator Byrd inverted a
jar of it at the witness table to show that it wouldn't even pour. Unfortunately, the jar had been left on a radiator while the Senator waited
his turn to testify. Whatever the resulting mess may have done to the
health of Interior's janitors, it reached no lobster pounds.

Despite a Presidential task force's recommendation of a "modest increase" in oil imports, Evans and IFOMA made no headway during the
Kennedy Presidency. The President's only actions affecting oil-import
controls were actually toward greater restrictions.* He was clearly

---

* There was one exception. The original program had contained an exemption for
overland (pipeline) imports, which in practice meant Canadian oil already going to
the Midwest and the West Coast. Mexico, despite the absence of any comparable
pipeline, requested equal treatment and threatened to sell the oil to Cuba. At the
behest of a State Department still reeling from the Bay of Pigs and on the rationale
that the oil could move in trucks in wartime, Kennedy granted Mexico a 30,000-
barrel-per-day exemption worth about $12 million per year.

The oil moved by tanker from Mexico to Brownsville, Texas. There it was offloaded
into trucks which, 150 times every 24 hours, rumbled back into Mexico, turned around
immediately and rumbled back into Texas, qualifying the imports as "overland" in
the process. Then the oil went back into tankers, expensive U.S.-flag tankers this time
because of the requirements of the Jones Act, to resume its submarine-vulnerable
voyage to East Coast refineries. Mexico was happy; shippers were happy; Brownsville

trading higher than necessary oil prices off against his hopes for major
gains in Medicare, tax reform, civil rights, federal aid to education,
Appalachian prosperity, and Southwestern support in 1964. He might
as well have been talking about oil-import reform as Vietnam withdrawal when he told Senator Mansfield and White House aide Kenneth
O'Donnell that, in part to avoid a McCarthyist revival, "I just can't do it
until 1965—after I'm reelected,"[6] but by 1965 it was Lyndon Johnson
who had been reelected.

Concurrently with the change in national administration came
changes in oil-refinery technology that enabled refiners to extract more
gasoline, home heating oil, and other profitable light oils from each
barrel of crude. Competition from coal and crude oil itself had kept
industrial-oil prices below the cost of refining the oil. Consequently,
U.S. refiners made as little of it as possible, and the production of
industrial oil did not keep pace with the growing demand.

Because New England was far from the coal fields, the declining
availability of industrial oil exacerbated a situation which had been
worsening since Eisenhower had imposed the mandatory controls.
Spurred on by Evans and IFOMA as well as by their home-state industries, the region's Congressmen made industrial oil a high priority at
the very time when it was becoming an even lower priority to major oil
companies. Outside the walls, the Venezuelan government sharpened
its suggestions that oil-import restrictions belied the oft-repeated U.S.
goal of freer trade with the developing economies of Latin America.*
The Venezuelans produced a crude oil more suitable than the U.S.

---

truckers were happy; hardly anyone else knew the difference, except for a few
refiners and dealers in Michigan, Illinois, Minnesota, and New York, who wondered
why they still couldn't import Canadian oil across the submarine-free Great Lakes.

The Brownsville Loop, as it was affectionately known, became the flamboyant flag-
ship in a post-1965 fleet of complex special exemptions, each of which made a few
people happy enough to be grateful while making no one unhappy enough to be
vindictive.

* Actually, Venezuela did not fare badly under the oil-import program. Most of the
imports into the uniquely high-priced U.S. market came from that country. Furthermore, the United States consciously permitted enough oil from the fields of western
Canada to come into the north central and western United States to reduce any
Canadian desire to build oil pipelines to eastern Canada. The eastern Canadian market
was largely supplied by Venezuelan oil, which reached Montreal refineries through a
pipeline originating in Portland, Maine. New England's irritation over the oil-import
program was heightened by the fact that throughout the late 1960s oil products were
more than three cents per gallon cheaper in Montreal than in Portland. The import
program had actually managed to bring the oil out of the pipeline cheaper than it
went in.

variety for the manufacture of high-sulfur industrial oil, and they were unconvinced that a tanker moving to New England from Venezuela was much more vulnerable to enemy torpedoes than one making the 300-mile-longer run up from Texas.

In the end, the coal industry was left alone to argue for continued controls on industrial oil against the fully aroused consuming industries, IFOMA, the Venezuelans, and those major oil companies (predominantly Esso and Shell) with extensive Venezuelan interests. The coal industry won in about 60 percent of the markets that it was defending, but it lost the territory from the Appalachians to the Atlantic, into which Secretary Udall allowed free importation of industrial oil "to combat inflation." Because of the Vietnam escalation, Udall's decision combated inflation the way a length of chicken wire combats a rising tide, but there were other consequences.

First, the price of industrial oil on the East Coast declined dramatically and soon reached foreign-source-plus-transportation levels. Most of the new imports came from Venezuela, which quickly increased its share of the East Coast industrial oil market from about 40 percent to more than 60 percent.

Second, some 2 million barrels per day worth of new refineries specializing in industrial fuel for the U.S. market, with some lighter products for Canada and Europe, were built in Venezuela, the Caribbean, and eastern Canada. Their construction was accelerated by provisions of the Western Hemisphere Trade Preference Act which enabled them to benefit from tax breaks in both the United States and the country they came to rest in. Thus, by freeing importation of a finished product while restricting crude oil, the United States exiled the refineries and deep-water terminals necessary to serve its domestic needs, for only by building abroad could anyone get access to foreign crude oil from which to make the unrestricted industrial fuel. With these refineries and terminals went the capital outlays and wages and salaries that were to contribute substantially to the balance of payments deficits associated with importing oil products.

This exporting of capital and facilities is virtually unique among oil-consuming nations. By the early 1930s, petroleum-deficient countries as diverse as France, Chile, Japan, Spain, and Germany were actively encouraging domestic refining. As long as the only U.S. shortages were in industrial oil, the balance-of-payments pitfalls were hidden by the fact that imported crude oil would have cost more than the imported refined oil, but no one seriously studying the U.S. oil situation could have thought that the shortage could be restricted to industrial oil even for a decade.

Third, because Venezuelan oil contained more sulfur than American oil, conversion to Venezuelan industrial fuel increased air pollution in the eastern United States. Since Venezuelan oil also contained metals that made sulfur removal difficult and expensive, it proved to be an inadequate source for low-sulfur oil at the very time that air-pollution standards eliminated coal in urban areas and increased the demand for low-sulfur oil.

Fourth, the situation in Maine relative to the rest of the East Coast actually worsened. Prices declined, but the C. H. Sprague monopoly in eastern Maine retarded the decline so that industrial fuel was comparatively more expensive in parts of Maine after the removal of controls than before.*

Fifth, the free importation of industrial fuel aborted a Jack Evans plan for a Maine refinery on deep water, especially designed for New England's heavy reliance on industrial oil. Hoping to capitalize on the new industrial-oil market structure created by his IFOMA victory, Evans planned to locate his refinery in a foreign-trade zone where the foreign crude could have come in safe from the quota system, to be made into industrial oil to enter the U.S. market under the new exemption. It was a good idea, but Evans didn't have it alone.

His rivals were the U.S. petrochemical companies, which had discovered that naphtha, ethane, propane, and other crucial feedstocks were becoming more expensive, even as the feedstocks of their foreign competitors and subsidiaries were becoming cheaper. To make matters worse, some oil companies were themselves going into the petrochemical business.

The petrochemical group first sought an exemption for feedstocks like the one granted to industrial fuel. The arguments were similar. Cheaper feedstocks were necessary to meet foreign competition and save American jobs. The difference was that petrochemical feedstocks were still so profitable a product that the oil industry and the Interior Department refused to exempt them from the quota system.

The petrochemical group then turned to plans combining refineries

---

* The attractiveness of the 1965 paper-company fuel-oil market in eastern Maine led the Pittston Company, a sizable marketer of coal and industrial fuel, to purchase land in Eastport for the construction of a competing terminal and distribution network. The terminal was never built, but Pittston's interest was to have other consequences.

and petrochemical plants in trade zones. Foreign oil would have come in to be refined into feedstocks, which would then be processed into finished plastics, pesticides, dyes, or other petrochemicals not subject to quota restrictions. These could have been imported and sold in the United States or reexported into the world market on competitive terms.

Although profitability, not national security, was the sole difference between industrial fuel and petrochemical feedstocks, Udall was persuaded to ban the importing of crude oil into trade zones even as he legalized the importing of industrial oil on the Atlantic coast. These measures aborted the petrochemical capers, and with them went Evans's plan for an industrial oil refinery on U.S. soil.

The New England market for home heating oil was similar to the market for industrial fuel oil, in that competitive fuels available in relative abundance elsewhere in the country were scarce in the Northeast. As coal and sometimes natural gas normally competed with industrial oil, so electricity and natural gas competed with home heating oil, but not in New England. New England was so distant from major gas-producing regions that the supply had never been plentiful, and aggressive marketing had been curtailed. At the same time, a historically inefficient network of private electric companies had priced electricity out of most of the home heating market.[7] Consequently, about three out of every four New England homes were heated by oil, and because New England is cold, those families spent an average of some $300 per year for their oil.

Because home heating oil was also cheaper abroad than at home, the New England homeowner, like his neighboring industries, had been paying a considerable and growing premium to protect a shadowy Presidentially imposed definition of the national security. Despite the similarities to the industrial fuel market, Evans could see three serious barriers to a 1965 repetition, oriented to home heating oil, of his earlier IFOMA effort.

First, he had no client. Citizens are infinitely more difficult to organize than industries. As a group, they were quietly accepting a drain of some $4.5 billion per year in the form of oil-import-control costs of six cents per person per day. A medium-sized power company asked to surrender $2 million through a fifty-cent-per-barrel fuel overcharge would have roused an entire Congressional delegation.

Second, the oil industry really cared about the home heating-oil market. Unlike industrial oil, home heating oil could not be replaced by crude oil, so the price was free to roam up to the usually profitable ceilings set by electricity, gas, or coal. Because this product was profitable, the oil industry resisted foreign home heating oil with a fervor that only the coal industry had shown toward imported industrial oil.

Third, Evans was basically a promoter. His aim was to find a money-making idea, develop it as far as necessary, and sell it, relieving himself of administrative responsibility but retaining a continuing share of the profits. By itself, the decontrolling of foreign home heating oil, socially necessary though it might have been, simply was not a business venture from which continuing profit would flow.

For a time, Evans was stuck. Only in the C. H. Sprague monopoly territory in eastern Maine could he find continuing discontent with the industrial-oil situation, but even there, the power and paper companies were interested in a potential refinery primarily as bargaining leverage with the Sprague Company. They were not eager to build. The home heating-oil grievance, while profound, was so diffuse as to defy mobilization against the massive resistance that it was bound to meet.

At this point, Secretary Udall breathed new life into the opponents of oil-import control. Inspired partly by his growing dislike of the program and partly by the fact that the supplicants had been wise enough to enlist such well-connected supporters as a former Interior Secretary, a present chairman of the House Committee controlling Udall's budget, and a future Supreme Court Justice, Udall granted special import allocations to a Phillips Oil Company refinery in Puerto Rico and later to a Hess Oil Company refinery in the Virgin Islands. In Puerto Rico, he justified the grant in terms of the need for jobs in depressed areas and insisted on some job-creating reinvestment from quota allocations worth several million dollars annually. In the Virgin Islands, which already had more jobs than people seeking work, he stressed skilled-job possibilities and the creation of a sizable conservation fund.

Once Udall had opened the import tent, he was plagued by camels' noses trumpeting demands for "equal treatment." These demands were strongly opposed by Interior's oil bureaucracy, which was content to distribute the existing annual allocations according to formulas that, however irrational, were at least fixed. Udall, gaining confidence in the absence of continuing White House supervision, felt instead that the national-security blanket should be lifted to permit economic development and pollution control in specific situations. Caught between his own dislike of the program and White House and Congressional insistence that it be maintained, he began to play philosopher-king, allocating or denying import tickets on the basis of undefined criteria of social benefit that were no more than casually related to the undefined national security. Because Interior's oil bureaucracy seemed to function primarily as an early-warning system for the oil-trade press, the Secretary often did not consult them, a tactic that, however necessary, made many of his decisions seem arbitrary.

The petrochemical industry persuaded Udall that since they couldn't have access to foreign feedstocks or foreign-trade zones, domestic refiners making feedstocks should be permitted to count them in the refinery output on which import allocations were calculated.* For a time this resulted in "double dip," under which a refiner claimed import rights based once on crude-oil input and again on petrochemical output. Even after that anomaly was corrected, the Standard Oil Company of Indiana (Amoco) found a way to claim an aromatic used in lead-free gasoline as a petrochemical, a ploy worth $2.3 million in its first and only year. When Senator William Proxmire discovered this wrinkle, Udall said that he had intended no such result and revoked the permits. Amoco sued; Udall had to give up the import tickets when the Justice Department refused to defend the belated revocation.

Next, Southern California Edison, the power company serving the Los Angeles area, teamed with several West Coast refiners to extract a well-intentioned regulation giving bonus imports to anyone making low-sulfur oil for sale to companies legally required to burn it to avoid air pollution. The oil producers successfully resisted any extension of this bonus program to the rest of the country, so the import program seemed to say that air pollution in Los Angeles threatened the national security in a way that air pollution in New York did not.

Meanwhile other Puerto Rican refiners and marketers sought treatment equal to that extended to Phillips. Sun Oil, Commonwealth Oil, and Union Carbide received import privileges in return for promises to employ, reinvest, supply, and beautify in Puerto Rico. Commonwealth enjoyed a one-year benefaction, permitting the sale of Puerto Rican–refined gasoline in California, and when annoyed West Coast

---

* The actual system of allocation of import tickets among refineries defies rational economic or security analysis. The basic formula was a sliding scale on which the less oil a refiner refined, the higher the percentage of imported oil he could use. This aspect of the program assured the political support of small refiners, particularly inland ones who could never have used real foreign oil but who did very well by selling their foreign-oil permits to their coastal brethren.

refiners persuaded Udall to revoke it, they pushed for a Phillips-type quota on the East Coast. Udall eased the pressure by persuading Union Carbide to take more Commonwealth oil. He remembered "twisting a lot of arms" on that one.[8]

Phillips protested that none of the Puerto Rican newcomers had made reinvestment promises approaching its own, and Texaco, the island's leading gasoline marketer, asked for allocations to construct its own refinery. That application was never acted on. To have granted it would have produced further demands from Phillips and Commonwealth. To have denied it would have invited a formidable lawsuit.

Several other refiners evinced an interest in joining Hess in the Virgin Islands, but Udall discouraged them, citing the need to protect the island beaches, a worthy concern but somewhat removed from national security and not shown for Puerto Rico, where the refiners were to damage a uniquely phosphorescent bay.

During this period (1966–67) the Oil Import Appeals Board, a separate branch of the Interior Department, was running a welfare program all its own. Using the value of the emergency permits that it was empowered to grant, the OIAB bailed out two small refineries that were less short on supply than on money and managed to revive one refinery that had been closed down for several years.

In 1967 all five executives of the Oil Import Administration spent a weekend running the first spot audit in the program's eight-year history. About 20 percent of the reports checked contained significant inaccuracies. After Udall left office in 1969, he reminisced, "It was a minor miracle that I got by without a major scandal."[9]

These indications of flexibility at the Interior Department revived Evans. Approaching Interior, where his role in the 1961 fund-raising debacle had been forgiven, he found a willingness to consider a foreign-trade zone in northern New England. Approaching Maine's political leadership, he found Senator Edmund Muskie and Governor Kenneth Curtis enthusiastic about the economic impact that such a project would have on Maine. Both men were veterans of the long struggle for respectability that the Maine Democratic Party had waged, based in no small part on Republican indifference to new economic development. Both had liberal and progressive records. Neither had any reservations about a properly sited oil refinery.

Not one to put all his eggs in one basket, Evans devised similar refinery proposals for three other states. In Georgia he invoked the bene-

fits that would flow from development of the port of Savannah. In
Virginia he spoke of the need for low-sulfur fuel, port development at
Norfolk, and the benefits to the coal industry of being able to use large
oil tankers to export coal. In Hawaii he pointed out that Standard Oil
of California, the island's sole refinery, had reached a zenith in abuse
of the import system by charging prices based on domestic oil products
shipped from California while actually selling products refined locally
from foreign crude imported from Indonesia and the Middle East.* In
each state, Evans and Business Development Fund, Inc., his one-man,
one-secretary, two-office, four-phone-number company, had no more
than a basic idea, a concept that anyone could steal while he sought oil,
transportation, refinery builders, refiners, marketers, and money.

During the spring and summer of 1967 he worked with the offices
of Governor Curtis and Senator Muskie to structure the Maine project
and choose a site. Under the environmental criteria that were to come
into being over the next five years, the site-selection process was
singularly casual and secretive, but it was responsible enough for the
times. The only people consulted were the director of the Maine Port
Authority, Maine's Commissioner of Sea and Shore Fisheries, the U.S.
Coast Guard, and the Federal Maritime Administration.

The Port Authority suggested an initial list of deep-water sites,
including Portland, the mouths of the Kennebec and nearby Sheepscot
rivers, and locations ringing Acadia National Park. Sites farther east
were not considered, because Evans objected to the additional distances
to market areas and to the absence of existing industry, transportation
facilities, and skilled labor.

The Kennebec and Sheepscot sites lacked either the turning room or
the shelter necessary to supertanker harbors; also, they included resort
areas. Senator Muskie's administrative assistant, Don Nicoll, rejected
the rest of the list except Portland because of the navigational problems
and the inevitable summer-resident and fishing-community opposition
in the Acadia National Park area. As he learned more about oil, Nicoll
realized that the additional costs of transportation that had eliminated
eastern Maine from earlier consideration were actually inconsequential.
Seeing the political and economic advantages of a major industrial

---

* Hawaii's situation illustrates the randomness of the "national security" definitions
underlying U.S. oil policy. As an archipelago without indigenous oil production,
Hawaii could be made secure against supply interruptions only by the storage of
reserves, an alternative the oil-import program ignored. The only effects of applying
quotas to the islands were higher product prices and less competition.

project in the state's most underdeveloped region, he asked the state's Sea and Shore Fisheries Department to evaluate deep-water sites well east of the national park.

Sea and Shore Fisheries Commissioner Ronald Green, wary of the difficult approaches, strong tidal currents, and extensive fogs at Eastport, advised Nicoll that Machias Bay provided the best combination of deep water with turning room and a partially sheltered offloading point. The Coast Guard and the Maritime Administration concurred, preferring Machias Bay over Portland because Portland's tanker lanes were already crowded and because its Casco Bay islands were second only to the summer havens of Penobscot Bay in the probable strength of their opposition to neighborhood supertankers and refineries.

By mid-1967 Governor Curtis and Senator Muskie were sufficiently impressed by the proposal to endorse and transmit Evans's two-page summary of it to Secretary Udall. Their letters stressed economic development and did not mention the environment. The summary itself hit all the notes that had opened Interior's doors to Udall's previous quota recipients. The score included:

—Abundant energy for satellite industries
—Feedstocks for petrochemical companies
—Jobs in a depressed area
—Increased national security (because Machias Bay was beyond likely areas of contamination in case of nuclear attack)
—Low-sulfur fuel for cities
—Stimulation of U.S. shipping
—Less exportation of capital and refinery capacity
—And even, à la Virgin Islands, a special marine resources foundation funded by a gift of twenty cents for each barrel of importable oil (10,000 barrels per day would equal $730,000 per year) to be used for "all aspects of education, research, and planning involved in the exploration, exploitation, and conservation of the marine resources of our nation to the end of that both our citizens and those of other friendly nations would benefit."
—Inspirational rhetoric in the form of a lead quote from Victor Hugo: "Stronger than all the armies of the world is an idea whose time has come."

The port having been chosen, Evans turned his attention to finding refiners and money. Because the project contemplated yet another roweling of the flanks of the oil-import program, the major oil companies and established independent refiners were out of the question. Maine's oil-consuming industries vacillated. The nationwide oil-consumer cooperatives, after an initial show of interest, turned him down. Finally, he turned again to his former IFOMA clients, several of whom were eager for the secure supplies inherent in part ownership of a refinery.* By the end of 1967 he had tentative commitments of sufficient capital support to build the refinery, and he had marketers for its output. Although he was gaining momentum, he still needed the crude oil and permission to import it. As he turned his attention to those problems, the support he had worked so long to build began to crumble.

His support had always been flawed in that it depended on the close cooperation of men and companies normally in competition for supplies and markets. After they had agreed to participate in a Machiasport refinery, they were unable to agree on anything else, least of all on what products the refinery was to make and who was to control them.

Concerned that some of his partners were beginning to wonder just why they needed him and knowing that disunity would hamper his search for political support and a crude-oil supply, Evans sought leverage of his own. Trading on the argument that only he could keep the whole package together, Evans was able to extract one of the most unusual property conveyances in the history of a state noteworthy for dubious land transactions with both its corporations and its Indians.

The document was a fifteen-line "Dear Jack" letter signed by the general manager of the Maine Port Authority. It purported to promise to convey to his Business Development Fund either a priority claim or an exclusive right (the letter is unclear) to lease "appropriate land" for the construction of an oil refinery and marine terminal in any future foreign-trade zone. No lease terms were mentioned.

The document was unenforceable for several reasons, but Evans, in a hurry and not a lawyer, had to gamble. The state officials were content

* The oil industry is, of course, dominated by major companies. The majors are fully integrated in that they explore for oil, produce it, transport it, refine it, wholesale it, and retail it. At each stage of the process there are nonintegrated or partially integrated independents that are almost invariably dependent on the majors as either suppliers, purchasers, or both. Thus an independent marketer is one who takes product from a combination of major and/or independent refiners. Such marketers are most visible to the public in the so-called "unbranded" gasoline stations, but some deal in home heating and industrial oil as well. Because a substantial part of their supply comes from majors with more product than their own retailers can handle, the independents lead a precarious existence during oil shortages and consequently are frequently interested in integrating backward into the refining business.

to give him a token. They knew that they had given nothing of consequence away.

Evans pocketed this putative option in early 1968, with Presidential
politics adding a new pressure to his multifaceted calculations. His
Norfolk project remained only an idea, but he had serious negotiations
under way in Maine, Georgia, and Hawaii. Simultaneously, Udall's
disagreement with Johnson over natural resource policies and the
Presidential candidacy of Robert Kennedy indicated that Evans's
friend in court would be gone and discredited even if Johnson were
reelected.

Knowing that he needed a crude-oil source, both for credibility and
for the political leverage that oil producers uniquely wield, Evans made
an effort to attract Continental Oil, the country's eighth largest oil
company, and one with a substantial supply of foreign crude looking
for a market. He was turned down cold. Conoco liked the idea but
would not jeopardize its close ties with the rest of the U.S. oil industry.

Immediately after this setback, Lyndon Johnson withdrew as a
Presidential candidate. Of his likely successors, Kennedy and Hubert
Humphrey were counted as friends; Eugene McCarthy and Nelson
Rockefeller as enigmas. Richard Nixon, who had entered politics under
the aegis of a group of Southern California oil, real estate, and banking
executives whose enthusiasm for him manifested itself in the secret
fund called to national inattention in the 1952 Checkers address,
seemed to promise the bowknot of negatives that his very name suggested.

In the week that Johnson withdrew, Evans was rejected by Shell and
by two other firms. Locally, his organizational problems were compounded by the C. H. Sprague Company, a New England fuel marketer
since it had first sold coal in Boston in 1870. As industrial fuel oil
replaced coal in the furnaces of New England power and paper companies, Sprague replaced its New England coal sales almost entirely
with oil, most of it Shell's. It established a lucrative monopoly among
the Maine paper mills east of the Penobscot River, and that position
was solidified by the 1959 oil-import restriction, which denied potential
competitors supplies at low enough prices to support invasion of the
monopoly area.

In 1967 Shaw Sprague sold the company to his son-in-law, Robert
Augustus Gardner Monks, who was looking for a business career that
would make him rich enough soon enough to get into public service at
an early age. Monks had realized during a seven-year stint with a

Boston law firm that a business career was a quicker route to the kind of money he had in mind, so he left the law a month after being made a partner in the firm.

Monks and two friends formed a venture-capital company and merged it with his family's investment-management firm. Meanwhile, he became more politically active, serving for a year as Republican finance chairman for Massachusetts. In 1967, with his father-in-law then sixty-six years old and looking to retire, Monks borrowed some $5 million and went into the industrial-fuel-oil business. He was scrambling to meet monthly payments of $30,000 on his loans when the 1966 decontrolling of industrial oil sharply reduced prices and profits outside of eastern Maine. Protection of that highly profitable earldom became essential, and Monks viewed efforts toward a local refinery with concern rather than enthusiasm. The possible competition of the Pittston Company at Eastport and the fact that the Evans refinery might actually be located in Sprague's monopoly area turned the concern into outright alarm. The Sprague Company therefore joined the refinery consortium and added another player to the continuing squabble over extents of participation.

Monks, not for the last time during his career in Maine, quickly demonstrated an aversion to the ground floor. Within three months of Sprague's inclusion in the project, he suggested to Evans that they forget about the eight other participants and build the refinery themselves. Evans knew that he would be better off allied with a single substantial joint owner, but his misgivings about Monks's inexperience in the oil business and about deserting companies with which he had been associated for several years caused him to reject the suggestion.

Burdened now by the increasing unwieldiness of his consortium, by his failure to get a crude-oil supply, and by an inexorable political timetable, Evans got the kind of break that befell Jonah when the whale spotted him floundering in the Mediterranean. In May, 1968, he was approached by the Occidental Petroleum Company, the nation's forty-eighth largest corporation and twelfth largest oil company.

Occidental, colloquially known as Oxy, had been the forty-eighth largest corporation for a month. In 1967 it had been 102nd but had merged with the Hooker Chemical Company in March, 1968. Ten years before that, it had been losing money and had been estimated to be worth $34,000, roughly 1/50,000 of its worth in 1968. The difference was a Russian gynecologist's son named Armand Hammer.

By 1921 Hammer was a self-made millionaire graduate of the Columbia Medical School who, having decided to get in a little pre-internship medical relief work in revolution-wracked postwar Russia, had discovered that the Russians needed food more than medicine and had brokered an exchange of a million bushels of U.S. wheat for Russian furs and caviar. The deal so impressed Lenin that he made the Hammer family the chief broker for all U.S.–Soviet trade.* In that capacity he represented thirty-eight American manufacturing companies and persuaded arch-capitalist Henry Ford to reverse his aversion to exporting tractors and training Russian mechanics. Lenin was so pleased that he gave Hammer his choice of manufacturing concessions as the Russians sought to strengthen their domestic industrial capability. The doctor wound up with an asbestos mine in the Ural Mountains and a pencil factory that he took on not because he knew anything about making pencils but because he didn't see how he could fail in a country where pencils cost fifty cents apiece and the government had just decreed a program of compulsory education. Within two years he had the price of pencils down to five cents, and the factory was showing a healthy annual profit.

Hammer used the pencil and asbestos profits to accumulate Russian jewelry, furniture, and works of art. When the Russians decided in 1930 to nationalize his enterprise (renaming the Armand Hammer pencil factory for Sacco and Vanzetti), he took his collection plus the Russian government notes paid for his companies out of the country with him. More bullish on Russia than most Western businessmen, he bought up the notes given to other dispossessed Westerners at discounts up to 72 percent and did handsomely when the Russians paid off in full. The art formed the basis for the Hammer Galleries and for his book, *In Quest of the Romanoff Treasure,* written in the early 1930s.

Hammer had wrapped up his first Russian phase just as Harry Sinclair, a multimillionaire ex-Kansan ex-druggist whose initial capital was insurance collected from the dubiously accidental shooting off of an expendable toe, tried to corner the production of Soviet oil with his winnings from the shortly-to-break Teapot Dome bribery, in which he had received an oil lease worth $100 million for a $100,000 gift to Interior Secretary Albert Fall.

This scandal broke over a nation hankering for normalcy in the

* Armand's father, Julius Hammer, was a founder of the American Communist Party. The Allied American Company, of which Julius, Armand, and Armand's brother Victor were directors, was the vehicle for much of the family's Russian commerce.

wake of the deep divisiveness that had attended Woodrow Wilson's doomed effort to assume an enlarged international role for the United States in the League of Nations. The elected purveyor of normalcy, President Warren G. Harding, mixed some strong appointments in foreign and monetary affairs with some appalling cronies at Justice and Interior. He died in the summer of 1923, just as he had begun to realize the extent of the cancer on his presidency. His successor appointed a team of special prosecutors who, together with a Senate investigating committee, uncovered and publicized a remarkable set of events of which a pale summary follows.

In late 1921 a group of oil executives, of whom Sinclair and Colonel Robert Stewart, the chairman of the board of Standard of Indiana, were the most prominent, formed the Continental Trading Company, which bought 33,333,333 barrels of oil for $1.50 per barrel and immediately resold it to the companies they represented for $1.75. The quarter-per-barrel difference, worth some $8 million, was used in part to buy Liberty Bonds for the creators of the Continental Trading Company. Much later the bright light of public disclosure persuaded these gentlemen that perhaps the bonds rightfully belonged to their companies, and they sheepishly surrendered them. Colonel Stewart maintained that he had been holding his $759,000 in trust during the seven years. As proof, he produced a trust agreement written in pencil.

Sinclair's $759,000 moved in two curious directions. Some $260,000 went to the Republican National Committee, where the bonds were laundered by being indefinitely loaned to others in return for money that concealed the immense single gift. Another $100,000 went to Fall, along with yet another $100,000 "loan" from fellow oilman E. L. Doheny. Pressed to produce Fall's note for the loan, Doheny could only find half of it, the half without Fall's signature.

The record was further blurred when one Archie Roosevelt, son of T.R. and an officer of the Sinclair companies, testified that a fellow Sinclair employee had told him of a $68,000 payment to the manager of Fall's New Mexico ranch. The fellow employee replied that this was a terrible mistake, that he had actually told Roosevelt of the transfer of "six or eight cows."

Other potential witnesses, including several founders of the Continental Trading Company, left the country. Cabinet officers suffered extraordinary lapses of memory and gave answers that volunteered nothing. Former Attorney General Harry Daugherty refused to testify about a related scandal before a New York grand jury, claiming five types of attorney-client privilege and noting also that his testimony "might tend to incriminate me."

Calvin Coolidge's aura of rectitude and the general economic prosperity diminished public interest in the complexities of the Harding scandals. After several quick resignations, public wrath turned against the persistent investigators. Senators Walsh and Wheeler were pilloried in the New York papers, which called them "the Montana scandal managers," "mudgunners," "assassins of character," and leaders of "a Democratic lynching-bee."[10] Superpatriot Fred Marvin of the Key Men of America attributed the oil scandals to "a gigantic international conspiracy . . . of the internationalists, or shall we call them socialists and communists?"[11]

John D. Rockefeller, Jr., a large stockholder in Standard of Indiana as a result of his father's holdings in the original Standard Oil Trust, ousted Colonel Stewart from his chairmanship of the company, but the public and the courts were generally more lenient. Fall was sentenced to a year in jail for having taken the same bribe that Sinclair and Doheny were acquitted of having offered. Sinclair did have to spend three months in jail for contempt of the Senate, whose questions he had declined to answer, and for having his jurors shadowed by private detectives. His jail sentence dampened Soviet interest in renegade American oilmen until Armand Hammer closed his one-man parenthesis around a half century of Soviet commercial intransigence by reappearing as a trader with President Nixon's unofficial blessing in 1972. The blessing may owe something to a $14,000 contribution to the Watergate legal defense fund and a $48,000 offering to Maurice Stans's coffers in the final April days before the 1972 campaign finance reporting laws took effect.

After leaving Russia, Hammer avoided the Depression with profits from transactions in livestock feed, raised a herd of purebred Black Angus cattle, arranged a sale of much of the bankrupt William Randolph Hearst's art collection by Gimbels department store, and celebrated the end of Prohibition by cornering the whiskey-barrel-stave market with Russian imports. In the early 1940s, with the country short on whiskey and long on potatoes, he produced potato-based bourbon and commercial alcohol. In 1955 he retired, selling off the whiskey part of his $100,000 potato investment to Schenley for $6.5 million and the commercial-alcohol part to Publicker Industries for $1 million.

Three years later he made a loan to the foundering Occidental Petroleum Company to drill two wells. One brought in a field. Then he made a much larger loan, resulting in the stock options that gave him control of the company. After a brief hiatus in which he bought the Mutual Broadcasting System for $700,000, found that he couldn't make it run to his satisfaction, and sold it for $2 million four months before it went into bankruptcy, he began to build Oxy. In 1961 it paid its first cash dividend in twenty-eight years. In 1963 it showed its first operating profit and acquired two fertilizer companies through exchanges of stock. In 1964 it picked up the Jefferson Lake Sulphur Company during what proved to be a low point in both Jefferson Lake's history and that of the sulfur market. Also in 1964 Oxy made two major discoveries. First it found extensive phosphate deposits essential to its fertilizer business. Then it found that there was no profit in fertilizers, so in 1965 it acquired the Permian Corporation, a Texas pipeline company, and went into California real estate development, another loser.

Oxy's real catapulting to oil and corporate status came in 1966, when the company was awarded two drilling concessions in Libya. If a suit filed by the investment-banking concern of Allen & Co. is to be believed, the phrase "was awarded" is a passive euphemism for a process in which Oxy either bribed or promised to bribe a group that included a bogus French general, who was really a notorious international swindler named Pegulu, and two Libyan ministers in the cabinet of King Idris II, after whom Oxy named its most successful well on the two wonderfully productive concessions.[12] By the spring of 1968 the company had acquired the Island Creek Coal Company and the Hooker Chemical Company while gaining effective control of the Signal Oil Company's European marketing structure. In May, 1968, Dr. Hammer turned seventy. His daily invigorator ("insurance policy" in his words) continued to be an early-morning clamber down a fur-covered spiral ladder to a half hour of sidestroking around his swimming pool.[13] He never practiced medicine.

Oxy's approach to Evans stemmed from a discussion at a March, 1968, meeting of oil marketers in Texas. At that encounter Herbert Sostek, an official of the Gibbs Oil Company and one of New England's largest independent gasoline and home heating-oil marketers, casually discussed the idea of a New England refinery with counterparts at Axel Johnson and Oxy. Upon returning to New York following the Texas meeting, the Johnson executive described the idea to John Buckley, a former editor of *Petroleum Intelligence Weekly* and a friend of Evans. The Johnson board of directors then voted not to pursue the project, but Buckley, stressing the need for additional political leverage in New England and the financial and marketing advantages of a more diversified consortium, persuaded Evans to include the Gibbs company and several additional independent heating-oil and gasoline marketers. Buckley then contacted Oxy, a brash newcomer seeking markets for a surfeit of extremely low-sulfur Libyan oil. Occidental was resented and snubbed by the established companies and had no reason to be solicitous of an import system that protected the U.S. production and markets in which it had no share. The company had already made three acquisitions that spring (Island Creek, Hooker, and part of Signal) of companies bigger than it had been the year before, and in less than a week it decided to consider a challenge to all the forces that were propping up the Mandatory Oil Import Program. By May 5, Evans was able to circulate an aide-mémoire which contemplated a refinery owned 30 percent by the IFOMA-descended group of industrial oil companies, 25 percent by Oxy, 20 percent by Evans and Buckley, and 5 percent by Refinery Associates, who were simply feasibility consultants willing to take their compensation in ownership participation instead of cash.

Evans was finally ready to begin drilling in Washington, D.C., and he still had a 20 percent share in his project. His calculations assumed that Maine would be granted a foreign-trade zone for Machiasport in early summer, that Udall would then allocate the import permits immediately, that refinery construction would begin in September, and that the refinery would be producing fuel oil for the 1969–70 winter. Like most losing wildcatters, he can today cite a plausible theory of geology ultimately proven inapplicable to the terrain with which he dealt, and he can maintain that the drill was angled wrong by his successors, who argue with equal retrospective fervor that the whole venture was nuts.

The rest of May and early June passed in further negotiations among the participants and in the preparation of the trade-zone application. The work on the application was done by the two-man Maine Port Authority working closely with the governor's office and the Maine Department of Economic Development. On June 10, four days after Robert Kennedy's death, Business Development Fund filed its request for an oil-import quota of 20,000 barrels per day with the Secretary of the Interior. Evans still didn't know which companies would participate in his refinery or to what extent, but he knew that time was running out on the Johnson-Udall administration. He knew also by then that his option from the Maine Port Authority was worthless and that without the quota application in his name as a tangible manifestation of Business Development Fund's essentiality, his shifting partners might find a way to resolve their own differences out of his 20 percent.

Nine days after Evans's application reached Interior, Maine's foreign-trade-zone application was delivered to Foreign Trade Zones Board headquarters at the Department of Commerce, where it was immediately and properly labeled "seriously deficient" because of its failure to indicate the boundaries of the zone, the identity and financial capacity of the tenants, or the manner in which the land would be acquired. Since both Walter Corey of the governor's office and Edward Langlois of the Port Authority had discussed the application with the board staff, these newly discovered shortcomings came as a surprise, but they were told that on so controversial an application extra care was necessary.

More dubiously, the Foreign Trade Zone Board staff also told the state officials that the board would not approve a full-fledged foreign-trade zone in an area which had no port facilities. They suggested that the zone application be shifted to Portland, with a subzone for the refinery at Machiasport. Not knowing of any industries interested in a Portland zone, Maine's representatives were dismayed, but they felt that the time available to them would be more wisely spent in proceeding with an imaginary Portland zone than in attempting a court appeal of the board's position. No one noticed that neither the application nor the list of serious deficiencies mentioned the environment.

Nine days after the filing of the application, the New England Governors' Conference met in Stowe, Vermont, for its summer session. Each of the governors had met with Corey and/or Evans and had been told by the independent marketers in their states of the benefits of the project. At the public session on June 28, the project was outlined by Governor Curtis. The other governors spoke briefly of the regional benefits that they anticipated from the cheaper oil. The governors then urged that the federal permits be quickly granted, pledged regional solidarity, and symbolized it by appropriating $500,000 in New England Regional Commission funds to pay the state and local shares of such necessary public works as site clearance and the fencing off of the subzone. Again the environment was not discussed, but the omission was not noticed in the banner headlines that spread the news from Stowe to Maine. These press accounts were the first public indication

that an oil refinery and supertanker terminal were planned for the
Maine coast, but no one complained either about the absence of consultation or about the silence on environmental matters.

The local reaction sampled by the Bangor *Daily News* on June 29
was typified by Gilbert Hanson, Machiasport's postmaster of twenty-
eight years, who saw "a tremendous boost to the economy . . . a new
pattern of living. . . . We have all the ocean to the south for any air
pollutants to blow into, and since this would be a new installation, I
just don't see any problem at all. We need what it can do for us and all
around us. . . . This just seems to have dropped out of the heavens."

Machiasport First Selectman Hammond Flynn, a seventy-year-old
retired ship captain, told the *Daily News,* "Now these young people
won't have to go away from their home to find work."

State Representative Robert Watts saw a considerable reduction in
unemployment and hoped "it will cause a chain reaction for the smaller
industries; perhaps it will even change our traditional reputation of
recreation to a highly industrialized site. We've got to be very careful
to protect the interests of those people who have already purchased
land and homes in this area."

Most accommodating of all was Millard Urquhart, a lobster dealer,
who said, "I'm not getting alarmed over the chance that the lobster
fisherman may decide to put his boat and traps away to work in a mill.
It's a good deal. It will leave a lot of money in circulation. If I can't
operate, I'll just have to find something else to do. And that shouldn't
be too hard."

The statewide reaction was typified by a *Maine Sunday Telegram*
editorial headed "Great News for Machias!" and continuing:

> The wheel for Washington County may be coming full cycle! Splen-
> did! Machiasport, fishing town and home of a sardine packing plant,
> may now become a deepwater port for the World's biggest tankers, site
> of an oil refinery, hub of an industrialized Atlantic World Port which
> could benefit all New England.
>
> Next in line may be Eastport, whose 60 feet deep harbor may make it
> too a magnet to the giant 350,000 ton supertankers bringing oil to
> United States. Fine upswing for Washington County!
>
> . . . All who read the exciting news should rejoice that this kind of
> active, forward thinking is taking place in the Governor's Office and the
> Department of Economic Development. Here is yet another good sign of
> Maine on the move.
>
> To advise caution against overoptimism, to urge care in planning to

protect Maine's beauties, we will leave to the Jeremiahs. We credit the
men who dreamed this one up to have foreseen those problems too.

Today our word is "Hurray for Good News!"

Maine's only consequential environmental organization was the
Natural Resources Council, experienced primarily in successfully urging the designation of the Allagash River as a wilderness waterway. It
stood silent. The only immediate Jeremiah was Bruce Sprague, who
owned the 200-acre tip of the Machiasport Peninsula where he had
recently set himself up as a farmer and contractor. Sprague announced
that he had rejected a $200,000 offer from the Port Authority for his
land and wouldn't sell it at any price. Told by a *Maine Sunday Telegram* reporter that the Port Authority might take it through eminent
domain, he asked, "Why didn't one of my gunnery sergeants tell me
this could happen to me back when we invaded the Marshall Islands
in World War II?"

Jack Evans was to have less than three weeks to contemplate his
publicly unveiled project. In mid-July the Securities and Exchange
Commission gave its final blessing to the Occidental-Hooker merger,
and Oxy was free to focus its full attention on the Maine project.
Evans was summoned to a morning meeting in his own living room
with Oxy vice-presidents Dorman Commons and Thomas Wachtell,
who explained, not to Evans's surprise, that the project now required
the capabilities of a large company and that Oxy must either own it all
or forget it. Aware of the new problems at the Foreign Trade Zones
Board and tired of the disagreement among his partners, Evans sold
Business Development Fund, its worthless option, its pending quota
application, its stationery, and its share of his two offices, four telephone numbers, and part-time secretary for a promise of roughly $3.9
million payable when Oxy received the approvals necessary to build
the refinery.

Knowing that the quota request would involve Udall in allegations
of preferential treatment that would inevitably exhume Evans's past
ties to the secretary, Oxy made the payment of $3.9 million contingent
on Evans's having nothing further to do with any aspect of the project.
With half the day left to them, Commons and Wachtell called John
Buckley, Evans's associate, informed him of the sale, and hired him
as a consultant for a moderate salary and a promise of a big payment,
in capital-gains form, when the refinery was complete.

Because the independent marketers had never been able to agree on a corporate structure and had put up no money, Evans's sale left them out in the cold. Their names were not on the application to the Interior Department, and they had no special relationship with Maine. They did have an existing marketing structure, and they did have political strength in New England, both of which Occidental needed, so the acrimonious multi-cornered negotiations, now complicated by the marketers' perplexity over Evans's sudden disappearance, continued.

Evans's consultants were released within weeks, and three months later he and the Savannah Port Authority parted company in Georgia without even the suggestion of future payment.

Before the Machiasport project was publicly announced, a flamboyant Colorado entrepreneur had dazzled the state with visions of offshore oil production. The entrepreneur was John King, whose King Resources Company had succeeded remarkably in the mid-1960s on the basis of a mutual fund approach to investment in oil-drilling projects. At the peak of his company's spectacular success, King was estimated by *Forbes Magazine* to be worth some $300 million, and he was boasting that his company would soon outdrill Esso.

In the early spring of 1968 King came to Maine to sign a lease for oil-exploration rights to 3 million acres of sea bed in the Gulf of Maine. He had been attempting similar arrangements in Massachusetts and later in New Jersey but had found the political and legislative going too slow for his style. Maine was much more to his liking. At the Augusta airport he climbed into the governor's car, noticed the telephone and the governor's absence, and, in the half mile between the airport and the capitol, asked that calls be placed to Governor John Volpe in Massachusetts and Governor Richard Hughes in New Jersey. Neither was available.

While in Maine, he negotiated a permit for King Resources to explore the 3 million acres. Announcements made headlines which had a benign effect on King Resources stock. The investors did not immediately realize that the waters in question were also claimed by the federal government, which was discussing their exploration with other oil companies. The United States immediately filed suit to invalidate the permit and prevent others like it.

Because the basic issue was whether colonial charters and treaties gave the original thirteen states a claim to the sea bed superior to that of the federal government, the rest of the Atlantic Coast states joined

Maine as defendants. Six years later, with King Resources in inextricable bankruptcy, the suit continued unresolved. Because the King incursion did not involve refining and because it was so quickly wrapped in litigation, no one in Maine realized what must, in retrospect, have been clear to King and Hammer from the moment they first thought about it—Maine's 4000-mile coastline wasn't big enough for both of them.

3: Summer, 1968

First, an end to refinery competition in Cleveland. Next, the big refineries must join Standard or be eliminated. The railroads must make more favorable rebate arrangements with Standard and its allies than with others. The railroads must also refuse shipments of crude oil for export, for Standard planned to refine oil for the world. Lastly, there were those wild fellows, the oil producers. They had no sense of order, much less the dangers of unrestrained competition.

> A description of John D. Rockefeller's
> master plan for the 1870s from
> Stewart Holbrook's *The Age of the Moguls*[1]

If a man anywhere in Oildom drilled a bad hole, or backed the wrong horse, lost at poker, dropped money speculating, stubbed his toe, or ran an unprofitable refinery . . . it was the fashion for him to pose as the victim of a gang of conspirators and curse Standard Oil vigorously and vociferously.

> John J. McLaurin, *Sketches in Crude Oil*[2]

A BRIEF LULL followed the refinery announcement. By late July, 1968, the Interior Department had made public the quota request together with a covering letter from Occidental noting that it was now the sole owner of Business Development Fund and the Maine refinery project, that it wanted an oil-import quota not of 20,000 barrels per day but of 100,000 barrels per day, and that it would promise to use the allocation to wholesale heating oil at 10 percent below prevailing prices. The twenty-cent-per-barrel offer to a New England governors' marine resources foundation remained in effect and would, given a 100,000-barrel-per-day quota, have been worth $7.5 million per year. The entire package could not have been better designed to infuriate the domestic oil industry and, to a much lesser extent, to stimulate the embryonic national consciousness of the need to preserve underdeveloped areas and clean waters.

The oil industry was already sullen toward Secretary Udall's handling of the oil-import program. U.S. oil producers attached the same fervid significance to the 12.2 percent ceiling on imports into the eastern United States that they felt toward the 27.5 percent deduction from taxable income available as a depletion allowance. While the 27.5 percent figure had been under unavailing public attack practically since its inception in the 1920s, the 12.2 percent import limit had been subjected to less public scrutiny but to more private erosion as a result of Udall's residual-oil exemption, the petrochemical feedstock shuffle, and Caribbean exemptions. While each of these reallocations had annoyed some segments of the oil industry, none had inspired the massive indignation of the Occidental proposal. That proposal came from an upstart outsider, and the requested allocation was five times larger than any previously granted by Udall. Most of the oil would come not from Venezuela but from the Middle East. The use of supertankers would make the oil cheaper still, and, least tolerable of all, the project carried with it a specific promise to cut the very prices that the oil-import program was designed to maintain.

Lloyd Unsel, a columnist for *The Independent Petroleum Monthly*, voiced the industry's scorn:

> Occidental has taken a leaf from Udall's book on how to set up refineries seeking very special treatment under the oil import program. It is disillusioning that the plant will not be operated by black ghetto dropouts. But aside from this shortcoming, it is plain guaranteed to help solve virtually every other grievous problem on the domestic scene. . . . Some even expect that this refinery would cure the clangs.
>
> Take inflation for example. Despite the fact that the federal government, through the Federal Trade Commission, has in times past frowned on price-cutters in the oil business, Occidental . . . starts right off by declaring that . . . it will undersell everybody in the business by 10 percent. This can be put down to industrial statesmanship.[3]

This piece caught the theme of the multiharmonied denunciations that echoed beaglelike through corridors in Washington. Some of the major companies even entered into a loose gentlemen's agreement that none of them would profit from a mainland refinery constructed on the basis of a special quota allocation.*

Letters of protest from the presidents and chairmen of the boards of most of the majors were sent to Secretary Udall and to Secretary of Commerce C. R. Smith, who served as chairman of the Foreign Trade Zones Board. Carbon copies were usually sent to the White House.

* As a result of this agreement, Bob Monks was told by Jock Ritchie of Shell's Asiatic Petroleum subsidiary to structure C. H. Sprague's Machiasport participation in such a way that none of the profits flowed to Shell's 25 percent of his company.

These letters acknowledged the need to increase international trade and abolish rural poverty. The writers felt, however, that oil imports were not the way to achieve such goals and that the Maine proposal was, in Amoco's words, "Nothing more than an attempt to circumvent the restrictions of the oil import program while gaining for a single company an advantageous position over its competitors in the oil industry." President Andrew Tarkington of Conoco furnished the most comprehensive nightmare, although each of its components was dreamed by others as well:

> These requests will have an extensive and detrimental impact upon the entire nation. If approved, the Mandatory Oil Import Program will be crippled or destroyed and the security of this nation will be seriously threatened; the real purpose and intent of the Foreign Trade Zones Act will be circumvented and distorted. Occidental Petroleum Corporation will receive enormous giveaway profits approximating one billion dollars, and the alleged benefits to New England will be illusory and far outweighed by the cost to other parts of the nation and by the inequities and dislocations that will result throughout the petroleum industry.[4]

For company shareholders and for federal officials who had trouble with printed arguments, the Union Oil Company published a copiously illustrated pamphlet on oil-import controls. Feeling one of these needs to condemn the getting of something for nothing which occasionally seized the holders of millions of dollars' worth of oil-import tickets, Union likened the Oxy proposal to the freeloading of hippies and depicted Udall and the New Englanders as hairy "politician hippies," with Armand Hammer and his predecessors in special exemption as "oil man hippies."

Independent producers and refiners, whose sheer number and local activism gave them political weight approaching that of the majors, expressed themselves vehemently at Interior, Commerce, and the White House.* Right behind them and their trade associations came a wave of "expressions of concern" from politicians. Virtually the entire Texas and Louisiana Congressional delegations weighed in on the

---

* The political strength of the independents is best illustrated by the fact that the quota system itself was largely their work. Most of the majors had sufficient overseas crude oil to be relaxed about the U.S. crude price, and some, notably Gulf in Kuwait, had such an abundance of foreign over domestic crude that they fought quotas bitterly. Only after realizing the benefits available through the annual multimillion-dollar allocation of quotas to their refineries did these sometime champions of laissez-faire government abandon free trade and support the independent producers.

side of national security and the oil revenues that supported public education in their home states. The Interstate Oil Compact Commission, consisting of every state that has ever had any oil or natural-gas production, put its entire thirty-three-state membership on record as opposed to foreign-trade-zone quota allocations despite the fact that several of its East Coast states, whose oil production was insignificant, could only have benefited from cheap petroleum products from Maine.

Udall's response to the protest was that he could make no decision until the Foreign Trade Zones Board had acted. However, he set in motion a review of his earlier decision forbidding the entry of crude oil into trade zones. This review, coupled with the secretary's earlier ventilations of the import program, encouraged the Maine project's opponents to fight in the White House and at the Commerce Department to make sure that the project never reached Interior.

Their strategy relied heavily on delay. Polls indicated the likelihood of a Nixon Presidency, and the industry knew him to be a reliable friend. Humphrey, an old foe of the 27.5 percent depletion allowance, had chosen Maine's Senator Muskie, a clear enemy, as his Vice-Presidential running mate, but even if the Democrats won in November, a barrage of procedural delays and time-consuming litigation might discourage Occidental. At worst, delay would give the existing permit holders a year or two more to enjoy their share before having to make room for a newcomer.

Meanwhile, in New England, the proponents of the Maine plan were gathering forces of their own. Occidental and the independents undertook to tell the New England homeowner how thoroughly he was being bilked. The New England Council, a regional chamber of commerce operating under the motto "A rising tide lifts all the boats," coordinated massive publicity among its member organizations. Editorials blossomed from Maine to New York City stressing such themes as high per capita oil use, high costs, and the bloated major oil companies.

At times the pack got somewhat out of hand and confused the valid point that New England, because of its distance from domestic oil wells and relative proximity to foreign sources, was hurt more than other areas by oil-import controls with the untrue but appealing claim that New Englanders paid the highest home heating-oil costs in the nation. The latter claim brought convincing rebuttals from oil-industry trade groups, who pointed out that New England retail prices were indeed higher than average, but only because New England marketers, including the independents, took higher than average markups.

The only economically dissenting voices in New England came from the state petroleum associations, which chided New Englanders for putting their pocketbooks ahead of their patriotism. Curious that a group calling itself the Maine Petroleum Association would take such a position, Governor Curtis's office learned that the Maine Petroleum Association was no more than one of the fifty tentacles maintained in state capitals by the American Petroleum Institute to make sure that the oil-industry view was communicated to the hinterlands and vice versa. Normally these state associations are leaders in campaigns for more and better highways, lower gasoline taxes, and environmental moderation, but they are available to speak out in local accents on any issue of concern to the oil industry.

As the economic impacts of the Occidental proposal translated themselves into the political forms, the New Englanders realized that the struggle could not take place in any orderly arena under known and reliable rules. They learned that the United States government, presiding over the world's heaviest consumers of oil, not only had no department charged with comprehensive oil or energy policy but also had developed no policy guidelines beyond a concept of national security vaguely based on a financially healthy domestic oil industry. Consequently, the most significant single petroleum-import proposal in American history drifted for decision to a Foreign Trade Zones Board and staff without experience or qualifications in national oil policy, there to be decided, under procedures guaranteeing confusion, on statutory criteria which meshed with the national security only by coincidence.

The Foreign Trade Zones Board staff did their best. Their rejection of Maine's June application had been entirely proper but had confronted the state with new requirements in the form of engineering blueprints, land acquisitions, and tenants for the Portland zone.

Reluctant to take the time or face the politics involved in seeking a special appropriation from a Republican legislature for an essentially speculative purpose, Governor Curtis's office looked instead to the refinery proponents to meet these expenses. Evans was out, his resources already spread thin; Oxy was not yet in, its buying-out of Evans still being some weeks away. It had to be the independents, so

Curtis contacted the two that did the most business in Maine, C. H.. Sprague (Robert Monks) and the Dead River Company.*

In many business ventures, the advancing of this front-end money to do planning, study, and design work before any real assets are acquired offers an inexpensive but risky (if the project doesn't go forward, these expenditures can rarely be recovered) way to gain a commanding position in the venture. So Monks viewed the Curtis request in this case. Worried about his eastern Maine monopoly and his loan payments, unable to establish any primacy within Evans's proposed coprosperity sphere, knowing that Occidental would be difficult at best to deal with, he quickly agreed to join Dead River in paying most of the costs of the foreign-trade-zone application and thereby established the kind of special relationship to the refinery project that he had been seeking all along.

The Sprague Company and Dead River formed the Machiasport Company, each owning half, to handle these expenses. The Machiasport Company undertook to underwrite any losses sustained by the Portland zone, a sure loser, and paid some of the costs involved in upholstering the Maine application. On his own, Monks began securing options on the key parcels of land, including the all-important deepwater terminal site on Stone Island. He had decided that the uniqueness of Stone Island's access to the deep water, coupled with the narrow peninsular refinery site, meant that control of the land would give control of the project.

Governor Curtis's staff realized the dangers in permitting exclusive control to go to one participant. Their hurried solution was another of those peculiar property documents so much in vogue in Augusta. This one was a "Dear Governor Curtis" letter from Monks stating that the options were being taken on behalf of the state and would be turned over at cost upon the granting of a foreign-trade zone. Again it was a unilateral commitment, without legal weight, but again it served the immediate interests of both parties. Monks at last had his foot in the door, and Maine's foreign-trade-zone application was advanced. Walter

---

* Dead River was a Bangor-based miniconglomerate founded in 1907 when two coal dealers purchased 5000-acre Jerusalem Township in order to provide wood to a cash-short Great Northern paper mill in order that the mill might continue to consume their coal until it made enough paper to earn enough money to pay for both the coal and the wood. Thirty years later the company went into the gasoline business when one of its land purchases contained an Esso station, and by 1968 it was Maine's largest gasoline and heating-oil dealer.

Corey, Governor Curtis's aide for oil matters, rationalized the documentary shortcomings by concluding that he had no reason to doubt Monks, that the threat of adverse publicity would deter Sprague from backing off its commitment, and that, if worse came to worst, the Maine Port Authority could take the land by eminent domain. He was privately appalled when subsequent research showed that such action would almost certainly be unconstitutional.

Monks's land acquisitions began none too soon, for after Occidental bought out Business Development Fund, it immediately began to assist in the preparation of the zone application. The Foster Wheeler engineering firm was retained and prepared detailed refinery descriptions and blueprints. Inquiring casually about the land itself, the Foster Wheeler people were told that the state had it under control.

Corey and Ed Langlois of the Maine Port Authority were given the task of preparing a viable application for Portland's clearly unviable trade zone. The effort began straightforwardly enough with a letter to Maine businessmen describing the advantages of a trade zone and asking if they were interested. None were.

Corey and Langlois then enlisted the aid of the New England Council and a leading Maine bank. Both organizations and Maine's Department of Economic Development told companies with which they did business that a letter indicating an interest in the Portland zone would not commit them to anything but would enhance the possibility of a Machiasport refinery and a rising tide for all their boats. On that basis, the Port Authority received more than 100 letters of interest which became part of its application to a flabbergasted Foreign Trade Zones Board staff that was fully aware that the Portland zone had been its own idea.*

On August 17 Corey and Andy Nixon of the Maine Department of Economic Development hand-carried the revised application to the trade-zones staff. The staff expressed astonishment that the revisions had taken so little time and acknowledged that the application now

* Only one letter was withheld from the parcel passed on to the Commerce Department. That one was a single sentence of warm endorsement from Bed Rock Dogs International, a Rhode Island firm involved in airline-flight kennels. Maine officials withheld it because they foresaw problems enough without arguing over whether the framers of the Foreign Trade Zones Act had foreseen the possibility of the European champion Irish setter mating with the all-American bitch on the duty-free ground of a trade zone and returning, untaxed in any financial sense, to Europe, puppies to be exported to the four winds ten weeks later.

appeared to be in order. Not suspecting that the staff had been instructed to take its time, Nixon and Corey returned to Maine. The
board waited four weeks before announcing that the Maine application
was complete and that public hearings would commence a month later
in Portland.

Four years later Langlois was going through some old correspondence seeking clues to firms interested in helping a new Maine Port
Authority drive to bring commerce to the Portland waterfront. Coming upon many enthusiastic expressions of interest in the Portland
trade zone, he excitedly began to consider reviving the idea. His enthusiasm waned as he dug deeper into the folders and found drafts of
all the letters he had just been reading. He remembered then that,
regardless of who had signed them, he had written most of them himself.

While New England and the Southwest circled for position in vague
federal arenas, Washington County was evaluating the proposal by its
own standards. Less exalted than the national security or the continued
prosperity of the oil industry, these standards were as firmly held but
no better defined. Two concerns were dominant: the need to bolster
the county economy and the need to protect the fishing industry.

For nearly a century the county's economic decline had paralleled
that of Machiasport. By 1960 the population was slightly more than
half what it had been at the turn of the century. The shipbuilding was
gone entirely, and one or two fish canneries operated part time on bays
which had supported a dozen. Scattered lumber mills remained, and
the offshore waters and clamflats still yielded a living to the few thousand able to harvest them. Inland, most of the textiles and tanneries
had long since gone South, and rocky soil and declining markets had
triumphed over most who had ever sought to farm. The only crop in
general cultivation was the blueberry, which grew in such abundance
on the burned-over barrens that Washington County boasted of supplying 80 percent of the nation's canned blueberries. The boast did not
usually mention that blueberries were picked by migrant workers,
many of them imported Canadian Indians, working at minimal wages
and living in minimal housing.

In an eastern corner, at once salvaging and ravaging, harvesting and
polluting, employing and exploiting, paying well and depriving, a
Georgia Pacific Paper Company mill squatted athwart the county's

patchwork economy, ambiguous as a garden toad, a continuing reminder that since 1900 most of the trees, men, and water in that part of the state had been employed in the manufacture of paper.

In 1968 the paper industry and its pulpwood suppliers employed roughly one fourth of Maine's workforce. The paper mills paid the best wages in the state, wages roughly equal to those in oil refineries elsewhere. The paper companies owned one third of the state's land area, and almost 90 percent of that (an area larger than Massachusetts and Rhode Island together) belonged to the seven largest firms. All seven had their headquarters in other states, and each had annual revenues larger than Maine's annual tax receipts.

The state's wilderness had been managed primarily for the production of low-cost pulpwood. Dubious early-cutting practices by some of the companies had left large areas tangled in brush and had ruined many small trout and salmon streams. Post-cutting neglect had imperiled reforestation.

Maine's major waterways, once abundant with trout and salmon, had been transformed into carriers of pulp-mill wastes. Some had been taken over by annual log drives which, for all their romantic aura, had denied the rivers to other users and had deposited a century's residue of boat-menacing logs and oxygen-depleting bark. Still other streams and watersheds had been impounded behind systems of dams raised and lowered to meet mill flowage needs without regard for bass and trout eggs sometimes laid in six inches of lake water. To those who regretted the loss, Maine officialdom reiterated versions of Governor Samuel Cony's 1865 valedictory:

> The mills and manufactories upon our rivers and streams, though they have banished the former denizens of these waters, furnish a compensation immeasurable as compared with all the fish that have ever floated in their bosom.[5]

For nearly a century, the state systematically undertaxed paper company lands, thereby shifting a tax burden to other landowners and taxpayers and subsidizing, for better or worse, the companies' inclination to let much of their holdings stand idle. Meanwhile, in the mill towns themselves, paper company stacks had deposited a mixture of chemicals and aromas which made breathing unpleasant and sometimes aggravated respiratory infections while peeling paint off cars and houses.

By the late 1960s mill managements elsewhere in the state had moved grudgingly toward alterations, sometimes corrections, of their worst abuses. Georgia Pacific marched at the rear of this trend.

For five years the company had resisted installing a $10,000 fishway in a small dam despite demands from both the state and the town of Grand Lake Stream. Georgia Pacific, alone among the Maine paper companies, obtained exemption from 1970 legislation ending Maine log driving. A waste treatment plant opened by the company amid promises to reduce water pollution by 82 percent had achieved less than 20 percent removal. At town meetings each year, the mill management and many employees had successfully spoken and voted against additional local expenditures for public schools because such expenditures would be reflected in the property taxes paid by the mill.

The declining economy had made Maine more acquiescent toward industry's exploitative side than a more prosperous and diversified state would have been. Knowing that they could not find other jobs, people would not jeopardize their workplace for better air or better fishing. The clichéd summary for the dilemma of midcentury Maine was "Payrolls or pickerels?" The state had always chosen payrolls.

Maine's distance from raw materials and major markets had discouraged advances by new industry after the arrival of the paper mills. Washington County's only vision of alternative growth had come early in the Depression when President Roosevelt had included in his public works program a billion-dollar proposal to convert the extraordinary tides of Passamaquoddy Bay into tidal power cheap enough to draw industry to eastern Maine as river dams had done for the Tennessee Valley and the Pacific Northwest. Plans were drawn up and a makeshift village was constructed, but opposition from private power companies and soaring cost estimates forced abandonment of the idea and left eastern Washington County with an unnecessary village, a surplus construction-labor force, and an enduring cynicism toward politicians' promises of economic bonanzas.

After the tidal power fiasco, Washington County, like most of Maine, had become a developmental wallflower, grateful for what industry there was, willing to sacrifice for more, skeptical of the intentions of persons suggesting that the risks might outweigh the benefits.

The Machias Bay towns were governed by selectmen, their budgets closely scrutinized by town residents at annual meetings. They had occasional planning boards, but with zoning nonexistent, a man could do what he pleased with his land. Such zoning-is-socialism, strike-your-

own-bargain values can rarely have been encountered in such pure
form by the U.S. oil industry since Dad Joiner inundated Texas's Rusk
County cattle pastures and drilling followed with such individualistic
abandon that loss of gas pressure (gas was good only for pressure then,
and trillions of cubic feet were just burned at the wellhead) sealed
millions of barrels of oil in the ground and forced governmental drilling and production controls. The people of the Machias Bay area still
had a real pride in this individualism, but their firm belief that a man
wasn't any poorer than he deserved to be had combined with fifty years
of economic decline to give the individualism a negative, sometimes
sullen twist.

Eastern Maine in 1968 was a less bleak form of what Charles Reich
in *The Greening of America* was to term "Consciousness I," still seeing

America as if it were a world of small towns and simple virtues. Invention
and machinery and production are the equivalent of progress; material
success is the road to happiness; nature is beautiful but must be con-
quered and put to use. Competition is the law of nature and man; life
is a harsh pursuit of individual self-interest. Consciousness I believes
that the American dream is still possible, and that success is determined
by character, morality, hard work, and self-denial. It does not accept the
fact that organizations predominate over individuals in American life,
or that social problems are due to something other than bad character,
or that the possibility of individual success, based on ability and enterprise, is largely out of date. Consciousness I still thinks that the least
government governs best. It votes for a candidate who seems to possess
personal moral virtues and who promises to return to earlier conditions
of life, law and order, rectitude, and lower taxes. It believes that the
present American crisis requires reducing government programs and
expenditures, greater reliance on private business, forcing people now
on welfare to go to work, taking stern measures to put down subversion
at home and threats from abroad, and, above all, a general moral re-
awakening of the people.[6] . . .

Consciousness I could not grasp, or could not accept, the reality that
the individual was no longer competing against the success of other
individuals but against a system. It could not understand that "private
property" in the hands of a corporation was a synonym for quasi-gov-
ernmental power, far different from the property of an individual. It
could not understand the crucial point that collective action against
corporate power would not have been a step toward collectivization, but a
step to preserve democracy in a society that had been collectivized.[7] . . .

If the people would not dominate the forces that were changing their country then those forces would dominate the people. Consciousness I, losing its own roots but holding tight to its myths, was ready game for manipulation by the organized forces of society.[8]

Despite the general applicability of Reich's analysis, three groups did not welcome oil. The summer residents, the few who preferred the real solitude of Maine's eastern coast to the more sociable rustications from Penobscot Bay south, were predictably appalled. The lobstermen and clam diggers, not conspicuously ecological in disposing of cars, boats, bottles, or sewage, depended for their livelihood on a clean ocean. Whatever it might do for their children or their taxes, an oil refinery could not help the fishing. The Washington County establishment, a near-feudal mixture of mill management, blueberry and sardine canners, textile and sawmill operators, and merchants and landlords, had mixed feelings about the impact of oil operations. Nice as it would be to have more money around, the reliable but minimally paid men and women who cut the wood, milled the cloth, and picked the blueberries would demand higher wages. Opposition to that possibility could not be voiced openly, but it provoked ecological sentiment from several prominent men who had never reproached Georgia Pacific.

Those making the case for a Machias Bay refinery in 1968 frequently compared the area to darkest Appalachia and suggested that the project would be a fine test of the usefulness of new-town construction and other federal spending tools in revitalizing rural America and checking the flight to the cities.* The analysis went no deeper, but the parallels between Machias Bay and other areas of rural America are more profound than mere eligibility for federal programs. William Faulkner and Harry Caudill, who never wrote of Maine, have more to say about the forces that shape life in these areas than all of the maddeningly saccharine "Down East" analyses that Maine inspires every summer.

Faulkner's Yoknapatawpha County, stripped of the moral taint of slavery and burdened by the memory of economic instead of military defeat, could pass for Washington County. The communication, com-

---

* Machiasport aside, this concern became inoperative. When President Nixon vetoed 1973 legislation providing funds for rural water- and sewer-facility construction, Office of Management and Budget Director Roy Ash explained, "It isn't the role of the federal government to overcome everybody's error of judgment as to where he lives."

merce, and humor are similar, and the land itself has character apart from those who people it. Individual good intentions, decency, and indignation are vulnerable to amoral force, whether from without or within. *Sanctuary*'s urban gangster, hating animals, spitting in a well, fearing an owl or a walk through darkened woods, would have been as unnatural and irresistible in Machias as in Jefferson, and declining communities seem easy prey to the amoral acquisitiveness of emergent Snopeses or their more polished counterparts among the aristocratic remnant.

Except for its concern with miscegenation, Faulkner's most wilderness-dominated work, *The Bear,* could be moved north without distortion. The scene at the novella's end, in which the wilderness is disappearing into a lumber mill and the last of the former bear hunters vainly asserts ownership of a tree full of chattering squirrels, is as appropriate to Maine as to Mississippi, and so is Faulkner's own 1957 perspective on the work.

> No matter how fine anything is, it can't endure, because once it stops, abandons motion, it is dead. . . .
> Change, if it is not controlled by wise people, destroys sometimes more than it brings. . . . If the reason for the change is base in motive —that is, to clear the wilderness just to make cotton land, to raise cotton on an agrarian economy of peonage, slavery, is base, because it's not as good as the wilderness which it replaces. But if in the end that makes more education for more people, and more food for more people, more of the good things of life—I mean by that to give man leisure to use what's up here instead of just leisure to ride around in automobiles, then it was worth destroying the wilderness. But if all the destruction of the wilderness does is give more people more automobiles just to ride around in, then the wilderness was better.[9]

Eastern Maine and Faulkner's Mississippi share the economies and sociologies of regions governmentally classified as depressed areas, but even at that they are pleasant habitats beside the Appalachian Kentucky evoked in *Night Comes to the Cumberlands,* Harry Caudill's history of the Cumberland Mountain region. That history shares with Maine and Mississippi the initial timber-company exploitation of the vulnerable self-reliance of mountaineers who thought themselves shrewd bargainers. The timber cutters' practices were as wasteful in Kentucky as elsewhere of the wood itself and of the stream beds used for log drives, but the definitive exploitation was sculpted by the coal companies.

Systematically buying up broadly worded deeds to subsurface mineral rights at trivial prices, coal's agents left the mountaineers with little of their land beyond the duty to pay property taxes. To get a job in the mines, the miner frequently had to rent a home in the company town, shop at the company store, and send his children to company-dominated schools. Working conditions were perilous and created cripples and widows in quantities rivaling those from the legendary feuds, which themselves made organization among the Kentuckians impossible.

Elected officials at all levels seem to have been company-chosen men, largely content to hold pardon hearings and issue commissions in the state militia. Their profoundest thinking on economic development perceived an overriding need for a prosperous coal industry. To that end they undertaxed coal properties while overtaxing individual land-owners. Since the individuals had little to pay taxes with, they were under pressure to grant more mineral leases while the tax revenues remained inadequate to support even the minimal schools and high-ways. These were financed by extensive borrowings against a future which proved unable to sustain them.

Prohibition brought the lawlessness and violence of a moonshine economy. Repeal brought further poverty. Indiscriminate logging caused disastrous floods which combined with rising national use of oil to drive the coal-mine operators to further gouging in the company towns. The miners responded with strikes which drove more of coal's customers to oil.

Coal rebounded after World War II on the strength of strip mining, which ruined the land, and automation, which held down employment. Oil prices kept coal prices down, and to the immediate south the Tennessee Valley Authority, until then a contrasting proof of what might be achieved in similar terrain by regional and federal planning, expanded into coal-fired power plants. These plants continued the outstanding TVA cheap-energy record by acquiring huge amounts of strip-mined coal and coal leases at bargain prices.

Many talented and ambitious younger people had been leaving the Cumberland Mountains for years. As employment and living conditions worsened, they were joined by most of the able youth of the region, many of whom were to wind up as refugees in slums in Ohio, Indiana, and Illinois.

The women's lives had never consisted of much more than hard work, teen-age marriage, and the rearing of many children through brief childhoods punctuated by attendance at the funerals or hospital beds of the impetuous men to whose uncontrollable futures their own were bound. As these women aged, their children moved away and the hopelessness around them increased. They found it harder and harder to preserve any semblance of neatness or order against the ceaseless rain of coal dust. First the streets, then the house exteriors, then even the interiors took on a smear-prone gray.

The original individualism passed through the unionism of John L. Lewis and then of Tony Boyle to a state of mind in which large efforts were expended to get entire families of cousins on the welfare rolls that forty years before had been beneath contempt. By the mid-1960s, even as Jack Evans traveled the East Coast in search of an import and refinery combination to lower the price of coal's competitor oils, Caudill's Cumberlands were a land in which

> Exhaustion is apparent on every hand—exhaustion of soil, exhaustion of men, exhaustion of hopes. Weariness and lethargy have settled everywhere. Nor has a single symptom of improvement manifested itself. . . . The plateau, almost unnoticed, continues to lurch toward a day when perhaps 80% of its inhabitants will be welfare recipients.[10]

Imagining gaunt women and crippled men listening in graying frame houses amid mud on cavitied hillsides as coal-powered radios and televisions, whose magnetism had already atrophied their once sociable folk culture, vexed them with the images and exhortations of a general prosperity, one can find much to value in the belittled Washington County way of life.

The general public's first real chance to debate the refinery proposal did not come until two months after its June, 1968, announcement in Vermont. In the interim, Governor Curtis had met with several Machias area officials, but the meeting was confined to exchanges of enthusiasm and agreement that any nation that could put a man on the moon could build a pollution-free oil refinery. In mid-August Charles Dorchester, a local minister, organized a meeting to which he invited representatives of Occidental and the state to discuss the proposed refinery.

Occidental, having only just acquired its first refineries (all in Europe), had no American employees involved in oil refining. Warned by Curtis aides that Dr. Hammer's notions of public relations were ill-suited to Washington County, the company sent Ted Davis, an engineer from the Foster Wheeler Corporation. Maine was represented by Ed Langlois and P. Andrews Nixon, a twenty-nine-year-old, Yale-educated New Yorker who had come to Maine eight months previously after a Peace Corps term in Sierra Leone. Nixon found a 200-year-old salt-water farm and a job in the state's Department of Economic Development, where he had planned to stay only until he found more permanent work. His talents blended well with the requirements of the Machiasport project, and he stayed longer than he had intended, never quite shaking the belief that his real place was out there in private enterprise.

Dorchester had scheduled his meeting for the Machias High School cafeteria but was forced by an attendance of more than 600 to move to the gymnasium. The meeting was orderly, and most of the questions were directed toward jobs (about 400 of them, for which local people would be trained and hired whenever possible), taxes (the value of the refinery facilities would be roughly $150 million, 100 times the total value of the property in Machiasport and twice the value of all of the property of Washington County), oil prices (Occidental promised to cut wholesale home heating-oil prices by 10 percent), effect on the fisheries (no one could guarantee against spillage, but major disasters were unlikely and small spills would not be harmful), and pollution generally (a modern refinery served by modern tankers would be much cleaner than the general refinery image, and Maine could, through the Foreign Trade Zones lease, write in special safeguards and close down the refinery if they were not met).

The only clearly voiced reservations came from a few outspoken lobstermen from neighboring towns, who had figured out that the refinery wasn't going to improve the fishing, and from summer residents. The most vocal of the latter was Gardiner C. Means, a leading New Deal economist and coauthor, with Adolph A. Berle, Jr., of a definitive work on the structure and behavior of corporations.

Means had been canoeing on the Maine coast and summering for twenty years on Machias Bay's Yellowhead Island in a house with a commanding view of both the refinery and the terminal sites. He had had a long-standing desire to do something for the Machias area economy, and had in 1966 designed a fiberglass rowboat, attractive to the elderly or the young, who could easily haul its light weight over the lengthy mud flats occasioned by Maine's extraordinary tides. Despite unfavorable economic prospects, he had set up an eight-man manufacturing operation in Machias which turned out some two hun-

dred boats before the fumes began to sicken the workers. Simultaneously, Means realized that he didn't have time to market the boats and
so discontinued production.

Although conscious of the need for a local economic stimulant and
not opposed to the refinery, Means was appalled by what he regarded
as the conspiratorial silence of oil's promoters and by the fatalism
with which many skeptical fishermen regarded the refinery's incursion.
Midway through Dorchester's meeting, he got the floor and depicted a
scene of devastation ranging from heavy air and blackened waters to
the honky-tonks that would be needed for the refinery workers and
sailors on leave. As he spoke the audience diminished substantially,
but many stayed to argue with him, leaving Davis, Nixon, and Langlois
as mere spectators. As they left at the meeting's end, they were several
times assured that the summer people and other opponents didn't
represent the real feelings of the community.

At the state level, the first tentative questionings also began in
September. The Governor's Council of Economic Advisers, an informal
collection of academicians, professional economists (including Means),
and businessmen who sometimes met annually, submitted a list of ten
questions concerning the economic, environmental, and social aspects
of the project. The governor's staff was chagrined to discover that only
three of the questions could be answered with any confidence. This
shortcoming, combined with the Machias gymnasium meeting, resulted
in Governor Curtis's setting up a planning committee to guide governmental action relative to the project.

Curtis created the committee with the same enthusiasm that he had
accepted the refinery proposal itself. Born in a farmhouse in central
Maine, the governor had progressed in fourteen years from high school
to the Maine Maritime Academy to a stint with the merchant marine
through a degree from the Portland Law School to two years on a
Congressman's staff and two more working for the Library of Congress.
Energy and enthusiasm, two qualities often missing from the general
Republican stuffiness that had dominated state politics since the end
of the nineteenth century, had propelled him successfully through a
primary campaign to the Democratic nomination for a Congressional
seat that he was to lose by 200 votes. Curtis was chosen secretary of
state by a Democratic legislature. In that office he built a successful
gubernatorial campaign on the need for economic development, highway safety, and the stand-pat incompetence of his opponent. He was
elected in 1966, the nation's youngest governor at thirty-five.

Knowing the overriding importance of a decent job to self-respect in Maine, he made economic growth his highest priority. He shared the general regret at the economically dictated demise of the state's major rivers, but he supported the temporary degrading of a northern Maine stream in hopes that a new beet refinery would diversify the region's one-crop potato economy. He had been profoundly annoyed that conservationists were aligned with the private power companies, in Maine as at Hetch Hetchy, in opposition to the damming of the St. John River for a publicly owned hydroelectric project aimed at lowering high regional electric rates.

In general, Curtis had more respect for industry than for industrialists and more regard for the environment than for environmentalists. With the adaptability that separates most politicians from most theorists, he assumed that conflicts over the refinery would be dealt with as the project progressed and did not need to be pigeonholed in advance. The appointment of the Machiasport Conservation and Planning Committee fifteen months after the serious work on the project had begun and two weeks before the final plan was to go to public hearing was shortsighted even by 1968 standards, but Curtis was never to waver from his commitment to codify the committee's recommendations.

The committee included Gardiner Means, four other environmentalists, six Washington County residents of various persuasions, thirteen state officials, four federal employees involved in economic development, and two state legislators. Andy Nixon was named chairman but was unable to attend the first and only meeting. That meeting was dominated first by Means's accurate insistence that neither the state nor Occidental had shown any concrete environmental concern and then by Commissioner of Economic Development James Keefe's pointing out that well-paying jobs in Washington County might be worth some environmental sacrifice. The Washington County representatives conceded that, while they wanted the refinery, they had never seen any of the relevant descriptive documents. They wanted and were promised a crash planning program to lessen the impact of the transient construction workers on their area. One environmentalist observed sympathetically that no one wanted to repeat the desecration wrought by the Navy in constructing its blinking radio towers over several square miles of the Cutler peninsula. Tom Maloy, the chairman of Machiasport's Planning Board, responded: "We don't mind Cutler. On a clear night, there's a lot of people that like to go down and look at the lights."

Two days later Andy Nixon named a seven-member conservation subcommittee to prepare the standards for air- and water-pollution control to be included in the eventual trade-zone lease with Occidental. Means was chairman of the subcommittee, and Nixon was one of the members.

This arrangement involved two risks. First, the subcommittee might simply have disintegrated, since its two leading members had little regard for each other. Means felt that Nixon was a brash young man, insensitive to local desires and unaware of the power and venality of the industry with which he was dealing, while Nixon felt that Means was essentially a preservationist, insensitive to local desires and without confidence in Nixon's ability to deal firmly with the oil industry. Second, if Means eventually did decide to oppose the entire project, he could go public not merely as a summer resident but as a chairman of the governor's conservation subcommittee.

Nixon took the precaution of stacking the subcommittee to ensure that Means would be outvoted if he proved unreasonable, but it never came to that. Instead, this inexperienced and incompatible group was to produce the seminal report for the nation's only comprehensive oil-pollution-control law.

Andy Nixon had missed the sole meeting of his full conservation and planning committee because it had conflicted with the first meeting of the post-Evans principals in the refinery project. Gathered on October 1 in Occidental's New York offices were Armand Hammer, Governor Curtis, attorney-author Louis Nizer, and the chief officers of five New England independent marketers, including Robert Monks. Hammer was represented by Nizer and Myer Feldman, a former counsel and speechwriter for Presidents Kennedy and Johnson and the director of Lyndon Johnson's little known Anti-Campaign, designed to embarrass Republicans by getting and staying under Barry Goldwater's skin. Feldman was generally acknowledged to be among the most successful of all Washington lawyers in dealings with the Interior Department and the White House. He had handled some oil matters while in the White House, and he and Hammer were fellow trustees of an Eleanor Roosevelt memorial foundation.

The independent marketers came to this meeting skeptically. At a previous session, they had been kept waiting for a total of four hours and had to walk out twice before Hammer consented to join them at all. Startled by Evans's disappearance and perplexed to find that Buckley had become a consultant to Occidental, they feared that they would be forced out of the project entirely or asked to settle for marketing the oil without participating in the refinery ownership. Because they had never reached a firm agreement with Evans, their only bargaining counters were their marketing network and political leverage. In addition, Monks had that oddly indefinite control of the real estate options. The marketers' suspicions were further provoked by the fact that Feldman, who already represented their Independent Fuel Terminal Operators' Association and its largest member (Northeast Petroleum), represented Occidental as well, and proposed to mediate between the parties since he now represented all of them.

The meeting was a shambles. Dr. Hammer was late. From the moment he arrived, a miniskirted secretary with a British accent interrupted the meeting at five-minute intervals to bring him phone messages, some of which he left the room to return. In his absence, Nizer philosophized about the importance of cooperation and the evils of the major oil companies while Feldman passed out political assignments. When the independents raised the question of their share of the refinery, they were told that such discussions were premature. Monks, from a far end of the table, wanted to discuss satellite industries and the role of Sprague and Dead River in view of their ownership of the land. For confirmation of a key point, he turned to Sam Hill, his Dead River associate, and said, "You tell him, Sam."

Hill, mindful that this same land had been promised to the state, remained silent.

"Go on, Sam, tell him," Monks urged.

Hammer frowned down the table and turned to Nizer. "Get that man's name," he instructed and returned to the telephone.

A few minutes later Hammer came back to summarize and announce lunch. Governor Curtis and his aides were to join him, Nizer, and Feldman in an upstairs dining room while the other Occidental executives took the independents to lunch at a nearby restaurant. The meeting had served the purpose of preparing for the forthcoming trade-zone hearings. True, some questions were unresolved, but they could wait. No afternoon meeting would be necessary.

The independents were convinced that Occidental was trying to kid them along as long as necessary, but they could do nothing until after the hearings. Monks alone was not unhappy, for he had been bluffing about the land. Bruce Sprague was refusing to sell the tip of the peninsula, and, more important, he could not even find the owner of

Stone Island. All told, he had optioned less than a third of the land that he had claimed to control.

Two days later, on October 3, Texas Congressman Robert Price made the first charges of corruption. His theme was that the quota request would be granted by the Johnson administration to bolster "the fizzling political drive by Vice-President Humphrey."[11] Describing the proposed marine resources fund as political payola, the speech recalled the Teapot Dome scandal, the rigged television quiz shows, and Jack Evans's fund-raising effort. It prophesied sheiks making hostages of New Englanders if the refinery were built and it demanded postponement of the October 10 hearings pending a congressional investigation in which no New Englander could participate. Price offered no proofs of his conjectured corruption, and he never pressed for the investigation. The statement is of continuing interest only because it is an early sample of the many that the industry now waves as evidence that they have been warning of Arab oil blackmail for a long time. The implication is that their warnings were ignored and chaos followed. In fact, they prevailed.

4: October, 1968

Today, with the strangling system of the Americans, certain people pay much too dearly for oil, whilst in other countries oil is thrown into the water. Because of this, many producers are at a standstill, many refineries are ruined, while subsidiary industries cannot make progress . . . We are happy when we are received as sincere and faithful allies, who succeed in finding a satisfactory profit for ourselves, as well as assuring prosperity and progress for our neighbors, thanks to the natural riches of the country, the work of the population side by side with us, and a community of interests and reciprocal good feelings.

> Henri Deterding, chief executive officer
> of Royal Dutch Shell, on the eve of its 1911
> world war with Standard Oil[1]

"Let me recommend to your attention this singular epidemic among the sheep."
"You consider that to be important?" Lestrade asked.
"Exceedingly so."
"Is there any other point to which you wish to draw my attention?"
"To the curious incident of the dog in the night-time."
"The dog did nothing in the night-time."
"That was the curious incident," remarked Sherlock Holmes.

> Sir Arthur Conan Doyle, "Silver Blaze"

In the presence of extraordinary actuality, consciousness takes the place of imagination.

> Wallace Stevens

FOLLOWING THE MEETING in Nizer's office, Walter Corey and Andy Nixon realized that Occidental would be a much more difficult partner than Jack Evans. The company clearly intended to control the project, and the state of Maine would get no more benefit or respect than it demanded. To Armand Hammer, friend of Lenin and of every Democratic President since Roosevelt, a thirty-eight-year-old governor and his state of less than one million people were objects to be used, albeit nicely, since the association was potentially a long one.

Consequently, when Louis Nizer and Occidental's four-man advance force arrived in Portland two days before the October 10 hearings, the governor's aides came warily to the drafting sessions at the Portland city hall. Occidental had thoughtfully prepared Governor Curtis's testimony in advance. It was rejected, with only a few paragraphs being carried into the final version.

Other disagreements arose, usually over Occidental's conception of the New England governors as glorified press agents, available, like Congressman Price, to make claims and charges that would be neither credible nor prudent if uttered by Occidental. Nixon and Corey felt that the governors should instead concentrate on making an affirmative case focused on national and regional economic issues and minimizing conflict with the rest of the country.

After a series of inconclusive skirmishes, Occidental Vice-President Thomas Wachtell requested that Governor Curtis come to Occidental's hotel to iron out remaining problems and prepare himself for likely questions at the hearings. To Nixon and Corey, Occidental seemed to be establishing a two-tier working arrangement whereby Wachtell and Nizer would work with and on Curtis at the hotel while John Buckley and public-relations expert George Bevel worked with Curtis aides at City Hall.

In terms of protocol, this arrangement seemed proper. In fact, the governor, a public official whose weekly routine ranged from ribbon cuttings to the complexities of tax and welfare reform, would have been at a serious disadvantage with Wachtell and Nizer, who had been immersed in the specifics of the project for weeks.

To Nixon and Corey, who may have been suffering from the aide's standard conviction that his boss is helplessly and sometimes dangerously uninformed without him, the prospect of an unaccompanied governor arbitrating areas of disagreement with Nizer and Wachtell was a nightmare. To avoid it, they kidnapped the governor.

The kidnapping will not rank with the Leopold-Loeb or Lindbergh atrocities, but it served its purpose. Unaware of the discord between his staff and Occidental, the governor was met at the Portland airport by his two aides, who drove him to the city hall instead of the hotel. There they found Buckley working alone among half-drafted statements. After a brief telephone skirmish during which Nixon and Corey persuaded the governor to stay where he was, the irritated Occidental team returned to city hall. The eventual compromise on the tone of the statements left Curtis on the high ground of economic development, with the Occidental team free to slip whatever bombast they could into the statements of the other five New England governors.

Dr. Hammer himself, knowing that the real trade-zone and quota decisions would be made far from the Portland hearing, had decided not to postpone minor surgery scheduled for October 10. When Wachtell called him from Portland on the evening of October 9, the hospitalized Hammer received a reassuring proof that his team still had their priorities in order. While the call was being placed, Governor Curtis was conferring with Nixon in another corner of the otherwise silent room. The connection having been made, Wachtell turned and glared at them. "Shut up," he said. "The Doctor's on the line."

October 9 was also the day that the middle-level federal civil servants who composed the Foreign Trade Zones Board arrived in Portland. To them the hearing was an explosive and challenging responsibility, by far the most controversial matter they had ever handled. Their duty was to run an orderly hearing, collecting relevant evidence. N. Norman Engleberg, the chief examiner, would then make recommendations to the Foreign Trade Zones Board of Alternates, who would make their own recommendations to the board itself. Although cumbersome, the process had gone smoothly enough for the dozen zones the board had granted in its thirty-year history. There had been no rejections.

The staff had been a focal point for growing pressure against the refinery. The letters from oil executives and Congressmen to Johnson, Udall, and Secretary of Commerce C. R. Smith had been only the most visible manifestations of that pressure. In the background had been dozens of phone calls and visits to the staff and to the board members themselves by representatives of every side. During the week before the Portland hearings were to begin, two concessions were made to the forces opposing the refinery.

First, a second set of hearings was scheduled in Washington for the week of October 15, ostensibly to accommodate those Senators and Representatives whose busy schedules would preclude their traveling to Maine. Since Congress was in recess, with most Congressmen campaigning in their home districts, the particular legislators whom the board desired to accommodate were not apparent.

Second, the staff ruled that the hearings would be run without verbal cross-examination. All questions would be submitted in writing to the hearing examiner, who would decide which ones to ask. Since the right to confront witnesses is usually a component of the constitutionally required "due process of law," this ruling risked invalidating the entire hearing in advance. Any party could appeal any decision with an excellent chance that a court would order that the hearing be repeated.

Governor Curtis protested both rulings but was told that they were firm. Privately the staff explained that several powerful Congressmen and governors who planned to testify against the project would not have time to prepare themselves carefully on specifics and did not wish to be embarrassed by cross-examination from Nizer or other attorneys.

Curtis was more successful with two other protests. First, he persuaded the board to reverse its ruling that Congressman Hale Boggs of Louisiana could, in deference to his busy schedule, be the first witness. Curtis was able to convince the Secretary of Commerce that the governor of the applicant state should at least be allowed to describe the project before the first opponent was permitted to attack it. Second, Curtis was able to dissuade Governor Richard Hughes of New Jersey from testifying as an opponent. Hughes had apparently been persuaded that the Maine project threatened New Jersey's own extensive refining industry. Curtis telegraphed sorrow that Hughes, "a colleague I have long admired for your sensitivity to the needs of the people and your sense of fair play," would come to Maine to testify against a project of great importance to the state and regional economy. He requested a chance to discuss the refinery and invited the governor to visit him while he was in Maine. Hughes canceled his appearance and rested his case on a letter to Udall which endorsed an earlier letter to the secretary from President Charles Jones of the Humble Oil Company, Standard of New Jersey's U.S. subsidiary.

In fact, New Jersey's refinery industry would probably have benefited from the Maine project. Because of their Atlantic location, New Jersey and Pennsylvania refined most of the foreign crude oil allowed in under the oil-import program. If the Maine project had resulted, as its critics contended, in the importing of more foreign oil, New Jersey refineries would have processed some of it. If, as Occidental suggested, the Maine quota were taken exclusively from the inevitable growth inherent in 12.2 percent of a growing number,* the New Jersey refinery industry would have lost only its fractional share of the annual growth in imports. Not one existing job or tax dollar was in jeopardy. On the

* If for example, U.S. production east of the Rockies had been 10,000,000 barrels per day in 1967, the 12.2 percent representing allowable imports would have been 1,220,000 b/d. With U.S. production growing at 4 percent per year, it would reach 10,400,000 in 1968, and the level of imports would go up by 48,800 b/d. Since the refinery would have taken two or three years to build, the requested 100,000 b/d allocation could theoretically have come entirely from the growth rate.

other hand, Standard Oil of New Jersey (Esso) had received some $22 million worth of import rights in 1968 and stood to lose several million dollars if an allocation to Occidental forced Esso to give up a part of its share or to reduce the price of any oil product in New England.

This tendency of politicians to identify their state's well-being with the prosperity of its leading industries frequently runs against the interest of many of the state's citizens. Governors and Senators from coal states have been leading opponents of mine health and safety laws; Maine leaders squandered much of the state's water power and timber resources; oil-state representatives argue for higher oil prices despite *The Oil Weekly*'s 1934 observation that

> most of the several million people of Texas are not sellers of oil . . . they are motorists, buyers of oil. If there is any rising of Texans in their might, it is more likely to be under the leadership of some astute politician claiming that high oil prices benefit the oil companies and Wall Street and that oil conservation laws are but generators of high prices.* [2]

Scholars of unusual administrative-agency proceedings should obtain the transcript of the October 10–12, 1968, hearings of the Foreign Trade Zones Board in Portland. The hearings were held in the U.S. District Court Room, a high-ceiling plaster-walled, wood-trimmed cavern, lined with large portraits of past district-court judges. At the rear of the room the spectators' benches, with a total capacity of about 100, were jammed with a mixture of curious Maine people and oil-industry representatives. A low barrier separated the spectator benches from the court arena itself. Inside the barrier, to the right of the bench, the press jammed into the jury box along with Congressman Boggs and his staff. In a box opposite them, like defendants in a criminal trial, sat the governors of Maine and New Hampshire, their aides, and Wachtell, Nizer, and Occidental consultants John Buckley and George Bevel. The witness table in the middle of the room was adorned with a metallic bouquet of microphones and a sweating water pitcher. Elevated two steps and facing the proceedings, Engleberg and his associates presided from the judge's wood-fronted dais. Immediately below them, hands poised to immortalize it all, the stenographer squirreled over his machine.

Engleberg opened the hearing with a summary of the application.

---

* *The Oil Weekly* (now *Oil World*) has changed its perspective considerably in the last forty years and now champions enlightened federal intervention on the side of high and stable prices.

He then began, with an Orientally copious deference, to explain the
new rules relating to cross-examination. After a minute or two, Congressman Boggs rose in the jury box and boomed, "Get on with it."
Flustered, Engleberg closed his peroration, announcing that Governor
Curtis would be the first witness, to be followed by other "dignitaries"
in favor, then by Boggs and other dignitaries opposed, then by ordinary proponents, then by ordinary opponents. Witnesses were asked
to remember that argument regarding the oil-import quota system was
irrelevant to the application for a foreign-trade zone and should be
made to the Secretary of the Interior.

Governor Curtis deferred his testimony to permit Assistant Attorney
General Robert Fuller to read the state's telegram protesting the
scheduling of the additional hearing in Washington. As Fuller finished
the telegram, he received unexpected support from the jury box:

CONGRESSMAN BOGGS: Mr. Chairman, I agree 100% with what the Governor has said. I think that it is perfectly outrageous that you have
  scheduled another hearing in Washington, and I can't imagine you
  running out on an agreement that you made with the Governor of
  this State.

CHAIRMAN: Thank you, sir . . . as everyone knows, this was done as
  an attempt to be courteous and to respect the Congress of the United
  States . . .

FROM THE FLOOR: There are three of them right here in front of you.

CHAIRMAN: I know that, but this was the decision. Thank you so much.
  We appreciate it.
                        [Mr. Nizer stands]
  We did want to hear the dignitaries first, Mr. Nizer.
                         [Laughter]

MR. FULLER: Mr. Examiner, I would be very pleased to yield a few minutes to Mr. Nizer.

CHAIRMAN: Governors, Senators, and Congressmen unless, but for a
  moment, yes?

MR. NIZER: I would like to add the objection of the Occidental Petroleum
  Company, for whom I speak, in respect to the matter on which even
  the adversaries of the proposal lend assistance. I stand in awe of the
  dignitaries, but I want to just register my objection.

CONG. BOGGS: Mr. Chairman, really we're out of order. I object to his
  testimony at this time.

CHAIRMAN: The objection is noted. May we try, at this time, to proceed
  in the way that the committee has said it will proceed. Let's see how
  it works. Let's try it, please, Mr. Nizer.

CONG. BOGGS: Please ask him to sit down. He's out of order.

MR. NIZER: I recess my objection for a later time, noting for the record that the only interruption thus far made before you were even through reading your statement was by the gentleman who is asking me to sit down.

CONG. KYROS: Mr. Chairman, I am Congressman Kyros from the 1st District. It seems to me that our Governor has specifically requested that you cancel the hearing on Tuesday.

CONG. BOGGS: Why don't you cancel it right now?

CHAIRMAN: Gentlemen . . .

CONG. KYROS: We are entitled to a ruling from the chair right now.

CHAIRMAN: Gentlemen, the matter will be taken under advisement . . . we will announce the decision of the Board later . . .

FROM THE FLOOR: May I read a telegram I wish to send to Senator Pastore?

CHAIRMAN: A telegram you wish to deliver to Senator Pastore? Is that it?

CONG. BOGGS: But he's out of order too.

CHAIRMAN: I know.

[Laughter]

CHAIRMAN: Now, we would like so very, very much to hear from Governor Curtis. Thank you, Governor.[3]

Curtis's testimony was essentially a recapitulation of the economic arguments in favor of the refinery. The governor stressed rural development as an antidote to urban ills. He also pointed out, in a prophetic surviving fragment from the Occidental draft, that the existing system of controls would result in more refineries being built on Caribbean islands and in eastern Canada and in an increased dollar outflow. Addressing himself for the first time to the environmental effects, he mentioned the Machiasport Conservation and Planning Committee and noted that the $7 million annual contribution to the New England Governors' Maine Resources Fund could be used to stimulate aquaculture to supplement the region's declining fishing industry.

At one point Governor Curtis stated that the Maine application would not disturb the oil-import program and that New England (a somewhat disingenuous euphemism for Occidental) was entitled to a share of the quotas. Congressman Boggs came alertly to his feet.

CONGRESSMAN BOGGS: I thought that we were not going to discuss the import quotas at this hearing.

CHAIRMAN: The import quotas?

CONG. BOGGS: Yes.

CHAIRMAN: I assume the subject is going to be brought out. We're not excluding any of it.[4]

Satisfied, Boggs subsided. With the import quota system out of the bag, the hearings were expanded, and the oil issue had spread from the uncertain confines of Udall's Interior Department into the safer custody of Secretary of Commerce C. R. Smith.

When the governor concluded his description of the most controversial refinery project in American history, Engleberg said that the examining committee had no questions and offered effusive thanks. He then invited written questions from the audience, at which Boggs, looking ahead to his own turn on the stand, took alarm.

CONGRESSMAN BOGGS: I share the admiration of New England for this great Governor. I think that he's one of the greatest . . .
CHAIRMAN: I know that you do.
CONG. BOGGS: And I certainly hope that we're not going to have questions from everybody sitting here. . . .
CHAIRMAN: I hope that we're not.
CONG. BOGGS: Well, why would you make such an invitation? It's very unusual . . . I'm not concerned with the procedure, only the etiquette of the Committee.
                [Question submitted to Committee]
CHAIRMAN: We have looked at the question. We do not think it is germane. It will not be asked. Anyone else have any questions?
                [No response][5]

Curtis was followed by Governor John King of New Hampshire, who delivered an Occidental-prepared attack on the major oil companies. King suggested that oil-import restrictions were based on reasoning that was

100% wrong. Why not do just the reverse. Rely mainly on foreign oil now and conserve our domestic supplies for national emergencies? . . .

And this so-called foreign oil is not foreign at all. Really it's produced by American companies that are overseas, through their subsidiaries. If anything, the increased development of foreign reserves by United States companies will help our balance of payments rather than worsen it.

Let me also speak very briefly to another, and to my mind, the strangest criticism of the major oil companies concerning the proposal before you this morning. This is the attack on Occidental's official offer to pay into a New England Conservation Fund 20¢ for each barrel of oil from this refinery which it sells in the United States market. This offer had been derided by a spokesman for one of the majors as a political payoff. Indeed, this kind of criticism can be expected from a group which has been less than notable for its efforts to improve the quality of the American environment. . . .

How typical of a group so bloated on depletion allowances and early write offs of intangible drilling expenses and so inconsiderate of the country which makes it wealthy, that it feels able to dismiss as cheap political gestures any effort by a competitor to shoulder some responsibility to society. This is the "public be damned" attitude of the 19th Century industrial robber baron.[6]

Following Governor King, Maine's two Representatives, Peter Kyros and Bill Hathaway, outlined the effect of the project on their districts. This concluded the testimony of the proponent dignitaries. Congressman Boggs moved to the witness table, where he began with an anecdote:*

CONG. BOGGS: Thank you very much, Mr. Chairman. I want to thank you and your colleagues and I want to subscribe in full to the nice things Congressman Kyros said about you.

CHAIRMAN: You are most kind. Thank you . . .

CONG. BOGGS: Now you know what Peter reminds me of, Peter Kyros and Hathaway both. They remind me of a story I tell about a fundamentalist preacher down in Louisiana. Now you fellows probably never have seen a fundamentalist preacher, but he's the kind of fellow that just takes up preaching. He doesn't go to any Seminary; he doesn't study Theology. He just becomes a preacher.

CHAIRMAN: Congressman, some of those people are not hearing you. Please turn up the volume.

CONG. BOGGS: I don't know how to operate this machine. I don't want to operate it. That's not my business. When I go to a doctor, I go to a doctor. I don't know how to operate any of the electrical stuff.

CHAIRMAN: I don't either. You and I are in the same boat. I don't either. . . .

[Laughter]

CONG. BOGGS: I want them to hear this story, because it's too applicable to Peter, who represents this district, and has done so much for Maine, and to his colleague Congressman Hathaway and to the next vice

---

* Two factors explain the partial incoherence of the following testimony. First, Boggs, under the pressures surrounding national Democratic politics in 1968 and faced with a serious challenge from one of those segregationist opponents who have the power to bring out the worst in a Southern liberal, had been drinking. He was later to describe the entire Machiasport project as "an episode I'd just as soon forget." Second, the quality of the transcript is erratic throughout, and some of Boggs's sharper turns appear to have lost the stenotypist in the bayous.

president of the United States and former Governor Muskie whose button I proudly wear on my lapel.

This fundamentalist preacher who just took up preaching. Now this preacher was given, my distinguished colleagues, a bit to the fermentation of the juice, if you know what I mean. And one night he was driving home like this, and a friendly deputy sheriff pulled him aside and said, "Reverend, you better let me drive you home." And his reaction was like all people who get into that condition; he protested his innocence. But the deputy sheriff looked back, and there were about five or six bottles of cheap wine, and he pulled them out, uncorked one and gave it to the preacher. The preacher smelled it, and looked right into the deputy's eyes and he said, "Sheriff, the good Lord's done done it again."

[Laughter]

Well, now I'll tell it. What Peter Kyros and Hathaway and Governor Curtis have done for Maine, and Vice President Muskie, is a miracle and I'm happy to pay tribute to them.

Now my presentation will take quite a while, because this is a very complex situation. First, if you don't mind, I would like to read the Portland, Maine, paper of Thursday morning, October 10, 1968. It says, "Second Trade Zone Hearing Shocks Curtis." That's the Governor, a very fine gentleman, believe me. . . . The Governor expressed "shock" at the Department's announcement that it has scheduled an additional hearing on the State's application for a Foreign-Trade-Zone for Tuesday, in Washington. "In a Wednesday night message, C. R. Smith"—a good friend of mine, the Secretary of Commerce, but he'd like to get this behind him, believe me—

FROM THE FLOOR: Congressman Boggs, I suggest that most of us have read the morning paper. I'd like to get on with the hearing.

CONG. BOGGS: Who are you, please? Would you have this man identify himself? Would you identify yourself?

MR. MERRILL: My name is Gary Merrill.

CONG. BOGGS: What is your job?

MR. MERRILL: I am an unemployed actor.

[Laughter]

CONG. BOGGS: A very good description.*

CHAIRMAN: Please, please.

* Congressman Boggs was apparently not a late-show devotee. Had he been, he might have recognized his adversary from a 1949–62 film career that included appearances in *Slattery's Hurricane, Twelve O'Clock High, All About Eve, Where the Sidewalk Ends, The Frogmen, Another Man's Poison, Night Without Sleep, Decision Before Dawn, Witness to Murder, The Black Dakotas, The Pleasure of His Company, Mysterious Island, Farewell in Hong Kong,* and *A Girl Named Tamiko.*

CONG. BOGGS: You make a ruling. Let me go on with my presentation, please. Let the unemployed actor go his own way. I hope he gets a job. May he get one somewhere. I voted for poverty programs. I'm the most liberal Congressman in the world, and I think that under some of these programs there must be some job for that poor fellow.

[Laughter]

Now let me read on. Curtis said, "Any contention made to you that the additional hearing is necessary for the convenience of Congressmen or Senators is specious. It's too bad they can't come up here and face us on our own ground."

Well, now I'm here. Right here in this beautiful city of Portland. At least, and believe you me, I love this state. I love this country. Anybody wants to give priorities I'll give them to you. First America, second my region, third my state, fourth my district . . .

Now, let's get to the subject. One other point to be made clear by Monday . . . This is where Sigmund Freud comes in, and I'll get to him later.

(FROM THE AUDIENCE) : Ho hum.

CONG. BOGGS: If you are bored, go home.

[Laughter]

There was more, much more.

On Louis Nizer—"The only oil company on this earth that I own property in happens to be Occidental [which is not] some little bitty kind independent, and I resent them dissipating their funds hiring this New York lawyer. . . . Why didn't they hire one in Portland? This is the place where people are unemployed."

On the Dickey-Lincoln public power project so dear to Maine Democrats—"Maine never had a better friend than Hale Boggs . . . One time the House killed Lincoln-Dixie I walked myself over to the United States Senate and got my Senator from Louisiana to put it back in." The man who killed it was Mr. Gerald Ford, who represents the Republican National Committee in Congress on certain ideas.

On foreign trade zones—"I wrote, with Congressman Celler, God bless him, the very amendment by which this hearing was made possible. Is that not a fact?" (Engleberg: "That is a fact.") Boggs: "Thanks. I'm not against the foreign trade zone in Portland, but I am against what Occidental is trying to do. The concept of the foreign trade zone, and let me tell you something, I'm no liberal in Congress, comes from the ancient city states like Florence, Venice, Hanover, Denmark."

Boggs made vague reference to a possibly illegal attempt by Oc-

cidental to keep him away from the hearing. He concluded by recommending to Governor Curtis that he turn his attention to oceanography,
preferably through private enterprise. He reinforced this admonition
with quotations on social self-reliance from James Reston, Sam Rayburn, and Saint Luke.

When he stopped, Engleberg rose to the occasion:

> CHAIRMAN: Congressman Boggs, we all deeply appreciate your most
> enthusiastic statement, and we knew it would be and it was. All your
> comments will be given our most careful consideration. Again, any
> questions? If not—
> FROM THE FLOOR [Stands up in back of the room]: Question?
> CHAIRMAN: It must be in writing, of course. No? No, we have no written
> questions.
> CONG. BOGGS: Thank you.
> CHAIRMAN: I'm sorry; I had announced that all questions be in writ
> ing. . . . Please let's have order. We must continue; we have not
> recessed as yet for lunch.[7]

Nizer had been reduced to elegant silence by Engleberg's refusal to
permit cross-examination. He had passed the time in drawing class-
yearbook-style sketch portraits, which he autographed and distributed.
After the noon recess, he held a press conference and then testified in
front of a blackboard containing some figures used by Boggs. His
testimony suggested that Boggs had exaggerated the Occidental proposal's impact on the oil-import program by some 700 percent.

When he had finished, Judge Jim Langdon, the 250-pound chairman of the Texas Railroad Commission,* rose to announce from the

---

* The Texas Railroad Commission sets the rate of production from Texas wells. The
Louisiana Conservation Commission performs the same function for Louisiana. The Hot
Oil Act, enacted in 1935, illegalizes interstate shipment of oil produced in violation of
state ceilings. Federal blessing was also conferred throughout the 1960s by the refusal
of the Interior Department to permit production in the Gulf of Mexico to exceed the
rates established in the adjacent states.

This regulation is said to be justified by the need to avoid the wasteful production
practices of the 1930s. The allowable production rate is termed the Maximum Efficient
Rate (MER), and any intent to influence prices by restricting supply is firmly denied.
Since the MER has grown from 60 percent to 100 percent in the last five years, during
which time the price of crude oil has more than doubled while the essential geology
of the wells has remained unchanged, it seems safe to conclude that the role of price
in these decisions has been understated.

The importance attached to this regulation by the industry emerges in a story told
on the TV program "Firing Line" to William F. Buckley and Beryl Milburn by Texas
reform Democrat Frances Farenthold, who once considered running for one of the
three seats on the commission. As she tells it, "I was encouraged by some environ-

back of the room that "This man doesn't know what he is talking about." Langdon, not scheduled to speak until the following day, was representing Governor John Connally.

Engleberg then resumed temporary control of the hearings and turned the floor over to the nondignitary proponents. The first of these was Commissioner James Keefe of Maine's Department of Economic Development.

Ten years earlier, Keefe had been a Chamber of Commerce executive in Presque Isle, then a city of 13,000 in Aroostook County, which is the home of the Maine potato and is similar in sparseness and poverty to Washington County, of which it was once a part. In 1961 the Air Force closed its Presque Isle base, on which much of the town's economy depended. Keefe headed a group of local merchants who organized the town's conversion of the airstrip into a commercial airfield. An industrial park constructed nearby attracted several new plants. Presque Isle survived with a moderate loss in population, and Keefe earned a reputation as a resourceful economic developer. As a result of his experience in economic development, he signed with the federal Area Redevelopment Administration at the same time that ARA's Maine coordinator, Kenneth Curtis, was first learning of Jack Evans's strong interest in the heavy-fuel side of the Maine economy.

Keefe stayed with ARA through its transformation into what is now the Economic Development Administration, while Curtis returned to Maine to wage his unsuccessful Congressional campaign, serve as secretary of state, and become governor in 1967. Curtis then invited Keefe to return to head the Department of Economic Development, whose revitalization had been one of his most popular campaign pledges.

Like Curtis, Keefe felt strongly that well-paying jobs were Maine's greatest need. He wanted his department to sell Maine to industries looking for new plant locations, and to this end he sought to anticipate and fulfill the needs of likely industries. He expanded the department's research capability and hired its first economist.

---

mentalists and so on. I had a phone call from a trusted adviser saying, 'Don't do this because if you do, you will have a million dollars up against you the day you announce.'" "Is it a lifelong job?" Buckley asked. "No, but I don't know when an incumbent has been ousted," Mrs. Farenthold replied. Mrs. Milburn added, "I do notice that each election year when one of the railroad commissioners is up for reelection, they pass the chairmanship to the man whose term is up, and of course, that lends an aura to the gentleman who seeks reelection."

He was more willing than his Republican predecessors to attract industry that would shake up the paper- and power-company domination of Maine's resources, but he shared the outlook common to all such offices, that their job was to attract and service anything that might provide jobs. Critical analysis of a company's social responsibility or environmental track record was unheard of. Some critics asserted that he guided his department by the fifth verse of the Twenty-third Psalm: "Thou preparest a table before me in the presence of mine enemies: thou anointest my head with oil; my cup runneth over."

Both his critics and his defenders were to build their arguments around a perception that he styled his department more often as industry's agent to Maine than as Maine's agent to industry. The perception was only occasionally accurate, but the occasions were major ones.

Keefe's statement at the trade-zone hearings was the most biting attack delivered on the major oil companies and the oil-producing states. It had originally been prepared by Occidental for delivery by Governor John Chafee of Rhode Island but had been rejected by his staff as not being "quite the Governor's style." Keefe, who had not been scheduled to testify, volunteered. Because he knew as little about the oil industry as most Maine people and because he was unfamiliar with the testimony, he did not attempt oratorical emphasis. The result was a strange blend of fiery words and a low monotone. At the conclusion of his testimony, the audience, unable to hear most of it, had no questions. Keefe successfully dodged reporters and returned to Augusta.

Behind him, the hearing turned its attention to the most substantial testimony it was to hear, that of Professor Maurice Adelman of the Massachusetts Institute of Technology. Adelman, long an opponent of oil-import restraints and one of the few petroleum economists truly independent of the oil industry, had infuriated many sections of the industry throughout the 1960s by arguing that world oil-producing costs were declining. Because prices were still (because of producing-nation taxes) well above the actual costs of production, and because of the emerging economies of supertankers, he predicted that the costs of foreign oil would continue to decline. He further argued that the rate of decline would increase if the United States ended oil-import restrictions and thereby made possible both greater competition for the U.S. market and the construction of supertanker terminals. His arguments were difficult for much of the oil industry to counter, for he was advocating broader application of the free-market principles that they claimed to hold dear.

Being careful to deny that he was a proponent of any special oil-import allocation for any particular company, Adelman made his points again in Portland, noting specifically that the increase in tanker size throughout the world was such that half of the tonnage then under construction was in vessels of 200,000 tons or more, while eight years earlier the same half had been in vessels of 45,000 tons or more. He pointed out that each quadrupling of tanker size halved shipping costs over long distances and that the per-barrel cost of refining in a 300,000-b/d refinery would be 40 percent less than in a 100,000-b/d refinery. In short, the trend throughout the world was toward immense economies of scale and toward increasing use of Middle Eastern oil. It was up to the United States to choose whether or not its East Coast would remain "a rather small-scale backward and inefficient terminus for oil shipments."[8] As Adelman concluded his testimony, Engleberg thanked him for "his very learned dissertation" and announced that the World Series game between the Detroit Tigers and the St. Louis Cardinals was scoreless after four innings.

Adelman was followed by Portland City Attorney Barney Shur, who pointed out that the decline of Portland's waterfront was directly traceable to a Canadian decision to require dry cargo bound for Montreal to be offloaded at a Canadian port and transported by truck or rail. This decision had rejuvenated the Nova Scotian port of Halifax, transforming it into a modern containerport, but it had saddled Portland, the closest port to Montreal, with a series of unused and rotting piers. Only the 500,000-b/d crude-oil pipeline from Portland to Montreal survived as a reminder of what had been a substantial and diverse commerce.

After Shur, Richard Morrell, a heating-oil dealer and state senator, testified that 8.3 million of New England's 11 million people (76 percent) lived in homes heated by oil and that they consumed 100 million barrels per year (275,000 barrels per day). Morrell too was warmly thanked by the hearing examiner, who added, "I don't know the final score. If anyone has it . . . the final score is 4–0, so we'll have another game tomorrow? . . . Oh? No game? It's over? See, I've been so confused."

The rest of the afternoon and the early evening were devoted to brief statements by proponents. Their words were unreported by newspapers. The press was fascinated with the Boggs-Nizer collision and the other dignitaries, but four of the midnight witnesses dealt with themes that were to prove at least as significant as those of the dignitaries.

The first represented the Federal Maritime Administration (MARAD), a subdivision of the same Commerce Department whose chairman was chairman of the Foreign Trade Zones Board. While careful to avoid taking a position with regard to oil-import policy, the MARAD spokesman put his agency strongly behind the construction of supertankers and supertanker ports in the United States. Like Professor Adelman, he foresaw adverse consequences to the consumer, to the national balance of payments, to the efficiency and competitiveness of American industry, and to the national security if the U.S. East Coast was bypassed by advancements in oil-transport technology.

Juxtaposed against MARAD, Adelman, and all of the preceding speakers were the environmentalists. The Natural Resources Council of Maine (NRC) submitted a moderate statement advocating an undefined principle of balanced and planned growth coupled with high environmental standards. It contained a series of questions about air- and water-pollution control and land planning. Like the oil-policy issues that dominated the hearings, those questions were of a legitimate and overriding importance that transcended the expertise and the mandate of the board that was being asked to consider them. The Natural Resources Council, unlike the oil spokesmen, was so unsure of itself that its representative was content to submit his unread statement for the record.

After the NRC interlude, Gardiner Means testified as a conditional proponent. Means agreed that the convergence of supertankers, deep water, and the economies of a large refinery offered Maine and the nation a major economic opportunity. He urged three preconditions to the granting of the zone: the preparation of a lease that would impose strict controls on refinery and tanker pollution, reevaluation of the apparently exposed Stone Island terminal against such alternatives as the free-floating discharge moorings in use in the Persian Gulf, and the removal of the refinery itself from the Machiasport peninsula to a site inland among the barrens, woods, and marshes back from the coast.

The board thanked him for his testimony and moved on to Thomas D. Cabot, chairman of the board of the Cabot Corporation, a company involved in petrochemical manufacturing. When not overseeing the company's petrochemical operations in England, France,

Germany, the Netherlands, Spain, Australia, Japan, Argentina, and Colombia, Cabot occasionally vacationed at his 1400-acre island in Machias Bay. Blending his interests nicely, Cabot opposed the Occidental refinery first as a summer resident because it would despoil the area; again as an experienced mariner (navigator of a fifty-foot yawl and chief executive of two companies, Cabot and United Fruit, with extensive shipping interests) because of the hazards of docking supertankers at Stone Island; yet again as a representative of the Cabot Corporation because the proposed quota would represent an unfair subsidy to a potential competitor; and finally as one who spent half a century in foreign trade because a surplus of imports over exports was inconsistent with the purposes of the Foreign Trade Zones Act.*

After Cabot, Engleberg adjourned the hearings for the night.

They resumed the following day with the opposing dignitaries. Led by Governor John Love of Colorado and representatives of Governors John Connally (Texas), John McKeithen (Louisiana), Stanley Hathaway (Wyoming), Dewey Bartlett (Oklahoma), and Robert Docking (Kansas), the opponents prophesied the ruin of their state economies if Machiasport and its inevitable descendants were allowed to drown domestic wells in a flood of cheap foreign oil. The presence of Governors Love and Hathaway at the hearings indicated how widespread the interest in high domestic prices had become. Colorado and Wyoming together produced less than 5 percent of the nation's oil. However, both states had extensive oil-shale and coal deposits that would be developed only under circumstances of high oil prices and limited supply. This perceived interest in high overall energy costs was the web that wove Colorado and Wyoming with such coal states as Pennsylvania, West Virginia, and Kentucky into a network opposed to any technological or governmental innovation in the direction of lower prices or reduced demand.

The opponents' testimony was partially countered by Governor Philip Hoff of Vermont, who reasserted the importance of the project to the New England economy and revived the images of New England as an oil-dependent region denied the opportunity to construct its own refinery and exploited by the predatory pricing practices of the major companies. Hoff had been persuaded to delay his testimony from the previous day in order to offset the media impact of an unbroken string

---

* Actually, the act speaks of the need to promote "international commerce." While Congress may or may not have preferred exports, zones in existence as of 1968 had consistently produced a heavy surplus of imports over exports.

of opponent dignitaries, just as Congressman Boggs had effectively swamped the bathtub of attention in which the proponents had expected to bask the day before.

The Hoff strategy assumed that Boggs himself was through with Machiasport. Actually, the Congressman had just been warming up in Portland. Returning to Washington, he requested time on the floor of the House to elaborate on his oblique Portland references to "honor." Since words spoken in Congress cannot legally be the basis for libel or slander suits, the House of Representatives may have seemed a safer forum for the charges that Boggs had in mind.

Before speaking, he had followed Congressional custom by notifying Senator John Tower and Republican Representatives Gerald Ford, George Bush, and Robert Price that he intended to mention them in case they cared to be present to reply. Uncertain of the tenor of Boggs's remarks, the Republicans chose not to be present but were able to prevail upon Representative Delbert Latta of Ohio to demand a quorum call. Since most Representatives were home campaigning, a quorum was not present, and the House adjourned for the weekend.

Furious, Boggs announced to the press gallery that he would instead make his statement at a press conference in his office. At the meeting Boggs reverted to the oratorical style that had enthralled Portland the day before. Brandishing copies of a Portland *Press Herald* article headlined "Boggs Steals Show," he reiterated his charge that Hammer was "dissipating my company's assets," and he threatened to sell his Occidental stock. In a remarkable finishing burst, he described his encounters with Louis Nizer ("Well, you should have seen his expression. He looked like one of those Arab sheiks. He had a cap on and a robe, and he is a very high priced looking fellow") and Gary Merrill ("They have a heckler. His name is Gary Merrill") and concluded with a reading from the scriptures. His centerpiece was an account of one of those occasionally transcribed meetings of improper motives that Watergate has since done so much to publicize.

As Boggs told it,[9] he had originally decided to attend the Portland hearing in late September as a result of requests received from Louisiana and Texas oilmen. He then talked with the Trade Zones Board and was told that the hearing was a mere formality.* Not desir-

_____

* The official involved made this statement under some duress. According to Boggs's press-conference account, he had just told him, "If you think for one moment you can do this, just forget about appropriations and all that kind of business."

ing to appear against the wishes of Maine Democrats, he told his oil-industry friends that he would not go.

Disappointed, they urged him to reconsider, and he somehow concluded that he would do the Maine Democrats less harm if he could find a powerful Republican to go with him to show that the opposition was bipartisan. He settled on Representative George Bush, then a respected Republican Congressman and oil millionaire, subsequently chairman of the Republican National Committee. Boggs's own words give some idea of how the levers operated:

> So I called my friend in Louisiana, an outstanding attorney with no official position, who was most anxious for me to go to Maine, despite the tremendous schedule which I had taking me across the continent and suggested that he get in touch with his friends in Texas to have my friend George Bush accompany me to Portland, Maine.
>
> My friend immediately saw the practicability of this suggestion and said that he would accomplish it. He said that he would contact the Nixon campaign manager in Texas and the Nixon campaign manager would get him there, meaning Congressman Bush.
>
> He had every reason to be confident because the name of the man he had in mind is James Postgate, vice-president in charge of production of Humble Oil and Refinery Company, who should, of course, be on the side of Texas and not Occidental. . . .
>
> As far as I can ascertain my Louisiana friend gave him a title that he does not enjoy. He is not a manager for former Vice President Nixon, but as far as I can ascertain supports him.
>
> The minute he said he would use a Nixon supporter to get Bush to Maine with me, I felt that I would not have to go.
>
> Whether the Nixon forces had anything to do with the fact that none of the Texas Representatives in Congress or Senators did appear is something that I do not know.
>
> But I do know that on Thursday, October 3, I called my friend in Louisiana and said "Is George Bush going? . . . If he does not go I could not go. I cannot embarrass my Democratic colleagues."
>
> But again I reassured him that my going there did not make any difference anyway.
>
> Now the story becomes very interesting. It is the old adage: "Truth is stranger than fiction." And this is the reason, Mr. Speaker, that I went.

As Boggs told it, he had been approached in late September by Occidental representatives who said that they were eager to contribute to his campaign. Again, Boggs's speech gives an unusual glimpse of the world of campaign finance.

They came to see me on Tuesday morning, October 1, at 10 A.M. They met with me in the Whip's office. In between the Friday telephone calls, and the Tuesday meeting in the Whip's office in the Capitol, I went on Sunday, September 29, to a Saints' football game in New Orleans, and I had as my guest a very fine gentleman named Julius "Duck" Sellers, the assessor of St. Charles Parish, who determines how much taxes the Hooker Chemical Company has to pay on its giant plant there.

During the game I casually asked Sellers about the Hooker Co. He said that they were fine people. I asked no further questions.

This plant is an invaluable asset to St. Charles Parish. It gives employment to many of our people and it is operated efficiently and ably.

I am sorry that Occidental bought it.

Now I am asking the SEC to investigate the transaction to see whether the insider rule was violated in its acquisition of Hooker Chemical on July 24, 1968.

In this connection I attach articles from the Wall Street Journal noting certain suits alleging just that sort of thing in previous transactions by Occidental. I think—I do not know—but I think the law was violated in this case. It is being made a matter of intense investigation and in due course we will know whether it was violated or not, and whether or not any indictment will be required.

Now returning to the meeting in the Whip's office on Tuesday, October 1. Present were Mr. James Baldwin of Occidental Petroleum Corporation, Mr. E. W. Mathias, treasurer of Hooker Chemical Company, and Mr. O. A. Mattison, Washington Manager of Hooker, and my whip administrative assistant, Mr. Gary Hymel.

When the gentlemen walked into the office we made a picture and then Mr. Hymel listened very carefully to the conversation.

I said in effect I am glad to see you gentlemen. I have much to do. What can I do for you?

They replied in effect we understand that you are in a campaign; we want to help you.

They said that they had helped me before. I learned that they had in a small amount in 1966. This was two years prior to their acquisition by Occidental.

I thereupon said, "What do you mean?"

They said, "Campaign funds."

Then Mr. Mathias asked me if I knew Mr. "Duck" Sellers. He was the man I had taken to the football game. He is a fine gentleman, an intimate friend of mine, and one of the ablest and most effective young leaders in my state. I predict for him a very bright future in Louisiana politics.

I said that I knew Mr. Sellers. They said, "Then we can make arrangements through him."

I said, "You are saying you want to give me a campaign contribution through Mr. Sellers."

They said, "Yes."

I thereupon turned to Mr. Baldwin; I asked him if Occidental wanted me to go to Maine and testify against its application for a Foreign Trade Zone; he blushed, but I asked him again, "Just answer the question yes or no." He replied, "No." I thereupon left the office and have not seen these gentlemen since that time. . . .

There is no question about this being a violation of the law. This was why I meant that it was a matter of honor.

. . . When NBC bugged the executive session of the Platform Committee, I said that was a violation of the law and it has been reported to the enforcement agency, as has this matter.

I suggest to Mr. Armand Hooker [sic] that he read the history of the Teapot Dome scandal.

The speech ended with the Teapot Dome admonition and was followed by 22,000 words of newspaper clippings related to Boggs's positions on oil imports in general and Machiasport in particular.

The most interesting appendix to the Boggs speech was an October 1 letter to the Congressman from Hooker Chemical Company treasurer E. W. Mathias. Written in apparent suspicion that he had been sandbagged, the letter outlined facts very similar to those alleged by Boggs. This was not surprising, for each side suspected the other of having taped the meeting. Consequently, neither could deviate much from the words that a possible transcript would saddle them with.

The crucial differences were (1) that Mathias claimed that the meeting had been called at Boggs's request and to his own astonishment and inconvenience, and (2) that he had said no to Boggs's question about whether Occidental wanted him to go to Maine only after Boggs had, to their surprise, raised the issue.

In an October 12 statement, Hammer dismissed the charges as "false and outrageous" and wondered how Boggs's aggrieved sense of honor had been able to wait ten days before making the meeting public. Hammer also noted that Boggs's administrative assistant, Gary Hymel, had called the Hooker executives after the meeting and stated that Boggs apologized for his rudeness and wished to consider the incident closed. In subsequent affidavits, prepared as a result of the FBI investigation demanded by Boggs, the Hooker executives said that Boggs's final question and his closing "That's it. You're in trouble" had been delivered in an unnaturally loud voice with his head turned strangely away from them toward an area concealed by a curtain.

Several newspapers and wire services ran the story once and then dropped it. *The New York Times* and the Washington *Post*, threatened by Occidental with libel actions and probably warned by saddened reporters of Boggs's condition at the press conference, did not carry the story at all. They subsequently printed mild reports that were safe from libel charges because other papers had already carried the same material. Disgruntled, Boggs complained, "The idea of the Democratic Majority Whip being offered a bribe has got to be news."

The best inference seems to be that both sides lost. Boggs did go to Portland; the Hooker group did not set itself up properly for the poised sandbags. Boggs never mentioned the episode again. He was narrowly reelected, buried his drinking problem, was elevated from whip to House majority leader, and disappeared in a small plane in Alaska during a 1972 campaign visit on behalf of Representative Nick Begich. The FBI investigation of the 1968 meeting uncovered nothing prosecutable.

Back in the Portland courtroom, the suddenly overshadowed hearings clanked on through Friday and into Saturday, their importance diminished by Boggs's allegation that they were a mere formality and that the trade zone would not be granted.

The ordinary proponents continued where they had left off on Thursday night. A representative of the New England Conference of Public Health Officials partially offset the environmental concerns of Means, Burk, and Cabot by pointing out that low-sulfur fuel was essential to the reduction of air pollution in Boston and Hartford. Two Maine executives testified that their companies would be seriously interested in using the Portland zone for manufacturing operations. Engleberg substituted progress reports on the Apollo launching for his earlier World Series scores.

Bob Fuller, Ed Langlois, and Walter Corey, testifying as a Maine governmental team, were barraged with written questions from oil-company attorneys as to whether Maine had made a special deal with Occidental to keep other refiners from using the zone. These questions were intended to compel the Maine officials either to admit to a special deal or to admit that the plan was so indefinite that the board could not find the necessary foreign commerce. To Occidental's displeasure, they resolved their dilemma by announcing that the subzone could be expanded to include other potential refiners. They assumed that none would apply.

Corey, Langlois, and Fuller were followed by Occidental's Wachtell, who banished any lingering pretense that discussion of oil-import policy would be excluded. After a brief wave at the Foreign Trade Zones Act, he devoted most of his testimony to proving that Occidental's 100,000-barrel-per-day quota request could be satisfied within the 12.2 percent ceiling and that the oil-import program had resulted in a ten-year direct gift of some $5 billion in import rights to oil refiners, not to mention the much larger indirect subsidy to producers in the form of unnecessarily high oil prices.

Wachtell was followed by John Buckley, Jack Evans's former partner, who had become an Occidental consultant. Nizer had instructed Buckley to rebut as much oil industry testimony as he could before Engleberg cut him off. His pugnacity toward the opposing dignitaries kept him in good-natured but constant conflict with the theretofore placatory hearing examiner, who had ruled all "oral rebuttal testimony" to be out of order. One example will give the flavor of their several exchanges:

> MR. BUCKLEY: . . . common sense would have directed that Esso [the largest single recipient of import permits] make the balance-of-payments arguments and stay away from the giveaway arguments and that Shell [a foreign-owned company repatriating most of its profits to England and the Netherlands] make the giveaway argument and stay away from the balance-of-payments argument. In any event, I give you Esso and Shell, two not-so-jolly green giants sitting in the green—
> CHAIRMAN: Mr. Buckley . . . Mr. Buckley . . . Mr. Buckley . . .
> MR. BUCKLEY: Yes.
> CHAIRMAN: I'm sorry, I thought my microphone wasn't working.
> MR. BUCKLEY: Oh, I heard you.
> CHAIRMAN: Then I expect you to stop when you hear me.
> MR. BUCKLEY: All right. I shall.[10]

The substance of Buckley's testimony focused on the allegation that the importing of 300,000 barrels per day of Libyan crude would have a disastrous balance of payments impact. Adopting Wachtell's conclusion that the 100,000-b/d quota could be accommodated within the 12.2 percent ceiling, he suggested that catastrophe could not result from shifting these import rights from other U.S. importers to Occidental. A total of thirty-eight questions were addressed to Buckley and Wachtell. One dealt with the environment, thirty-seven with the oil-import program.

The proponents concluded their case with Buckley's testimony. Then the oil-industry attorneys, who had spent the first day and a half lobbing written questions from the spectators' benches, had their chance. Perhaps feeling that they had to testify to earn their fees, they ignored Engleberg's frequent pleas that written testimony be orally summarized or simply submitted in the record. Following each other in outraged succession, lawyers for Amoco, Sinclair, Shell, Ashland, Getty, two independent refiners, the Independent Petroleum Association of America, and the Rocky Mountain Oil and Gas Association predicted the ruin of the domestic industry, with the oft-invoked independent wildcatter the first victim. They also foresaw an inequitable subsidy to one of their competitors and prophesied that New England would rue the day that its economy became dependent on Libyan oil.

Asked whether harm to established importers might be offset by gains to Occidental that would leave the industry as a whole unharmed, G. E. Medin of Sinclair replied, "The damage which will be done to the domestic market is not directly proportional to whatever financial benefit Occidental might gain. The price damage which can be done to the domestic market can be many times whatever Occidental might gain." Few less oblique statements of the industry's goal for government programs are likely to be made to the general public. High and stable prices came first, subsidies second. Free competition, national security, unfettered economic development were not mentioned.

Two refinery opponents managed to vary the theme somewhat. Thomas Matthews, representing Atlantic Richfield, confined himself to two narrow and relatively ingenious legal points. First, if Occidental truly did not seek to break the 12.2 percent ceiling and upset the U.S. balance of payments, the company could not show the new foreign commerce that the trade-zone law required, for the refinery would merely reallocate existing imports. Second, if Occidental actually built a 300,000-b/d refinery, it would preempt the entire regional oil market, and the award of such a privilege must be on some sounder basis than "first come, first served." The cause of Matthews's circumspection was to become clear four months later when Atlantic Richfield announced its own plans for a Machias Bay refinery.

The second unorthodox opponent was Reddington Fiske, a summer resident of Roque Bluffs, a community of 150 immediately west of

Machiasport. Fiske disputed the statistical portrait of Washington County as a depressed area:

> A depressed area is defined largely by statistical computations dealing with family income. In a community where people very largely do not work for wages or salaries, where they live on nature, where a man can go out on the tide and earn twenty-five dollars digging clams, where he can run a string of lobster traps, where he can go in the woods and cut pulpwood or firewood, where he doesn't necessarily report a good portion of his income, any statistics based on family incomes are most unreliable.
>
> I do want to point out a characteristic of the people of fishing towns along the shore of Washington County because they represent something that is not too apparent any longer in America. They represent an independent breed of men who are self-reliant, who don't want to be wage slaves, don't want to work for employers. They prefer nature as their employer and nature can be rugged. . . .
>
> It has been suggested that 85% of the employees of the proposed refinery project could be local people.
>
> Gentlemen, I have tried, and friends of mine have tried, to hire people to do various jobs in the Machiasport and Machias and neighboring areas. There is simply not labor available. . . . [These people] are making out very nicely in other ways and the fact is that they don't necessarily report some substantial income and some may even be drawing unemployment relief, a rather notorious situation in some areas, including Machiasport.[11]

Fiske doubted that the Maine government, so committed to promoting the refinery, had the sophistication or the will to control it. As precedent, he cited Maine's most notorious plunge into industrial promotion, the Aroostook County sugar-beet factory.

Aroostook County shared many of Washington County's economic problems. Landlocked, it depended on potato farming to complement the pulp and paper industry, much as Washington County relied on fishing. Fluctuations in the potato crop or market had drastic effects on the quality of life, and county and state agricultural planners had always sought a second crop to stabilize the fluctuations. In the early 1960s sugar beets seemed to be that second crop.

The politics of sugar beets are oddly similar to those of oil. Both the production and the importing are tightly controlled by U.S. Department of Agriculture acreage and quota allocations. Acreage allocations and quotas for beets and sugar have at times been whimsically assigned.

Under the unanimous blandishments of Maine's political leadership, including Senator Muskie and Secretary of State Curtis, the Agriculture Department had made an acreage allocation to Maine despite some doubts about the suitability of the soil. The state then sought to attract a sugar-beet refinery to process the crop. After initial rejections elsewhere, Maine found Fred Vahlsing, whose Vahlsing, Inc. was already a major processor of Maine potatoes at its plant on Aroostook County's Prestile Stream. Vahlsing, an ebullient man given to boasting of his extensive political contacts, was a heavy contributor to Maine Democrats, although not above an occasional side bet on a friendly Republican.

Because the processing of sugar beets at a new factory dependent on land that had never grown them before was a high-risk enterprise, the Maine Industrial Building Authority was willing to join the federal Economic Development Administration in guaranteeing to the banks involved that any defaults by Vahlsing would be repaid. With the active support of Muskie's office, Vahlsing induced the Maine legislature to lower the water-quality standard on the Prestile Stream to class D, the state's lowest. Although he promised that his new refinery would ultimately be pollution-free, he said that he needed to be assured that normal first-year malfunctions would not cause the plant to be shut down or heavily fined for water-quality violations. In fact, the machinery worked perfectly, and the refinery was pollution-free from the outset. The venture failed for other reasons.

The first sugar-beet harvest was far below expectations, in part because Aroostook County soil was not well suited to the new crop and in part because the potato market had had its first good year in a decade. The farmers, discouraged by the poor results and by Vahlsing's slowness in paying them, then refused to plant the full acreage allocation, and the underfed refinery ran well below capacity every year thereafter.

The only beneficiary of the downgrading of the Prestile Stream was Vahlsing's upstream potato plant, which had been violating the original standards. The new class D standard meant that the potato plant could not be prosecuted for nearly a decade. Indeed, after the reclassification, Vahlsing actually increased the amount of potato discharge, choking the stream to a pestilential level by the summer of 1968. In midsummer he had tried to process a trainload of predominantly rotten potatoes, most of which wound up in the stream with extraordinary results described in a subsequent Muskie biography:

"Piles of filthy gook built up around bridges and coated rocks. Fish leaped out of the water and died. People who lived near the stream vomited in their homes. The paint on their houses turned black and formed bubbles."[12]

At the border, Canadians with fond memories of pulling trout from the Prestile dammed the stream, forcing the waste back into the choking Maine village of Easton and creating a small but dramatic international incident. Maine finally forced Vahlsing to improve his waste-holding lagoons, but the D classification prevented more effective enforcement.

This was the history that Fiske had in mind when he questioned Maine government's willingness to be environmentally firm with an industrial project to which much prestige had been committed. Had he possessed three years' worth of clairvoyance, he might have added that the unwillingness of both the soil and the farmers to grow beets for Vahlsing would eventually force the beet-refining company into bankruptcy, leaving Maine and the federal government to bail out the banks.

Atlantic Richfield's Matthews asked Fiske why no one from the Machias area had testified in favor of the refinery.* Fiske pointed out that Gardiner Means had testified as a proponent, but he intimated that Means had been a steadfast opponent until the governor had turned his head by making him chairman of the conservation subcommittee of the Machiasport Conservation and Planning Committee.

The charge that a burdensome unsalaried subcommittee chairmanship on that nondescript committee could have swayed an internationally renowned economist and former Presidential adviser seemed a strange one. Four years later, however, Jack Evans shed some light on Fiske's perspective.

Shortly after the Stowe announcement, Evans had been approached by Fiske, an old acquaintance with some experience in international

---

* Actually, three town officials from Machias and Machiasport came prepared to testify on the first day. Machiasport Selectman Herbert Rose testified briefly. The others, not having been called after nine hours of dignitaries, not being able to give up another working day, and perhaps not being sure, after Boggs, just what they had gotten into, returned to Washington County unheard. The stenographers lost Rose's testimony, along with that of Lieutenant Governor Ben Barnes of Texas, who was then, before his brush with the Sharpstown bank scandal, often referred to as "the golden boy" of Texas Democratic politics.

trade. Fiske offered his services as a consultant to further the project in any way possible. Only after Evans turned him down did he discover environmental objections to the refinery.

Shortly after Fiske's Saturday-morning testimony, Engleberg adjourned the Portland phase of the hearings, closing with a reassurance to "each of you—and I repeat—each of you—that in our book, in the very finest sense of the word, you are truly a dignitary."

The special Washington hearing that Curtis had protested was held the following Tuesday. Perhaps alarmed by the aura that Boggs had lent to the proceedings, the opposing Senators and Representatives for whose convenience the hearing had been scheduled did not appear. The sole witnesses were Congressmen Hathaway and Kyros, joined by Senators Thomas McIntyre of New Hampshire and Edward Brooke of Massachusetts. The only question came from the ubiquitous Matthews of Atlantic Richfield.

Matthews so annoyed Engleberg by dropping a small Rhode Island asphalt plant on McIntyre's claim that New England was without refineries that the examiner disallowed his written question to Senator Brooke about an inconsistency between his testimony and that of Professor Adelman. Engleberg pronounced the question "a rebuttal question, and rebuttal testimony is not being permitted. Also, it's a question not within the particular knowledge of the Senator. . . . I regret that we will not ask this question."

Kyros then moved to strike most of Boggs's testimony as "extraneous," including "all allusions to the Bible and the patronizing and condescending suggestions to our Governor as to what we should do with our lobsters." He accused Boggs of "tainting and tarnishing" the proposal. The motion was taken under advisement, never to be ruled on, and Engleberg attempted to recess the hearing until 1:30 to allow Rhode Island Representative Robert Tiernan, who had been delayed, to testify.

Louis Nizer leapt to his feet, objecting that many people would be inconvenienced and that the hearings should end.

Engleberg began to reply that the Congressman was "flying all the way from New York." As he spoke, Nizer was pulled back by an aide for a whispered conference, after which he interrupted Engleberg:

I am advised that this Congressman is *for* the application. In view of that situation, we . . . are willing to undertake the unpleasant burden of advising our own supporters not having been here in time, that we have recommended that his statement be filed. . . .

We appreciate that these arduous hearings have been conducted in such a manner as to delimit the anguish that may be caused, both to you and to us, by considerations that might otherwise have applied.[13]

On that note the hearing adjourned. The only additions to the record were letters from Senators Gordon Allott (Colorado), Clifford Hansen (Wyoming), Fred Harris (Oklahoma),* Roman Hruska (Nebraska), and John Tower (Texas), who joined Representatives Speedy O. Long of Louisiana and John Dowdy of Texas in opposing the project and requesting further hearings. Congressman Robert Price of Texas went a step further. He said that the very holding of the hearings constituted a threat to the national security and that he would therefore have nothing to do with them. He added that if the application were granted, "my answer will be to pursue with all my energy in the next session of Congress, legislation to repeal the Foreign Trade Zones Act."

Verbose though the hearings record is, it has some eloquent silences. Along with the absence both of organized environmental opposition and of enthusiastic Washington County support, the silence of the Interior Department and of Maine's two U.S. Senators was more striking than most of the fourteen-pound transcript.

The absence of the Interior Department meant that those responsible for federal oil policy had, after nine years of mandatory oil-import controls and thirty-five years of general responsibility for oil, no position to communicate. Various Presidents may have traded coherent oil policy for other noble achievements, but the corollary abandoning of basic responsibility for national energy security to private companies, responsible by the terms of their charters not to the nation but to their stockholders, must now haunt the U.S. energy situation into the 1980s, perhaps beyond.

The silence of Maine's senior Senator, Margaret Chase Smith, was more understandable. The lady from Skowhegan had always been perceived by Maine Democrats as a shrewd political infighter. One of her trademarks had been an astonishing ability to squeeze mileage out of relative trifles. Her perfect attendance record, her daily red rose, her prompt replies to her mail, her wars on cut-rate lunches at the Pentagon, all buttressed her deserved reputation for independence on

* The same Fred Harris who was later to run for the Presidency as an anti-corporate populist. In 1968 he still hoped to continue to be an Oklahoma Senator.

Maine's front pages as often as Senator Muskie's most carefully prepared speeches. In addition, she was a master at the Congressional
game of announcing federal grants to projects for which she frequently
had played no more than a supporting role. These announcements by
their nature suggested to a casual reader that the concept may have
been hers from the outset.

Jack Evans's Maine contacts had necessarily been Democrats, for he
needed President Johnson's help. The governor and Senator Muskie,
both on shaky terms with Mrs. Smith, were worried about confiden-
tiality and were not eager to share the credit. Consequently, those planning the refinery told her only the barest details and hardly even those
until the June announcement in Vermont. Bob Monks, then Republican
finance chairman for Massachusetts, met briefly with her in mid-July to
outline his concept of the project and to solidify his own position. He
was later to cite her unpreparedness and "vindictiveness" at this meeting as formative of his decision to run against her four years later.

At the time, the meeting yielded nothing. Senator Smith, incapaci-
tated in any case by major hip surgery, remained far apart from the
project during late 1968, and she signed only one perfunctory statement of support. Later to say that she regarded the entire quota proposal as an unconscionable special deal for Occidental, she did not
move actively to support the foreign-trade zone until after the inauguration of President Nixon.

Senator Muskie's situation was more complex. Although his had
been the Senate's strongest early voice on behalf of the environment,
his Maine background was similar to the governor's. He supported
environmental regulation, but not prohibition of new industry. He
encouraged Don Nicoll's efforts to steer Evans into the best deep-water
port. That having been achieved, his support became temporarily unequivocal.

In September, Muskie had been chosen by Hubert Humphrey to
help him try to overtake Nixon. Muskie's selection assured Humphrey
of Maine's four electoral votes, but the Democratic ticket was still
critically short of both money and support in the South and Southwest.
This shortage put immense pressure on Muskie to lower his Machiasport profile. Political wisdom, the fact that he was more needed elsewhere, and the knowledge that the hearings had little real importance
caused him to leave Maine's showing to Curtis, Kyros, and Hathaway.
In later years, some members of his staff were to ascribe his absence in

part to environmental misgivings, but his postcampaign statements about the refinery were environmentally optimistic for months.

Some oilmen were not satisfied with Muskie's diminished support for the Machiasport refinery. Jacob Blaustein, a director of Standard of Indiana, arranged a meeting with Muskie through Humphrey. As Muskie remembers the meeting, Blaustein argued strongly against Machiasport and suggested that Muskie's support of the project would drive Texas into voting for and contributing to Nixon. Muskie is firm in pointing out that specific contributions were not discussed. Others, who were not present at the meeting, say they are sure that Blaustein was prepared to offer a six-figure contribution to the Humphrey-Muskie ticket if they would abandon such regional preferences as Machiasport in favor of the more national preferences already in effect. In any case, Blaustein made no headway. When asked, Muskie and Humphrey reaffirmed their long-standing positions of opposition to the depletion allowance and the quota system. Nixon supported both, and, while he lost Texas, oilmen supported him ten times more lavishly than his Democratic opponent.

A week after the trade-zone hearings ended in Washington, Vice-Presidential candidate Spiro Agnew met with a group of oil executives in Midland, Texas, at the behest of chief Republican fund raiser Maurice Stans. The campaign had not been kind to Agnew, but here at least he was among friends. He was authorized, he said, to promise that any gimmick to get a refinery at Machiasport would be killed.

Standing with Agnew, Texas campaign finance chairman John Hurd was even more unequivocal. He said that Agnew had assured him "that the Occidental effort at Machiasport is dead. If he and Nixon are successful, there will be no refinery." Then he added, "I sure hope there are no Occidental people here!"

"There sure are," said Walter Davis of the Permian corporation, an Occidental subsidiary.[14]

5: November, 1968–January, 1969

Finally, Gulf favors free market pricing and fair profit as the most likely tools to assure balance between supply and demand, and to stimulate new discovery and development of the energy the nation needs. After all, a helping hand is a far more productive tool than any number of pointing fingers.

To find energy, find facts—not fault.

> Gulf advertisement in *The New York Times*,
> February 13, 1974

The U.S. team, they finally seem like fighting for country; always before they seem like playing for Gulf Oil or somebody.

> Kresimir Cosic, Yugoslav basketball player[1]

Dear Mr. Bradford:

I have your letter. I see no need to re-open the Machiasport matter: it is for me a part of history and the records are in the Commerce Department.

> Sincerely yours,
> C. R. Smith

EVEN BEFORE the Portland hearings, Occidental's Washington representatives had begun to hear from friends on the White House staff that the President had been thoroughly briefed on the project both by White House aides and by Frank Ikard, a close friend who had given up a Texas Congressional seat to become president of the American Petroleum Institute. Johnson had decided that he didn't want the last days of his Presidency enmeshed in an oil scandal. Furthermore, as one aide pointed out, he was going home to Texas.

Occidental's executives didn't believe it. In view of the corporate and personal prestige by then committed to the project, they probably could not have changed course if they had. Dr. Hammer was confident that his association with every Democratic President since Roosevelt would assure him a fair hearing and that Muskie's involvement would guarantee success if Humphrey won the election. As insurance, Occidental was in close touch with Marvin Watson, a John Connally protégé who had become one of LBJ's closest political consultants, both as a White House aide and as Postmaster General. After Nixon's inauguration, Watson was to join Occidental first as a Washington representative and later as a close assistant to Hammer. His preelection position in the White House was one source of Hammer's unwarranted optimism.

Another cause was Hammer's miscalculation of his own importance. He was able to arrange White House meetings, to get Cabinet officers on the telephone, to be named to Presidential commissions, but these were trappings traditionally available to large contributors. Valuable though they could be, they were not to be confused with real power. A better measure of Hammer's real power was a vignette offered two years later by a Johnson administration official sympathetic to Occidental's efforts to break the oil-import program. "Sure," he said, "Hammer would always arrive with one or two letters from people at the White House asking that he be extended every possible courtesy and assistance. When I got a letter like that, I always called the writer later to ask how strongly he intended that it be taken. In Hammer's case they were always just courtesies."

Misled by the Doctor's apparent strength, Occidental permitted itself to be drawn into a war of attrition, the first battle of which ran from October 29, 1968, until January 20, 1969. The Foreign Trade Zones Board had set an October 29 deadline for additional written comments and for rebuttals of material presented at the hearing. As the deadline passed, the proponents of the Machiasport refinery had eighty-three days to extract their permits from the Johnson administration. Those days passed as follows:

October 29—The executive secretary of the Foreign Trade Zones Board extended the posthearing period for comment and rebuttal by ten days because of "delays in completing the transcript." The transcript had indeed been delayed. Expected five days after the close of the hearings, it did not arrive for five weeks.

October 30—Sinclair Oil filed suit in New York to prevent any further consideration of the Maine trade-zone application. Sinclair alleged that the granting of the import rights should precede the granting of the zone. Hammer, responding with the top-hatted rhetoric in which he and Nizer specialized, said that the suit was "an incredible and outrageous effort that will undoubtedly meet its just deserts."

The Doctor was clearly correct in his belief that the suit's only purpose was delay. The proper and obvious procedure would have been for Sinclair to withhold its appeal until the zone was granted. Competent company attorneys cannot seriously have believed that a court would intervene to forbid the mere processing of a genuine application, but they could have been confident that a pending lawsuit would afford an excuse for various delays.

The suit did provide insight into the casualness with which oil companies shuffled import data. Sinclair alleged that Occidental's import request would never be granted because home heating oil was plentiful in New England. Occidental's reply brief pointed out that six months earlier Sinclair itself had requested a special 12,000-barrel-per-day home heating-oil quota because the fuel was so scarce that the company could not get enough to supply its Northeastern customers at competitive prices.

November 1—"Informed sources" disclosed to reporters that Mr. Nixon, having been briefed on the Maine project by "influential New England Republicans," had agreed to remain neutral until the November 5 election.

Also on November 1, the New England Refining Company announced its interest in building a refinery in the Machiasport subzone. The company had been formed especially for this purpose by the Shaheen Natural Resources Company, a privately held corporation controlled by John M. Shaheen, who claimed to be an old friend of candidate Nixon's.

Shaheen's first petroleum venture had been an unsuccessful attempt to build a refinery in Puerto Rico. He then participated in the construction of a small refinery in Newfoundland. During the Newfoundland venture, he became close to Premier Joseph Smallwood, whose passion for bringing development to his chronically destitute province made the eagerness prevailing in Maine and in the rest of Canada seem diffident by comparison.

Smallwood was convinced that he could best attract industry to Newfoundland and Labrador by the most generous tax and grant-in-aid programs. In addition, he was hostile to organized labor and never considered conservation. His methods ultimately did lead to considerable iron-ore development and to Labrador's impressive Churchill

Falls power plant, in which a once-spectacular waterfall has been re-routed to produce as much as 48.2 billion kilowatt-hours of inexpensive electricity per year.*

Smallwood would go to considerable lengths to aid or defend his developers. On one occasion he interceded unsuccessfully with Attorney General Robert Kennedy to prevent the indictment (for tax evasion) of an iron-ore magnate. Such enthusiasm for development was appealing to Shaheen, who perceived Newfoundland's port potential at the same time that Evans began to consider Maine's. He was able to talk Small-wood into a truly extraordinary package of grants, loans, and tax exemptions to encourage a 100,000-barrel-per-day refinery at Come-by-Chance. The refinery was to have been followed by a petrochemical complex and paper mill.

Late in 1967, inspired by the grant of import rights to the Hess refiner in the Virgin Islands, Shaheen had applied to Udall for a 30,000-barrel-per-day allocation to his proposed Newfoundland plant. A supporting letter from Premier Smallwood offered a novel justifica-tion—that the U.S. owed Newfoundland a favor in return for England's 1941 grant, with the consent of Canada, of free access to certain harbor and other land areas as part of the Allied effort in World War II. Smallwood's letter noted that Shaheen had "always been keenly inter-ested in developing and furthering the welfare of Newfoundland." Udall never acted on the request, but Shaheen was more successful in his dealings with the Canadian government. His original financial pack-age, negotiated by attorney Richard Nixon, was so favorable to Shaheen that the Canadian government reconsidered it and compelled a partial renegotiation, which, by November of 1968, was forcing the Shaheen company to seek outside assistance to pay for the refinery. Because Shaheen was having trouble financing the Newfoundland refinery, his interest in building a second one seemed unusual, particularly since his letters to Governor Curtis and Secretary Udall stressed that his project required no quota allocation.

Although Shaheen seemed to be in no position to undertake a Maine refinery of his own, his reasons for concern about the Occidental project were apparent. His Come-by-Chance refinery contemplated supplying the same jet fuel and petrochemical markets that Occidental

* If the entire 300,000-b/d output of the Occidental refinery were burned in power plants, it would generate about 58 billion kilowatt-hours of much more costly electricity per year.

sought. In addition, Shaheen's hopes of selling home heating oil in the New England market would diminish sharply if Occidental achieved a dominant position with a U.S. refinery.

Both Occidental and Governor Curtis's office concluded that Shaheen's announcement represented an effort to protect his own position and was not a serious refinery bid in itself. His request would, if rejected, put him in a position to allege in subsequent lawsuits that Maine was in collusion with Occidental, and his effort also supported oil-industry claims that (1) an import quota wasn't really essential to the construction of a Maine refinery, (2) any granting of permits to one company would deluge the government with demands for equal treatment, and (3) if any import permits were granted, they should go pro rata to all would-be importers. In addition, the mere existence of a second applicant complicated the issues on which Maine sought to force a quick decision.

November 3—Congressman Wayne Aspinall (D-Colorado), chairman of the House committee with jurisdiction over the Interior Department, wrote a letter to President Johnson suggesting that action be halted on the Maine project until completion of the investigation of the Boggs bribery charges.

November 4—Word began to filter out of the Interior Department that Udall did not see how he could grant the import permits before leaving office on January 20, 1969. For one thing, the Foreign Trade Zones Board had given itself until December 31, 1968, to act on the zone request. For another, before approving any particular allocation, he would have to rescind the ban on oil imports into foreign-trade zones that he had imposed when petrochemical companies had first proposed the concept three years earlier. Knowing this, Aspinall had already extracted Udall's promise to allow ample time for public and industry comment on any new regulations. Such a request was reasonable enough, although Aspinall had not previously been known as a stickler for procedure.

Also on November 4, the State Department disclosed that it had received an expression of "most serious concern" about the project from the Venezuelan government. The Venezuelans were concerned that some of their sales of industrial fuel to the U.S. East Coast would be replaced by Libyan oil.

November 5—Richard Nixon was elected President; the probability of a Machiasport refinery under a Humphrey-Muskie administration became irrelevant.

November 6—Bob Monks finally obtained the last of the Machiasport options that he had been bluffing with for six weeks. While continuing to assure the Maine governor's office that the land was being
held for the state, he had offered no such reassurances to Occidental.
Instead he had sought to use his options to secure his participation in
the refinery ownership along with an exclusive opportunity for the
C. H. Sprague Company to market much of the industrial-fuel output.
He also wanted a guarantee of payments to him to be used to establish
certain satellite industries.

Occidental had no intention of letting the independent marketers
participate in the refinery ownership. As the independents began to
realize this, the negotiations grew more difficult. Hammer was
astounded and infuriated to learn that Monks held key land options,
and he did not want to rely on Maine to enforce Monks's weakly documented commitment to cooperate. Instead he concluded that Walter
Corey and Monks had planned the situation to extort concessions from
Occidental, and he gave vent to his anger by berating his vice-president, Tom Wachtell. Wachtell in turn called Governor Curtis to suggest that his aide, Corey, was involved in illicit land speculation. When
the governor requested specifics in order that he might initiate prosecution, Wachtell abandoned the allegation.

November 7—Governor Curtis visited the Commerce and Treasury
Departments to press the case for the Maine foreign-trade zone. Meeting with Under Secretaries at both places, he came away with another
assurance of a decision on the foreign-trade zone by December 31.
During the plane ride back to Maine, he mused, "One of the things
that worries me about Nixon is that he gives politicians a bad name."

November 12—Curtis met with officers of Shaheen's New England
Refining Company to discuss their interest in Machiasport. To his surprise, they told him that they would prefer to build at Northport, a
small community on the eastern shore of Penobscot Bay, in the middle
of one of the most beautiful stretches of the coast. The tankers would
pass within easy spilling range of Acadia National Park and close to
islands and bays that were a mecca to East Coast sailors. The governor
told Shaheen's representatives that Maine would not consider applying
for a subzone away from the Machias Bay area.

He also told them that Maine could not amend its trade-zone application until it had received information describing the proposed refinery,
the port and tanker plans, possible satellite industries, probable construction timetables, the local economic impact, and the measures to

be taken to protect the environment. These requests served two purposes. As the governor said, they were necessary to any attempt to redesign the trade zone. They also got Shaheen out of the way during the sixty-nine days that remained until January 20.

November 11—Occidental dispatched a letter to President Johnson urging him to ignore Representative Aspinall's request that all action be suspended pending investigation of the Boggs charges. Hammer's letter denied the charges and pointed out that, even if they were true, they did not allege any effort to influence the Foreign Trade Zones Board and therefore could not result in the scandal that Aspinall professed to fear. Unfortunately for their cause, Nizer and Hammer didn't stop there. The letter, backed up by an eighteen-page memorandum, went on to attack Boggs's judgment and credibility, noting that he was "concededly serving the large oil companies."

After the letter reached the White House, incredulous Johnson aides warned that it had been a major error. Johnson and Boggs were close friends, and the President didn't need or like to be told that the Congressman's judgment was sometimes erratic. He had been more irritated than soothed, which didn't matter much because he wasn't going to help Occidental anyway.

November 13—Campaign-spending reports filed with the Clerk of the House of Representatives showed John Shaheen to have contributed $7000 to the Nixon-Agnew campaign.

Jack Evans warned Governor Curtis that Assistant Secretary of the Interior Cordell Moore, a defender of oil-import restraints, had told a Society of Petroleum Engineers meeting at which Evans was present that the Johnson administration would make no decision on the trade-zone application.

November 14—The acting executive secretary of the Foreign Trade Zones Board announced that the deadline for filing comments on the Maine application had been extended until December 6 because the hearing transcript had been found to be of "unacceptable quality" and had been returned for correction.

The acting executive secretary added that review of the evidence would continue during the additional time and that the board still expected to issue a decision prior to December 31. He is reported to have laughed at suggestions that the delay might have been caused by political pressures.

Also November 14—The Georgia Port Authority filed an application for a foreign-trade zone at Savannah to house a 200,000-barrel-per-day oil refinery to be operated by Tenneco. This was the sprouting of the second of Evans's three beanstalks, the one from which he himself had been weeded earlier in the summer.

In Evans's place, Tenneco had retained Washington lawyer Thomas Corcoran, who had been a White House counsel to Franklin Roosevelt. Having fallen from FDR's favor in 1940, he had left the White House promising to make a million dollars in a year and return to government service for the rest of his life. Less than a year later, he had told a friend that he would "have to raise the price or shorten the time." Labeled "the prototype of a legend most Washington lawyers wish they could expunge from the public's conception of government," Corcoran had, by his failure to return to his idealism of the 1930s, inspired attorney Joseph Rauh to remark that

> Corcoran's case is particularly sad because he spent his youth slaying dragons. I considered myself lucky to carry his briefcase. Then he had his seventieth birthday party, and he got up to make a speech, and one of the first things he said was, "One of the greatest things in my life is that I represent the largest pipeline company in the world and the biggest . . ." and on and on and on. I almost got sick. I looked across at Wayne Morse and he was shaking his head and looking sad.
>
> I understand Tommy. He had to be the best. When he was in government, he had to be the best government lawyer there was, get more accomplished than anyone else. The same now that he's with the corporations. He wants to be the richest and the most influential, the most highly regarded.[2]

Corcoran's role on Tenneco's behalf was ambiguous. He called Walter Corey several times to propose an alliance between the two projects, and tentative arrangements for mutual Congressional support were discussed. Little came of these, in part because the Maine participants were reluctant to enhance fears in the industry of a host of special deals, in part because the Southerners were leery of the notoriety achieved by the Maine project. Some Occidental employees still swear that Corcoran opposed the Maine project, while some former Senate staffers are convinced that he was working for Occidental. One even remembers that he claimed to have originated the idea while cruising the Maine coast with President Roosevelt.

The Georgia application itself was clearly legitimate, with none of Shaheen's apparent diversionary motive, but it nevertheless added to the complexity confronting the Foreign Trade Zones Board, and it fueled oil producers' nightmares of legions of Machiasports.

November 17—The state of Hawaii applied for a foreign-trade zone
to include a 30,000-barrel-per-day-refinery on Oahu. This was the most
modest of the three Evans originals, and the only one with which he
was still associated. Because the refinery planned to make only products
not subject to oil-import controls, it required no special import permits.

November 18—*The New York Times* came out in editorial opposition to the oil-import quota system. *The Wall Street Journal* had
reached the same conclusion a month earlier, both papers asserting that
the program imposed unnecessary costs on the consumer and invited
governmental scandal.

November 20—Michael L. Haider, chairman of the American
Petroleum Institute and chief executive officer of the Standard Oil
Company of New Jersey, called for a reevaluation of the oil-import
program.

Speaking at the annual API meeting, Haider told the group that
special-interest allocations had recently begun to undermine the basic
national-security justifications for oil-import controls. Noting that "We
can all agree that, by and large, the program has served the national
interest," he concluded, "There is a need for reevaluation of how the
program is to be administered if it is to continue to serve national
goals rather than special individual or group interests."[3]

November 21—The State of Oklahoma filed suit in Oklahoma City
to block further consideration of the Maine application by the Foreign
Trade Zones Board. Oklahoma claimed that the board lacked jurisdiction to hear the Maine application. Dr. Hammer termed the suit mere
"execution of the wishes of the major oil companies," and branded it
"audacious and arrogant and a new low in expressing contempt for
the public interest."[4]

November 22—John Buckley, having completed the transition from
Evans partner to Occidental consultant, traveled to Texas to try to split
the opponents of the Maine project. Addressing the Southwest chapter
of the American Petroleum Institute, Buckley aimed his remarks at
the independent oil producers, men and companies of considerable
political importance who were not involved in refining and marketing.

Buckley pointed out that their sector of the industry was interested
primarily in retaining the 12.2 percent ceiling on foreign crude-oil
imports. The carving up of that 12.2 percent was not their concern. He
indicated that Occidental had no intention of breaking the ceiling and
that the majors were asking the producers "to pull their chestnuts out

of the fire." Pointing out that Congress contained more representatives from consuming states than from producing states, he said that rejection of the Occidental proposal would "sow the seeds of frustration, and, when the harvest is gathered, the whole oil import program could go up in smoke, and part of the depletion allowance along with it."[5]

In suggesting that the producers were being manipulated by the majors, Buckley scratched an old and still open wound, but the threat to the oil-import program was too terrifying for the producers to break ranks. The speech had no impact visible from Maine except for a few laudatory Southwestern editorials suggesting that import tickets go to producers rather than refiners. It may, however, have helped to stimulate a remarkably educational column in the June 25, 1969, issue of the Wichita, Kansas, *Eagle* by Ted Brooks. Cast as a "Letter to Major Firms" from "the Independent Independents," it said:

We are writing to ask you to remove yourselves, your membership, your people and your influence from our trade associations and political groups. . . . We insist that [in state and national politics] you stop pretending that you speak for us too.

We remember the day when many of you were small independents too. You grew and you changed. . . . Now our needs and goals are vastly different.

By our nature, we are tied to local and regional economic communities. The proceeds of our small achievements stay with us. . . . The harvest you reap goes elsewhere. . . . And when the harvest ends, you go with it. . . .

We are grateful that many of your fine people have given much of their time, effort, and money to local and regional projects. But on the corporate level you clog our courts with your reluctance to pay taxes. You subvert the interests of our politicians with contributions we cannot hope to match. Your money warps our legislative process. Our officialdom is constantly reminded that those who play your game go on to greater awards than those who act only in the public interest. . . .

Your prime interest once was to import all the crude oil you could. It still is, but it is now tempered by your greater desire to protect your domestic manufacturing and marketing investments and obstruct new entrants into the petrochemical and refining field. So you shout murder in Machiasport because it takes in one bite what you planned to take in little nibbles; and you hoodwinked us into taking your side. The real issue revolves around a quarrel among petroleum buccaneers as to how to divide up the foreign oil booty.

Our interest, and we believe it happens to be the public interest, lies in restricting foreign oil imports to the levels necessary to supplement domestic production.

We credit to your political influence the design of the mandatory import system through which all quotas were given to refiners. Knowing better, you sold the idea that the benefits would flow down to producers. Then, through your monopoly you put a rock on crude prices for 10 years. It was a very clever way to make a lot of money, ruin the domestic industry and run your country out of oil.

You have spoofed the President of the United States into going on record favoring [the depletion allowance].

Now, with tax reform under way, there is a cry for bloodletting from the petroleum industry. You are making sure that it is our blood, not yours. With a set of exclusive figures lifted out of the most carefully guarded books in the world you purport to show that you are paying adequate taxes. You even claim in these the $7.5 billion paid by the public in the form of excise taxes.

Not content with ordinary political propaganda maneuvers, you invade public institutions other than our political parties. The state commissions, still thought by old fashioned economists to be price-setting mechanisms, are your supply-setting valves. They believe what you say and do what you say.

The Interstate Oil Compact Commission, following the politically acceptable and profitable line that wells up from regulatory officials, repeats your propaganda line for line. The governors, ignorant or ambitious, give notibility [sic] to your goals.

Through a different route you get the same results from the Independent Petroleum Association of America.

Whenever power, money and threats will obtain allegiance, you obtain it. The conventions and pronouncements of the American Association of Petroleum Geologists, a great scientific body, are beginning to sound like waterfront precinct meetings. The American Association of Petroleum Landmen is dedicated to proving your worth. You have terrorized almost all of the marketing and jobbing associations into rubber-stamping your doctrines. The National Petroleum Council serves as your point of government infiltration and outright government-industry job-swapping. The American Petroleum Institute is your body and soul and the focal point of your political and ideological collusion.

You are not content with this. Your American Petroleum Institute floods our civic organizations with its propaganda. Shockingly you even extend this to our schools, where our children are exposed to indoctrination in the beliefs that could insure the acceptability of your domination forever. Our schools are full of your literature and heroic charts and

posters which drum into our kids your claim that your corporations—
not ordinary mortals—are the fountainhead of all good things. Your
API openly brags about this and recounts its success in terms of tons of
propaganda successfully fobbed off on unsuspecting educators. We
wonder if you would approve of the beer industry doing this.

You have provided the world with immense and efficient corporate
structures. These provide the only adequate means of assembling the
effort and technology necessary to find and distribute the world's energy
resources.

But in doing this you have been contaminated by the corruptions of
power. You have acquired the insane idea that in order to serve the
world the world must serve you. Let us set you straight while you remain
in one piece: It is you who must accommodate yourselves to the requirements of living among us—not contrariwise.

November 25—The acting executive secretary of the Foreign Trade
Zones Board told Walter Corey that the board was sure to be sued
regardless of its decision and that it was proceeding with caution in
order to be sure that the suit would be groundless.

November 27—Governor Curtis persuaded Secretary Udall to postpone the issuance of regulations covering the importing of crude oil
into foreign-trade zones. Curtis had learned that the proposed regulations would be unfavorable to the Maine project.

November 29—Curtis and Udall met to discuss the Maine project.
Udall agreed to review the proposed regulation personally and said
that he would make every effort to decide the oil-import issue before
January 20.

December 1—Occidental's Tom Wachtell mentioned to a Boston
Globe reporter that the company was also considering deep-water
refinery sites in the Canadian provinces of New Brunswick and Nova
Scotia. Such sites, he admitted, would be less profitable to Occidental
and would aggravate the U.S. balance-of-payments problems.

In the same interview, the Occidental vice-president aimed concilia-
tory remarks at the company's opponents. He said, "We're not about
to ruin any markets. We are responsible people in the community."
The comment summarized the Occidental dilemma: the New England
community wanted the market "ruined" or at least shaken up; the
oil community wanted the opposite. Occidental wanted to get into
both communities at once and then to close both doors behind it.

Wachtell ended the interview in a burst of geniality: "About the
only thing we haven't said about Machiasport is that it's going to be

operated by Negro ghetto dropouts." Neither Wachtell nor columnist Lloyd Unsel, who had first coined this little jape, realized that fear of city labor imported from ghetto areas, which on television had been depicted in frequent riot, did underlie some Washington County opposition to the refinery.

December 4—Governor Walter Hickel of Alaska ordered his state's attorney general to file suit in Anchorage to enjoin the Foreign Trade Zones Board from proceeding with the Maine application. The complaint was identical to those in the Sinclair and Oklahoma cases. It can only have been filed to extend the delay and travel time of the government attorneys defending the case. According to his book *Who Owns America?* Hickel had agreed to become Secretary of the Interior four days earlier, but announcement of the appointment was still five days away.*

December 6—The board closed the record of the Machiasport hearings. The staff announced that the decision would still be reached before December 31.

December 9—The Shaheen company announced that it would expand its Maine refinery from $97 million and 80,000 b/d to $207 million and 300,000 b/d. The change was being made "because of an unexpected increase in European sales after the original announcement of refinery construction in Maine." Commenting on the fact that its new refinery was $57 million more expensive than Occidental's, the company explained that the refinery would be "more sophisticated," which was true, and that its products had to be of higher quality to suit its worldwide markets, which was nonsense.

For a company that had not yet raised its $10-million share of the Newfoundland refinery, a $207-million refinery was no more of a financial strain than a $97-million refinery, as long as it was never actually built. The company's claim of 220,000 barrels per day of new sales to Europe never materialized, but Shaheen did raise his project to a public-relations par with the Occidental proposal.

Also December 9—The Interior Department announced that it would invite comment on two sets of regulations governing oil in

---

* In the five-day interval before Nixon announced that he had selected Hickel, Carl McMurray, one of the Secretary-designate's assistants, attended what Hickel gleefully described in his book as "a small reception given by Dita Beard, congressional liaison in Washington for ITT. . . . Only after he arrived did he learn that the purpose was to celebrate the pending nomination of Maryland Congressman Rogers Morton as Secretary of the Interior. Dita and her friends were excited about having in this post an Easterner familiar with the corridors of Capitol Hill."[6]

foreign-trade zones. An Occidental employee divulged that he had seen
both proposals several days previously and that one set was favorable
to the Maine refinery and one was not. Udall had added the favorable
set after his talk with Governor Curtis ten days before.

December 10—Udall promulgated the alternative sets of regulations.
Proposal A permitted unlimited importing of foreign crude oil to
trade-zone refineries with quotas for finished products to be awarded
on the traditional ad hoc basis "consonant with the objectives of the
oil import program." This proposal was perfect for Machiasport.

Proposal B limited the importing of finished products into U.S.
Customs territory to the amount of domestic crude oil used in the zone.
Thus Occidental would have had to use 100,000 barrels per day of
high-cost U.S. oil transported in expensive tankers from the Gulf Coast
to earn the right to import 100,000 b/d of home heating oil. The costs
under Proposal B were prohibitive to Machiasport and would have
guaranteed that future foreign-oil-oriented refineries would be built on
the Gulf of Mexico, close to domestic wells.

Udall gave the interested parties thirty days to comment, leaving ten
days from January 10 to January 20 for action on the Machiasport
zone. This action heightened oil-industry suspicions of the Secretary's
intentions. It also further undermined his crumbling relationship with
his President, for not only had Udall overruled his own bureaucracy in
issuing Proposal A at all, but he had done so in a way that gave him
time, if he dared, to contravene Johnson's wishes and act on Machiasport during the President's last ten days in office.

One of the Udall subordinates responsible for Proposal B will remember December 10, 1968, for other reasons. Tom Snedeker, assistant administrator of the Oil Import Program, had sent a postelection
letter to executives in the oil industry and its trade associations. With
a naïveté and vague impropriety matching the 1961 Evans solicitation,
Snedeker pointed out that

> The position of Administrator of the Oil Import Program will be
> vacated by Mr. Elmer Hoehn when the Administration changes.
>
> As you know, I have been Assistant Administrator since the Program's
> inception in 1958. My own beliefs with regard to the fundamental
> philosophy of the program have been uniform from the beginning. I
> believe the program is necessary to the purpose for which it was es-
> tablished (our national security) and the most equitable program is
> one of strict controls without the all too numerous exceptions which
> have been granted in recent years. In many instances, I alone objected

to the granting of these exceptions. Now, I would like very much to return the program to the basic principles upon which it was founded.

Any support you may give me in this behalf: whether through Members of Congress or through other individuals will be greatly appreciated. For your information, both my wife and I have been registered Republicans for many years. . . .

P.S., Any support should be sent to Mr. Harry Fleming [sic], Office of the President-Elect, c/o the White House, Washington, D.C. 20500

The letter appeared in the December 10 Washington *Post* and ruined Snedeker's chances for the job.

December 11—During the television special in which President-elect Nixon presented his Cabinet of "men with that extra dimension," Governor Hickel was proclaimed Secretary of the Interior. Of Hickel, Nixon said, "You can see that his eyes are looking over the horizon to things unseen beyond. He's going to bring a new sense of excitement, a new sense of creativity, to that department."[7]

These kind words, only slightly milder than Nixon's tributes that evening to the extradimensional attributes of John Mitchell and Maurice Stans, were lost in a rash of newspaper articles mentioning Hickel's contempt for any philosophy of "conservation for conservation's sake" and his statement that "Whatever Udall can do by executive order, I can undo." To Machiasport opponents disturbed by Udall's behavior, help seemed clearly on the way.

Some hours before Nixon unveiled his Cabinet, Governor Curtis had attended a startling briefing conducted by TEMPO, a part of the research and analysis division of General Electric. TEMPO had been retained a month earlier to help Maine prepare the economic sections of the trade-zone lease and had concluded that the state was on the verge of being taken.

TEMPO's basic calculation was that after Occidental had paid all the costs of producing, transporting, and refining the oil, the net revenue from the refinery would be $97 million per year even with the 10 percent reduction in heating-oil prices. Allowing Occidental $22 million for interest, depreciation, and a fair return on the investment, the TEMPO calculations showed an extra $75 million per year going to the firm. Occidental would move its refinery elsewhere long before it would give up the entire $75 million, but Maine now had good reason to be firm in negotiating the trade-zone lease. Suddenly the

$7.3-million marine resource fund seemed less generous, and this knowledge strengthened both Curtis's hope for significant investment in satellite industry facilities around the refinery and his determination that cost be no objection to preventing pollution.

December 12—Assistant Secretary of Commerce Larry McQuade spurred hopes and fears that the import decision would fall to Udall rather than Hickel. Speaking in St. Louis, he emphasized that the trade-zone issue should be decided apart from the oil-import issue and that if the board found that the general purposes of the Foreign Trade Zones Act would be accomplished, it had to grant the zone.

December 13—With thirty-nine days to kill, the opponents played their ace. Secretary of Commerce C. R. Smith, a Texan with friends throughout the oil industry, announced that the board would take no final action on the Maine application during the Johnson administration. The Secretary said that the board wanted to "give the new administration an opportunity to examine the far reaching policy implications of this application." He listed the issues raised at the hearing plus the three lawsuits, Udall's proposed regulations, and a theretofore undisclosed request for a balance of payments study by the Treasury Department. He later admitted that he was acting without benefit of a board meeting.[8]

Smith's decision, like Johnson's own refusal to have the issue decided during his administration, was reasonable in itself. However, it contradicted previous assurances of a December 31 decision, and it was another piece in the mosaic of decisions made under pressure, without standards or planning, that compromised all there was of United States energy policy in 1968.

December 14—New England politicians of both parties reacted to Smith's announcement with furious impotence. Curtis, accompanied by a group of New England Congressmen, went to the White House to protest. The group was told by W. Deviers Pierson, an Oklahoman risen from Senator Mike Monroney's staff to White House responsibility for oil matters,* that Johnson would not interfere.

---

* Since he left the White House, one of Pierson's primary involvements with quotas and production restraints has been as Washington counsel for the Republic of Mauritius, whose sugar quota he helped to raise by 61 percent in 1971. By contrast, his White House colleague in oil and trade responsibility has gotten caught in the teeth of the government-industry zipper. Jake Jacobsen went back to Texas to practice law. He eventually involved himself in what would once have been thought to be the economist's task of replotting the supply-demand-price curves of the milk industry. Early in 1974, he was indicted for lying to a federal grand jury investigating connec-

Before meeting with Pierson, the New Englanders had assembled in a White House waiting room. Because of the contingent's size, no one knew everyone, and the Curtis aides assumed that the dour individual on the corner sofa was a senatorial aide named Joe Fogarty from Rhode Island. Not until the real Fogarty arrived did they realize that they had spent fifteen minutes discussing grievances and strategies in front of Attorney General-designate John Mitchell.

Also December 16—The Sinclair suit was thrown out of court in New York. The judge ruled that the suit was "premature" and that the application before the Foreign Trade Zones Board "was not ripe for judicial action."

December 17—Eugene Foley, president of an Occidental subsidiary, former Assistant Secretary of Commerce for Economic Development, and close friend to Hubert Humphrey, persuaded Senator Thomas McIntyre of New Hampshire to hold hearings on Smith's refusal to decide on the Maine application. As McIntyre's legislative assistant later put it, "We didn't know a thing about the oil industry except that we didn't like their special status around here, but it was a slack time with Congress out of session. And it was a terrific chance to investigate an issue that had really stirred up New England."

That evening, the Occidental staff took the McIntyre staff to dinner. The hearing stratagem took final form over wines that live on in the memories of the participants. The hearings were announced the next morning and began a day later. Foley remarked afterward that it was the only time he had ever seen the Washington oil network taken completely by surprise.

Also on December 17—Senator Edward Kennedy urged litigation to challenge the constitutionality of the oil-import program. Kennedy felt that the program denied New Englanders the equal protection of the law to which the Constitution entitled them. The suit was discussed with Harvard law professor Archibald Cox, who suggested research approaches but was pessimistic. Eventually the idea was dropped. By the time it was revived on better grounds four years later, it was too late.

December 18—Governor Curtis filed suit to force Secretary Smith to act on the Maine application. This action was as legally hopeless as

---

tions between campaign contributions and the price of milk. Although Pierson had a hand on the bucket during the frantic money shuffle designed to pasteurize one of the contributions, he managed to avoid the hooves that got Jacobsen and John Connally.

the three opposing suits, for even if Maine was clearly entitled to the zone, no judge would force action before January 20 simply because the governor doubted that the incoming President would treat Maine fairly. In fact, the action never even got that far. Instead, the judge pointed out that the Commerce Department did not have to answer the complaint for sixty days, or well beyond the end of Smith's incumbency. The suit benefited only Secretary Smith, who immediately declined to appear at the McIntyre investigation because of this additional pending litigation.

December 19—The McIntyre hearings were an all–New England affair. Senators McIntyre and Brooke presided while Governor Curtis and two New England Congressmen took turns belaboring the absent Secretary of Commerce. They pointed out that one of the lawsuits mentioned by Smith had already been dismissed and that the Treasury Department had said that its balance-of-payments questions could easily be answered by the end of the month. The New Englanders also noted caustically that the policy issues cited by Smith as important were precisely the ones that his subordinate N. Norman Engleberg had insisted were irrelevant.

A written statement submitted by Senator Kennedy provided perspective for the immediate controversy by reviewing the ways in which the oil-import program inhibited competition and reduced supplies. After dwelling on the workings of the oil lobby, it put in more rhetorical terms the threat implicit in John Buckley's November speech to the independent producers:

> The oil industry has overreached once too often. It will be haunted by its unwillingness to accept the Machiasport proposal. The people will want to know why large corporations are permitted to band together to prevent the entry of competitors into the market. The people will want to know how it can be within the confines of equal protection and due process of law to let some oil marketers who do not need imported oil have it, while others who need it cannot get it. The people will want to know why the $500 million a year in profits produced by the federal oil import program should go to private industry at all rather than benefitting the public.
>
> I think when those questions are answered, the oil industry will have much more to worry about than stopping Machiasport.[9]

Senator McIntyre closed the hearing by announcing that he would subpoena Smith unless the Secretary agreed within twenty-four hours to appear voluntarily.

December 20—McIntyre agreed to give Smith until Monday to reconsider his position.

Hearing examiner Engleberg submitted his report to the Foreign Trade Zones Board of Alternates. It recommended approval of both the zone and the subzone.

Washington County residents told a roving Bangor *Daily News* reporter that the proposed oil refinery was now being discussed with traces of the cynicism evoked by Roosevelt's defunct Passamaquoddy tidal-power project.

December 26—Smith's Monday deadline having been Christmas Eve, McIntyre had again extended it. On the day after Christmas, Smith reasserted his refusal to appear, claiming that his testimony might prejudice the processing of the trade-zone application by his subordinates. McIntyre denounced Smith's explanation as "inadequate" but said that he would not subpoena the Secretary. Instead he scheduled a new hearing for December 30.

In fact, McIntyre was powerless to subpoena anyone. Before beginning his subcommittee hearings, he had cleared them with Alabama Senator John Sparkman of the parent Senate Banking and Currency Committee. Under an informal agreement with ranking Republican John Tower of Texas, the Republicans agreed not to challenge the jurisdiction of the subcommittee as long as the subcommittee avoided issuing subpoenas or trying to write legislation.

December 30—The McIntyre hearing was inconsequential. Several New Englanders reviewed the nature of their regional hopes and hardships. The only disclosure of note was that C. R. Smith would shortly be joining the investment banking firm of Lazard Frères, described in a previous issue of *Fortune* magazine as "long the investment banker for Royal Dutch Shell."*

McIntyre was joined in presiding at these new hearings by Senators Muskie and William Proxmire. This was Muskie's first public appearance on behalf of the Maine project. Throughout the Presidential campaign, he had necessarily been overshadowed by Senators from Massachusetts and New Hampshire. His office explained that he was working "quietly behind the scenes in order to avoid making enemies," but Occidental's Washington representatives continued to hear that Muskie's low profile and the complete silence of the still recuperating

---

* Three months later, Smith was to deny that Lazard Frères did any banking for Shell. He noted that his new firm had, however, arranged the merger of Occidental with the Island Creek Coal Company.

Senator Margaret Chase Smith were not helping whatever slim prospects remained for the refinery.

Wisconsin's Senator Proxmire was at the hearing to lend the weight of a non–New England state to the protest against oil-import controls. He and Philip Hart of Michigan had been the Senate's most persistent and coherent critics of the various special incentives offered to the oil industry. Proxmire's iconoclasm on oil issues, like that of Illinois Senator Paul Douglas before him, had helped to exclude him from positions of power in the Senate even as it enhanced his image among consumer and public-interest groups.

January 2—Governor Curtis received an aide-mémoire from Jack Evans suggesting that Secretary Smith's obstructionism was one side of a deal in which President Johnson vetoed an American Airlines route to Japan "in order to subtly support American's application for rights to Hawaii, which is all that American really wanted."

Smith had been president of American Airlines before becoming Secretary of Commerce, but Johnson would hardly have needed to bargain with his own Cabinet officers. More likely Evans simply passed along one of many Washington rumors impugning Smith's motives.

January 4—The Bangor *Daily News* reported that speculation surrounding the refinery project had

> spurred real estate transactions both inland and along the coast to the point where planning boards and zoning ordinances were drawn up almost overnight. On the other hand, property tax valuations were lofted to the point where numerous landowners were forced to sell.

January 8—Stewart Udall granted permits to three companies to import fixed amounts of high-sulfur industrial oil on the East Coast for rerefining into low-sulfur oil and other finished products. No press release was issued, and the action passed unnoticed until January 23. When it did become public, the industry trade press demanded an investigation. Secretary Hickel, while suspending the rule under which the allocations had been made, permitted the allocations to remain in effect. His investigation of Udall soon went beyond the permits in question, and some Udall associates attribute its scope and persistence in part to Hickel's desire for revenge for the embarrassing questions prepared by Udall's staff for Hickel's confirmation hearings, in part to the urgings of a then scandal-hungry White House staff, and in part to Republican desire to prevent Udall from challenging Arizona Senator Paul Fannin in 1970. The investigation, which focused primarily on a contract between the Virgin Islands and the environmental consulting firm that Udall formed after leaving Interior, was not formally dropped until after Udall let the Arizona senatorial primary filing date go by.

January 9—Premier Smallwood of Newfoundland disclosed that the Shaheen company had raised its $10-million share of the $120-million Newfoundland refinery despite an alleged "murderous battle" fought against the project. He enthused that, if all went as scheduled, "You won't need to worry then about the future of Newfoundland." He urged his radio and television audience to "Pray for the refinery, praise it, speak up for it."[10]

January 10—Various New Englanders having spent the week charging C. R. Smith with conflicts of interest, the Secretary announced that he would disqualify himself from further action relating to the Maine refinery. Since Secretary of the Treasury Henry Fowler and Secretary of the Army Stanley Resor hastened to disqualify themselves because they owned stock in oil companies, the conflict-of-interest charges eliminated the entire Foreign Trade Zones Board.

During the various investigations of Smith's motives, Walter Corey had told Senator McIntyre's office that he had located a witness prepared to testify that the blind trust set up by Smith at Lazard Frères had not been blind and that Lazard Frères had not charged the commissions required by the rules of the New York Stock Exchange. McIntyre's staff enthusiastically scheduled a set of mid-January hearings to hear Corey's special witness when, according to Corey, the witness was summoned before Lazard Frères senior partner Andre Meyer and told that he would "never find a job on Wall Street again" if he continued to discuss the affairs of either Secretary Smith or Lazard Frères with the McIntyre subcommittee.

Corey told McIntyre aide Alan Novins that he had concluded that his own telephone or one of McIntyre's was being tapped, for Meyer could not have learned of the witness in any other way. Corey mentioned the same concern to the Occidental Washington team, who offered him the services of an electronics surveillance expert in whom Dr. Hammer had confidence.

The expert swept McIntyre's offices and found them clean. He then boarded a plane for Maine, landed in Portland, rented a car, and drove to Augusta, arriving at Corey's office right at closing time on Friday, January 10. Introducing himself as Ron Shelby, he told Gerry Dick, Corey's secretary, that he would lock up.

Shelby began by checking Mrs. Dick's office. He dismantled the telephone and poked a wandlike instrument into nooks, crannies, and filing cabinets. He declined a cup of coffee.

He moved into the office that Corey and I shared,* seated himself at Corey's desk, and again dismantled the telephone. Looking up at me, he said, "You know, I think I could use that coffee after all."

The trip downstairs to the coffee urn and back took about seventy seconds. When I returned, Shelby was sitting in the fireplace with his head partially up the chimney and a small transmitting device in his hand.

"I think this is what we're looking for," he said.

The device was very cold to the touch, and the telephone was still disassembled on the desk. Metal will usually be colder than other materials in a room, but the transmitter seemed even colder than that, as cold in fact, as the tools in Shelby's bag, which had just traveled fifty miles in the back of a car after sunset in Maine in January.

Noting my perplexity, Shelby himself pointed out some oddities. For one thing, the batteries were dead, which was why his wand hadn't found them. Even had they been live, the device had a maximum range of seventy-five yards. For another thing, the switch was in the OFF position, a fact that Shelby attributed to its fall from the ledge off of which he claimed to have knocked it when, in sudden inspiration after I had gone for the coffee, he had leaned back and run his hand along the lower rim of the inside of the chimney.

More puzzled than suspicious, I asked, "Who would have put a short-range transmitter with the switch maybe off, in Walter's chimney and let the battery go dead?"

"I don't know," he replied, trying unsuccessfully all the while to balance the bug back on the half-inch ledge from which he said it had fallen. "Maybe one of your local newspapers or the Repub-

---

* I apologize for surfacing so abruptly, but there was no occasion for it earlier, and no way to avoid it here. I had been hired by Governor Curtis early in 1968, while still at law school. A summer working with Ralph Nader's study group on the shortcomings of the Federal Trade Commission had kept me away from Maine until September, 1968. I had been assigned upon arrival to the nonoil side of Corey's federal-state coordinator's job, which he had been forced to neglect in favor of the refinery. Except for serving on the Machiasport Conservation and Planning Committee, drafting peripheral testimony, and driving witnesses between the Portland Airport and the October 10 hearings, I had had little to do with the refinery project. Nevertheless, I had found it intriguing, and, never having seen an office debugged, I decided not to go home.

licans. I'll tell you one thing, though. It wasn't the major oil companies. They'd bribe somebody at a central telephone office before they'd do anything as stupid as this."

Shelby then left Augusta for Portland, where he was to debug Corey's house and report his Augusta findings. As soon as he was gone, I called Corey from a neutral phone. Because I no longer trusted his home phone, I told him no more than that he should watch Shelby very closely and treat his report with skepticism. Since Corey and I were to meet the following afternoon, I promised to explain my concern at that time.

Before leaving for home, I switched the amplifier disc from the mouthpiece of Corey's phone to that of an Office of Economic Opportunity employee in the next office. The OEO employee was leaving at the end of the month and had no very sensitive responsibilities, but I really chose his phone because he had once told me that he usually came to work stoned. I had no idea whether the disc was a bug, but I liked the idea of someone waiting at the other end for oil intelligence and hearing only deep breathing and whistled choruses of "Yellow Submarine."

January 11 (a Saturday)—Corey, knowing that Shelby had found a transmitter but knowing little of the surrounding circumstances, called Novins to report the bug to him and suggest that the episode be used in place of the Lazard Frères witness at the forthcoming hearings. Corey reached Novins in McIntyre's living room, where the New Hampshire Senator and his staff were conferring with Under Secretary of Commerce Joseph Bartlett about the Maine trade zone.

Bartlett was in a difficult position. C. R. Smith's disqualification had made him the acting chairman of the Foreign Trade Zones Board. He had been a major Commerce Department contact point for the White House staff and was fully aware that President Johnson did not want the quota granted during his administration. At the same time, he was planning to return to his native Boston in ten days to practice law, and he had close ties to Senator Kennedy's office, from which he received frequent phone calls requesting his help and urging approval of the trade zone.

Corey's call arrived just as Bartlett, after stressing the glee among the Republicans at this worsening squabble among Democrats, proposed that McIntyre cancel the hearings in return for last-minute approval by the Board of Alternates. This would leave both the routine approval by the board itself and the entire quota question for the Nixon administration.

While this package was being discussed, Novins returned from his conversation with Corey and passed McIntyre a note to the effect that a bug had just been found in the office of the governor of Maine. McIntyre pocketed the note without revealing its contents to Bartlett. The Under Secretary's offer was rejected on the grounds that it gave the Nixon administration a chance to put the refinery under study indefinitely. The McIntyre staff began to plan anew for an extraordinary hearing.

Four hours later I met with Corey and explained my growing conviction that Shelby had found his own transmitter. We agreed that Governor Curtis could hardly go before the McIntyre subcommittee brandishing the little brown box and demanding an FBI investigation that would immediately be subverted by his own staff. Corey called Novins back and asked him to forget about the hearing on the transmitter until completion of a Maine state police investigation.

January 13—Neither Corey nor I nor two state policemen were able to get the transmitter to stay on the ledge from which Shelby claimed to have knocked it. The police were unable to find records of a car or hotel room rented to a Ron Shelby, but a call to a Maryland number left with Corey tied him to the Blackhawk Private Detective Agency of Rockville, Maryland. The proprietor of the Blackhawk Agency, Doyle C. Burke, had rented a car at the Portland airport and had stayed at the Portland Holiday Inn on the night of January 10.

Doyle Burke spent that afternoon in Novins's office explaining, at his own request, that he had indeed used an assumed name in Maine. Because Corey had not told Novins that the bug itself was false, the McIntyre aide did not question Burke about it.

Since Burke had come to Corey from Occidental's Gene Foley, to whom he had been recommended by Hammer himself, we could see only three possibilities. First, perhaps the transmitter was, as Burke had claimed, the holdover effort of a local politician or reporter, and the state police had simply butterfingered their efforts to put it back in the chimney. This seemed extremely unlikely. Second, Burke was a self-promoting fool who thought that he had to seem to find something to satisfy his employer. Again, unlikely. Third, someone at Occidental thought that the New Englanders would be further energized (and the incoming Nixonians appalled) by the sight of the governor of Maine waving an electronic eavesdropping device at a Senate hearing. No further investigation was conducted, but Governor Curtis's Machiasport conservation subcommittee began rewriting its penalty clauses.

McIntyre's third hearing, which took place on the morning of Burke's visit to Novins's office, was anticlimactic. It had been scheduled first for testimony by Corey's Lazard Frères witness and then for discussion of the bug. It finally evolved into a two-witness show in which Occidental's Gene Foley recounted all of the pre-December 13 assurances of a decision by December 31, and Donald O'Hara of the National Petroleum Refiners Association repeated his association's charge that the quota would be an unfair subsidy to a single refiner.

January 15—At Governor Hickel's confirmation hearings, Senator Muskie asked the Alaskan how he could be impartial toward Machiasport in light of the lawsuit he had filed a month earlier. Hickel responded that as Secretary of the Interior he would take a national view and wondered facetiously if he "couldn't just toss this back to the White House like they tossed it to Interior."[11]

Muskie had no way of knowing that the confirmation hearings were moot. Six days earlier, Hickel had met with President Johnson, who said of the environmental and other forces opposing Hickel, "Governor, I really don't like what's happening to you.* They should give a man a chance. . . . I want to help you. . . . I'd like you to go down and see Senator Long and Senator Russell and Senator Anderson." Johnson then had an aide call the three Senators.

Hickel visited first with Senator Russell Long of Louisiana, who had amassed considerable power both as chairman of the Senate Finance Committee and as disburser of oil campaign funds to reliable Democrats. Long, a substantial oil investor who had received $330,000 tax free from oil investments in the preceding four years, had stated that he could vote on oil matters without conflict because his personal interests were "completely parallel" to those of his state. Long greeted Hickel with "Governor, I have twenty-three votes for you. The President says you're okay." Senators Clinton Anderson of New Mexico and Richard Russell of Georgia were also supportive.[12]

---

* One of Hickel's foremost opponents was the late Drew Pearson, who joined Jack Anderson in a series of nationally syndicated columns on "Help Yourself Hickel," "I am the law" Hickel, and "Leap before you look" Hickel. Three anti-Hickel columns in a five-day span were titled, in order, "Hickel Embarrassed over Swedish Ferry," "Governor Hickel Is a Careless Bungler," and "Ethical Standards Lower for Nixon Cabinet." Much of the material in the columns had been provided by Occidental (the ubiquitous Feldman was an attorney-adviser to the columnists), and some of it proved inaccurate. These columns may have been the basis for Johnson's displeasure.

Also January 15—Columnists Rowland Evans and Robert Novak reported on the curious behavior of one Peter Lewis, an assistant budget director of the Bureau of the Budget. In the preceding months, Lewis had inexplicably devoted increasing amounts of his time to absorbing federal government procedures and information on offshore oil. During his final weeks in office his curiosity reached a frenzied pitch, and when he left office he was a gold mine of federal offshore-oil expertise. He was joining Lazard Frères.

January 16—The Foreign Trade Zones Board of Alternates met to consider the Maine application. Most questions were settled, but because the Treasury Department was still concerned about the project's impact on the nation's balance of payments, no decision was made.

January 17—Larry McQuade, C. R. Smith's designee on the Board of Alternates, called the Treasury Department to see if they were ready to vote. They were not.

January 18—Senator McIntyre gave up, telling a reporter, "It is apparent we have lost."

January 20—At 10 A.M. Lyndon Johnson left the White House to attend the inauguration of Richard Nixon, giving Stewart Udall two hours to work on oil policy with real independence.

Udall was furious at Johnson's rejection of a proposal to add 7.5 million acres to the National Park system. In his anger, he had drawn up amended regulations that would permit Jack Evans's Hawaiian foreign-trade-zone refinery, which required no import quota, to go into operation. While the new regulation could not approve Machiasport, it would open the door to trade-zone refineries.

Knowing that Johnson had forbidden him to take such action, Udall had given the promulgation to an aide the weekend before. The aide was ordered to disappear to a place where neither Udall nor anyone else could find him until the morning of the inauguration. Then he was to go straight to the *Federal Register* to have the regulation published. He was to take care not to arrive until Johnson had left the White House.

The aide performed superbly, which is how Jack Evans got permission to build a Hawaiian refinery that has done very well for him. Johnson learned of the subterfuge on January 21 at his ranch in Texas, from which he had his ex-White House oil aide Deviers Pierson call several Udall aides to express the former President's extreme displeasure.

6: Spring, 1969

You economists are going to come here and tell your story, but in the final analysis the governmental officials, the White House, which has jurisdiction over the mandatory provisions, the Congress of the United States, who may reexamine that provision, are going to have the final analysis. . . .

> *Governmental Intervention in the Market*
> *Mechanism: The Petroleum Industry,*
> Hearings of the Senate Subcommittee on
> Antitrust and Monopoly, remark of Peter
> Chumbris, minority counsel, March 11, 1969,
> p. 73.

Howard Hunt's taste in food moves from steak in the early books . . . to French wine and lobster. As a student of H.H., I was pleased to learn that H.H. and his fellow burglars dined on lobster the night of the Watergate break-in. I think I know who did the ordering.

> Gore Vidal, *The New York Review of Books,*
> December 13, 1973

"You don't really appreciate this [Glen Canyon] Dam unless you're on the transformer deck looking up," Dominey said. . . . "Suicides come down that wall sometimes. They don't realize how unvertical it is. When they're found at the bottom, there isn't a god-damned bit of flesh left on them."

Brower said, "My advice to suicides is 'If you've got to go, take Glen Canyon Dam with you.' "

"Read *Desert Solitaire,*" Dominey said. "Page 165. The guy who wrote it is way ahead of you."

I eventually bought a copy of *Desert Solitaire* and found that on page 165 its angry author—Edward Abbey—imagines "the loveliest explosion ever seen by man, reducing the great dam to a heap of rubble in the path of the river. The splendid new rapids thus created we will name Floyd E. Dominey Falls" (after the Commissioner of the Bureau of Reclamation, which built the dam).

> John McPhee, *Encounters with the Archdruid*

WHEN THE FEDERAL GOVERNMENT dragged tacklers across the January 20 goal line with both the trade zone and the quota allocation still in its hands, the refinery opponents had reason to feel confident that they had saved the quota system and kept American markets free of Dr. Hammer's price-cutting nostrums. Their confidence was based on Richard Nixon's consistent advocacy of views congenial to oilmen.

Nixon had been lured into politics in 1946 by a group of conservative Californians seeking someone to run against liberal Congressman Jerry Voorhis. This group, in which oil was well represented, backed him strongly in his successful campaigns against Voorhis for the House in 1946 and Helen Gahagan Douglas for the Senate in 1950. In both campaigns anti-Communism, free enterprise, and national security were determinative issues.

The general anti-Communism of the early 1950s was enthusiastically supported and funded by much of the oil industry. Its impulses were useful both abroad and at home. In foreign countries, it helped to assure the uncritical support of the State Department on behalf both of friendly regimes and of the fullest possible expansion of American capitalism. Within the United States, it created a climate conveniently hostile to any postwar expansion of the government role in energy development. Critical definitions of the federal role in offshore oil, coal gasification, oil shale, Alaskan exploration, nuclear development, and natural-gas pricing were resolved at this time, and only in natural gas did the industry come to resent the role assumed by the government.

Each of the other decisions went in favor of the same intellectual and political impulses against Communism that tied U.S. national security to Chiang Kai-shek in China, to Emperor Bao Dai in Vietnam, and to the monarchy in Iran—the same impulses toward free enterprise among fettered peoples that such idealistic young men as E. Howard Hunt and Robert Kennedy (then on the staff of Senator Joe McCarthy's investigating committee) were simultaneously positioning themselves to uphold in the service of a government that seemed to see things their way.

Nixon was at this time a moderate in a Senate dominated on the Republican side by Senators McCarthy and Robert Taft of Ohio. His moderation and his record of party loyalty (along with some neat pro-Eisenhower undermining of California favorite son Earl Warren at the 1952 Republican convention) made him an acceptable running mate for Eisenhower, the newcomer above politics.

Nixon was perfectly acceptable to oilmen, for he had stood firm for the oil-depletion allowance and had worked for inclusion in the 1952 Republican platform of an endorsement of the rights of individual states to control and lease offshore oil lands. The latter issue was important to oil producers, for they were confident that Texas and Louisiana would not drive hard bargains, and they feared that federal control might mean federal drilling and production.

Pleased with Nixon's comprehension of their problems, his supporters set up a special fund to pay expenses that his government stipend would not cover. When disclosed during the 1952 Presidential campaign, this fund triggered the "Checkers speech," which, for all its cornucopia of cloth coats, mortgages, old cars, and cocker spaniels, did not mention that oilmen outnumbered any other group of donors.

Nixon played no major role in oil decision making under Eisenhower. He did brush by the subject in 1957, when, as president of the Senate, he joined Majority Leader Lyndon Johnson in sidetracking an investigation into South Dakota Senator Francis Case's allegation that an oil-company lobbyist had tried to bribe him to vote for a bill stripping the Federal Power Commission of its duty to regulate natural-gas prices. Nixon and Johnson were able to steer the investigation away from the appropriate Senate committee into a friendly special committee with members pledged to a speedy and limited inquiry. It was so limited that it failed to call the director of the oil and gas lobbying effort. The director, a close friend and political ally then of Johnson, later of Nixon, was Texas attorney John Connally.

Nixon's only other notable involvement with oil during his Vice-Presidency was entirely passive but very nearly derailed him. It occurred in 1956, when Robert B. Anderson was paid a million-dollar finder's fee by Stanolind, a Standard Oil Company of Indiana subsidiary, for finding a driller to explore certain Stanolind properties. The driller was Sid Richardson, a multimillionaire Texas oil producer, client and benefactor to the same John Connally. This transaction troubled authors Morton Mintz and Jerry Cohen, who mused,

> How Richardson could have been so hard to find as to warrant a $1 million finder's fee is not easy to see. In Midland, Texas, for example, Stanolind could have found Richardson's office only one block away from their own; and in Fort Worth both had offices too. . . .
> Nossiter* cited an explanation that he brought up in an interview with Anderson, but that Anderson refused to discuss. It concerned a purported effort by President Eisenhower to have Anderson, whom Ike greatly admired, replace Mr. Richard M. Nixon as his running mate

* Bernard Nossiter, from whose July 16, 1970, Washington *Post* article Mintz and Cohen drew much of this account.

in 1956. According to this wholly credible report, for which Nossiter found independent support, Anderson was willing but told Mr. Eisenhower that he would need $1 million to afford this. The President . . . told Richardson of the problem, and Richardson devised the $1 million finder's fee. . . . But Mr. Nixon had influential friends. . . . The upshot was that Mr. Nixon remained on the ticket and General Eisenhower managed to keep his esteemed friend Anderson close at hand by making him Secretary of the Treasury.[1]

Anderson had managed the $300-million W. T. Waggoner estate, which included extensive oil operations, and he had been a member of the National Petroleum Council,* a director of the American Petroleum Institute, president of the Texas Midcontinent Oil and Gas Association, and chairman of the Texas Board of Education. As Secretary of the Navy, he had in 1953 advised that the promising naval oil exploration in the Prudhoe Bay area of Alaska's North Slope be halted and that these lands be opened for private development, which did not find the Prudhoe Bay oil field until 1968.

After Eisenhower named him Secretary of the Treasury, he vigorously supported the Johnson-Rayburn push for import controls, even though the fact that certain contingent clauses relating to $450,000 of his $1-million finder's fee were tied to the price of domestic oil. Discussing the contingent arrangement with Nossiter, Anderson said that his stake in domestic oil prices "never crossed my mind. I think anybody who comes into these things tries to think of the national interest."

The Eisenhower oil record included the abandoning of federal jurisdiction over billions of dollars' worth of offshore oil, initial opposition to natural-gas price controls,† abandonment of any meaningful federal role in oil shale and coal-gasification research, the imposition of mandatory import restraints, the dropping of a Truman-initiated antitrust action, and a heavy preponderance of pro-industry appointments to key regulatory positions. Three appreciative oilmen gave $500,000 toward the upkeep of Eisenhower's Gettysburg farm.[2]

Eisenhower may well have been far removed from both the quid and the quo, but the oilmen, more sophisticated, hoped that his Vice-President would carry on administration traditions. In both 1960 and 1968, persons with oil interests contributed between ten and twenty times more to Nixon than to his opponent. Mintz and Cohen document two

* A group of oil executives set up to advise the federal government on oil policy.
† This opposition was dropped after the alleged attempt to bribe Senator Case.

1968 episodes like the Blaustein meeting with Muskie, in which support was withheld from Humphrey because of his refusal to temper his opposition to the 27½ percent depletion allowance, of which candidate Nixon said, incorrectly as it turned out, "As President, I will maintain it."[3]

The Nixon team took office pledged to restoring orderly decision making to the federal government, and for a time that pledge seemed to include Machiasport. Nine days after the inauguration, the Nixon Trade Zones Board of Alternates met and discussed the Maine refinery. While the new alternates reached no decision, Secretary of Commerce Maurice Stans, who had replaced C. R. Smith, seized the occasion to send a letter to all New England Senators and Representatives pledging that no time would be lost in processing the application. Twelve days later the Board of Alternates voted their approval of both the zone and the subzone, and Stans announced that the board would make its decision by the end of February.

The New England victory came tarnished. On January 27, 1969, the Union Oil Company's Platform A had erupted out of control in the Santa Barbara Channel. Losing some 500 barrels of crude oil per day for twelve days, it resulted in a slick over several hundred square miles of ocean, and it fouled beaches, birds' wings, and oil's nationwide image. It was finally capped the day before the Board of Alternates voted.

After initial hesitancy, Walter Hickel met the Santa Barbara problem with a firmness which came as a pleasant surprise to conservationists, even as its private reverberations started the Interior Secretary's skid in administration esteem that culminated in his sacking in 1970. In Maine, Gardiner Means calculated that Platform A could pump out of control for eleven years without losing the oil contained in one 300,000-ton supertanker.

Despite that transcontinental sour note, the vote by the Board of Alternates occasioned nothing but favorable comment in New England. It was generally hailed as "a step in the right direction," with Republicans seeing it also as a sign of a "new responsiveness in Washington."[4] Senator Smith was particularly pleased. She had surfaced on behalf of the zone for the first time in a late January meeting with Under Secretary of Commerce Rocco Siciliano, Joe Bartlett's replacement. She had been careful not to support the Occidental quota request, so her meeting with Siciliano in effect supported the Shaheen quotaless refinery, which was not identified with Curtis and Muskie. To emphasize that the zone was at last in good hands, she dispatched a letter to President Nixon praising him for his "credibility, responsiveness, and promptness with the people of Maine" and contrasting his performance with "the shocking delays, procrastination, and non-action of the preceding administration."[5]

Senator Smith and her fellow New Englanders were unaware of another letter that had been sent to Nixon via Counselor to the President Arthur Burns. That letter and an accompanying memorandum asserted that the oil-import program had been harmed by Udall's "ad hoc administrative changes . . . to achieve objectives that, although possibly desirable in themselves, are not readily identifiable with the basic security goals envisioned in the original program." The memorandum concluded, "It is critical that a complete review be undertaken immediately before further changes or exceptions are made." The letter was signed by Frank Ikard, president of the American Petroleum Institute, on behalf of himself and Michael Haider, chairman of the board of the API and chief executive officer of the Standard Oil Company of New Jersey.

Through the rest of February the Maine trade zone application and the Ikard-Haider letter, which was supplemented by several meetings involving Burns, Hickel, and Stans, raced each other across the desks of Cabinet officers and White House aides. The probable resolution seemed to be the granting of the trade zone and the withholding of the quota allocation pending a full review of the entire oil-import program.

This appears to have been John Shaheen's interpretation of the situation. After two months of relative silence, the Shaheen company suddenly surfaced in mid-February with a nearly completed trade-zone application. To Andy Nixon, who met the Shaheen officials in Portland to review the new application, it seemed to lack only one element—a letter of credit or other proof that the Shaheen company could really finance a $207-million oil refinery. The only mention of financial capability was in a one-sentence letter saying, as Nixon remembers it, "A 150 million dollar refinery is well within the capacity of the Shaheen Natural Resources Company." Only it wasn't signed by a bank; it was signed by John Shaheen.

When Nixon asked for supporting data, he was told that it would be forwarded from New York. What came from New York instead was a late-evening phone call from Shaheen himself, who began with allusions to leverage with "your uncle in the White House"* and concluded by

* Nixon and Nixon are not related.

accusing the Curtis aide of obstructing the refinery and Maine's economic progress.

While Shaheen sought to solidify his position in Maine, his President moved to consolidate power over oil matters. Noting that Johnson had delegated oil policy to Interior only because of his own oil-state ties, the essentially stateless Nixon pulled the responsibility away from Hickel and back into the White House. His first action was to be a review, indefinite in duration, of national oil-import policies, including the Machiasport quota request.

Stans still promised a trade-zone decision before the end of February, and Hickel breakfasted with the New England governors to reassure them that economic law would cause private enterprise to build a New England refinery if one was really needed. The Secretary was reported undaunted when someone pointed out that private enterprise had once built New England refineries but that oil-import controls had closed them down.

"All right," Hickel replied. "I know what I know. If you people think you're entitled to a quota, why don't you send your senators to see Russell Long. He's got twenty-three votes against you." The Secretary's later account of the Johnson-Long role in his confirmation* makes clear that the number was not so randomly chosen as the governors may have believed.

Hickel's assertion that private enterprise would build a New England refinery under the existing import restrictions could have been rooted in his unfamiliarity with the East Coast oil market, but he may also have known that ten days earlier Corey, Andy Nixon, and I had been jolted out of our puzzlings over Shaheen by a telephone call from Tom Matthews, the Atlantic Richfield lawyer whose irreverence toward dignitaries had so distressed Engleberg. Matthews had called to say that Atlantic Richfield wanted to build a refinery at Machiasport and would appreciate an opportunity to meet with Maine's refinery and tanker experts as soon as possible.

Corey and I flipped a coin to determine where the refinery and tanker expertise lay. Andy Nixon was ineligible only because he had to spend the same morning attending the Hickel breakfast as the New England governors' oil-policy expert. For the three of us to have been shifting these nonexistent expertises so blandly back and forth did not,

* See page 120.

as we sometimes admitted, portend particularly well for the safeguard-
ing of Maine interests, but real oil experts weren't available at the
Maine salary scale.

On the morning of February 26, while Hickel was promising the New
England governors that private enterprise would eventually bring
them the refining end of the industry whose producing end he had
just had to shut down in the Santa Barbara Channel, Corey and I met
with the Atlantic Richfield representatives, and the Foreign Trade
Zones Board was scheduled to hold its first formal meeting in twenty-
seven years.

Corey and I went to our meeting as skeptics. We remembered Matthews's Portland testimony that Occidental's 300,000-barrel-per-day
refinery would preempt the regional market and his doubt that other
refiners could possibly receive the required equal treatment. Atlantic
Richfield board chairman Robert O. Anderson (no relation to the
Eisenhower Treasury Secretary) was known to be a $50,000 contribu-
tor to the 1968 Nixon campaign,[6] and the company's year-old discoveries on the North Slope of Alaska would obviously be more valuable in a U.S. market undisturbed by foreign competition. Under the
circumstances, we saw a substantial possibility that Atlantic Richfield
had no real interest in a refinery but was just hoping that Maine would
violate the Foreign Trade Zones Act by exhibiting some overt preference for Occidental. At the very least, its application could, like Shaheen's, cause further confusion and delay during which its own import
privileges were worth more than $18 million per year. We were only
half right in our skepticism. Matthews was indeed prepared to raise
havoc if he had found that Occidental had Maine locked up, but his
client was really interested in a Maine refinery.

Arco had attained major-oil-company status almost as recently as
Occidental, although its origins were less modest. Both the Atlantic
Refining Company and the Richfield Oil Company had been substantial regional operations eight years earlier. In 1963 Atlantic had acquired the Hondo Oil Company, owned by Robert O. Anderson, a
New Mexico cattle rancher and the largest individual landowner in
the United States. Anderson joined Atlantic's board of directors, of
which he was quickly elected chairman. In 1966 he merged Atlantic
with Richfield, whose greatest assets were producing wells in southern
Alaska and leases on the North Slope.

Anderson had a reputation as an individualist and an iconoclast. Under his leadership Atlantic Richfield was among the forerunners in experimenting with oil shale and the Canadian tar sands. In the mid-sixties, he had a company short of crude oil in a time of general crude-oil abundance. He immediately broke with the reluctance to drill that had restrained the several other companies with North Slope leases. In March, 1968, Arco struck an oil pool estimated by the conservative DeGolyer and McNaughton petroleum geology firm to be "one of the greatest petroleum accumulations known to the world today . . . [perhaps] a field with recoverable reserves of some five billion to ten billion barrels of oil."* The November 20, 1968, *Wall Street Journal* article that reported this estimate continued:

> A field that size would be the largest in North America, probably sur-passing the five billion barrel East Texas Field, discovered in 1930. But that might not be the end of it. Oil experts say that other sizeable pools might well be found in the vicinity. "I don't know of any major sedi-mentary basin with only one field," says E. R. Scott, president of De-Golyer and McNaughton.
>
> Alaska's Governor Walter J. Hickel, who has seen geologists' reports on the region, has estimated that the total North Slope contains some forty billion barrels of oil. This amount would put the total region al-most in a class with Kuwait's Burgan Field, the world's largest with estimated recoverable reserves of fifty-five billion to sixty billion.

Later in 1968 Atlantic Richfield merged with Sinclair, unloading in the process the Sinclair vice-president who had dreamed up the suit against the Maine trade zone. The merger left the company with more market than product on the East Coast, and its only East Coast re-finery was surrounded by Philadelphia and could not expand. This shortage of refinery capacity was exacerbated by the possibility that North Slope oil would move eastward above Canada to New York and New England in icebreaking tankers. When Arco analysts combined their corporate problems with the trend toward supertankers and the possible liberalization of the oil-import program, they saw that the best location for an East Coast refinery would be on the Alaska–New York route close to deep water, meaning Machiasport. Against this background, Matthews had returned from the October hearings in Portland disturbed by the image of the entire oil industry fighting both against the New England states and against a lone potential com-

---

* Five billion barrels of oil would have run the Occidental refinery for forty-five years or supplied the U.S. for about one year at 1968 consumption rates.

petitor, and Atlantic Richfield had realized that good politics and good business both justified the Maine move.

Matthews opened the meeting in his office by stressing that the company wanted its preliminary interest kept absolutely confidential, a posture which contrasted with the Shaheen tendency to hand out press releases like business cards. At the time, the difference seemed a reassuring proof of seriousness. By subsequent standards, it might seem clandestine.

The Arco lawyer indicated that his client would not seek a quota unless Occidental received one and was not, for the time being, interested in a trade zone. He said that the company's real estate, tanker, and refinery experts would like to fly over and visit Machias Bay within two weeks to choose a site. Corey and I did our best to convey the impression that we encountered similar requests once a week, thus probably revealing ourselves as the plumpest of pigeons. We said that Governor Curtis certainly welcomed all interested parties, and we left the meeting realizing that we had never met Occidental's real estate and tanker experts.

We were not given time to dwell on the Atlantic Richfield meeting, for we learned that Secretary Stans had been taken suddenly ill and had canceled the meeting of the Foreign Trade Zones Board. A Commerce Department spokesman announced that he hoped to reschedule the meeting for later in the week. Suspecting nothing, we caught up with Andy Nixon, who told us of Hickel's confidence that private enterprise would build a Maine refinery if Maine deserved one. Reassured, we returned to Maine the next day, a Thursday.

Snow had fallen heavily over the state all that week. Beginning Monday, the blizzard had snowed Corey into Boston during Nixon's meeting with the Shaheen group and then had locked the Shaheen group into Portland for so long that they needed Ed Langlois's endorsement on their checks to buy new clothes. Somehow *Time* reporter Richard Saltonstall had pushed through the weather to keep a Tuesday interview appointment with Governor Curtis and Andy Nixon in the deserted State House in Augusta. Nixon had called Corey that night to mention that the interview had gone well except that the governor had at one point remarked, "You know, the Maine coast is thirty-five hundred miles long. I don't see why conservationists would make such fuss over a couple of miles of it." We braced ourselves for a *Time* story headed "What's a couple of miles of the Maine coast?" but Saltonstall didn't use the quote. Two years later he explained that it didn't seem to be an accurate summary of the governor's position.

The storm had passed to sea when we got back from Washington on Thursday. Maine was buried from the Aroostook potato fields to the deserted summer cottages jammed along the southeastern beaches. A cold wind on a flurrying night buffeted us when we deplaned in Portland. As I drove home, an evening broadcast reported that Secretary Stans had remarked offhandedly to a British reporter that the Machiasport trade-zone decision would not be made until after completion of the pending review of the oil-import program.

Senator Smith had issued a statement of "shock." She was not to take a leadership position on oil again. Senator Edward Kennedy stated, "Today's action is like the local elevator inspector refusing a certificate for a perfectly safe elevator in a TV studio until he sees whether the Federal Communications Commission renews the station's license."[7] Senators Muskie, McIntyre, and Brooke said that the oil industry was at it again. Republican Minority Leader Everett Dirksen of Illinois, one of the Senate's foremost defenders of the oil and gas industries, was reported to have boasted openly that he had advised Stans to postpone the decision.[8] Secretary of Labor George Shultz, the newly appointed chairman of the Presidential Task Force on Oil Import Controls, said that his group would conduct a general review but would not make decisions on specific projects like Machiasport.

I did not slow down quite enough on some packed snow on a sharp corner. The car fishtailed in three increasing arcs and buried its rear half harmlessly in a gigantic snowbank during an optimistic weather forecast.

Maine was colder and clearer by the weekend. While skiing at an area closed all week by the storm, I lost the circular basket off a ski pole. The entire five-foot shaft went into the new snow before it encountered the base packed the previous weekend. It had been a big week for home heating oil.

Atlantic Richfield's interest had an immediate impact on the task of the Conservation Subcommittee of the Machiasport Conservation and Planning Committee. Andy Nixon and I, the only two members of the subcommittee aware of the new player, realized that the foreign-trade-zone lease was no longer an adequate vehicle for environmental standards. Because Atlantic Richfield might locate outside the zone, the antipollution measures would have to be written into state law.

By this time Gardiner Means had established himself in the same graying and jovial bird dog role vis-à-vis Machias Bay integrity that Senator Sam Ervin was four years later to seek to play to the U.S. Constitution. Hectoring, cajoling, accumulating, and persisting, Means ranged from his Virginia home to New York, Philadelphia, Baltimore, and Washington, prying from consultants, oil companies, and federal agencies whatever they would yield about oil pollution. He interrupted business and vacation trips to Puerto Rico and the Virgin Islands to visit the Udall-spawned island refinery complexes. The Hess plant in the Virgin Islands particularly impressed him, for it had no apparent effect on the transparency of the Caribbean waters, and it gave off so little odor that he had to ask whether it was actually operating.

From these sessions, he drew together draft standards for air and water pollution, for tanker safeguards, and for emergency procedures. He was satisfied that the refinery could be built and operated cleanly, provided extra money was spent and strong laws were enforced. Tankers and their attendant overwater transfers of oil were more of a problem. To deal with them, Means assembled a mound of regulations from oil ports and sifted it down to specific recommendations incorporating the strictest provisions from every category. As drafts were completed, they went to the subcommittee for comments and legal analysis.

Because the subcommittee made no interim reports and issued no press releases, it had been inconspicuous to environmentalists, who were beginning in the wake of Santa Barbara to realize that a possible refinery and supertanker port on the eastern Maine coast was something to be regarded skeptically. They had been silent until Santa Barbara for two reasons.

First, in the view generally preferred by conservationists, the Machiasport refinery presented complicated questions of environmental and economic fact and philosophy which could not have been quickly evaluated. The prudent position seemed to be to avoid any firm stand, to raise questions, to oppose generalized evils until a consensus developed around firm answers or their absence. Thus the restrained informational meetings, the Natural Resources Council's unread set of questions at the trade-zone hearings, and an NRC brochure entitled "20 Questions for the People of Maine," which contained twelve solid questions padded to twenty by eight redundancies.

Second, in a view popular in the governor's office, conservation in Maine had a long history of well-meaning ineffectuality, of which

Machiasport was only the latest example. Adherents to this view doubted that Maine conservationists, who had never lobbied or sued, had the organization, the personnel, or the will to have a real impact on the refinery, particularly since much of their limited strength came from summer residents who had been gone since September and would not return until June.

Governor Curtis himself felt that Maine conservationists had allowed themselves to be used by private power companies in opposing the Dickey-Lincoln dam. He feared a similar ploy by the major oil companies regarding the refinery. Nor was his staff's confidence in the cutting edge of the movement enhanced on the March morning that a top NRC official strolled into a legislative assistant's office, picked up a draft air-pollution ordinance, scanned it for twenty minutes, and remarked as he left, "If this passes, we'll have clean water even before 1980."

As a result of the lack of a real conservationist presence, Andy Nixon and I both felt that environmental safeguards would come only from the Conservation and Planning Committee. Consequently we consulted little with conservationists other than those on the Conservation Subcommittee. In turn, those who were not consulted concluded that we weren't doing much. In the void thus created between the Conservation Subcommittee and the increasing number of people concerned with oil's impact on the Maine coast, two groups found room to maneuver. The first was the *Maine Times,* a newly formed weekly newspaper. The second was the Sierra Club.

The *Maine Times* and Jack Evans's Machiasport project took form simultaneously. The idea of an independent weekly newspaper in Maine had grown over several years in the minds of John Cole and Peter Cox, both editing daily newspapers in towns some fifty miles east of Portland. Both were from out of state, Cole from New York, Cox from Washington. Cole was Yale '48, Cox Yale '59. Before settling into Maine journalism, Cole had tried public relations and commercial fishing, and Cox had run a paper in New York's Adirondack Mountains.

Exasperated by the political conservatism and commercial Babbittry of Maine's leading daily papers, they concluded that Maine was ready for a weekly specializing in in-depth investigative reporting about the state's environment, economy, sociology, government, and politics. In particular, they felt that Maine's thousands of devoted summer residents would use the paper to stay in touch while they made their livings and investments elsewhere.

Cox and Cole raised money from family and friends, nearly all summer residents or recent immigrants. They hired their reporters primarily from among Maine immigrants, and the first issue of the paper came out during the week of the trade-zone hearings in October, 1968. The early issues featured the Muskie candidacy and Maine land development, as well as columns on Maine arts and Maine restaurants aimed at the summer residents. From the outset, the paper's heaviest advertisers were real estate agencies, who saw it as a superb pipeline to an out-of-state clientele with money and an unending interest in events affecting Maine land. Even Cole, who had developed something of an eye for Maine real estate, acquired and advertised one speculative property per year in its pages. Only once did he fail to double his money within two years.

From the outset, the *Maine Times* differed from other Maine papers on the oil issue. Neither Cole nor Cox was an admirer of the oil industry, and the paper shared the general disgust over the oil-import program and the treatment Maine was getting in Washington. Simultaneously, however, it began to raise the environmental questions that the daily papers, often content with vacuous "local color" stories, had been so willing to "leave to the Jeremiahs."

In January, 1969, the *Maine Times* was briefly distracted from Machiasport by a proposal to build an aluminum smelter and a nuclear power plant at the very edge of Acadia National Park. Alone among Maine papers, the *Maine Times* covered the proposal extensively, exposing several contradictions. Eventually, 500 local townspeople rejected the smelter by a 2–1 margin. Commissioner James Keefe of the Department of Economic Development, annoyed by an exaggerated attack on his role in promoting the project, publicly questioned the motives of a Maine newspaper that would oppose jobs for Maine people. The *Times* responded with a suggestion that Commissioner Keefe "take a tour of Harlem and see how many fat children you can find enjoying their slum life at the dirty and polluted center of one of the world's largest industrial complexes."[9]

The editorial went on to suggest that hunger in Maine was less attributable to the absence of heavy industry than to the refusal of several towns and counties to avail themselves of federal surplus-food programs because they feared that such welfare might sap individual initiative even more than would an inadequate diet. In this exchange, the *Maine Times* and the Department of Economic Development joined a mortal if sporadic combat whose deep-seated causes were sometimes obscured by the clashing of trivial but noisy weaponry.

In March the *Maine Times* turned again to Machiasport, with an article superimposing the sights and smells of Bayonne, New Jersey, on the Washington County landscape. A March 28 article cautioned that the silence of the fishermen meant only that many "think it's sacrilegious or un-American to speak out against such figures as Senator Muskie and Governor Curtis." This article was followed by an editorial entitled "Government Gone Sour," which asked, "How many ways is Maine being raped?" and answered, "Too many ways to count. And among the ugliest faces at the scene is the face of the state's government, encouraging the ravagers instead of defending the state against them."

On April 4, Cole editorialized:

Giving Governor Curtis the benefit of the doubt has not been difficult to do. We want desperately to believe that there is someone in top-level state government who sees the need for preventing the industrial spoilers from destroying what's left of Maine's unspoiled natural resources. So when the Governor gives a major speech about the need for conservation, we support and applaud him.

It begins to look, however, as if our applause is destined for a short life. Enough indicators have begun to turn up to let us know that while the Governor and others in Augusta may mean business about new business, they are not quite so serious about the business of conservation.

We read carefully a full-page advertisement in Maine's largest newspapers about the Department of Economic Development—that "go-go department," as the ad puts it, and nowhere in the entire page is there one word about conservation or the need to protect Maine's resources. Instead, there are many words about ways to streamline the DED so it can bring in more industry.

These indicators are not designed to encourage anyone who wants to believe that the much proposed oil refinery at Machiasport will be safeguarded with stiff laws to prevent it from destroying that part of Maine's coast. We think those laws will never be written, and we think that while there is a great deal of State House talk about conservation, there are few if any deeds to back up what is becoming nothing more than a breath of hot air from capitol hill.

Because of these and other indicators—and until there is a definite and meaningful evidence to the contrary—we now join the forces that are fighting hard to keep the Machiasport oil refinery out of Maine. Nothing that has happened or is happening in Augusta convinces us that Maine will be properly protected. That being the case, no riches the oil men bring to Maine will replace the treasures that they destroy.

Since no conservation group had yet come out against the refinery, the "forces that are fighting hard to keep the Machiasport oil refinery out of Maine" that the paper was joining consisted primarily of the major oil companies, the Southwestern states, and several oil producers' and refiners' associations. To Governor Curtis, this alliance of conservationists with industrial reactionaries was Dickey-Lincoln all over again, but to an environmental historian an equally intriguing point of reference would have been the Hetch Hetchy debate, circa 1910, when the proponents of the dam and its cheap electricity had warned that last-ditch opposition could be expected from "short-haired women and long-haired men" and from "misinformed nature lovers and power interests who are working through the women's clubs."[10]

The Sierra Club itself had initially maintained silence on the Maine project. It had never been strong in the East, and, despite Maine's status as the only remaining wilderness area on the Northeastern seaboard, the closest Sierra Club presence was the Eastern New England Group in Boston. This group had set up a four-member task force to evaluate the refinery proposal.

Their report, released in mid-1969, began by noting that Machiasport posed a dilemma different from the spectacular struggles over the Colorado River:

> While the values threatened by the Machiasport development differ from those at stake in the Redwoods or Grand Canyon controversies, they are, in a sense, more crucial for the conservationist. His love of nature and the out of doors, and the style of life which it permits, is probably kindled and sustained by places like Machiasport, within reach of many millions, rather than by occasional glimpses of more spectacular and remote areas. Indeed as Frederick Jackson Turner recognized long ago, the American spirit has been moulded by the frontier, by the knowledge that somewhere out there one can start anew, find renewal, or merely retreat to beauty and quiet. This knowledge, today, may depend more on the continued existence of places like the northern Maine coast than on the well-viewed vistas of a Grand Canyon.
>
> If Americans indeed prefer the abstract virtues of the outdoor experience over the delusive exactness of economics, the arguments against the

Machiasport project presented in this report should be conclusive; if not, the arguments will inevitably be less persuasive. The romantic may deplore debating such fundamental questions of value in a language of economics and statistics; indeed conservationists long tended to counter the engineers' calculations with poetry. But by now they have realized, as David Brower puts it, "If you can't measure a thing, measure it anyway for those who won't know anything about it unless you do." This report is written, therefore, in terms of ecology and economics; but the fundamental question of values still permeates the Machiasport problem, as it will most conservation problems of the future.[11]

Despite occasional analytical shortcomings,* the report reached the indisputable conclusion that the refinery would change the character of much of the last remnant of the East Coast capable of conveying within a day's drive for millions of people "a sense, among the farms and villages, that things must have been like this a hundred years ago." Because this value to the nation seemed to the Sierra Club to outweigh any possible economic benefits to Maine, the report concluded that no port should be developed on Machias Bay.

Realizing that Maine would not forgo economic gain for so speculative a loss to the nation, the Sierra Club report sketched a "possible solution" in which the federal government would buy the zoning rights of the towns along the eastern Maine coast. The Nixon administration would then try to preserve through zoning a federally supervised aura of Maine writer Sarah Orne Jewett's land:

> On the coast of Maine, where many green islands and salt inlets fringe the deep cut shore line; where balsam firs and bayberry bushes send their fragrance far seaward, and song sparrows sing all day, and the tide runs plashing in and out among the weedy ledges; where cowbells tingle on the hills and herons stand in the shady coves . . . All the weather-beaten houses of that region face the sea apprehensively, like the women who live in them. . . .
>
> These houses seemed to be securely wedged and tree-nailed in among the ledges by the landing. They made the most of their seaward view and there was a gayety and determined floweriness in their bits of garden ground; the small paned high windows in the peaks of their steep gables like knowing eyes that watched the harbor and the far sea

---

* For example, the report predicted that an additional population of 18,000 would overburden the Machias area. In fact, such an increase would have just about restored Washington County to its 1910 population, and the Machias Bay towns would have been supporting 25,000 people in an area the size of Boston.

line beyond, or looked northward all along the shore and its background of spruces and balsam firs.[12]

The Sierra Club proposal urged that the payments go to towns rather than to individuals. The zoning power would be exercised by "a board appointed by Maine officials" under guidelines set down by the federal government. Under this system, the payment,

> being indirect, does not become a substitute for working for a living, nor does it humiliate individual recipients. The problems of welfare are thus avoided, as are psychological problems which might arise through direct payments, even though the payment is earned, and not a charity. The payments to the towns would presumably go to such benefits as lowered taxes and increased community services. Persons living in the area would be faced with the following sort of choice: continue to live here, have the benefits of excellent community services and a fine environment, but still have to work hard for a relatively meager income (assuming that farming and fishing do not become more lucrative than they are now); or, move away, lose the community benefits and environment, but earn more.[13]

The proposal represented the best creative conservationist thought evoked by the Machiasport dilemma, but it was foredoomed. Maine was committed to the refinery, and neither Congress nor the executive branch would undertake so radical a proposal without the support of Maine's governor and Senators.

The strongest reaction came from the *Washington County Times*, published weekly by Marc Nault, a former Northrop Aircraft public-relations official who had come to prefer his in-laws' home town of Machias to the environment of Washington, D.C. Nault's paper had consistently favored the refinery, but it had always insisted on the strictest of environmental controls and had welcomed conservationist concern. The Sierra Club report struck a nerve. The *Washington County Times* editorialized that it was

> wildly incredible, unrealistic and socialistic, coming as it does from a national organization of reputed great power and influence and noble goals. . . . The premise on which it is based defies reality and violates the cherished democratic right of self-determination. The plan presumes that residents of coastal Washington County would willingly submit to federal controls. Those who would not could move away. . . .
> If it were not advanced under the name of the Sierra Club, we would be inclined to dismiss the scheme as the product of a crackpot. This is

the very sort of selfish scheme we had in mind when we commented last week on the selfishness of some in the conservation movement.

An analysis of the conservation movement published in this newspaper three weeks ago pointed out the risk of alienating neutrals and causing the defection of supporters from the battle lines of the conservationists. The plan to create a federal reservation strikes us as the sort of absurdity that level-headed people are finding increasingly difficult to tolerate.

We make no apology for our strong distaste of the Sierra Club plan with its wholly repugnant choice of living here as paupers under federal jurisdiction or of getting out if we don't like it. That's little more than totalitarianism permits where it prevails. We do not think the political climate in this nation or any part of it has so deteriorated as to fear the plan will ever see the light of day except as a figment of the imagination of a few distorted minds. We invite comment on the plan from any Washington County resident who is moved to express a reaction.[14]

Governor Curtis regretted the Sierra Club opposition but asserted his belief that "the poor housing, insufficient education, and present pollution which result in large part from the inadequacy of our present tax base are more of an environmental blight than a modern refinery and terminal operating under the strictest possible regulations."[15]

Wyoming Senator Clifford Hansen, no admirer of the Sierra Club in normal circumstances but willing to oppose Occidental for any available reason, praised the report for its "sincere concern" and inserted it in the *Congressional Record* for the "sincere consideration" of his colleagues.[16]

While the Sierra Club circulated its soon-to-be-forgotten report, the Natural Resources Council of Maine scattered its "20 Questions" leaflet to its members and to the press. Governor Curtis's reply ran to seven single-spaced pages, restating the economic case and summarizing the planning and environmental measures undertaken and contemplated. It did not promise freedom from spillage, but it seemed thorough in all other respects. It went unacknowledged for three months, until mid-July, when the NRC formally adopted a resolution opposing the refinery proposal. Among the resolution's "whereases" was a statement that the twenty questions had been "unanswered in any substantive manner and have been largely unstudied." Andy Nixon and I were furious; the governor wasn't. He had never expected anything else from "that bunch of conservative Republicans. They like Maine just fine the way it is."

The NRC did introduce one new element into the Machiasport maelstrom. It proposed that Maine government forget about oil and direct its attention instead to aquaculture, loosely defined as the farming of the sea. Pointing to results achieved in Japan and on the U.S. West Coast, the NRC and the *Maine Times* suggested that Maine's river mouths were ideally suited to the commercial rearing of salmon, trout, lobsters, scallops, and oysters. The state's Department of Sea and Shore Fisheries estimated that if the right 10 percent of the Maine coast were devoted to aquaculture, the retail value of the product could approach $2.2 billion per year, four times the market value of the products of the Occidental refinery. The refinery, however, didn't need 10 percent of the coast, and if that much coastline had been devoted to large oil refineries, say 100 of them, the annual market value of their output would have been $50 billion. They would have produced twice as much oil as the nation then consumed.

A little of this numerical hypothesizing confirms warnings by some marine scientists that aquacultural extrapolations of small-scale successes into large-scale results will lead to meaningless conclusions. Some of the perils emerged in America's first flight into rural aquacultural fantasy, the fictional California frog ranch in Owen Wister's 1902 novel, *The Virginian.* That venture collapsed despite the best advice of "the government Fish Commission," the careful separation of "the bulls from the cows," and a brief run of frogs at the top of fashionable New York and Philadelphia menus. The frog ranch had branding difficulties, compounded by pelicans and poachers. Ultimately, two leading chefs decreed that the legs should not be fashionable, and the market collapsed under the weight of a webfooted glut.

The problems that defeated the froggers have counterparts awaiting the first company that tries to market $2.2 billion worth of Maine clams, enough to provide fifty bushels for every American since Columbus. For example, Maine law provides that any fish, shellfish, or vegetation below the high-tide line is available to anyone caring to harvest it. A corporation raising shellfish, salmon, marine worms, or seaweed in the open water would have no defense against poachers gathering the crop. Attempts to rewrite the law failed because Maine fishermen were no more disposed than Texas oil producers to see their prices depressed by alternative sources of supply.

Repeated miracles of loaves and fishes would have ruined bakers and fishermen; and Congressman William Hathaway tells a fable about a group of French candlemakers who petitioned their government to order the shuttering of all Parisian windows in order to foreclose un-

fair competition from the sun. In this vein, Maine lobstermen had long
since achieved legislation excluding South African lobster tails from
Maine. They joined clam diggers, who perennially sought to exclude
outsiders from town flats, to defeat laws encouraging the aquaculture
through which conservationists sought to protect them from an oil
company eager to pay $7.2 million per year into a fund available for
aquacultural research.

At times the fishermen's self-defense smacked of guerrilla warfare.
Research scientists Ed Myers and Bob Dow, two of Maine's leading
aquaculture advocates, attempted to hire local clam diggers to plant
marked seed quahogs in specific areas. After one planting proved
particularly unsuccessful, Dow became suspicious and discovered his
quahogs rotting behind his digger's barn. Another digger, perhaps a
pioneering recycler, erased most of the markings from the quahogs and
attempted to sell them back to his supplier for a second planting.

Quite apart from the empirical setbacks suffered by the Dow-Myers
team, Governor Curtis had commissioned several independent projections of Maine's aquacultural potential. None approached the $2.2-
billion estimate being bandied by conservationists. Some were modestly
optimistic regarding particular species in particular locations. Others,
including a six-month review by Walter Corey, who had decided early
in 1969 to leave state government to become involved in venture capital
for new industry in Maine, said flatly that most forms of aquaculture
were commercial losers for the foreseeable future. All analysts agreed
that extensive aquaculture was impossible until a company could lease
and protect areas of the sea bed, and the fish lobby annually defeated
legislative proposals to permit such leasing.

Conservationists and fishermen had little leisure for quarreling
among themselves over aquaculture. Even as Nixon's Cabinet Task
Force review of oil-import controls shelved Machiasport, the King
Resources Company announced plans to construct a supertanker off-
loading facility among the Casco Bay islands a mile from Portland,
Maine's largest city with a population of 65,000.

King Resources was the company on whose behalf John King had so
casually taken exploration rights to 3.3 million acres of the Maine coast
in early 1968. The $335,000 price would have been a steal if Maine
had owned what it was selling, but the federal government, claiming
the same acreage and unwilling to lease it before major companies
were ready to bid on it, had filed a suit to nullify the transaction. While

that suit dragged on, the King company set up an Atlantic Division in Boston under the direction of John J. (Donny) McNamara.

McNamara had twice been an all-American swimmer at Harvard (class of '53) and had come within ten yards of a gold medal sailing 5.5-meter yachts in the 1964 Olympics. The manner in which the gold (and silver and bronze) medals eluded him is worth keeping in mind. His boat went into the final race needing to finish either first to Australia's third or second to Australia's fifth. At the race's end, he was above the finish line, second to Sweden with Australia fourth. As he told it in a subsequent book, he asked,

> "Could we clear Sweden?"
> "I don't think so" came the reply. "Look for yourself!"
> I glanced over my shoulder at Sweden's bow and made the judgment of an instant. "OK. We're going for it. We came for the gold." I knew we risked the silver but it didn't matter at all. I took her around, and in the next seconds realized that Sweden could take the last ten feet off our stern. I flipped back with less way, but in doing so made Sweden alter course. . . . As soon as we returned to Enoshima I withdrew from the race. . . . The ultimate irony of that day was that Germany . . . sailed over Australia's wind in the last ten yards to shove her back to what would have been a fifth. . . . My chance was needless, but there had been no way of knowing.[17]

Between sailing races, McNamara had pursued a career in investment banking and stock brokerage. An eye for the tax advantages of oil investing had brought him into contact with King Resources, because the King complex of companies owed its uniqueness to the way in which it parlayed packages of oil investments into tax shelters normally available only to very wealthy investors.

McNamara had remained an avid sailor. Mention of his name in Massachusetts sailing circles still evokes reminiscences of Irish temperament and cutthroat racing tactics. Some of the stories are true enough; he once drove his brother overboard after a disappointing second-place finish. But some of them are ascribable to Yankee Bostonian resentment at frequent whippings absorbed at the hands of an upstart Irishman. Bob Monks once said of him, one big Harvard man interested in oil in Maine blackballing another, "That guy has been thrown out of every yacht club he ever walked into," but Monks speaks sympathetically of McNamara's "Kennedy-type" will to combat upper Boston's disdain for upward mobile Hibernians.

McNamara attributes the King Resources venture into Casco Bay in part to his continued interest in sailing. He recalls having been be-calmed on Casco Bay during the 1967 race from Monhegan Island to Portland. His charts showed that he was in waters 100 feet deep close to several islands. One of these, Long Island, contained oil storage tanks that had been used to refuel the U.S. Navy during World War II. The water near the oil terminal was eighty feet deep on the sheltered side of the island and ninety-five feet deep on the seaward side.

Subsequent research showed that the Navy was in the process of disposing of Long Island as surplus property. Moving quickly, Mc-Namara obtained the 173-acre property for $203,000 and began pur-chasing land on several Casco Bay Islands.

At this point, King Resources was confronted by a variant of the old Evans problem. It had an idea. It had deep water. It had land, but it had insufficient money and less oil, no tankers, and no import per-mits. Because King Resources was built as much on money manipula-tion, tax avoidance, and salesmanship as on any true process of re-source development, these shortcomings had to be dealt with in terms of image as well as resource acquisition.

This public-relations approach was also dictated by Occidental's political and economic head start on Machias Bay. To offset Occiden-tal's inside track to federal quotas and to New England politicians and marketers, King Resources needed to make an announcement of some sort. A refinery was out of the question. Not only was the company without oil, but McNamara had been sailing long enough to know the resistance awaiting anyone trying to build a refinery on a Maine island. Instead the company announced that it intended to use Long Island as a transshipping point, a terminal where other companies could transfer their oil from arriving supertankers into the smaller tankers and barges required by the relative shallowness of U.S. oil ports. Whether the terminal would handle Alaskan or foreign crude oil was unclear, but the announcement implied savings to U.S. refiners similar to those provided to Europe by a Gulf Oil Company transshipping operation at Bantry Bay, Ireland. Like several other King Resources proposi-tions, the terminal was plausible and attractively packaged, but it lacked customers.

A century earlier Congress had passed several measures designed to bolster the U.S. merchant marine. One legacy of that era was the Jones Act, which provided that cargoes had to move between U.S. ports in vessels built and registered in the United States and manned by Ameri-can seamen. As U.S. shipbuilding costs and maritime wage scales rose far above those of the rest of the world, the Jones Act became increasingly costly to consumers of goods shipped between U.S. ports. It would have imposed a substantial cost on the King Resources plan, because any transshipment operation forced to use U.S. vessels for the final leg of the voyage would have had to compete with Bantry Bay or any similar facility in eastern Canada able to use foreign vessels and seamen.

McNamara was fully aware of the Jones Act, but he believed the transshipment terminal was still the soundest idea with which he could go public. As an unmentioned supplement, he hoped to use Long Island as a terminal for a pipeline connected either to an inland refinery site or to the pipeline in Montreal. The refinery would have been similar to the Occidental proposal; the terminal would have passed on to central Quebec the supertanker savings that the United States was denying itself through both the quota system and the Jones Act. Neither concept could become public until King Resources had secured the cooperation of some real oil companies.

The decision to go public with an embryonic plan did King Resources no immediate harm, for the company could not be cross-examined in detail until it actually applied for permits. The Portland city council, attracted by the possibility of a multimillion-dollar addition to its tax base, put the King property under an industrial zoning classification without serious scrutiny. The Maine press had never mastered oil-import complexities and was, in any case, not given to unfriendly examination of major industrial developments. The *Maine Times* went after the proposal like a dog after a fire hydrant, but its objections were limited to environmental impact and did not penetrate the economic difficulties. Governor Curtis welcomed King Resources as further evidence of industrial interest in Maine, but he acknowledged that a terminal providing twenty-four jobs without a refinery entailed very large risks for very small benefits.

Within days of King's April announcement, a group of Casco Bay property owners formed Citizens Who Care, a group strongly opposed to oil in the Portland area. Citizens Who Care campaigned to rescind the Portland city council's zoning action. Although unsuccessful, the group emerged with a membership of more than 2000, a telling difference between the relatively affluent Portland area and the poverty of Washington County.

A group calling itself Keep Oil Out (the acronym KOO modeled on the angry Santa Barbarans who styled themselves Get Oil Out, or

GOO) announced an antioil march on Augusta. The march attracted a crowd of fewer than 100, and KOO declined thereafter. Its founder claimed to have had evidence that Governor Curtis and Senator Muskie owned large blocks of King Resources stock, but the evidence was never produced. He called John Cole at the *Maine Times* to announce that his phone was tapped, but his relationship with Cole subsequently collapsed following a 4 A.M. telephone call in which the KOO impresario claimed that he was being followed through the Portland night by relays of taxicabs.

McNamara had no reason to regard environmentalists as serious threats. He was determined to build the safest possible terminal, and no state or federal law then in existence could have been used to reject his project. Only the Portland city council could have done that, and since he had them by their tax base, he was free to concentrate on seeking an agreement with the Portland-Montreal pipeline and on discrediting the competitive Occidental project.

The negotiations with the pipeline never came to much. The Portland Pipeline Corporation was a wholly owned subsidiary of the Montreal Pipeline Company, which was in turn owned by the Canadian subsidiaries of six of the largest oil companies in the world. The Canadian companies were not interested in buying Long Island until the U.S. oil-import rules were clarified. A joint venture was unattractive because the pipeline was already a profitable operation which gave its owners effective control over Montreal's oil supply. They had little incentive to embrace a highflier like John King. The publicity surrounding such a joint venture might have led to disclosures that could have been expected to infuriate Canadian consumers and, in the words of a pipeline representative, "cause a field day for the likes of Ralph Nader. This public-has-the-right-to-know nonsense has gone too damn far."

The only alternative was a simple terminal operation for the supertankers of one or more of the six majors. If one company would use Long Island for its Canada-bound oil, the others would be under considerable pressure to do the same, and the joint venture would be a reality. This was one of several plans that McNamara felt he had nurtured to the verge of success a year later when King Resources exploded into one of America's most star-spangled post-Depression bankruptcies.

Long before then, King Resources made its run at Occidental. McNamara made the rounds of Maine Congressional offices with the gloomy news that King studies showed a clear need for a $75-million breakwater in Machias Bay, a cost which he asserted would wreck the Occidental project. The King company then printed up a striking four-color brochure comparing Machias Bay to Portland and concluding that Portland was superior in terms of fog, tide, current, wind, approaches, available land transportation, and surrounding market area. The brochure, not drawn to scale, distorted the approach-route comparison, and it ignored the considerations of ship traffic and heavy recreational use that had originally swayed Curtis, Muskie, the Coast Guard, and the Maritime Administration against Portland. It did prove that reasonable men emphasizing different characteristics could justify either port, but by carrying the argument further and attacking Machias Bay's suitability, King Resources succeeded only in irritating New England politicians whose help the company would later need. The support for Occidental's $150-million, 400-job refinery could not have been swayed by a $30-million, 24-job tank farm. On McNamara's behalf it can be said that games without rules invite expensive mistakes and that subsequent King Resources blunders for which he was less responsible reduced the brochure to a mere historical curiosity.

During the Portland controversy stimulated by the King Resources announcement, Andy Nixon and I took a group from Atlantic Richfield on a site-inspecting foray into Washington County. Driving down the Machiasport Peninsula, we mentioned the King proposal. With us for the first time was Atlantic Richfield executive vice-president Louis Ream, the No. 3 man in the company, an executive whose supervisory responsibilities touched every aspect of the oil industry. Ream's first reaction to King's name gave us a new perspective on his company's concern over the Maine coast's most clamorous suitor, the sole permittee to 3 million subsea Maine acres, a man who called governors on car telephones, who challenged the plans of billion-dollar corporations, who was soon to be President Nixon's personal emissary to the world trade fair in Osaka. Ream wrinkled his brow and asked, "Who on earth is John King?"

No one at Occidental needed to ask any similar question, probably because Mike Feldman, in addition to representing Occidental, the New England independent marketers' organization, and its largest individual member, was also a director and legal counsel of both Royal Resources Exploration, Inc., and the Imperial-American Resources Fund, Inc., both of which were wholly owned oil-exploration investing

subsidiaries of management companies which were wholly owned subsidiaries of the Denver Corporation, which was a wholly owned subsidiary of the Colorado Corporation, which was 95 percent owned by
the chairman of its board, John M. King, who was at the time considering merging the Colorado Corporation with the publicly owned King
Resources Company, of which he was also chairman.

The King announcement and the Portland-Machiasport debate gave
Andy Nixon justification for expanding the mandate of the Machiasport Conservation and Planning Committee. The first Atlantic Richfield meeting two months earlier had shown that the foreign-trade-zone
lease alone would not be an adequate environmental control device for
companies not interested in zones and that only state legislation could
apply equally to all refiners. Because Atlantic Richfield had requested
absolute secrecy regarding its interest, Nixon had no plausible pretext
to broaden the subcommittee's work beyond the foreign-trade-zone
lease. The King announcement provided that pretext even as it called
attention to another shortcoming in Maine law, namely that Maine
had no control over the siting of major industrial facilities and no land-
use planning framework within which such controls could have been
exercised. Since few Maine towns had zoning ordinances, most of the
coast was open to anyone capable of putting 200 acres near deep water
together with a press release. The subcommittee began to consider
giving a state agency veto power over the siting of developments with
exceptional potential for environmental harm. Our search for prece-
dents revealed that in the last decade of the United States' second century, the American fascination with industrial development and the
correlative municipal officials' dreams of property-tax bonanzas were so
dominant that none of the fifty states had such a law.

The Conservation Subcommittee had to deal with several matters before reforming national land-use law. For one thing, it was still struggling to digest and analyze the flow of chemical, biological, and technological standards that Gardiner Means kept ferreting out of corners
from Los Angeles to Rotterdam to Harris County, Texas. For another,
the subcommittee found itself confronted again with Means's proposal
that any refinery near Machias Bay be located well away from the
coast. When Means had offered this suggestion the preceding summer
and again at the Portland hearing, it had been jeered into eclipse.
Occidental spokesmen had estimated the pipeline cost at a million

dollars per mile and had said that such a figure would make the refinery unfeasible. Governor Curtis and Andy Nixon had echoed these
figures when first questioned about the inland suggestion. In Machias
some suggested that Means was merely seeking to protect the view
from his island. Means himself let the idea drop pending completion
of the Conservation Subcommittee's other work.

While the idea languished in the background, much of the case
against it melted away. First, the TEMPO report revealed that the
potential annual profit to Occidental far exceeded the cost of any
pipeline to any conceivable inland site. Next, articles about the Alaskan
discoveries used a million-dollar-a-mile estimate to describe the costs
of a much larger trans-Alaskan line, which had to cross not only
shifting permafrost but also the forbidding Brooks Range and the
sometimes rampant Yukon River. The Occidental estimate was nearly
twice what it should have been.

Even as Governor Curtis's office realized that the barriers to the
inland site were less formidable than had been asserted, the advantages
came to seem greater. The Atlantic Richfield proposal showed that the
Machiasport Peninsula was barely big enough for one refinery, not
to mention satellite industries or a second refinery. On the other hand,
the hilly peninsula, with its many views of the two bays and the open
Atlantic, contained excellent home sites that would not have been im-
paired by the Stone Island tanker terminal as long as the refinery went
inland.

Atlantic Richfield was willing to option land as far inland as Maine
demanded, provided only that Occidental too was moved away from the
more economical coastal location. Governor Curtis was willing as long
as Armand Hammer's already acute discomfort over Monks and the
Machiasport land situation was not exacerbated. Hammer himself remained publicly opposed to the idea, but he told his subordinates to
keep the possibility open. Atlantic Richfield agreed to protect that
flank by optioning enough land not only for its own use but for the
proposed foreign-trade zone as well. Maine had only to formalize its
new position in favor of an inland site.

The appropriate forum for such a declaration was hard to find. The
legislature, in the final month of a difficult session and fighting over
the enactment of a state income tax, would never have passed a law
zoning either the entire coast or the land around a particular bay.
Governor Curtis could not regally move oil refineries around the Maine
map, particularly in a manner which might appear to make him the

servant of one company (Atlantic Richfield) acting against another (Occidental).

By happy inspiration, Nixon remembered the State Planning Council, a group of citizens who met irregularly to offer policy guidance to the State Planning Office. Two friendly members of the council were alerted; Nixon prepared the resolution; Gardiner Means, fortunately a council member, introduced it. The council bemusedly endorsed it between a report on Maine's public-investment needs and a discussion of appropriate boundaries for planning subzones. The resolution, one sentence long, concluded that "the refinery portion of the development should be located far enough inland to minimize any undesirable impact on the coastal environment." It received considerable attention in the press. Governor Curtis accepted it. Atlantic Richfield embraced it. Occidental took the matter under study. In its 149th year of statehood, Maine had taken its first step toward reviewing industrial-site location.

Meanwhile in Washington, President Nixon's task force had begun the first comprehensive review of the Mandatory Oil Import Program. In New England, the review was openly regarded as a joke, a delaying tactic to get rid of Machiasport and provide a blanket endorsement of existing import controls. In the Southwest, where it was interpreted no differently, it was hailed as an act of deliberative statesmanship.

Governor Curtis made one final effort to prevent the trade zone from disappearing into a task force whose chairman had already stated that his group would concern itself not with specific controversies but with general principles. In mid-March he arranged a meeting with Arthur Burns, then a special counselor to the President with Cabinet rank and oil-policy responsibility. Four years later, Curtis was to remember this as "the only meeting on oil I ever had with a federal official who gave me a straight answer." Burns actually gave the governor two straight answers. First, Secretary Stans had canceled the granting of the foreign-trade zone because the administration feared that such action would generate so great a momentum for the project that it would ultimately compel the granting of the quota as well. Second, Burns told Curtis that no respectable economist in the federal government would defend the import-quota program, that it belonged to the generals and the politicians, and that they too had to be heeded.

Curtis responded with an impulsive request which, luckily for him, Burns ignored. "Why not," asked the governor, "at least give us the

Portland zone now? That doesn't involve oil, and Maine is entitled to it."

Burns's reply was noncommittal. Had the request been granted, it would almost certainly have boomeranged on Maine. All of the letters in support of the Portland zone had come from businessmen who would have signed unsworn letters of intent to open retail outlets on Saturn if such letters would have added an oil refinery to the Maine economy. If the Portland zone had been granted and no businesses had occupied it for a year or more, the entire application would have been discredited. Fortunately, Burns let the idea pass, and Maine was spared losing an oil refinery at Machiasport because various shoe manufacturers, textile producers, and dog breeders had falsely asserted an intent to do business in Portland.

The same week in March that Curtis met with Burns, New England's five Republican Senators met with President Nixon to discuss oil. The President promised them a decision on overall oil policy before the next winter heating season but refused to include a decision on the Machiasport refinery in his commitment.

Shortly after this meeting, Senator Smith closed down her brief run on Machiasport's center stage. She wrote two letters to Jack Evans. The first expressed some surprise that the creator of the Machiasport idea had never seen fit to contact her. It concluded: "I prefer to keep it that way, for anything that I do in this matter will be for the people of Maine and not for the Occidental Petroleum Corporation or any other oil company or oil individual."

Evans responded that he had conceived the plan "believe it or not . . . from a desire to help my adopted state. I love Maine, it reminds me of my birthplace in North Wales."

Apparently unmoved, Senator Smith rejected this overture, noting in a second letter that

> Senator Muskie made it abundantly clear that I was to be excluded—
> that is, until the Johnson Administration failed to deliver and the project
> ran into trouble. . . . In short, the operation of this project from the
> outset until it ran into serious trouble and negative response from the
> Democratic Administration was as crude and brazen a partisan Democratic operation as I have ever witnessed in my nearly thirty-three years
> of congressional association.

In March, 1969, Machiasport's Phase I came to an unremarked end. The New England–Occidental offensive had been halted, the oil-import program had shuddered but had held. Both sides took to trenches and embarked on a war of attrition. The New Englanders were vaguely confident that no impartial review could fail to see that they had God on their side; the oil producers grew increasingly certain that with Udall gone oil-policy formulation had reverted to old jokes and familiar punch lines.

Occasionally one side would poke a hat up to see who fired from where with what. Senator Russell Long delivered a two-hour attack on the Occidental proposal in which he was supported by Senators Gale McGee (D.-Wyoming) and Ted Stevens (R.-Alaska). A month later, Senators Muskie, Brooke, McIntyre, Proxmire, and Kennedy delivered the appropriate rebuttals.

Senator Long was on solid ground in asking the New Englanders and Proxmire to explain their hostility to oil quotas in light of their efforts to erect similar barriers against foreign shoes, textiles, and dairy products.* The New Englanders could reply only that their industries, being labor-intensive and in financial difficulty, were in more urgent need of protection. Only Senator Kennedy, the sole New Englander to have consistently opposed most trade restraints, was able to argue in comfort.

In other areas, Senator Long was less convincing. He repeatedly depicted the drowning of independent producers and refiners in a sea of imported oil, a nightmare which ignored Occidental's suggestion that its share of the quotas could come from the normal expansion of import needs. At one point he asked, "How can we do this for Occidental Petroleum Company, which is a relatively new company, and deny it to the older companies which have made great sacrifices to maintain this Nation in good times and bad times at considerable sacrifice and cost to themselves?"†[18]

---

* Proxmire on dairy imports sounds curiously like Long on foreign oil. An increase in 1974 cheese imports drove the Wisconsin free trader to charge in a newsletter to his constituents that "the administration has decided to sacrifice the dairy industry on the altar of so-called 'free trade.' They are giving other countries the privilege of dumping subsidized dairy products on our shores in order to preserve foreign markets for wheat, soybeans and feed grains. . . . The result? An increasing dependence on other countries for milk and cheese. If you think dairy prices are high now, wait until the bulk of our dairy farmers have been driven out of business by these misguided policies."

† This passage exemplifies a two-generation reversal in Louisiana political formulas. Russell's father, Huey Long, had risen to prominence in the 1920s and 1930s on the strength of a vitriolic feud with the Standard Oil Company of New Jersey over the

The debate reached a nadir of sorts after a suggestion by Senator Proxmire that Canadian oil, being safe from the pillaging of submarines and sheiks, need not be excluded as rigorously as Senator Long believed. Long would not agree:

> MR. LONG: How does the Senator know whether a war would not break out between the United States and Canada? . . . That could happen. Has the Senator ever heard of the War of 1812?
>
> MR. PROXMIRE: Is the Senator from Louisiana really serious about that?
>
> MR. LONG: It is not inconceivable.
>
> MR. PROXMIRE: Canada and the United States would engage in a prolonged war that could hold up our ability to import oil into this country?
>
> MR. LONG: It's entirely conceivable to the Senator from Louisiana.[19]

No Senator pointed out that New England and Wisconsin had been at war with Louisiana fifty years more recently than with Canada.

As the trench war ground on, Gulf and Occidental gassed each other with brochures entitled "Some Important Facts about Machiasport" and "Let's Keep the Record Straight on Machiasport." Perhaps because Occidental's effort was prepared in specific rebuttal to exaggerations in the Gulf brochure and was wrapped in banners of consumer benefit, rural development, and an end to (or at least a broadening of) special treatment, it was more effective, but the decision was not being made on debating points.

Sniper fire included C. R. Smith's appearance as a private citizen before the McIntyre subcommittee to charge that the New Hampshire Senator had maligned his reputation. Smith was correct in asserting that several of the charges of improper conduct made in early January had gone unproven, but the confrontation became a standoff when the former Secretary of Commerce could not justify the bizarre events

---

inadequacy of Esso's Louisiana taxes and the unfairness of its pipeline practices. Huey's trump was to threaten expropriation of a Standard refinery.

Oil did not replace cotton as the prime mover in Texas-Louisiana politics until after World War II. House Speaker Sam Rayburn had weathered a purge attempt by oilmen in 1944. Russell Long was elected to the Senate at the age of thirty in 1948, thirteen years after the assassination of his father. Oil's other two most powerful senatorial defenders, Lyndon Johnson and Robert Kerr, were elected in the same year. Tom Connally, a Texas Senator more solicitous of cotton than of oil, was driven from office four years later. After that, only Senator Ralph Yarborough dared to cross oil on important votes. Yarborough was defeated in 1970 by Lloyd Bentsen, a conservative Democrat with oil industry ties.

surrounding the processing of the trade-zone application. Smith asserted that the original December 31 deadline had been an unrealistic target. He pointed out that the average span between hearing and decision of foreign-trade zones had been six months, a persuasive fact at the time of his testimony in 1969 but less convincing in view of the several years that have since elapsed without a decision.

For the other side, Occidental leaked the story of Spiro Agnew's Midland, Texas, promise to kill "any gimmick to get a refinery at Machiasport"* to Drew Pearson and Jack Anderson. To Occidental's horror, the Pearson-Anderson column virtually attributed the story to Oxy's Walter Davis, thereby telling an infuriated White House staff to blame the story on a corporation with a $93-million-per-year oil refinery dependent on a Presidential decision.

Stewart Udall announced in mid-April that he would have approved a quota allocation if the Machiasport application had reached his desk. He added that he "would have attached the most stringent possible environmental controls." Udall went on to defend his Virgin Islands quota allocation as "one of the best decisions I ever made. The St. Croix refinery is an example of how clean refineries can be maintained. You might say that refinery is located right in the middle of a park; and they still have their beautiful beaches."[20] Udall was accurate enough at the time. The Virgin Islands' first big oil spill and the eruption of murderous racial tensions caused in part by St. Croix's growing industrialization were still thirty months away.

Udall's successor, Walter Hickel, had his own theories on the construction of a Maine refinery: "It's my opinion that a refinery will be built there, and it will use domestic crude. If that happens, then the problem goes away. That's my recommendation for solving the problem."[21] Hickel, like Governor Curtis, was a man more interested in actions than words. Content to get a general thought across, he did not use language with the precision expected of diplomats. Careful searching through his statements for significant nuances is at best a waste of time. Nevertheless, with all allowances for linguistic imprecision, his talk of a Machias Bay refinery running on U.S. crude cannot be made to make sense. The Secretary himself insisted that he did not mean the Alaskan oil that Esso was considering transporting to the East Coast by icebreaking tanker. He can only have meant oil from the Gulf Coast, which could not have been refined economically in Maine.

* See page 95.

The only other explanation is conjectural but has at least the virtue of economic and political plausibility. In a vigorously denied post-campaign report, Drew Pearson and Jack Anderson asserted that Atlantic Richfield chairman Robert O. Anderson had secretly ridden a service elevator to the Nixon suite in New York's Pierre Hotel, where he was able to prevail on the President-elect to switch the Interior Secretaryship from Montana Governor Tim Babcock to Hickel. Anderson wrote to Pearson to deny that such a visit ever occurred, suggesting that the story might have resulted from a meeting between Nixon and Robert B. Anderson, Eisenhower's former Treasury Secretary. The letter concluded, "In any case, I do not ride in service elevators."

Whether or not Anderson actually visited Nixon, his company had adequate pipeline capacity to Hickel's office. Atlantic Richfield and the governor had been on excellent terms as a result of the company's willingness to push ahead with exploration of Alaska's North Slope. In 1969 Hickel's brother was hired to construct Atlantic Richfield's Anchorage office building. Company officials privately joked about Hickel's frequent boast that he told them where to drill, but the jokes remained private. The company may well have told the new Secretary that it was considering running a Maine refinery on Alaskan crude simply to assure that he did nothing precipitate to aid Occidental. Under this hypothesis, Hickel's denial that Alaskan crude was involved would have been necessary to conceal Atlantic Richfield's identity, since any mention of Alaskan oil would have narrowed speculation to the three companies (Arco, Esso, and British Petroleum) with proven North Slope finds.

Whatever the motivation, the statement as given was absurd. Since a Secretary of the Interior is generally presumed to know what he is talking about on oil matters, it provided a considerable distraction. When it went without confirmation or reiteration, it dwindled to further proof that U.S. oil policy was not being made by the nominal policymakers.

A more symbolic and less subtle confirmation of the same point came in mid-April, during Vice-President Agnew's first postelection visit to New England. An Agnew advance man aroused some resentment by his handling of the press at a dinner at Manchester, New Hampshire. He forbade photographs during the dinner and announced that Agnew would only answer a few questions on specified subjects. An annoyed reporter checked the identity of the "advance man" and discovered him to be Spencer Schedler, an official of the Sinclair Oil Company on salaried vacation at the time.*

Sociologist Michael Harrington has observed that "the Government of the United States had carefully counted, classified, and computer taped all of the outrages which it does so little about. The statistics would frighten a Jeremiah, but the laws must be written to satisfy stolid businessmen."[22] Oil-import controls began to experience this process of unconsummated analysis on two fronts during the six chaotic weeks beginning with Secretary Stans's abrupt reversal on the trade zone and including the arrivals of Atlantic Richfield and King Resources in Maine and the Arthur Burns, Russell Long, and Spiro Agnew episodes.

The first scrutiny came from Nixon's Cabinet Task Force on Oil Import Controls. The President appointed Secretary of Labor George Shultz to chair the task force. Shultz's inexperience in oil policymaking suggested different things to different people, but his independence of mind quickly manifested itself. Given a free hand to choose his staff, the Secretary picked Harvard Law Professor Philip Areeda as his staff director. Areeda had been on the Eisenhower White House staff when import controls were imposed but was generally regarded as being both capable and independent. The staff of lawyers and economists that he assembled soon earned a similar reputation.

The oil industry, expecting the task force to reproduce the endorsement of mandatory import controls that had emerged from the original Eisenhower task force, was jolted almost immediately. The task force's first public document was a no-nonsense statement of procedures governing the submission of information. Simultaneously, in a regulation unusual in contact-conscious Washington, the staff were instructed to submit memoranda of conversations to the publicly available files. Only classified information, proprietary corporate data, and internal task force working papers were exempt from disclosure.

With these procedural regulations, the task force promulgated an eighty-two-item questionnaire delving into all aspects of import con-

---

* Although the Sinclair–Atlantic Richfield merger had been consummated earlier in the year, Sinclair maintained a separate identity for several months. Schedler did not survive the completed merger. In May, 1969, he became Assistant Secretary of the Air Force for Financial Management, where he supervised Air Force efforts to ignore the $2 billion cost overrun in the C5A transport plane as it was pointed out by his subordinate, A. Ernest Fitzgerald, whom he reassigned and fired, a process that the Civil Service Commission eventually refused to uphold.

trols, including the cost to consumers, the security interest actually being protected, alternative means of protection, and ways and consequences of eliminating or altering quota restraints. Scarcely had the questionnaire been distributed when Robert Ellsworth, the Nixon aide with staff responsibility for oil policy, left the White House to become the U.S. ambassador to the North Atlantic Treaty Organization. Columnist Marianne Means reported on April 10 that Ellsworth's handling of oil matters and airline routes coupled with his willingness to talk to reporters had annoyed two aides named John Ehrlichman and H. R. Haldeman, who had moved him out.

As the Cabinet Task Force began its work, it was spurred on by some noteworthy testimony before the Senate Subcommittee on Antitrust and Monopoly, chaired by Michigan Democrat Philip Hart. Hart had just led his subcommittee through a set of eight-volume, 5000-page hearings on economic concentration. He was commencing what was to become a five-volume, 2250-page effort on governmental involvement in petroleum-industry market mechanisms. These hearings were encyclopedic compilations of governmental economic malfunctions. They failed to give rise to any legislation, but they did some spadework for the Nixon task force while giving warning that its work would be closely watched.

Senator Hart's hearings on the oil-import restraints were a Washington response to the tangible consequences emerging in places like Machiasport. Senators Hart and Kennedy pressed consumer perspectives and dissatisfactions. Senators Roman Hruska (R.-Nebraska) and John McClellan (D.-Arkansas) and, until his death in September, Everett Dirksen defended the existing quota and prorationing systems as natural free-market norms from which any change would constitute burdensome governmental interference. The subcommittee's chief economist, responsible to the Democrats, was Dr. John Blair, brusquely intolerant of disagreement from friend or adversary and monumentally prepared. Ranged against him were minority counsel Peter Chumbris and minority economist Kirkley Coulter, both basically faithful to the Dirksen-Hruska positions. Senator Hiram Fong (R.-Hawaii) made occasional appearances to stress his state's particular burdens and to plug Jack Evans's Honolulu trade-zone refinery. The remaining subcommittee members, Sam Ervin of North Carolina and Thomas Dodd of Connecticut, missed every session.

The first round of hearings, held in March, 1969, was devoted exclusively to professional economists and to academicians. Their esti-

mates of the annual cost of import controls to the American consumer
varied from a low of $2.7 billion ($54 per family) to a high of $7.2
billion ($144 per family). During the hearings, Senator Hart con-
firmed one of Arthur Burns's observations to Governor Curtis by noting
that the subcommittee had been unable to find a single independent
economist willing to support the program. Those who opposed it had
many complaints.

Dr. Walter Mead of the University of California at Santa Barbara
asserted that the combination of tax subsidies, state prorationing, and
import controls resulted in a system that paid $3.42 to develop a barrel
of oil worth $2.10, a resource misallocation resulting in a lower na-
tionwide standard of living. One source of relatively expensive oil that
would not have been developed without subsidy was the Santa Barbara
Channel, which had erupted six weeks earlier. To Dr. Blair, Mead's
testimony was uniquely valuable in showing

> how one form of governmental intervention in the market mechanism
> breeds another . . . starting with percentage depletion which results
> in excessive production which then must be limited by state proration-
> ing . . . Then because there is a limitation on domestic production but
> none on foreign supplies, import quotas must be established.[23]

Mead was followed by Dr. Paul Homan, an economist with Resources for the Future, a nonprofit research group. Addressing himself
solely to the way in which import permits were assigned without any
regard for national-security considerations, frequently going to refiners
unable to use them,* Homan asserted:

> We are under the impression that those responsible for adopting the
> allocation system never regarded it as having any importance for meet-
> ing the national security objectives of the import system. . . .
> We are not aware that those responsible for framing the allocations
> system engaged in any serious analysis of the alternatives open to them.
> . . . And the administrators of the established system have never
> bothered to give an economic justification for their decisions. . . .
> Probably, however, the administration of the system is so affected by

---

* Because quotas were assigned to all refiners on a sliding scale based on refinery inputs, substantial allocations went to inland refiners with no access to imports.
Those who could not use the oil exchanged their permits for domestic oil. Thus on
the day the program went into effect, the government began making a daily present
of 3000 barrels of foreign oil to every owner of a 30,000-b/d refinery. In 1968 this
was a present of $4500 per day or $1.6 million per year, in return for which the
refiner was subject to less scrutiny than most welfare recipients.

claimant interests and political pressures that any effort to establish an economic rationale would be a losing game from the start. . . . The exercises in economic reasoning which are to be found in the record can only be described as feeble.[24]

Dr. Walter Adams, professor of economics and acting president of Michigan State University, opened his testimony with a summary of the late Professor Joseph Schumpeter's analysis of the functioning of the capitalist process, a statement that must have sent a cold wind whistling through the audience crowded with oil lobbyists:

> The capitalist process was rooted not in classical price competition, but rather the competition from the new commodity, the new technology, the new source of supply, the new type of organization—competition which commands a decisive cost or quality advantage and which strikes not at the margin of the profits and outputs of existing firms, but at their very foundation. The very essence of capitalism, according to Schumpeter, was the perennial gale of creative destruction in which existing power positions and entrenched advantage were constantly displaced by new organizations and new power complexes. This gale of creative destruction was to be not only the harbinger of progress, but also the built-in safeguard against the vices of monopoly and privilege. . . .
>
> By manipulation of the state for private ends, the possessors of entrenched power have found the most felicitous instrument for insulating themselves against, and immunizing themselves from, the Schumpeterian gale.[25]

Dr. Adams was sufficiently concerned about "the existence of a government-created, government-supported, and government-subsidized cartel"[26] to point out that oil was one of the few subjects on which he agreed with conservative economist Milton Friedman, who had said:

> Few industries sing the praises of free enterprise more loudly than the oil industry. Yet few industries rely so heavily on government favors. . . . The political power of the oil industry, not national security, is the reason for the present subsidies to the industry. International disturbances simply offer a convenient excuse.[27]

Adams added his own condemnation:

> The problem before us is a problem in political economy. This is not just an economic problem. Most economists I know have arrived at substantially the same conclusion. . . . That is, on economic grounds there simply seems to be no rationale for the perpetuation of the honey-

comb of restraints that the Government has built up in the oil industry. The Government here is a mask for privilege. The Government is an agent for creating monopoly. And this, of course, is doubly ironic because we have on the statute books the antitrust laws, the basic objective of which is to install a competitive market in the United States, and here the Government subverts these antitrust laws by doing precisely that which private individuals are prohibited from doing for themselves.[28]

Professor Henry Steele of the University of Houston addressed himself to the system of state production controls which flourished only because the oil-import program excluded foreign competition. He concluded that oil-import controls shielded inefficient production because the states restricted wells capable of producing thousands of barrels of oil daily to outputs of less than twenty barrels per day in order to make room for wells incapable of producing more than that. Thus thousands of small high-cost wells produced the same amount of oil that a few much larger wells could have produced much more cheaply. Steele estimated that the price drop caused by the elimination of oil-import controls might eliminate 50 percent of the oil wells in the United States but would reduce U.S. oil production by only 5 percent because the efficient wells would increase production to fill any gap.

Chumbris interjected a concern for the jobs involved in the oil wells that would be lost. Steele replied:

There is trade-off here . . . you may be increasing the total cost of producing 98 percent of the country's oil by 20 or 30 percent or so in order to keep on producing the last 2 percent.

Senator Hart asked if this made sense. Steele answered:

I think not. More intensive development of the lower cost fields would be much more in the interest of optional longrun development of the Nation's supplies than continuing overemphasis on the marginal wells.[29]

Three British witnesses testified that oil-import controls could only harm the overall ability of all U.S. industry to compete in international markets. One, Edith Penrose of the University of London, noted that

For the United States to maintain this barrier to the flows of oil is not in the interest of American investment and American companies abroad. It is also not in the interest of the United States and it is really quite absurd, it seems to me, that this country on the one hand subsidizes them and on the other makes their positions so much more difficult in the long run.[30]

Economist Michael Rieber and political scientist Robert Engler added noneconomic condemnations to the subcommittee's deliberations. Rieber issued a prophecy that events have dramatically borne out when he remarked,

If the Occidental proposal and others like it are rejected, it is difficult to see from where any large amounts of low sulphur oil are going to come. . . . The result will be . . . the strong probability that shortfalls of supply, whether programmed or unavoidable, will keep the price to the consumer high.

SENATOR HART: There is a conflict, then, between the maintenance of the import quota and the reduction of pollutants in the air, is that correct?

DR. RIEBER: That is what I think, yes.[31]

Professor Robert Engler, whose *The Politics of Oil* is a staggering account of oil's role in American politics, summarized the political history of the market controls that culminated in the import program. He noted that the problem began with the post–World World I efforts of the five largest American companies (Esso, Texaco, Mobil, Gulf, Standard of California) to explore for oil overseas. Their success and the immense East Texas discoveries created problems of world surplus, solved temporarily by intercompany agreements and state prorationing. After World War II, immense discoveries in the Middle East threatened these arrangements and led ultimately to import controls to protect domestic producers. Engler summarized this translation of economic into political power thus:

With 32 states having oil or gas production and one fourth of the land area of the United States under lease to oil corporations . . . there is a very potent oil lobby. Law firms, tax experts, public relations consultants, vice presidents in charge of governmental relations and numerous trade associations including the American Petroleum Institute, the Independent Petroleum Association of America, and those reflecting specific segments of the industry, keep close surveillance over parties, candidates, and all relevant governmental actions. Personnel and policies of the Federal Power Commission, the Federal Trade Commission, the Departments of State, Defense and Interior and the executive offices of the White House are carefully studied. . . . Segments of the Congress also function as spokesmen for their regions and industry. Sympathetic members on congressional committees dealing with oil policy are viewed as important assets.

Oilmen have developed intimate relations with key administrative agencies. There is a steady flow of personnel from the industry to the Oil and Gas Offices of the Interior Department and to other agencies dealing with oil. Staff of the Oil Import Administration and the Bureau of Mines tend to see the industry, not the public, as their client. Advisory bodies such as the National Petroleum Council provide opportunity for oil and gas leaders to work within the Federal bureaucracy, furnishing information and guidance for the Secretary of the Interior on topics ranging from pipeline construction and civil defense to national oil policy.

Among the consequences of these governmental interventions in the market mechanisms are:

1. The wasteful investment of capital and also the dissipation of irreplaceable energy supplies because of the eagerness to extract and then use oil without full knowledge of or sensitivity to genuine conservation considerations.

2. The continuation of scarcity practices which attempt to keep production under tight controls while areas such as New England are fuel hungry.

3. The perpetuation of the myth of "national security" while the industry resists full use of crude and blocks the building of pipelines in Canada and the United States for carrying oil to the East Coast.

4. The furthering of inflation. Despite an abundant world supply and a decline in crude oil prices, within the United States prices are kept artificially high. . . .

5. The expanded profits of the major international oil companies, each of whom in 1968 had at least a 10% rise over 1967.

6. The furthering of the concentrated power of multinational oil companies. . . . These corporations are now moving into other energy areas.

7. The corrosive impact of oil at every level of political life. . . .

8. The identification in the developing nations of the United States with exploitative practices. . . .[32]

Despite the often savage attacks on the program, the Senators who favored it rarely cross-examined the economists. The reasons for this reticence may lie in the experiences of Senators Dirksen and Hruska with Maurice Adelman, the MIT economist who had condemned the import program at the Portland hearing five months earlier. Dr. Adelman was the first witness and the only one whom Dirksen and Hruska were to challenge.

Adelman testified that the existing import restraints seemed to promote various inefficiencies in the production and transportation of oil. Because these inefficiencies resulted from governmentally caused deviations from the free market, he felt that they should either be terminated or be justified in ways that had never been attempted. His own opinion was that any impartial review would inevitably lead to larger volumes of imports.

Senator Hruska, startled by Adelman's charge that governmental oil policies had "never been seriously discussed, least of all by the Cabinet Committees of the '50s," brandished a bibliography of works totaling several thousand pages at the MIT professor while asking,

> What explanations would you give to the many men, Senators, Congressmen, Cabinet officials, sub-Cabinet officials, the members of loyal dedicated staffs that are many in number, what explanation would you give to them when they came to you and asked you what you mean? Are all of these printed pages and these laws and all of these actions subjects that have never been seriously discussed and debated? What answer would you give to a well meaning good faith question from that congregation?

DR. ADELMAN: I think I would have to say that I have most of those hearings in my office and that is one reason why I have a space problem there, and that I looked at them before I wrote that sentence, Senator. Sometimes the truth is inadvertently painful, but I think I have to stand on that, that all of these voluminous writings and hearings were concerned with the preservation of one or another interest, special interests usually, the general interest sometimes, but they were not devoted to the basic facts that would permit anyone to make an intelligent choice in the national interest. And that was why, under questioning by one of your colleagues, I had to say repeatedly that I did not know, nobody else knew, and that it will take a good deal of time to find out.

With all the pile of paper we have, we have not gotten the knowledge or even an approach to the knowledge that we should have.

SENATOR HRUSKA: Well, the act of 1954 as amended by the Extension Act of 1955 was the basis for the President's mandatory oil import program.

DR. ADELMAN: Yes, sir.

SENATOR HRUSKA: And the thrust of those acts is national security.

DR. ADELMAN: Those are the words.

SENATOR HRUSKA: Not individual investments, not individual industries, not even the economics of the thing, the thrust was national security.

Now do you mean to tell me that all of this legislation and all of these things taken on behalf of preserving our national security is not a serious discussion and debate and effort?

DR. ADELMAN: The tone is a serious one, Senator, but the substance, I am afraid, was frivolous.

SENATOR HRUSKA: Was what?

DR. ADELMAN: Frivolous, light-minded, not concerned with the basic facts, and I must say that reading, and I have spent many more hours than I like to recollect reading them—was like hearing the same scratchy records played over and over again. . . .

SENATOR HRUSKA: Well, it is your testimony, and I just wanted to have it explained, because I imagine some of my colleagues are going to wonder if they should not change their ways and maybe consult you before they go further into discussions, so that they can get something meaningful and something that will not be frivolous. . . . And I think they might profit greatly by such a consultation.

DR. ADELMAN: They have seen fit to do it.[33]

Senator Dirksen fared no better:

SENATOR DIRKSEN: By that you mean you would sort of remake the industry and remake policy and let a lot more petroleum come in from outside, let other countries exhaust their resources and then put what you call the uneconomic wells and all their appurtenances out of business and then you would have a nice compact industry right under the hand of government so you can control it at every step along the line, is that it?

DR. ADELMAN: On the contrary, Senator. What I wish we would have done, and it is never too late to get started, is to remove the dead hand of bureaucracy from the domestic oil industry, give them a very simple mandate which is to file a prorationing plan, which is something like a health and safety requirement, and then leave them alone.

I wish this had been done many years ago but it is not too late to start now.

SENATOR DIRKSEN: Well, Doctor, that will give government the opportunity to plow in—

DR. ADELMAN: I beg your pardon—

SENATOR DIRKSEN: And violate every aspect of the Sherman Act, Clayton Act, Federal Trade Commission Act, Robinson-Patman Act, everything we have got on the books, while at the same time, if private enterprises did that they would be put in jail. But government can do it.

It is like the old NRA days when I first came to Washington. We

set up trade associations, imposed fair prices and then if someone
in New Jersey charges 10 cents less than that price, put him in the
can, is that it?

DR. ADELMAN: That, Senator, seems like a fair description of the system
we have now.

SENATOR DIRKSEN: I give up.[34]

Unanimous and convincing though the economists were in their case
against the quota system, two factors have come to overshadow the
testimony itself. First, almost all of the economists were significantly
wrong in one aspect of their analysis. Second, as Robert Engler could
have told them and Peter Chumbris did, there was never any serious
possibility of corrective legislation.

The economists' error was their prediction that world oil prices
would continue to decline. The opposite happened. World oil prices
more than quadrupled within five years.*

This error, significant though it was to prove, did not discredit the
economists' basic point, that the United States should take advantage
of favorable prices in the world market. An implicit corollary to that
argument, too obvious to have needed frequent restating, was that if
the unexpected happened and world prices rose, free importation would
not damage the domestic industry, because its high-cost wells would
then be competitive with world prices. This happened in 1973.

The oil industry did not seem worried by the hearings. No doubt
oilmen concurred in the pleasure that minority counsel Chumbris took
in confronting several of the economists with the concession wrung
from one of them that "this is a problem for the politician, not the
economist." Furthermore, while the economists made some headlines,
they did not sway the Senate.

* In the economists' defense, three points can be made. First, to the extent that
they were talking about production and transportation costs rather than prices, they
may well have been right. The 1972–74 world increases resulted from massive increases in producing-nation taxes and royalties. Basic production and transportation
costs appear to have diminished slightly. Second, the error was essentially political
rather than economic, since it lay in the dual assumptions that the producing nations
would continue their historic inability to cooperate effectively among themselves and
that the consuming nations would in any case be strong enough and clever enough
to subvert such cooperation. Third, the prophecies were for the long term, and the
world price increases of 1972–74 could yet prove aberrational. Those increases have
created an immense gap between cost and price in the producing nations. This gap is
like a balloon skin separating air and helium. Let the barrier of producing-nation unity
leak, and the helium of price will diffuse into the air of cost with an explosiveness
dependent on the size and source of the puncture.

Following a second round of hearings, in which industry witnesses challenged the ability of economists and academicians to protect either the national security or industrial well-being, *The Oil and Gas Journal* reassured its readers that

> Industry witnesses made committee members sit up and take notice. The testimony of hostile witnesses was put in perspective. The industry couldn't reverse the publicity tide, since by last month the general press had lost interest. But the industry did stop Hart and Kennedy from talking about elimination of import controls. . . .*
>
> The subcommittee itself can't do anything about the subject it was probing. It has no legislative jurisdiction. It may, at most, produce a majority staff report, and a minority staff report or dissent.
>
> Dr. John Blair, chief economist for the subcommittee, whose hostility toward the industry is quite open, will write a report mainly reflecting criticism of the 18 academic economists who testified. They agree with him. But the minority staff, relying on industrial testimony, will be able to write a strong dissent.
>
> Dr. Blair's report may never get beyond the "staff" status. It is doubtful that he can get anything through the subcommittee, let alone the parent Judiciary Committee.
>
> Besides Hart and Kennedy, the subcommittee includes Democrats Thomas J. Dodd of Connecticut, John L. McClellan of Arkansas, and Sam J. Ervin of North Carolina, and Republicans Everett M. Dirksen of Illinois, Roman L. Hruska of Nebraska, and Hiram L. Fong of Hawaii. McClellan, Dirksen, and Hruska left no doubt about their support for import controls during the hearings, and one more vote would stymie any subcommittee action.[35]

Not even Hart and Kennedy pressed for subcommittee action. Perceiving that the best hope for reform lay with the Cabinet Task Force,

* The oil industry has one of the most self-congratulatory trade presses in the nation. It does an extraordinary job of keeping its readers informed of developments in the industry and in Washington, but its biases infuse its columns. Anyone reading them over time is a long way toward understanding the mixture of pride and paranoia which infuses the industry's attitude toward the citizenry. Senators such as Hansen or Long invariably annihilate the Kennedys, Proxmires, "unrealistic environmentalists," and "theoretical economists" in debate. If a Hansen or a Long is not present, the oil press will itself point out shortcomings in critics' arguments in sentences with beginnings like "The Senator overlooked . . ." In the paragraph quoted above, the *Journal* is indulging another favorite ploy, that of assigning preposterous views to opponents. In fact, neither Hart nor Kennedy had ever favored complete elimination of import controls. Kennedy did, however, imprudently rebuke Senator Hruska for asserting that the world price of oil might soon climb to $4.00 per barrel. "Now we're getting into the realm of the ridiculous," asserted the Massachusetts Senator.

the Senators were content to hold hearings and wait. Thus the task force achieved its creators' first purpose, a sullen truce on the Washington side of the struggle over oil imports. The struggle continued unabated among oil companies and in Maine.

7: Summer, 1969

What we ask is an essentially free market for energy, in which each energy source can compete as nearly as possible at its true economic value. This means the least possible imposition of discriminatory taxes, tariffs, quotas, regulated prices or other barriers to fair competition. It means avoiding excessive or inflexible protection for non-competitive energy suppliers.

> Michael Haider, president of Esso,
> in a speech in Paris, 1968[1]

Being basically a free trader, I object to anything that impedes trade among nations. . . . But as a citizen I am opposed to anything that would jeopardize our country's security, and uncontrolled imports would do just that.

> Michael Haider, 1969 Report to Esso stockholders

What would be important to me is that I would like to have a little assurance about what the running rules of the whole game are going to be a little bit further down the road . . . to have them nailed down so you are sure of what environment you are going to have to operate in.

> Charles Jones, president of Humble
> (Esso's U.S. subsidiary), 1967[2]

We're flexible. We can play the game anyway you want—if somebody will just tell us what the rules are.

> Michael Haider, chairman of the board of Esso, 1968[3]

Jersey's main purpose is to enhance the value of the shareholder's investment, and its greatest achievement is to have survived at all with so large a share of a rapidly growing market over a long period.

> An Esso director[4]

There has been no contrivance, but I don't know how to convince the man on the street.

> C. C. Garvin, president of Exxon, January, 1974[5]

There has to be a certain kind of discipline and order and respect for an honest answer . . . long term we will build a sense of credibility and honesty that is absolutely fundamental to the future of this country.

> Lelan Sillin, chief executive, Northeast Utilities, 1971[6]

OIL TRAPPED millions of years beneath rock builds upward pressure from both water encroachment and the action of natural gas. A crack or a well through the rock will release gushers of gas, oil, and sometimes water in the fashion of a shaken soft drink. The escape of enough gas and oil will eventually relieve the pressure. Since an oil pool, unlike a soft drink, cannot be tilted, whatever remains when the pressure is gone is expensive or impossible to recover. To check the flow of a large gusher is difficult, but it can be done.

When Stewart Udall first penetrated the traprock of oil-import controls with his Puerto Rican grants in the mid-1960s, he tapped a huge pool of pent demand pressure for foreign oil. His subsequent acrobatics sufficed for a while to control the eruptions and to restrict to minor spillage several episodes that threatened real blowouts. The Machiasport proposal was the greatest threat of all, analogous in its way to the worst of the faults in the unpredictable geology of the Santa Barbara Channel. Taking no chances, Nixon capped the well with the appointment of his Cabinet Task Force, but the unspent pressures in the trapped reservoir still sought the surface. One of the most insistent of these, seeking fissures the length and breadth of the traprock, was the ambitious energy of Robert Augustus Gardiner Monks.

Nineteen sixty-eight had been an exciting but frustrating year for Monks. He had begun it newly in charge of the C. H. Sprague Company, saddled with sizable debts but backed by substantial family and personal resources. He had joined with Evans in order to protect his uniquely profitable eastern Maine flank, but Evans had rebuffed his effort to take over the refinery project. Monks had achieved his protection by helping Maine acquire key pieces of land, but Occidental, annoyed and confused by the land's shifting status, had rejected his demands for a favored position in marketing the refinery output or in developing satellite industries. His political aspirations had gone unencouraged. He was later to say that his 1968 meetings with Senator Smith convinced him that he could unseat her, but in 1969 he was not sure enough of that route to refrain from telling Boston associates about White House urgings that he run against Senator Kennedy.*

* The White House must have had quite a Republican Senatorial primary in mind for Massachusetts. Upset because leading Kennedy challenger Josiah Spaulding seemed unlikely to make an issue of Chappaquiddick or to support Nixon on Vietnam, Nixon aides Charles Colson and Murray Chotiner searched for some unlikely corners for a replacement. The level of company in which Monks found himself is indicated by serious White House efforts to persuade Massachusetts Governor Francis Sargent to support the conservative and acerbic Al Capp, creator of the

While Nixon's election appalled most of the proponents of a Machias Bay refinery, it opened new fissures for Monks. A lifelong Republican and a recent Massachusetts Republican finance chairman, he was well connected to the country's new centurions. As he put it, "I woke up one morning, and I said to myself, 'Gee, those are all my friends down there now.' "

Among his friends were former Massachusetts governor John Volpe, Nixon's Secretary of Transportation; Elliott Richardson, the Under Secretary of State; a dovecote of Volpe and Richardson aides who went south with their bosses; and Charles Colson, a Massachusetts lawyer, influential in Washington, whose asserted willingness to walk over his grandmother for his President's sake was taken as proof of the toughness so necessary to employment on the White House staff.

A man in whom a considerable intelligence was sometimes undercut by a matching ego, Monks had a tendency to assess a political disequilibrium quickly and accurately and then overestimate his own ability to affect it. He saw that Dr. Hammer was stymied, his Democratic connections now a liability. New England still had a compelling case for relief from the disproportionate regional burdens of the oil-import program. Even within the oil industry, many were convinced that something had to be done for New England as long as "we don't have to swallow Armand Hammer."[7] Monks realized that a well-connected Republican with a plan to slake New England had a chance to walk off with Occidental's marbles. Why not he?

In mid-April Monks suggested to Hammer that the C. H. Sprague Company take over the Machiasport refinery project under a commitment to use Occidental's Libyan and Venezuelan oil. This would have given the project a Republican rather than Democratic veneer, with other arrangements remaining unchanged. Hammer had been around long enough to realize that once Monks had added import permits to his landownership, Occidental would be unable to resist whatever demands the Sprague company might see fit to impose. Since the Doctor had begun to open his own lines to the Nixon administration, Occidental was far from ready to concede defeat.

Undaunted, Monks formed his own company to wrest the project from Occidental. Remembering that the New England governors had supported the original Machiasport plan with a brochure entitled "How

Li'l Abner cartoons and a nominal Democrat, for the Republican Senatorial nomination. These efforts did not cease until Sargent berated Chotiner, "Murray, do I have to tell you exactly what you can do with Al Capp?"

the Atlantic World Port Will Serve the National Interest," Monks named this company Atlantic World Port, Inc., a choice that did not amuse the author of the governors' pamphlet, Occidental public relations man George Bevel. Monks then told Governor Curtis of his feeling that the project could go forward only under Republican sponsorship, and he asked for an endorsing letter to accompany his oil-import application.

Although Curtis was concerned that Monks's independent course might be used to justify further federal delay, he saw a gain to be had in return for the requested letter. Specifically, he now had a chance to obtain a real and enforceable agreement committing Monks to turn the land options over to the state if the trade zone were granted. To this end, he told Monks that he could not permit one of the potential refiners to control the trade-zone site and requested that Monks sign a formal contract with the Maine Port Authority giving the state a one-year option on Monks's options on the Machiasport Peninsula. Monks readily agreed and received in return a letter from Curtis acknowledging his cooperation in furthering the project and continuing:

> As I have stated many times, my policy is to welcome all responsible parties wishing to construct and operate a refinery in the proposed Machiasport Project Subzone.
>
> In my judgment, your proposal, in addition to meeting the consumer problems, would provide substantial economic assistance to the people of Maine in particular and New England in general.

What Curtis knew but Monks did not was that Atlantic Richfield, a real oil company with far stronger White House ties than Atlantic World Port, had its own plans for displacing Dr. Hammer.

Throughout May and June the real company and the pretender, each ignorant of the other, do-si-doed through a miraculously collision-free reel from Machias Bay to Augusta to Washington. By late June, Monks executed the first half of the coup which he had hoped for when he gave up his legal partnership in 1965 for a business career in order to make enough money quickly enough to go into politics. He sold his 75-percent interest in the C. H. Sprague company's oil properties to a subsidiary of Royal Dutch Shell. He was left with the company's Westmoreland coal properties, which he later sold for the multimillion-dollar profit that freed him for public service.

Monks had been trying to sell his company to Shell for some time with little success. Concerned with the antitrust laws, Shell was satisfied to own 25 percent of the company while supplying most of its product requirements. The Sprague company's potential involvement in a trade-zone-plus-quota refinery had already necessitated the extraordinary arrangement to shield Shell's 25-percent ownership from any of the profits from that venture,* and when Occidental took over the project, Monks decided to involve the two corporations in a Dutch auction based largely on the irritation that he was causing them both.

First he gave Hammer a chance to buy the Sprague oil business except for the land options, which belonged to the Machiasport company. This offered Hammer a marketing outlet for his industrial oil and an apparent diminution of the Monks nuisance factor. The Doctor opened serious negotiations.

Monks then returned to Shell, where he confronted Jock Ritchie, president of Shell's Asiatic Petroleum subsidiary, with the prospect of direct competition from Armand Hammer's abundant supplies of low-sulfur Libyan oil. Ritchie wanted time for Shell to think about it, but Monks told him that he was on his way to Occidental's offices, implying that Hammer had made an acceptable offer. Ritchie replied, as Monks remembers it, to the effect that he wouldn't do business at gun point, and Monks departed for Occidental's offices. Arriving there, he found a call from Ritchie awaiting him and, when he returned it, a better offer. Hammer was furious when he found out that Monks had solicited the Occidental offer only to pressure Shell. For revenge, Occidental convinced Senator McIntyre to complain to the Justice Department that the purchase was part of a pattern of acquisitions of independents by major companies that was driving competition out of New England. McIntyre's complaint had merit, and the resulting successful Justice Department suit embarrassed Monks slightly at the outset of his political career. It resulted in the 1971 divestiture order forcing Shell to relinquish the Sprague properties, which were then acquired by Axel Johnson, the Swedish company that, even though it had chosen not to pursue an early Machiasport role, was still seeking a U.S. market outlet.

One of the losing bidders to Axel Johnson on the Sprague properties was a consortium formed by Donny McNamara, by then long gone from the bankrupt King Resources Company. McNamara later felt foolish for having taken the time to get together a consortium to make a bid, since he came to believe that the Justice Department had arranged with Shell to accept the Axel Johnson bid for the properties. His reasoning was that since Shell supplied much of the Swedish com-

* See footnote, page 45.

pany's crude oil, Axel Johnson's successful bid enabled Shell to maintain its share of the sales of the crude oil that eventually went to New England.

Monks still talks of his sale to Shell with more enthusiasm than any other aspect of his Machiasport involvement, and with good reason. All of the nerve, the bluff, the aggressive manipulativeness that were later to be just a shade too obvious in his political ventures were precisely the qualities he needed to succeed in playing Shell and Occidental off against each other. In discussing this sale, Monks quotes New York merchant and banker James Seligman's advice that "To sell something you have to someone who wants it—that is not business. But to sell something you don't have to someone who doesn't want it— *that* is business."[8] It is often politics as well.

From its outset the Machiasport refinery had inspired more than its share of bizarre announcements. Even among these, the press conference at which Monks unveiled Atlantic World Port must have startled anyone in Maine who still believed that an orderly process of free-enterprise development would follow the uncovering of new natural resources such as a deep-water port site in a state eager for industry.

The June 25 press conference took place in a caucus room in the U.S. House of Representatives. It began with the unveiling of Atlantic World Port's oil-import quota application, which had that afternoon been filed with the Department of the Interior. Landing at Interior was in itself something of a comedown. The application had been addressed to "The President, The White House, Washington, D.C. Dear Mr. President . . ." because, as Monks put it,

> I read in the newspapers that President Nixon had rescinded the Authority granted by President Johnson to the Secretary of the Interior with respect to oil import matters. . . . [In attempting to file my application at the White House] I was told that I was filing it in the wrong place and to please go file it with the Secretary of the Interior.*

The application proposed that a 100,000-barrel-per-day quota be assigned to Atlantic World Port instead of Occidental. Unencumbered by such trappings as crude oil, tankers, markets, refinery experience,

---

* This process cannot have been quite so naïve as it sounded. Atlantic World Port's Washington counsel, the firm of Gadsby & Hannah, had represented the New England Council in the successful 1966 struggle to remove controls from industrial fuel, and Charles Colson, the partner who had handled that effort (doing, as Jack Evans remembers it, "one hell of a job"), was at that moment poised at the beginning of the Nixon fork in his unusual road to Christ.

or substantial capital, Atlantic World Port would then undertake to oversee the refinery project in either of two alternative roles.

Role A was as the refinery operator, in which case Atlantic World Port was prepared to buy its oil on the world market, refine it, and distribute it to New England through the independent terminal operators. The refinery size, output, and economics were copied without significant change from the Occidental proposal, except that Atlantic World Port proposed to offer 60 percent of its stock for sale to New England residents only. Occidental's promised 10 percent drop in home heating–oil prices was included. The only significant change was the dropping of the $7.2-million marine research fund. In its place, Atlantic World Port promised to pay Maine 15 percent of the gross profit of the refinery operation, with another 10 percent to be distributed among the other five New England states "in direct relation to the consumption in those states of petroleum products produced at the Machiasport refinery." Since this promise appeared to mean a payout of some $25 million per year, it actually exceeded Occidental's marine fund.

If the Interior Department found fault with Role A, the application included an alternative under which Atlantic World Port would transform itself into a de facto public utility, limiting its return to the average of the returns permitted to New England's power, telephone, gas, and water companies. In Role B, Atlantic World Port would build the terminal and refinery and lease them to whichever refiner would, in the judgment of the New England governors, "most effectively deal with the New England regions' problems of cost and pollution and offer the largest payments to the six states."

Other conditions beyond the guaranteed return to Atlantic World Port and the New England state treasuries were that the winning refiner promise a 10 percent reduction in home heating-oil prices, that it guarantee significant quantities of low-sulfur industrial oil to meet air-pollution problems, and that it undertake to distribute all products through the independent terminal operators.

Atlantic World Port made several further gestures. First, it promised to use American supertankers to import the crude oil as long as the U.S. government subsidized the immense difference between these costs and those of comparable foreign vessels. The company also promised that products would go from Machiasport to market in U.S. vessels ever without subsidies. This was actually no more than a promise to obey the Jones Act. Last, in a gesture whose nerve must have startled even Armand Hammer, Atlantic World Port magnanimously added, "In order to clarify any possible misunderstanding, World Port states its desire that Occidental be one of the competitors."

In seeking to reduce Occidental to "one of the competitors," Atlantic World Port was playing a con game that Hammer may have recognized from his knowledge of the Romanoffs, particularly Anastasia. Specifically, Monks was attempting to present his company as the returned heir, arrived as the false will was to be probated or the pretender crowned, just in time to steer the estate into the proper hands, partially his own. Not only had he borrowed the Atlantic World Port title from the New England governors' 1968 announcement; he had also prepared a slightly doctored family tree showing his company as the legitimate offspring of a union between Evans's New England Refinery Associates and the New England Governors' Conference. Hammer was inferentially an adopted bastard with oedipal tendencies.

Jack Evans was not included in Monks's rewritten history. Instead, his New England Refinery Associates had become a creation of the Independent Terminal Operators, with the C. H. Sprague company playing a leading role. Occidental was depicted as an interloper who had gained possession of New England Refinery Associates without the knowledge or consent of the terminal operators and had then perverted the original regional effort into a scheme for the enrichment of a single company.

The truth was that the terminal operators had never been able to reach agreement either among themselves or with Evans as to a corporate framework. Consequently, New England Refinery Associates had existed only as a shell for a corporate mollusk that had never moved in. The original application had been the property of Evans's Business Development Fund until Occidental had taken advantage of the terminal operators' disagreements to acquire both Business Development Fund and the quota application, a development for which the terminal operators, including C. H. Sprague, had only themselves and each other to blame. Evans had given them their chance, and he did not take kindly to Monks's press conference. He got Occidental's permission to speak out on this one occasion, and he then issued a statement noting that Monks had had no part in conceiving the original refinery and had no legitimate claim to the quota permits. His statement reflected more than pride of authorship, for his seven-figure arrangement with Occidental would have been worthless if the quota had gone to Atlantic World Port.

Despite the liberties with history, Atlantic World Port's application contained some truth. Occidental had indeed refused to come to ownership or marketing arrangements wtih the terminal operators and had claimed for itself a quota allocation that was being sought to relieve a regional hardship. By upping the kitty to the New England states, Monks was saying, in effect, "To relieve a multimillion-dollar New England injustice by trickling down a $97-million annual subsidy through a California (Democratic) company is nonsense. Instead, give my New England (Republican) company the same subsidy, and I'll trickle more of it down."

The dialogue of the press conference suggests the formal mendacity of a professional wrestling match. The reporters, unable to grasp what Atlantic World Port was, played it safe by conferring upon Monks and the company the legitimacy they hoped for. Vague stories described the new firm as a direct competitor to Occidental and the six-foot-six Monks in terms varying from "rising Republican force in Massachusetts" to "dashing."

The most revealing exchange came not with a reporter but with Maine Congressman William Hathaway, who asked why Maine shouldn't "bypass you and simply make the trade zone subject to the conditions that you've got there as leasor?"

Monks replied, "It has always been my view that the proper role of government is to encourage the private companies to undertake as much of the burden of the economic process as possible. On the other hand, there is nothing in logic incorrect with your suggestion in my view. . . .

"My only question, Bill, would be whether the question you ask is a fair one. . . . Where has this governmental agency been coming forward in making this proposal?"[9]

In fact, the Maine state government had planned to make demands in the foreign-trade-zone lease very similar to those under which Monks proposed to auction off the quota, except that Maine had stated its intent to trade some of the cash payment in return for the added cost of an inland site and extraordinary pollution controls. In devising their respective demands, Maine and Atlantic World Port were both playing the old Udall game of inventing socially beneficial ways to auction off multimillion-dollar subsidies. They had not learned that with Udall gone the game's new croupiers did not recognize social benefit as valid currency.

Armand Hammer put out a relatively mild statement suggesting that Monks was simply doing the bidding of C. H. Sprague's new owner, Royal Dutch Shell, and was trying to generate Machiasport confusion. In fact, the reverse was true. Shell had not been pleased by the Sprague company's active involvement at Machiasport and had just bought the Sprague oil interests outright at a price inflated by the offer Monks had extracted from Occidental for the same properties.

As Monks was gluing together the Atlantic World Port montage, Maine's most substantial suitor was following more conventional blueprints to refinery construction, blueprints not without their own pitfalls.

While other companies sent public-relations experts, lobbyists, and entrepreneurs, Atlantic Richfield had approached Maine with refinery experts, tanker captains, and real estate evaluators. After the February meeting in Washington, Atlantic Richfield's Machiasport task force twice visited the Machiasport Peninsula. I went on the task force's second visit, in early June, 1969, a visit which included a hike along a rail line seven miles back from the coast. The surrounding land was a 3000-acre tract owned by the St. Regis Paper Company. It seemed boggy, but the weather had been wet, and the Atlantic Richfield people, wearing the first neckties ever seen by the resident frogs, decided that they had found a refinery site.

We returned to waiting cars to discover that we had been located by Clayton Beal, an enterprising Bangor *Daily News* reporter who had taken to tracking down the passengers of the occasional unfamiliar aircraft that landed at the Machias airfield. He introduced himself, and I experienced the comic-strip sensation of having companions vanish, leaving dotted lines where their bodies had been.

"Those men with you," Beal asked, "might they be with an oil company?"

"Well, not exactly," I lied.

"Not exactly?"

"No. You remember the State Planning Council's recommendation that the refinery be built inland? Well, those men are refinery experts helping us evaluate the feasibility of different sites."

"Funny, all of them needing to crowd into a service-station rest room like that."

Beal was not satisfied. Remembering that Esso had just announced the forthcoming voyage of the icebreaking tanker *Manhattan* to Alaska's North Slope to assess the feasibility of bringing Alaskan crude to the East Coast, he decided to try a shot in the dark. He called Governor Curtis's press secretary, Roy Whitcomb, and demanded to know what Peter Bradford was doing showing a team of Esso people around Machias Bay.

Whitcomb, not among those who knew about Atlantic Richfield, had no idea what I was doing near Machias Bay and said so, adding that if Esso people were looking at the bay, they were probably interested in a refinery there. Beal filed a story accurate in every respect except for a strong suggestion that the unnamed officials were with Esso. Over the next six months, as several unnamed oil companies made or were rumored to be making forays into Maine, Esso had repeatedly to deny, with increasing annoyance, that it had any interest whatsoever in a Maine refinery.

During the Beal encounter, a classic Maine coastal fog had rolled in, closing the airstrip and diverting the plane that was to return us to Augusta, to an inland field. Thanks to a ride from the state police, available in Maine as elsewhere to assist in economic development, we reached the plane, but the fog precluded a flight over Atlantic Richfield's chosen acreage. This seemed insignificant at the time, but such an overview might have saved the company the expensive embarrassment of optioning 3000 acres of hopeless swamp.

The embarrassment was enhanced by the price. When Atlantic Richfield attempted to option the land from the St. Regis Paper Company, it was astounded to come up against a sale price of $400 per acre. Anxious to keep its intentions secret, the company was in no position to shop around among other landowners for alternative 3000-acre blocks and finally agreed to the price. Even then, St. Regis wanted to retain the subsurface mineral rights. No one thought that any commercially exploitable deposits existed, but Atlantic Richfield, unwilling to have its oil refinery undermined, refused. The stalemate might have lasted indefinitely if a Maine Department of Economic Development official hadn't stopped by St. Regis headquarters in New York to ask whether the company would mind if the state taxed the rest of St. Regis's 750,000 Maine acres on the basis of the company's $400-per-acre asking price. Since Maine was then valuing St. Regis land at less than $50 per acre, this suggestion meant an eightfold increase in the company's tax burden. St. Regis got the idea and completed the optioning within a week.

Atlantic Richfield operated with the same impressive but accident-prone professionalism on environmental matters. Andy Nixon circulated the Means refinery and terminal standards to relevant Arco engineers and learned that they were no more stringent than those the company was planning to meet at a refinery under construction at Cherry Point, Washington. After these exchanges had been digested by the conservation subcommittee, Nixon and I went to New York to discuss the final draft standards with Atlantic Richfield and Occidental representatives.

For this occasion the two Atlantic Richfield engineers with whom we had been dealing decided to involve three members of their company's newly formed environmental division. Because they had both come to Atlantic Richfield in the Sinclair merger, the engineers were unfamiliar with the environmental group's work but were sure that it would give us a different perspective.

That it did. One of the environmental men never said a word. Another was long on platitudes but underinformed as to their chemical, biological, numerical, and statutory foundations. The third was the most expansive, launching himself on the strength of a lunch on the rocks into several rambling denunciations of the incompetence and irresponsibility of the conservation movement.

The two engineers brought the meeting to an early close. Transparently angry, they were still better team players than to criticize their environmental colleagues. Their only acknowledgment of fiasco was to state that such meetings would not be repeated, that they would continue the previous arrangement under which the refinery engineers assumed responsibility for environmental standards.

During the environmental discussions, the Atlantic Richfield personnel realized that neither Nixon nor I had ever seen a refinery in operation. Tom Matthews subsequently called to offer us a tour of the company's Philadelphia plant, but this offer was withdrawn because "The Philadelphia refinery's a very old one. We'd hate to have you think that we still build them like that." In place of Philadelphia, we were offered Los Angeles.

The proposed trip to California troubled us for a good ten minutes. We could not have justified the cost of round-trip plane tickets, but

Atlantic Richfield was offering a company plane, leaving us only the cost of accommodations and meals. We had been critical of politicians who had arrived at the foreign-trade-zone hearings in oil-company planes, but such travel now seemed a good way to save the Maine taxpayers some $600. The Nader maxim is that if it's not worth billing to the taxpayer, the public official has no business going. Wanting to see the refinery and confident that Matthews didn't think that we could be had for a plane ride, we went anyway.

The trip through the refinery was not conclusive. The refinery manager reconfirmed our generally high opinion of Atlantic Richfield's personnel, but the Los Angeles atmosphere did not permit precise naked-eye appraisals of its sources and their volumes. Still, the refinery didn't stink, and it didn't roar. The processing units were compact, unsprawling. The water discharges were oil-free. The only visible airborne emissions were steam. At the waterfront a small tanker was discharging oil into storage tanks. The water was a mess, but the mess was from the wastes of an urban industrial area rather than the particular transfer operation.

Not for the first time, we realized that the siting problems of coastal oil terminals were virtually unique, more comparable to offshore oil exploration, nuclear power plants, and plane rides than to other industries. In each of those cases, the day-to-day operations could be controlled or did not horrify. It was the remote but total catastrophe, whose image outweighed its probability, that inspired fears even more compelling than the daily toxicity of a paper mill, an automobile, or a sewage outfall.

We realized also that even if Maine decided to accept the risks of a refinery served by supertankers, the choice among companies would be difficult. On one hand, Maine was offered a Hammer, a Shaheen, or a Monks—each clawing for a place in the protected U.S. market and willing to make valuable price concessions to get it, but each without any demonstrated competence in running environmentally attuned refineries and tanker operations. The other hand was Atlantic Richfield, an established major oil company, though not in quite the same league as the seven giants,* with an environmentally progressive top manage-

* The seven largest U.S. oil companies in 1969 were Esso, Mobil, Texaco, Gulf, Standard of California, Shell, and Standard of Indiana. By the way of perspective Atlantic Richfield was the twenty-ninth largest U.S. company and the eighth largest oil company. Occidental, the forty-fourth largest company, was the twelfth oil company. The combined assets and sales of the oil companies that have shown an interest in Maine do not approach those of Exxon.

ment possessed of the technical expertise and the resources to build and operate the cleanest possible refineries and terminals. Atlantic Richfield had this expertise because the company was firmly established in the U.S. market and was satisfied with that market as it was. The company would not consider price-slashing schemes, undermining the oil-import program, or contributing to special funds. In short, the most desirable marketers were unknown environmentally, and the most environmentally responsible refiners were committed to the preservation of an unsatisfactory marketplace.*

After the day at the refinery, we passed an hour with a group of Atlantic Richfield's Los Angeles executives. With the company's interest in Maine still secret, only Matthews knew where Nixon and I were from. The result was an unusual hour in which the conversation skirted apparent price-fixing techniques ("Out here Gulf isn't listed as a major at all. They're just listed as price cutters." "What list is he talking about, Tom?" "For God's sake, don't ask") and ended with a Texan's good-natured response to some intracompany ribbing about the thickness of his drawl ("Well, you people may think I talk funny, but you ought to go to Maine. I was back there once, and I hardly understood a word. Sometimes I didn't think they were talking English").

Shortly after the Los Angeles trip, Atlantic Richfield marketed the common-stock issue whose pendency had been a prime reason for the secrecy surrounding the company's venture into Maine.† With that obstacle removed, a formal press conference announcing the company's interest in Maine was set for July 2, exactly one week after Bob Monks had launched Atlantic World Port in a Congressional caucus room.

The press-conference preparations went smoothly. Behind the diversionary excitement of the Atlantic World Port announcement Atlantic

* A similar insight occurred to Daniel Chasan, writing about the Alaskan oil dilemma in his *Klondike '70*. Discussing the construction of a road to the North Slope, he wrote, "The road will open the interior to every 'gypo' driller who wants to prospect on federal land. 'If you know how, big corporations are easy to regulate,' William Van Ness [special counsel to the Senate Interior Committee] says, 'but gypos can't be regulated. They can't afford the extra expense of conservation.' . . .

"A TAPS man with whom I spoke agrees. . . . 'Well, the little guy will really mess up the country. He operates on a shoestring, and he can't afford to paint oil tanks or clean things up. In east Texas the ARCO tanks are all painted, and they're beautiful—or at least as beautiful as something like that can be, compared to nature. But if you look over onto the next lease, which is held by an independent operator, it's a mess.' "[10]

† Securities and Exchange Commission regulations prohibit announcements or actions designed to influence the market for a forthcoming stock issue.

Richfield's cherished secrecy was easily maintained. Late on the afternoon of July 1, the Maine Department of Economic Development sent
a cryptic telegram to a dozen newspapers and released the text to the
wire services. It read:

> You are invited to send a representative to an important press con-
> ference to be held at the Sheraton-Eastland Hotel in Portland, Maine,
> on July 2 at 1:00 p.m. . . . The subject of the conference will be an
> announcement by a major U.S. corporation relating to Machiasport.

The telegram touched off a struggle among Maine reporters to un-
cover the full story in time for their morning editions. They and Oc-
cidental public-relations consultant George Bevel pursued a variety
of fruitless hunches. Finally, following the Alaskan oil hypothesis, Joe
Brooks of the Bangor *Daily News* reached Atlantic Richfield president
Thornton Bradshaw at his home in New York. Using the same stratagem that Clayton Beal had tried on Roy Whitcomb, Brooks asked
Bradshaw to tell him about his company's plan for a Maine refinery.
Just back from a business trip to Cincinnati and on his way to bed,
Bradshaw was confused on dates, assumed that the press conference
had already been held, and talked. Brooks had a scoop shared only by
the Washington *Post,* which had been tipped off by Bevel as soon as
he learned it from Brooks. Bevel's only other self-indulgence was to call
Andy Nixon one more time for as much of a gloat as his discovery's
ominous implications for Occidental would allow. After that, Nixon
left his phone off the hook for the night.

Maine's morning radio and television news reports were full of Atlantic Richfield's forthcoming announcement, but neither Nixon nor I,
on our way to meet the Arco plane, learned of the source until we
bought a copy of the Bangor *Daily News* at the airport. Our perplexity
was a mere raised eyebrow beside the astonishment of Lou Ream and
the Atlantic Richfield officials who deplaned, all unsuspecting, moments
later.

We greeted them with the paper at the edge of the runway. The
headline brought annoyance to their faces—obviously state officials
couldn't quite resist temptation after all. Then they read the first paragraph (which revealed Bradshaw as the source) and bolted, aghast
beyond any cordiality, for telephones. Calls to New York established
the cause of the seepage and secured immediate release of the press kit
to aroused New York and oil-trade papers unaccustomed to losing such
announcements to the Bangor *Daily News*.

The anticlimactic press conference went smoothly. There were more than enough theretofore unpublicized details to mollify the reporters. Ream stated that Atlantic Richfield had optioned a 3500-acre tract of land and would immediately commence a one-year feasibility study for a 100,000-barrel-per-day gasoline refinery. He emphasized that his company was primarily interested in processing Alaskan oil and would seek no special quota or foreign-trade zone unless "special privileges" were given to a competitor. Ream also refused to promise any price reductions, noting only that "prices usually come down in an area where a refinery is built."

With regard to the land, he confirmed that Atlantic Richfield endorsed Maine's preference for an inland site. Indeed, the company's 3500 acres included an allowance for 2000 acres firmly committed to the state for a foreign-trade subzone. Ream didn't say it, but this arrangement showed that Monks wasn't the only one who knew the value of controlling the land.

Reaction among Arco's competitors varied. Although it was not immediately apparent, Atlantic World Port was ruined. If the Nixon administration was looking for a Republican oil company to relieve pressure in New England, it now had a real one. Monks's only hope for leverage had been his control of the terminal land, but that had been traded to the Maine Port Authority in return for the governor's letter welcoming Atlantic World Port's application. Nonetheless, Monks's nerve was still with him as he told a Bangor *Daily News* reporter:

> This is the biggest day in the history of Maine.
>
> This proves we have made a breakthrough. We have now a major company interested enough in Machiasport to make a move. This is bound to cause industrialization the likes of which Maine has never experienced.

Hammer was less ecstatic:

> This is still another attempt by a large oil company to sidetrack Maine's application for a foreign trade zone . . . a transparent attempt to defeat the inevitable relief which the entire New England Congressional delegation, 6 New England Governors, and 11 million people of New England will insist upon: a foreign trade zone, a refinery built by Occidental with its associated independent companies in New England, and home fuel at a price at least as low as other regions of the country enjoy.[11]

John Shaheen's reaction was baffling. He said that his New England Refining Company was no longer interested in the Machiasport sub-zone but that it had narrowed eleven other sites down to two and would announce a 100,000-barrel-per-day refinery for somewhere in New England within thirty days.

The Shaheen refinery was to run on domestic oil from the Gulf Coast, a clear economic impossibility. Shaheen asserted that his company would use a hydrogen process in use in thirty-nine refineries elsewhere in the world, and that this process would alter the unfavorable economics by extracting five barrels of end product for every four barrels of crude oil.

This statement, if it was as reported, is beyond sober analysis. Shaheen's four-will-get-you-five hydrogen process was in a scientific class with alchemy and phlogiston. The oil industry did have a hydrogen process, hydro-cracking, which increased both the amount of gasoline and the total yield available from a barrel of crude oil, but hydro-cracking would not have improved the relative economics of a refinery running Gulf Coast crude in Maine, and it would have increased the yield by an amount closer to 5 percent than 20 percent. In any case, more than five years have now passed without the announcement that Shaheen promised within thirty days.

Three weeks after the Portland announcement, Robert Howe, Atlantic Richfield's Machiasport project manager, traveled to Machias to brief the locals. The briefing was well received. Again, no one questioned why contact by the company with its prospective neighbors should have come so late.

A month later, Atlantic Richfield optioned another 3500 acres, this time from the Georgia-Pacific Corporation. The purchase was explained as "simply to allow an alternate site if the refinery proves feasible." In fact, it was the consequence of that fogged-out overflight and hasty negotiation with St. Regis in June. Atlantic Richfield geologists visiting the first site later in the summer had sunk to their hips in undrainable swamp, optioned from St. Regis under the pressure of the July 2 deadline at a purchase price of $400 per acre. Arco's silver lining in having to take the Georgia-Pacific option was the knowledge that at least St. Regis would never collect its exorbitant purchase price.

The Atlantic Richfield press conference and Maine's decision in favor of an inland refinery site were two last straws for Armand Hammer. He had been chafing since his late 1968 discovery that neither his company nor the state had complete control over the land, but in early 1969 he had been uneasily willing to live with Governor Curtis's assurances that the key acreage could be taken by eminent domain if necessary. Whatever reassurance he may have derived from the agreement that Curtis had extracted from Monks before endorsing Atlantic World Port's application was more than offset by the mid-summer entry of the two new competitors and by Maine's decision to move the trade zone inland, probably to a site held by Atlantic Richfield under another of those troublesome trusteeship arrangements.

Annoyed beyond endurance by conflicting land demands, Hammer decided to acquire his own refinery site. This would at least improve his bargaining position with Monks and Atlantic Richfield, and he might actually use it. This step was entirely consistent with Hammer's proven trading ability, but he combined it with a quest for leverage beyond land in the person of Fred H. Vahlsing, Jr., whose avoidance of bankruptcy or jail in the wake of the economic and environmental disasters at his Prestile Stream beet refinery did seem to bespeak a certain influence in the right places.

Hammer's connection with the Vahlsing family went back to a friendship with Fred's father. Because of this friendship, Fred, Jr., had had sufficient access to Hammer to belabor him with his standard boast of influence among Maine Democrats, a boast which in its most brazen form sometimes came out as an assertion to the effect that he had Ken Curtis and Ed Muskie in his hip pocket.

Vahlsing did possess the trappings of influence. For history, he could point to his success in getting the Prestile Stream declassified.* For style, he could recall his ebullient provision of transportation and entertainment to the Maine delegation to the 1968 Democratic national convention. For present muscle, he could demonstrate his continuing access to both Curtis and Muskie.

In view of his land problems, Hammer felt badly in need of just such influence. He did not believe that he could simply accept the inland site and let the state deal with Monks and Atlantic Richfield. Perhaps he shared Occidental vice-president Thomas Wachtell's conviction that one or more state officials were in collusion with Monks. In any case, Hammer and Vahlsing agreed on an alliance symbolized by a partial stock swap in which Occidental became the second largest shareholder in Vahlsing, Inc., while Vahlsing, Inc., acquired 20 percent of the common stock of the Oxytrol Corporation, an Occidental

* See pages 90–91.

subsidiary specializing in atmospheric control devices to preserve perishable goods during transportation.

Neither Hammer nor Vahlsing realized that Vahlsing's real influence among Maine Democrats was very much on the wane. The Prestile Stream episode had received nationwide attention right at the dawning of American environmental awareness. Muskie's early Presidential campaign was dogged by his involvement in the environmental downgrading of the Prestile. Nixon "ombudsman" Clark Mollenhoff, a once and future Iowa newspaper reporter, shipped a distorted version of the episode to Iowa Representative H. R. Gross, who inserted it in the *Congressional Record,* from which other reporters exhumed and reprinted it. Virginia Congressman Joel Broyhill, infuriated by a Muskie endorsement of his more environmentally concerned opponent, aped Agnevian alliteration in denouncing Muskie as "that mousy meddler from Machiasport, that pussyfooting polluter of the Prestile."

Much of Vahlsing's remaining influence lay in the fact that the failure of his beet refinery had made hostages of unpaid Aroostook farmers and other creditors, along with the Maine industrial-loan-guarantee agency and the federal Economic Development Administration. All would lose money and some would lose prestige if the beet operation failed entirely, and most were consequently willing to do what they could to help.

As climbers roped to a dangling mountaineer are unlikely to be much moved by his shouted enthusiasms for shared future conquests, so Vahlsing's coerced Aroostook County support did not transfer well to a Washington County oil refinery. This may have begun to dawn on Dr. Hammer on the day in early 1970 when Vahlsing called Muskie's office to confirm the Doctor's appointment already arranged by Marvin Watson, LBJ's Postmaster General, who had become an Occidental vice-president. Furious at so transparent a use of Vahlsing, Muskie canceled the appointment altogether.

One of Vahlsing's first contributions to Hammer's land problem was to suggest Sears Island at the head of Penobscot Bay. Muskie and Curtis had warned Jack Evans away from Penobscot Bay because of the certainty of overwhelming opposition from the wealthy and powerful summer residents whose retreats and yachts surrounded the water. Others in the Occidental organization perceived this danger, and Hammer rejected Sears Island.

Instead, he choose Perry, a small community on the western shore of

Passamaquoddy Bay. As a refinery and terminal site, Perry was superb. Low hills and an unindented shoreline meant that a refinery located a mile inland would be invisible from the water. The ocean close to shore was more than 100 feet deep and sheltered from all directions. The site offered ample turning and anchorage room. The terminal area was, if anything, superior to the relatively exposed berths at Stone Island in Machias Bay. The problem (and the reason why Sea and Shore Fisheries Commissioner Ron Green had not recommended the site to Jack Evans) was, in the vernacular of the Maine folk tale, that you couldn't get there from anywhere else.

Jean-Claude Killy would have hesitated to slalom a supertanker through the approaches to Perry. They were narrow, current-beset, fog-prone, and dominated by a 100-degree turn at the narrowest and trickiest point. Spillage from a tanker aground in the approach channel would have smothered the shorefront of Campobello Island, site of a Franklin Roosevelt summer home which had passed out of the former President's family after World War II. In 1963 it had been given to the United States and Canada to become a jointly administered bi-national park, a truly splendid gesture by its owner of eleven years, Dr. Armand Hammer.

To preserve anonymity, Hammer placed the acquisition of the Perry refinery site in Vahlsing's hands. Vahlsing in turn retained Searsport realtor Al Miliano, who did some of the work himself and some in association with a Perry agent. Much of the land that they were seeking was easily optioned. By late September they had accumulated some 3500 acres, but owners of a few key tracts were reluctant to sell. Miliano decided to increase the pressure, and his tactics reportedly included telling recalcitrant owners that their tracts were not essential and that if they insisted on remaining they would be neighbors to "a stinking oil refinery."

Such encounters inevitably attracted press attention. Asked for his comment, Governor Curtis "doubted that a major oil company is involved because they have dealt more straightforwardly with us."[12] Concerned that the tactics of an unknown oil company would arouse resentment that could imperil the Machiasport project, Andy Nixon and I undertook to find out what company was rattling the underbrush. Three of our first calls were to Occidental publicist George Bevel, Washington attorney John Zentay, and consulting economist John

Buckley. These three made up Occidental's Machiasport project team and had excellent oil-industry sources. Each replied that he had no idea but would start looking.

Four days later we learned of Miliano's connection to Vahlsing. Andy Nixon called Bevel. The pertinent part of the conversation went roughly as follows:

NIXON: Have you learned anything about the outfit buying land at Perry, George?
BEVEL: Not yet, Andy. How about you?
NIXON: We know who it is, George.
BEVEL: Well, maybe I do too then.
NIXON: Who do you think, George?
BEVEL: It's a nice day, Andy.

We then called Zentay and Buckley, neither of whom had learned yet. We were told, "We know now, but we can't tell you. The only advice we can give you is, for your own sakes, stop looking."

Although furious at first, we came eventually to believe that none of the three members of Occidental's Machiasport team knew of the Perry caper when we first called them. They all knew of Hammer's concern over the land situation at Machiasport, and Bevel and Buckley knew that Hammer was considering an alternative site. Nevertheless, Occidental's major projects were orchestrated by Hammer, and a direct arrangement between him and Vahlsing was entirely plausible.

This general plausibility was enhanced by the fact that none of the other three were regular Occidental employees. Each was paid for time actually worked or by a retainer, and each had dealt with Maine officials constantly and generally candidly for nearly a year. Concealment of a matter of this magnitude, since it could not have been done effectively, would have been objectionable to each of them.

Bevel inadvertently established a further circumstantial proof of their unawareness. After our first phone call, the public-relations consultant called reporters at both the Portland *Press Herald* and the Bangor *Daily News* to find out what they knew. His third call, to Occidental's Los Angeles headquarters, alerted him to the fact that he was chasing his own tail. Had he known the truth any sooner, the calls to Maine newsmen would have been idiotic, for the subsequent revelation of his client's involvement must have driven the reporters to conclude that their friend had misled them in a singularly gratuitous and heavy-handed way.

The Maine newspapers connected Miliano to Vahlsing almost as quickly as we had. They were temporarily sidetracked by a rumor that the land was to be used for experimental sugar-beet plantings, and matters were complicated by an unavailing attempt by Bob Monks to tie up a coastal tract large enough to cut Occidental's second refinery site off from the sea. Nevertheless, the trail quickly led to the Hammer-Vahlsing tie. Disapproving editorials and landowner complaints were brought to Occidental's attention, and the company became unwilling to accept responsibility for its second site strategy. When the puzzled Bangor *Daily News* reporter Joe Brooks finally contacted Bevel for comment, he was told only that "Every day someone offers us another refinery site in Maine."[13]

These maneuverings posed several serious problems for Governor Curtis. Occidental had been a close ally in fighting federal intransigence and the major oil companies. It was the company most substantially committed to the refinery, the jobs, the revenues, and the cheaper oil that the governor so strongly desired. In addition, he hoped that Occidental might provide a financial transfusion to save the faltering sugar-beet refinery and diversify the Aroostook County farm economy beyond potatoes.*

The governor did not object to Occidental's seeking a separate site from which to deal with either Monks or Atlantic Richfield. On the other hand, Maine was to be the landlord of the foreign-trade zone. No site that was not environmentally equal to Machiasport could be acceptable, and Maine could not certify a site acquired through dubious tactics and without serious environmental study. Maine people would have concluded either that the governor had condoned the Perry foray in advance or that Occidental took Maine government too lightly to keep its chief executive closely informed. He now knew that the latter was the case, but he still hesitated to jeopardize the benefits that he hoped for from the Hammer-Vahlsing team in Aroostook County.

Curtis had also to weigh the Perry move in light of the newly enacted National Environmental Policy Act of 1969 (NEPA). This measure required any federal agency granting a permit for any project with an environmental impact to prepare an assessment of that impact,

* Hammer himself cultivated this connection at a mid-September, 1969, meeting at the beet refinery attended by both Vahlsing and Curtis. He told several hundred assembled members and friends of the Maine Sugar Beet Growers Association, "I and my company are closely associated in business with Maine Sugar Industries and to Vahlsing, Inc. You may rest assured that I will do whatever is possible to help promote the welfare of the people of this state."[14]

including the ways in which it might be minimized and alternative ways to use the site and to meet the demand for the products. Applications already on file were subject to a more lenient review.

NEPA was enacted by Congress all but unnoticed by the industries among which it was shortly to cause convulsions approached in twentieth-century peacetime legislation only by a few New Deal statutes and the early enforcement of the antitrust laws. Occidental was no more perceptive than the rest. The Machiasport subzone qualified for the exemption for applications on file, but an application for a Perry subzone would in all probability have forced a new hearing and a full-fledged environmental review by N. Norman Engleberg.

Under these mixed constraints, Curtis took two actions calculated to contain the damage that might arise from Hammer's lunge. First, he authorized his staff to warn Occidental that Maine would not amend its trade-zone application to include Perry unless the state was convinced that the Perry site was equal to or better than Machias Bay. Second, he accepted the recommendation of a statewide environmental task force that he support legislation giving the Maine Environmental Improvement Commission a power to veto projects sited without due regard for the environment. The task force, which functioned separately from the Machiasport Conservation and Planning Committee, had first focused on the problem of siting heavy industrial plants at the time of the King Resources announcement the preceding spring.*

The governor's position and the aroma hanging over the Perry tactics sufficed to postpone any immediate Occidental announcement of its new home. Instead the news stories died off after recounting the overwhelming circumstantial evidence of the company's involvement. Most of the townspeople of Perry never really knew who wore the cloak that had brushed by them in the night. An ad hoc local anti-pollution committee met once to question Miliano's joint broker for Perry and a county commissioner whose dairy farm had been one of the first areas optioned by the unknown company. Both men said that they saw nothing to be alarmed about and doubted that most Perry residents were averse to potential industrial development. They would not disclose the name of the company.

Marc Nault's *Washington County Times* editorialized that the unknown company was performing with the inferiority of Brand Xs everywhere. Nixon and I took some pleasure in forwarding this and

* See pages 147–48.

similar comments to Bevel and Buckley, who passed a sampling on to Hammer. The Doctor's response was an evening phone call to the governor admonishing him that his aides were seeking to undermine Occidental's relationship with Fred Vahlsing.

Curtis had given his personal approval to our pointing out to Occidental that its move into Perry posed problems, but it is doubtful that he anticipated the enthusiasm with which we undertook the job. He was certainly unaware of the specific material that we had relayed to Occidental. Nevertheless, his reply to Hammer was that Perry required further study and that everything we had done had been "on my direct orders."

The Perry caper was Occidental's second unilateral departure from the original Machiasport plan. The first had come in late July at the third round of the Hart subcommittee hearings, when Hammer told the subcommittee that his proposed refinery would process two barrels of Venezuelan oil for every barrel from Libya, a reversal of the original proportions.

This announcement had two aims. First, it sought to draw the Venezuelan government into the quota struggle on Occidental's side. Venezuelan oil interests had demonstrated considerable past leverage with the State Department,* and Occidental was hoping that the leverage would influence Secretary of State William Rogers's conduct as a member of the Cabinet Task Force on Oil Import Controls. Second, Occidental had submitted bids for exploration concessions on Venezuela's Lake Maracaibo, and his offer of a large U.S. market share would make those bids more appealing to the Venezuelan government. Because Venezuelan crude was exceptionally high in sulfur and difficult to desulfurize, the doubling of the Venezuelan role made the refinery less compatible with the promise of low-sulfur fuel for the East Coast. Furthermore, because Venezuela had no deep-water ports, the supertanker savings dwindled. Added to the higher cost of Venezuelan

* The Nixon administration sampled this leverage when it named John Hurd as its ambassador to Caracas. In addition to serving as a leading fund raiser and Texas state chairman for the Nixon-Agnew ticket, in which capacity he had allegedly filled coffers with Agnew's promise to kill any Machiasport gimmicks, Hurd was chairman of the Independent Oil Producers Association, a group strongly committed to protecting U.S. producers from foreign oil, Venezuelan or other. In the words of the August 3, 1969, Washington *Sunday Star*, he was as welcome in Venezuela as "a Ku Klux Klan member would be in Tanzania." Venezuelan protests and Congressional doubts ultimately persuaded the White House to withdraw the nomination at Hurd's request.

over Libyan crude oil, these changes reduced the likelihood of the promised 10 percent price reduction in home heating oil, a ramification not mentioned in Dr. Hammer's statement. It escaped notice because public attention to that round of the Hart hearings was dominated by two other complainants, the petrochemical industry and, on the day that Hammer testified, by Governor Curtis.

The petrochemical industry depended on petroleum-based feedstocks for its basic raw materials. However, unlike makers of gasoline or home heating or industrial fuel, the petrochemical producers converted their oil into plastics and dyes rather than energy fuels. The shutting off of their supply would have had little effect on the national security. Consequently, they felt that the 5 percent (650,000 barrels per day) of U.S. demand that they represented* should have been free of import restraints. To bolster their case, they pointed out that foreign petrochemical imports could come into the United States freely and that they therefore were being forced to compete at home and abroad with products made from cheaper petroleum. Every dollar of sales that they lost was also lost to the U.S. balance of payments and was a further incentive to build new petrochemical plants outside of the United States.

Although sometimes exaggerated, the testimony of the petrochemical witnesses was essentially irrefutable. Neither Senator Hruska nor the minority staff seriously disputed it. One reason for their restraint was that the Chemco Group had known better than to challenge the entire oil-import control system. They portrayed themselves as no more than "the unintended victims" of a basically wise import policy. They asked, they humbly said, for no more than the treatment accorded to East Coast users of industrial fuel since 1966, namely complete decontrol of the one product that they cared about. If granted that much, they would join in the defense of the overall program. Those hoping for more general reform of oil-import policy had to regard this private pleading as being of the same consumer usefulness as Colonel Sanders endorsing a beef boycott, and John Blair, the chief economist to the Hart subcommittee, fumed at the continuing inability of consumer groups to form effective coalitions.

In contrast to the Chemco approach, Governor Curtis had decided to

---

* The witnesses testified together on behalf of the Chemco Group, a trade association formed especially to seek a more liberal import policy. Its members were Dow Chemical, Dupont, Eastman Kodak, Monsanto, Union Carbide, Olin Mathieson, Publicker Industries, Celanese, and National Distillers & Chemical Corporation.

use his appearance before Senator Hart to move Maine and New England away from single-minded pursuit of the Machiasport refinery into a position supporting overall oil-import reform. The New England governors had already made this transition in a midsummer submission to the Cabinet Task Force, but the Hart hearings provided Curtis's first chance to advance the position in public debate.

Senator Hart picked up the change quickly, commenting in benign impotence: "I am struck by the fact that you did not belabor the Machiasport issue, although you made very clear your attitude on it, but rather spoke to the national concern—the effect that this import quota system has on each of us."[15]

Hart then turned the questioning over to Hruska. The governor and the Senator were not prepared for each other. Curtis's previous Congressional testimony had been before the completely friendly McIntyre subcommittee and had required no special preparation. Overconfident, he had confined his homework for the Hart hearing to the taxi ride from the airport to the hearing room.

Hruska, his defense of the right of mediocrity to representation on the U.S. Supreme Court still ahead of him, had not performed well in the subcommittee's earlier sessions. To prop him up, Washington's ever helpful oil lobby usually supplied him with questions for adverse witnesses. Since Hammer was to follow Curtis, Atlantic Richfield had thoughtfully provided the Nebraska Senator with a few questions for the company's chief Machiasport rival. To avoid any misunderstanding, Curtis aides were told that this had been done* and that Hruska probably didn't have many questions for Curtis. No one anticipated that Hruska would get confused and ask his Hammer questions of the Maine governor. The result was a shambles partially concealed by aides who edited the transcript before it appeared in final form.

The skirmish began with Senator Hruska asking Governor Curtis how he could justify his advocacy of quotas for shoe manufacturers and sardine canners. Curtis replied that his real objection was that both issues had been resolved against New England's interest and that the oil industry had successfully draped a cloak of national security over economic arguments no better than those advanced in vain by the New England industries.

---

* Atlantic Richfield's involvement in Maine had not diminished the company's support for oil-import controls. We could hardly resent their helping Hruska, for both we and Occidental had frequently done the same for friendly Senators, and we felt that the public interest could not suffer much from the source of a Senator's questions.

Hruska dismissed this with:

> We are worse off in the middle west than you are. In Nebraska we
> have no sardine packers, and we have no shoe factories. Do you suppose
> we ought to arrange something whereby we suspend the economic laws
> and build shoe factories there and pack sardines there?

And later:

> I know some argument has been made here from time to time, you
> raise it yourself, you do not have any petrochemical industry. Of course
> not. You do not have any grain industry either, or corn industry and
> you do not have any coalmining. You do not have any oil production.
> But that goes in the nature of things, and a petrochemical plant is built
> where the source of supply is. That is where it is built.
>
> Now, we would like to have some petrochemical industry in our state
> and we cannot get it. And I do not know just how much we are going
> to gain by trying to remove certain government intervention, as you call
> it, in the marketing process of oil and we get into another kind of
> government intervention, and we say we are going to suspend all laws
> of economics and finances and fiscal affairs and we are going to put the
> petrochemical industry in New Hampshire or Vermont.
>
> Have you any comment on that line of reasoning which we have had
> here again and again and again?

GOVERNOR CURTIS: Well, I think one of the great values of this particular
    subcommittee itself is to bring in the testimony and the facts of all of
    these points of view. My advisers that I have sitting beside me, as you
    have, indicate that testimony has been brought out before this Com-
    mittee that only some five percent of the domestic production would be
    cut if controls were removed . . .

SENATOR HRUSKA: What is that?

GOVERNOR CURTIS: Only five percent of the domestic production would
    be cut out or lost if there were a change.

SENATOR HRUSKA: What is the source of that information? This is some-
    thing new and strange.

GOVERNOR CURTIS: That comes, I believe, from Professor Harry [sic]
    Steele, who I think testified here on March 20, 1969.

SENATOR HRUSKA: Who is this?

GOVERNOR CURTIS: Professor Henry Steele, University of Houston.

SENATOR HRUSKA: He was talking about existing wells, was he not? He
    was talking about existing wells.

GOVERNOR CURTIS: I do not know. I was not there.[16]

At this point Hruska shifted gears, laid down a marginally relevant
quotation from a Texas Congressman, and plowed ahead with the ques-

tions intended for Dr. Hammer. Governor Curtis parried a barrage of queries about ways to allocate quotas between Occidental, Atlantic Richfield, and other potential claimants. His appearance ended on a pleasant note:

> SENATOR HRUSKA: Well, the people of Maine and New England have a staunch advocate in you and a very persuasive one. I do not know that you changed my convictions very much but you speak well.
>
> GOVERNOR CURTIS: I enjoyed the visit.
>
> SENATOR HRUSKA: And I speak not egotistically at all because this is a point of view. This is a point of view. Witness the debates on the floor of the Senate and elsewhere, and the testimony of the record is a point of view.
>
> GOVERNOR CURTIS: We think that people in Nebraska and the Dakotas have some very beautiful farmlands. We envy the way they maintain their farms. We wish we could do as well.
>
> SENATOR HRUSKA: Thank you very much, Governor.
>
> GOVERNOR CURTIS: Thank you.[17]

Many Congressional appearances end in just such pleasantries. This one is noteworthy only because it formed the entire basis for the next day's front-page story in the Portland *Press Herald*, a story headlined "Senatorial Foe Praises Maine Governor."

The Curtis-Hruska exchange consumed so much time that the hearing ended before Hruska could question the next witness, Dr. Hammer. Hruska asked that Hammer make himself available at a later date, and the Doctor agreed. However, Occidental's Republican contacts were improving, and Washington liaison man Tim Babcock, a former governor of Montana, director of the Nixon campaign in ten Western states, and runner-up to Walter Hickel as Secretary of the Interior, talked Hruska out of holding the follow-up hearing. Consequently, Atlantic Richfield's question never found the intended target.

Neither the Hart hearings nor the Perry debacle can possibly remain large among Dr. Hammer's memories of the summer of 1969. Libya's extensive oil discoveries coupled with the passive administration of the aging King Idris II had given birth to most of the corruptions of sudden wealth. Seething over Idris's refusal to give full support to Nasser during the Six Day War in 1967 and infuriated by the loose morals, personal abuse, and general exploitation that accompanied the foreign oilmen, a group of Libyan army officers ousted Idris even as Hammer was testifying before Hart. The monarchy was replaced by a twelve-member Revolutionary Council headed by Muammar el-Qaddafi, a twenty-eight-year-old colonel guided by a ferociously puritanical and nationalistic vision of anti-Zionist union among the Arab nations.

Qaddafi's post-coup forays among his people while disguised as a peasant were the most publicized element in a program stressing the return to basic Islamic principles, including disdain for alcohol and resort to amputation as punishment for robbery. Unnecessary foreign influences were expelled, and an oil company with most of its oil in Libya, a Jewish chairman, and close ties of suspect propriety to the deposed King Idris had good reason to worry.

Qaddafi's actual moves against Occidental and other oil companies were some months away. Spectacularly successful, they were to precipitate a revolutionary realignment in prices and patterns of Arab oil production. Whether damned as blind and amateurish greed or praised as just retribution, the young Libyan's attitude toward oil and his nation's well-being were similar in origin to the observations of an equally young Texas reporter writing in 1968 that

> The loss to Texas of its natural heritage, sold for pottage, had been one of the great shames of a state in which social services contrast so dramatically with basic economic wealth. If an enlightened tax program had been applied to oil and gas two decades ago, Texas in the 1960's might have had the best and most progressive state government in America. It was in this perspective that the constant destruction of decent appropriations took on deeper shades of meaning than in the legislatures of other, less endowed states. The reformers in the Texas legislature never missed an opportunity to argue that theirs was a state which ranked first in the nation in oil, with about half the nation's underground reserves; first in gas, with over 45 percent of the nation's underground reserves; first in cattle; first in cotton; first in everything from livestock and mohair to goats and pecans. Yet in basic social services the State of Texas ranked 40th in public assistance programs in general, with almost three-fourths of these funds from the federal government; 40th in literacy; 42nd in aid to dependent children; 50th in vocational rehabilitation for injured workers; and close to the bottom in educational services. Despite its impressive natural beauty, its state parks were a travesty, and it could be judged nothing less than criminal in its negligence of the mentally ill.
>
> Such arguments, made almost in desperation, were greeted, depending on the moment, with smugness, high hilarity, inattention, or a simple

lack of intelligence. On the *Observer* we were sometimes overcome with futility and anger. The flaws seemed too great to be measured in terms of our own private contempt, and the sheer enormity of the task of reform within the system made our occasional optimisms seem a waste of good energy. "If Texas won't," it was said bitterly, "then Washington will." . . .

One night while the Senate was considering a gas tax bill, I was in a private club in Austin with a well known county judge from El Paso noted chiefly for his capacity for whiskey sours. He began exploring the place and came back and told me, "I've just uncovered a covey of old birds." He led me to a back room and pulled the curtains. Seated at the table were the chairman and five members of the tax committee of the state Senate and the four biggest oil and gas lobbyists in Texas. "Senator Regan," the judge shouted, sticking his head through the curtain, "y'awl decidin' on that gas tax?" The Senator turned and said, "Judge, it's got us all up in the air."

A man could not have edited a newspaper with the acute degree of contempt one felt in those first days. As often happens to people deeply involved in everyday politics in America, I think I relaxed, or perhaps weakened as a means of survival. In the Texas legislature at the time, even when one saw human decency violated, and many of the violations actually put into law, one learned that there was little future in indulging outrage and anger at the personal level. Otherwise one's existence among politicians would have consisted of more or less uninterrupted physical violence.[18]

The conditions that were to nurture and exhale a triumphant fanaticism from the Libyan desert had shaped no more than a compromised journalistic indignation in Texas. There are obvious reasons—different constitutions, different traditions, different countries, different vitalities, different men. Still, these reformations through taxation must be paid for by consumers, and neither New Englanders nor Japanese nor Fiji Islanders can be expected to greet them with much enthusiasm, at least not until they find their own oil or its replacement. This is the blandishment offered to Maine in the mid-1970s by oil-state politicians supporting oil-company efforts to drill off the New England coast, a peculiar solicitude whose most extraordinary expression occurred at a September, 1973, hearing in Boston sponsored by the President's Council on Environmental Quality. The stated purpose of the hearing was to expose the Council to New England sentiment and knowledge regarding offshore oil drilling. Inexplicably, Senators Paul Fannin of Arizona and Clifford Hansen of Wyoming, both from noncoastal states, addressed the hearing on the pleasures of producing oil. Fannin spoke warmly of Yankee ingenuity while Hansen extolled the virtues of Pilgrim self-sufficiency and the Puritan ethic.

Hansen, it should be remembered, had enthusiastically endorsed and placed in the *Congressional Record* a description of the Sierra Club's opposition to the Occidental refinery because of the grave threat of spillage along the priceless Maine coast. Inconsistency aside, his posture has precedent. The following welcome was sent by Oklahoma to North Dakota upon the discovery of oil in the latter state in 1951: "It will be exciting to be in the oil business in North Dakota where such divergent philosophies as the state and the industry have are bound to clash. The oil will finally prevail. There is nothing so soothing of passion as monthly production of royalty checks."[19]

The ownership of the oil off New England's coast is clouded by the fact that the suit precipitated by Maine's giving a permit to King Resources in 1968 has gone unresolved into its seventh year. In 1973 Southwestern Congressmen began introducing bills permitting the Interior Department to lease the outer Continental Shelf anyway, provided that substantial royalty payments were made to state conservation programs. Thus it seems that because of oil perhaps trapped under the sea that they have been trying to ship oil over, New Englanders are to be offered their own turbans, garments of mixed significance in past struggles for crude-oil control.

8: Winter, 1970

It is very hard to remember that events now long in the past were once in the future.

F. W. Maitland[1]

There is treasure to be desired and oil in the dwelling of the wise; but a foolish man spendeth it up.

Proverbs 21:20

All of them . . . constructed at infinite cost to themselves these Maginot Lines against this enemy they thought they saw across the frontier, this enemy who never attacked that way—if he ever attacked at all, if he was indeed the enemy.

John Knowles, *A Separate Peace*

The economic clauses . . . were malignant and silly to an extent that made them obviously futile . . . The multitudes remained plunged in ignorance of the simplest economic facts, and their leaders, seeking their votes, did not dare to undeceive them. The newspapers, after their fashion, reflected and emphasised the prevailing opinions . . . No one in great authority had the wit, ascendancy, or detachment from public folly to declare these fundamental brutal facts to the electorates; nor would anyone have been believed if he had . . . everybody seemed pleased and appeared to think this might go on forever.

History will characterise all these transactions as insane . . . a sad story of complicated idiocy in the making of which much toil and virtue was consumed.

Winston Churchill on the reparations sections of the Treaty of Versailles[2]

O lastly over-strong against thyself!

Milton, *Samson Agonistes*[3]

THROUGHOUT 1969, Occidental, Atlantic Richfield, Atlantic World Port, King Resources, and Shaheen had maneuvered in an empty pool. They could not bring oil into Maine until President Nixon's Cabinet Task Force put the handle back on the faucet. By September the task

199

force's examination of the relationship of oil imports to the national security had attracted some 10,000 pages of submissions and had provoked outlays of more than $2 million by the oil industry and less than $200,000 by independent or consumer-oriented groups. Environmental groups, not realizing their stake, did not comment at all.

Most of the submissions stressed the need for continued protection for the domestic oil producer. The stated reason was invariably enhancement of national security, but the logic was cast in terms of industry prosperity. There was certainly a relationship between the economic well-being of the domestic industry and the availability of sufficient oil to meet security needs, but these submissions rarely sought to define it. The major companies and the independent producers were nearly unanimous in stating that very high costs were acceptable when the security of the nation was at stake.

The phrase "national security" came during the Watergate months to evoke emotions ranging from national paranoia to a vague urge to count the spoons. The following examples, largely taken from one source,* suggest that we have been slow to understand the phrase's flexibility and that corporations formed to make money cannot be expected to give it a content inconsistent with business relationships and profits.

1. Despite the oil industry's stated commitment to minimizing dependence on foreign oil, it opposed the creation of the naval petroleum reserves† and harassed their administration.

The opposition was due in part to fear of governmental involvement in any form of oil production and in part to simple desire for the oil. The most famous harassment was the Teapot Dome bribery. Others have included drainage resulting from an artificially created wartime shortage scare in California, successful pressure for the halting of ex-

* The source is Robert Engler's *The Politics of Oil*. One should read the list that follows without forgetting that many oil executives have served in government in wartime at a personal sacrifice only sometimes lessened by salary supplements from their companies or by access to subsequently useful information. Nor would it be prudent to forget the opinion of historian Allan Nevins that "without our powerful industrial units . . . the free world might have lost the First World War and most certainly would have lost the Second."

† These reserves are at Elk Hills and Buena Vista, California; northern Alaska; three oil shale areas in Colorado and Utah; and Teapot Dome, Wyoming. In attempting to maintain federal control of undersea oil in the Gulf of Mexico, President Truman set aside these submerged lands as additional naval reserves at the end of his Presidency. This action was quickly rescinded by the Eisenhower administration.

ploration on the Alaskan reserve, and constant efforts by neighboring private leaseholders to siphon off the reserves.

2. The oil industry also opposed governmentally sponsored research into the extraction of petroleum from oil shale and from coal. Upon the recommendation of the National Petroleum Council and the U.S. Chamber of Commerce, promising research programs into both sources were terminated during the Eisenhower administration as unwarranted governmental interference in realms better left to private enterprise. In 1956 coal-to-gas research appropriation requests were cut and several demonstration projects were abandoned on the recommendation of the National Petroleum Council. Work at the experimental shale pilot plant owned by the Interior Department at Anvil Points, Colorado, was curtailed in 1956, once again on the recommendation of the National Petroleum Council.

The saga of oil shale is a first cousin to the oil-import problem. In aggressive or governmental hands, shale oil might have challenged the structure of the existing U.S. oil industry. The Green River shale deposits in Utah, Wyoming, and especially Colorado contain enough oil to supply the entire United States for more than a hundred years, even if only a third of it is recoverable. Experiments have established the technical feasibility of shale oil production, apparently at prices somewhat above the three-dollar-per-barrel range of crude oil prices during the 1960s. The major oil companies have bought up considerable shale land, but, with the exceptions of Atlantic Richfield and Union Oil, they have made no serious effort to produce oil and have actively discouraged government efforts.

The desire to produce shale oil moved Governors Love (Colorado) and Hathaway (Wyoming) to oppose increased oil imports and the development of Maine's deep-water port, but they were no more able than Governor Curtis to get the oil industry to develop their states' obvious resources. This has produced a paradox in the nation-security advice so often tendered by oil spokesmen, for, in the words of one economist,

> Oil men have to turn their national security doxology around when they talk about shale. They like to claim it's worth paying more for crude because of the national security benefits. But when they discuss oil shale, which would have the same benefits, they say you shouldn't have to pay the extra money it might cost to bring shale into commercial production.[4]

Since the location of shale is well known, no one needs tax breaks to search for it, and it is absolutely invulnerable to Arab cutoffs. However, the extension of the depletion allowance to wells in foreign countries coupled with the denial of similar treatment to domestic shale has actually encouraged U.S. companies to find Arabian rather than domestic sources.

After an extensive research effort on oil shale, Chris Welles, then *Life* magazine's business editor, concluded that the major oil companies have acted "individually in a fairly uniform way" to "spend millions of dollars obtaining control over most of the privately owned shale land and to constrain or stifle potentially productive research efforts."[5] As the 1968 publication date for Welles's article approached, *Life*'s publisher estimated that the story might cost the magazine between $5 million and $20 million in advertising, and Shell decided not to sign a major advertising contract until "we get a chance to see how the story turns out." After putting Welles through a dozen rewrites, *Life* killed the story. Welles then sold it to *Harper's Magazine*, for which he was fired by *Life*.

3. As with oil shale, suggestions that the government guard against wartime shortages by building up subsidized standby production, refining capacity, pipelines, and storage were opposed publicly as wasteful, privately because such surpluses posed a constant threat to the price structure. Standby surpluses were rejected by P. C. Spencer, president of Sinclair, because

> It seems to me . . . that the greatest cushion in the world for petroleum reserves is in the elasticity of and flexibility of civilian demand. Take it away from them, if we are going to have a war. . . . We have tried to make war too comfortable and too convenient for civilians. . . . War should be tough. We should cut back civilian demand. I think that is the greatest reserve cushion we have.[6]

This statement, made in 1954, anticipated the events of 1973–74. The flexibility in civilian demand certainly existed, but it argued as strongly against controls on oil imports as against surplus oil facilities.

4. Throughout the 1930s Esso cooperated closely and extensively with I. G. Farbenindustrie, the giant German chemical company allied with the German government before and after Hitler came to power. This cooperation was based on an agreement by I. G. Farben to stay out of the oil business outside of Germany in return for Esso's staying out of chemicals. Discoveries and information by one company in the

other's realm were to be shared through joint companies. Under these arrangements, I. G. Farben gained access to tetraethyl lead despite the national security–based reservations of Dupont, then involved through its controlling interest in General Motors, Esso's partner in tetraethyl production. Esso's contribution to the security of the United States was described as follows in a "to be destroyed" I. G. Farben folder found by American forces in Germany:

> Without lead-tetraethyl the present method of warfare would be unthinkable. The fact that since the beginning of the war we [I. G. Farben] could produce lead-tetraethyl is entirely due to the circumstances that shortly before the Americans had presented us with the production plans complete with experimental knowledge. Thus the difficult work of development (one need only recall the poisonous property of lead-tetraethyl which caused many deaths in the U.S.A.) was spared us since we could take up the manufacture of this product together with all the experience that the Americans had gathered over long years.[7]

Tetraethyl was not the only German gain from the ties with Esso. The Wehrmacht was able to purchase high-grade aviation fuel for stockpiling, and as late as 1939 an Esso subsidiary helped to design German facilities for refining aviation fuel.

Esso also retarded the prewar development of an American synthetic-rubber industry while waiting in vain for I. G. Farben to get permission from Hitler to develop its buna process in the United States. Despite the delays, Esso continued to turn over the results of its research on synthetic rubber to I. G. Farben and even acquired thousands of Farben patents of all sorts, occasionally without the technical knowledge necessary to use them, under an agreement subsequently characterized by a U.S. federal court as a "sham transaction" for the purpose of camouflaging I. G. Farben's assets to prevent their seizure in several Allied nations including the United States. As Assistant Attorney General Thurman Arnold saw these arrangements:

> What these people were trying to do was to look at the war as a transitory phenomenon and at business as a kind of permanent thing: The war is bound to be over in a couple of years and let's not have it interfere any more than necessary with commercial relationships that are bound to exist.[8]

5. Also in apparent contradiction of their nation's World War II security interests, some oil companies opposed the cutting off of oil supplies to a Japan preparing for war and, in Engler's words, "resisted

or ignored efforts to prevent indirect shipments by way of neutrals or independent brokers and even were reluctant to stop the refueling of Axis ships."[9] As in Germany, Esso aided in the construction of aviation fuel refining facilities in Japan as late as 1939.

Oil companies also attempted to use the war to reestablish their hold over Mexican fields nationalized, with compensation, in 1938. Deputy Petroleum Administrator for War Ralph Davies, himself a former executive vice-president of Standard of California, described this effort as a "shameful hindrance in the prosecution of the war."[10]

Yet another group of companies insisted, as a precondition to their cooperation in the war effort, that all pending antitrust litigation against the industry be suspended, including a staggering $2-billion treble-damage suit arising from alleged pipeline rebates. According to Thurman Arnold, "they felt that it was impossible for them to participate in national defense as long as this suit was hanging over them."[11] The lawsuits were suspended, and the government "in the confused and hurried situation" waived two thirds of its $2-billion rebate claim.

Texaco solved a separate problem by removing its board chairman, Torkild Rieber, after press exposure of his enthusiastic reception of Nazi visitors to the United States in 1940. "I considered it simply good business,"[12] he explained.

6. Lest their country pursue its national security not merely by guarding against wartime contingencies but by actually promoting peace, oil representatives "warned the State Department against accepting the United Nations' proposed Covenant of Human Rights because of a provision asserting the right of peoples to self-determination including permanent sovereignty over their national wealth and resources.' "[13] *The New York Times* described the State Department's behavior as "a drive to scuttle a section of the proposed Covenant of Human Rights that poses a threat to its business interests abroad."[14]

In its final report the Cabinet Task Force summarily dismissed the oil industry's blanket assertion that the nation's security "must be protected against any contingency."[15] Noting that the law authorizing the President to control imports was part of a larger statute asserting that the nation's overall security was best protected through free international trade, the task force found that oil-import restraints should have only two main objectives:

(1) . . . protecting military and essential civilian demand against reasonably possible foreign supply interruptions that could not be overcome by feasible replacement measures in an emergency. . . .

(2) To prevent imports from causing a decline in the petroleum sector of U.S. industry that would so weaken the national economy as to impair the national security. . . . The purpose . . . is quite clearly not to give protection *per se* to domestic industry. Section 232 (c) makes the impact of imports on individual industries relevant, but only to the ultimate determination of whether such weakening of our internal economy may impair the national security.[16]

These objectives were to be accomplished

. . . with minimum cost and maximum advantage to the economy, to various regions of the country, to consumers and producers, and to other segments of the industry . . . also minimum disruption to and maximum opportunity for the free play of competitive market forces [without] undue adverse effects on either our balance of payments or foreign relations.[17]

And how did the oil-import program, tolerated and encouraged by four Presidents and estimated by the Cabinet Task Force to have cost consumers $5 billion in 1969 alone, measure up to these complex criteria? Part IV (c) of the report concluded:

The present import control program is not adequately responsive to present and future security considerations. The fixed quota limitations that have been in effect for the past ten years, and the system of implementation that has grown up around them bears no reasonable relation to current requirements for protection either of the national economy or of essential oil consumption. The level of restriction is arbitrary and the treatment of secure foreign sources internally inconsistent. The present system has spawned a host of special arrangements and exceptions for purposes essentially unrelated to national security, has imposed high costs and inefficiencies on consumers and the economy, and has led to undue government intervention in the market and consequent competitive distortions. In addition, the existing quota system has left a significant degree of control over this national program to state regulatory authorities. If import controls are to serve the distinctive needs of national security, they should be subject to a system of federal control that interferes as little as possible with the operation of competitive market forces while remaining subject to adjustment as needed to respond to changes in the over-all security environment. A majority of the Task Force finds that the present import control system, as it has developed in practice, is no longer acceptable.[18]

Later sections conceded that because of Middle Eastern unrest and vested interests in the existing system, any sudden abandonment of import controls "might on present evidence be deemed to threaten the security of supply."[19] The report nevertheless concluded that "liberalization of import controls over a suitable period would not seriously weaken the national economy . . . to the extent of impairing our national security."[20]

The reason that liberalization would not threaten national security was that the existing oil-import restraints were not protecting it. In assessing events that might cut the United States off from essential oil, the Cabinet Task Force concluded that

(1) In the event of large-scale nuclear war, oil shortages would not be a problem. Destruction of refineries and consumers would be so great that domestic crude oil would more than supply the demands of the shattered economy.

(2) In limited wars, such as Korea and Vietnam, dependence on foreign oil would not pose special problems. Indeed, 90 percent of the oil used by the United States in Vietnam had been of foreign origin.

(3) Even if a major non-nuclear war or a prolonged boycott by the world's exporting nations were to deny oil to the United States for a period of one year, such an "extreme contingency" would leave "only a modest portion of the United States and Canadian demand unsatisfied," and this deficit "could be met with tolerable rationing."[21] Any one-year wartime interruption would pose a serious threat to East Coast and Hawaiian oil supplies regardless of import restraints, for oil shipped from Texas to the East Coast or from Alaska to either the West Coast or the East Coast was no more secure against submarines than oil shipped from Venezuela or via Mexico's soggy overland route to the Brownsville Loop.

The Cabinet Task Force suggested that a nation seriously concerned about protecting its submarine-vulnerable shores could do so through pipeline and storage facilities rather than a program of random protections under which the least secure areas paid the most.* Then, in

* The task force rejected almost all regional claims for special treatment. However, an appendix to the report acknowledged that home heating oil "is probably in artificially short supply in the Northeast relative to the rest of the country because the quotas have their greatest effect there. The Northeastern states are at the far end of the country from the source of domestic supply but are readily accessible to foreign sources. . . . With free importation, home heating oil would retail for about

perhaps the most controversial paragraph on oil policy ever to have emerged from the federal government, the task force stated:

> National security will be adequately protected by adopting as a first step a revised control system and a modest immediate reduction in import restraints. . . . A prudent course, in other words, would be to adopt a system of tariff restrictions, to take effect no later than January 1, 1971.[22]

In short, the task force's majority urged that the Mandatory Oil Import Program be abolished. In its place, they recommended an initial tariff of $1.45 per barrel on imported oil. This would have raised the cost of imported oil to a level roughly equal to the prevailing Gulf Coast price of domestic crude oil. At that cost, imports would not have drastically affected U.S. oil producers.

The task force then urged a one-year analysis of the impact of the new tariffs on domestic production and exploration. If the effects were acceptable, the tariffs could be gradually lowered to permit further import increases and consequent price declines. The task force's calculations suggested that the price of crude oil could have fallen by as much as two cents per gallon without damaging the national economy or causing overreliance on insecure sources of oil. To be safe, specific recommendations were made for tariff preferences to Western Hemisphere oil, and an upper limit was placed on the tolerable level of Eastern Hemisphere imports.

The task force saw several advantages to tariffs over quotas. Tariffs were more flexible, and they permitted the import market to operate under conditions of minimal government interference. Like quotas, they could have been used to give preference to "secure" oil from nations with historically stable relations with the United States. Unlike quotas, however, they did not build any vested interests among governmentally chosen beneficiaries, and they put no ceiling on the amount that could be imported in a given year.

Spot shortages of the type that had sent importers scurrying to Washington with pleas for special allocations which, once granted, usually outlived the alleged shortage would not have occurred under the proposed program, for anyone could have imported needed oil

---

three cents per gallon (17 percent) less in New England than it does now."[23] The task force also made a state-by-state estimate of the costs of the program. The national average cost for a family of four was $96 in 1969. The corresponding figure for New England as a whole was $144; for Maine it was $160.

simply by paying the tariff.* Because so many more potential competitors would have had access to imports, consumer prices could have
been expected to decline, and deep-water ports and refineries might
have been built in areas where the market and the environment would
have supported them.

A further advantage of tariffs over quotas was that they would have
taken the government out of the business of dealing out quota rights
like chips in a poker game. The task force condemned this practice in
exceptionally strong language:

> No single aspect of the present system has engendered so much con-
> troversy as the allocation of valuable import rights among recipients.
> Some of the more dubious features of past practice can no doubt be
> corrected, but there are inevitable strains and distortions in the adminis-
> trative process of favoring some at the expense of others. The hazards
> of fallible judgement, combined with the ever-present risks of corrup-
> tion, counsel strongly in favor of getting the government out of the
> allocation business as rapidly and as completely as possible.[24]

A tariff system would have taken the states as well as the federal
government out of the allocation business. The Texas and Louisiana
prorationing boards could have continued to function, but they would
have been responding to federal decisions instead of dictating them. As
long as the quota system was geared to 12.2 percent of domestic production, the agencies that controlled domestic production also controlled imports. Under a tariff system, any state effort to increase price
by cutting production would probably have been defeated by increased
imports.

A final advantage of a tariff system was that it put the value of
import rights into the U.S. Treasury rather than into the pockets of
the importing companies. With each barrel per day of import permits
worth roughly $1.50 to the importing company, the imposition of a
$1.45 tariff in 1969 would have had the effect of reclaiming for the
Treasury most of the $22.5 million given to Esso, the $22.1 million
given to Atlantic Richfield, the $21 million given to Gulf, the $19
million given to Shell and Standard of California, the $15.8 million
given to Texaco, and the $14.2 million given to Amoco. The govern-
ment could have used these funds to develop petroleum reserves,

---

* This would have been as true for refined products as for crude oil, since the task
force recommended that products be imported under a charge of ten cents above
crude-oil tariffs.

standby storage or pipeline capacity, or research programs into alternative sources of oil or other energy.

Of course, the imposition of a tariff initially serving to raise the cost
of foreign oil to prevailing domestic prices offered little consumer
benefit, a fact that dissenters Walter Hickel and Maurice Stans were
prompt to join the oil industry in pointing out,* but the recommended
eventual lowering of tariffs from $1.45 to $1.00 per barrel would have
produced consumer benefits of some $2.5 billion. Furthermore, the
benefit of tariffs to the consumer as taxpayer would clearly have been
sizable, for the $1.45 tariff would have yielded about $2 billion in the
year that President Nixon vetoed housing and education bills that exceeded his budget by a slightly lower amount.

Tariffs would have been a vast nationwide improvement on quotas,
but the report offered little hope to Occidental or to Atlantic World
Port that a Maine refinery would receive special consideration. Despite
an acknowledgment that New England bore exceptionally high costs
and despite tacit recognition that the Maine foreign-trade-zone application had been mishandled,† the task-force majority rejected the proposition that inequities could be remedied through a continuing series of
special deals. Calling Udall's Robin Hood use of privately negotiated
awards to promote particular socioeconomic goals "highly discriminatory" and "indefensible," the task force recommended that these
awards be phased out wherever possible, and, to the chagrin of Armand
Hammer and Robert Monks, that such awards "not be repeated."[25]

The Hickel-Stans minority report,‡ hostile though both men had

* Indeed, Hickel and Stans went a step further and suggested that the recommended tariffs would force prices to rise because the importing companies could no
longer pass on any of the benefit of their access to cheaper oil. In reply, the task
force's majority challenged the minority to prove that such "passing through"
existed at all. For its purposes, the majority put an annual value of $300–$600 million
on "passing through," less than 12 percent of its estimate of the cost of the controls.

† With the Maine application clearly in mind, the task force's majority had said of
trade zones: "Their administration can and should be kept distinct from any oil import program. . . . This would mean that zone applications satisfactory to the Foreign
Trade Zones Board could be approved in the ordinary course. In no way, however,
would such approval be considered as committing the managers of the oil import
program."[26]

‡ The report was also signed by John Nassikas, chairman of the Federal Power
Commission, a curious circumstance only because Nassikas was not a task force
member. His signature bolstered the minority from 5-2 to 5-3 and added his weight
to their analysis of the relationship of oil imports to natural-gas supplies, which are
indirectly regulated by his agency.

been to New England's complaints, was more to the liking of Occidental, Atlantic World Port, and the New England Independent Terminal Operators. Strongly influenced by political realities, the minority differed with the majority on its two most important premises, that the infusion of additional foreign oil could lower U.S. prices without harming national security and that imports should in any case be controlled by tariffs rather than quotas. The minority saw the New England situation differently from the majority. To the majority, any special New England problems would be solved in a system of reform that treated all regions equally. To the minority, New England and the petrochemical companies were the squeaking wheels that threatened the tranquillity with which consumers generally were accepting their fuel bills. Special oil allocations were the logical and proverbial remedy.

Beside the majority report, the minority effort was laughably bereft of meaningful security or economic analysis. Its logic, unstated, was political. The independent producers and producing states wanted no part of cheaper imports and lower domestic prices. Those majors and independent refiners who could have used cheaper oil did not want to be deprived of their multimillion-dollar quota transfusions. Inland refiners were particularly upset, for the majority would have deprived them of the import rights which they had never used but had traded handsomely to their coastal brethren for crude oil, some of which came from inefficient wells that owed their very existence to import controls. A tariff system would have put several independent refiners out of business,* because ten years of unearned grants had subsidized some inefficiencies in refinery size and operation comparable to the fatal dependence warned against by the Yosemite Park sign reading "Please do not feed the bears. You are not really being kind to them, for they will lose the ability to forage for themselves."

To preserve the basic quota system while placating the complainers, the minority recommended three steps. First, imports east of the Rocky Mountains should be liberalized at a rate of 1 percent per year for five years, to a level of 17.2 percent of domestic production by 1974. This step was a minimum acknowledgment of inevitable increases in demand. Second, the petrochemical companies should be given increased

---

* Going out of business would, in fact, have been profitable in the short run for some refiners. The task-force staff found examples of refiners who could have made more money in 1969 by simply selling their quota and shutting down than by bothering to refine oil.

access to foreign oil. Third, the New England terminal operators should be given special quotas for home heating oil.

The third recommendation was ingenious, for it gave the value of the permits to the terminal operators while bypassing Occidental entirely. The terminal operators would get access to foreign products on terms worth as much as $2 million per year to certain companies. Since Hickel and Stans assumed that the terminal operators rather than Occidental or consumer sentiment were the moving force behind New England oil politics, a proposal which satisfied them was expected to quiet the New England politicians.

Even Occidental had to prefer the minority recommendations, because they preserved the principle of special deals by offering them to the independent terminal operators and the petrochemical companies even as the authors professed to scorn the special deal approach. The minority report said little more to Occidental than "You haven't squeaked loudly enough yet." By contrast, the tariff recommendation did offer Occidental an East Coast refinery and outlet for its Libyan oil, but only on the same terms as any other potential importer. Had Libya remained under King Idris, Occidental might have secured its special deal at the producing end and done nicely under a tariff system, but Idris was gone and his successors were less likely than Hickel and Stans to make the kinds of deals that Occidental had in mind.

In stressing political over economic or military considerations, Hickel and Stans came up on the winning side. The initial Cabinet Task Force deliberations had been remarkably free of political overtones, but a series of events late in the summer of 1969 alerted the oil industry that this task force was a maverick. As Southwesterners, the oilmen knew that corrals and patience are often as effective as spurs and apples.

The first jolt to the industry came in a task-force working paper on Alaskan oil which estimated that crude oil from the Alaskan North Slope could be delivered to the East Coast at a cost of ninety-six cents per barrel (2.3 cents per gallon). The industry had been claiming that Alaskan oil would cost two dollars per barrel at the wellhead and at least three dollars on the East Coast.* Television advertisements

* The Alaskan oil-cost shuffle had been briefly exposed during the testimony of M. A. Wright, chairman of the board of the Humble Oil and Refining Company (Esso's largest U.S. affiliate), before Senator Hart's subcommittee. Senator Kennedy, noting that Michael Haider, chairman of Esso, had boasted that North Slope oil might

featuring howling winds and plunging tankers had suggested that reduced oil prices or lessened tax incentives would make production of
Alaskan oil too expensive to undertake. The staff study suggested that
Alaskan oil would be profitable even if all import controls were removed and U.S. prices fell from $3.30 per barrel to the prevailing
world price of two dollars.

In publicizing its Alaskan estimates, the task force's staff was not
certifying their accuracy. The estimates were no more than highly
educated guesses and were made public out of dissatisfaction with the
refusal of the private companies to provide more accurate data. The
staff was saying in effect, "These are the numbers we'll use unless you
give us some better ones." In a government where the several agencies
regulating the oil and gas industries rarely audited or disputed the
information provided to them by the companies under their jurisdiction, this fumigation produced considerable trade-press gagging about
"out-of-date figures" and "whiz kids."

A week after the appearance of the Alaskan estimates, the industry
received a heavier jolt. The Antitrust Division of the Justice Department submitted a recommendation that the quota system be scrapped
entirely and that the national security be protected by tariffs. The
Justice Department submission criticized quotas both for their consumer costs and for the manner in which they allocated foreign oil to
a few companies. It also included an unusual breach of interagency
etiquette, in which Justice remarked that a pro-quota submission by
the Interior Department had been drawn up by the Foreign Petroleum
Supply Committee, "an industry committee . . . [which] does not
appear to provide wholly objective consideration of national interest
and foreign policy matters."[27]

Startled oil lobbyists hastened to learn whether Attorney General
John Mitchell had approved the position of his Antitrust Division.
Mitchell had emerged in the early months of the administration as
President Nixon's dominant domestic policy adviser. If he opposed
quotas, the system was in real trouble.

The answer came quickly. Texas Congressman George Bush, a
Nixon favorite in training for a 1970 Senate race, met with Mitchell

---

be sold in Europe, asked Wright how such expensive oil could compete in world
markets where the going price was less than two dollars per barrel. Wright replied
that Haider couldn't have meant what he seemed to have said.

and reported that the Attorney General had been taken completely by surprise. Richard McLaren, Mitchell's representative to the task force, received an unreported rebuke, and John Lamont, the writer of the offending submission, was relieved of further responsibility to the task force despite his twenty years of experience with federal oil law.

The industry's next surprise was more comical. The Interior Department, usually oil's closest friend among government agencies, had asserted that the quota system was necessary to protect the national security and was well worth the $2.2–3.5 billion that Interior acknowledged to be the cost to consumers.* A month later a separate division of the department released its own estimate—that import quotas would cost consumers $7.1 billion by 1975 and $8.1 billion by 1980. This estimate was discussed with several reporters by an official in Interior's Office of Oil and Gas on September 23. On the morning of September 24, Secretary Hickel ordered that the new study be kept secret, and several reporters who hadn't seen the estimates the day before were told that they were "internal working papers" which had been released through "an honest error."

By the evening of the twenty-fourth, the journalistic uproar was so great that Hickel reversed himself with a statement that "any statements that the report was being withheld from the public were made without my knowledge or approval." Lewis Helm, a personal assistant to Hickel, added that the new analysis "isn't really that important. It's just one of a series of studies to try and get as many divergent views as possible."[28]

Who Owns America?, Secretary Hickel's 328-page saga of his twenty-two months at Interior, contains several extensive and righteous discussions of existing oil-government relationships and ways in which they must change. Despite Interior's role as administrator of the Mandatory Oil Import Program, his role in the Cabinet Task Force on Oil Import Controls is never mentioned.

---

* Secretary Hickel was ultimately to shave the official Interior estimate to less than $1 billion, largely by dismissing most consumer costs as "transfer payments" to state and local governments and to other sections of the economy, such as the companies themselves. About this estimate the Hart subcommittee economist John Blair was to say, "Exactly what its meaning is is somewhat unclear to me. If I am walking down the street and somebody puts a gun in my back and robs me of $10, that is a transfer payment from me to him. Just as I no longer have $10, the consumer will no longer have $5 billion."

None of the rumors surrounding the task force in late 1969 encouraged the industry. At one point the task force was falsely reported ready to recommend replacing quotas with an extensive storage program.* More accurate rumors, usually from the Interior Department's oil bureaucracy, described probable tariff systems. By early November these rumors had inspired sharply escalated political maneuvering.

The governors of four oil-producing states† demanded a meeting with the task force. All such requests had previously been rebuffed, but at the insistence of White House aide Peter Flanigan‡ this one was granted, and was attended by Secretaries Shultz, Hickel, Stans, and David Kennedy.

The session was nothing more than a show of strength. The governors, supported by telegrams from their colleagues in thirteen other oil-producing states, stressed the catastrophe that increased oil imports would bring to their state economies. They offered no new information, and the only surprise was a telegram of support for the quota system from Governor Nelson Rockefeller of New York, a state whose oil production had peaked in 1882. In the next eighty-seven years, production had fallen to a daily average of less than one barrel per well and to an annual value of less than $6 million. The task force estimated the cost of oil-import controls to New York consumers in 1969 to have been $429 million, or some eighty times greater than the value of the oil production.

Feeling that a corresponding show of strength was an indispensable waste of time, Governor Curtis contacted Flanigan and was assured that consuming states could have their own meeting. He was joined by Governors Francis Sargent of Massachusetts, Frank Licht of Rhode Island, and Walter Peterson of New Hampshire. In addition, New

---

* The task force's report did note that storage could help vulnerable areas to respond to supply cutoffs. Although limited by considerations of space, a storage program could have provided a one-year supply of crude oil for half of the annual cost of the oil-import program if steel tanks were used, or a third of the cost if the oil were pumped into available salt domes.

† The governors were Preston Smith of Texas, Stanley Hathaway of Wyoming, Robert Docking of Kansas, and Richard Ogilvie of Illinois. Ogilvie's presence was remarkable in that the task force estimated the cost of oil-import controls to Illinois at $254 million. This exceeded the total value of Illinois oil and gas production by more than $75 million.

‡ Flanigan sat as one of seven "observers" of the task force's deliberations. He is the only one of the seven not listed as an observer in the final report, although he is given that designation in interim documents.

Jersey,* South Carolina, Hawaii, Vermont, and New York City sent
representatives while seven states sent telegrams.

Andy Nixon and I, telephoning for support, were astounded by the
number of governors' aides who had never heard of oil-import controls
or who were indifferent to their impact. No amount of effort could stir
response in such oilless states as Georgia, North Carolina, Delaware, or
Wisconsin. Several coal states wanted no part of competition from
cheaper oil, and Governor Daniel Evans of Washington was unwilling
to take any step that might imperil his state's hopes of refining North
Slope crude.

Our one clear triumph came in New York, where Governor Rockefeller's telegram had drawn protests from Senators Jacob Javits and
Charles Goodell of New York along with a flaying by Senator William
Proxmire of Wisconsin. While we were pressing his staff, nationally
syndicated columnist Marianne Means charged that Rockefeller had

> . . . identified himself with his family's vast oil interests against the
> consumer good and raised once again the ancestral specter of greed.
> . . . Standard Oil of New Jersey does most of its banking with Chase
> Manhattan Bank, headed by Governor Rockefeller's brother David. . . .
> [When his telegram came to light] Governor Rockefeller, suddenly
> faced with a public conflict between big business and big politics, began
> to wobble. . . . A Rockefeller oil expert said he didn't know what the
> governor would do because "the question hasn't arisen as a public issue
> in the last few years." In other words, it is one thing for Governor
> Rockefeller to help out Standard Oil when nobody is looking—but quite
> another if people start to notice.[29]

Rockefeller ultimately sent a telegram supporting the consuming
states' position. Since the second telegram made no mention of the first,
the task force was presumably free to draw its own conclusions.

Between the task force's meetings with the two groups of governors,
The Oil Daily carried a story proving that the oil industry had not forgotten to whom the task force was reporting. The story reported a press
conference held by Michael Haider, the recently retired chairman of
Esso and still chairman of the American Petroleum Institute. The story
said that Haider had originally been dissatisfied with industry access
to the task force but that "the situation has changed completely in the

---

* Governor-elect William Cahill quickly perceived a truth that had always eluded
Governor Richard Hughes, namely that an Eastern Seaboard refining state would gain
rather than lose industry if controls were relaxed.

last one and one-half to two months, and Jersey had been afforded 'quite adequate opportunities' to make its views known."*

The story reported that Haider had also met recently with President Nixon, on whom he had successfully pressed the task-force concept nine months earlier. He emerged from the meeting

> feeling more optimistic about the handling of petroleum industry prob-
> lems in Washington. . . . Haider said that he had "a very good con-
> versation with the President" but declined to detail what they had
> talked about.
>
> He indicated later he believes Nixon has a good grasp of the problems
> surrounding oil import controls and is more confident that the outcome
> will be favorable . . . he believes the President also has a good under-
> standing of the tax problems of the oilmen.
>
> He commended Nixon's statement advocating retention of the $27\frac{1}{2}\%$
> depletion allowance but said the President had to go along with the
> position taken by Congress.†
>
> "I think I would have done so too," he added.[30]

Senator Proxmire suggested that both the governors' meetings and Haider's conference with the President had tarnished the impartial and factual nature of the Cabinet Task Force review and had prejudiced its Presidential reception. Proxmire's attack drove *The Oil Daily* to exacerbate the mutually reinforcing paranoias with which the consumer representatives and the industry regarded each other. Arguing that Haider and the four governors were merely exercising their constitutional right to be heard, the editorial reassured its readers:

> One of the best recent examples of the malice and ill-will held for
> the petroleum industry by a certain type of industry-baiting legislator
> is furnished in the latest outburst of Senator Proxmire. . . . For
> smear and slur, the doughty senator, in his long-continuing campaign
> against this industry, its policies and people, has become a recognized
> past master. With him virtually everything in and about the industry
> can be and is bitterly criticized.
>
> For some months, much misgiving had been aroused in the industry
> over the approach of the administration to petroleum issues and policies.
> It was feared that the White House was unduly depending on the filter-

---

* Haider may have been speaking just for Esso and not for the API membership. The Esso submission had, through both the quality of its data and its willingness to see quotas expanded and auctioned off rather than given away, impressed the task-force staff and led to considerable further contact not afforded to other companies.

† Congress had just cut the depletion allowance to 22 percent.

ing of information on industry matters and problems through a system of a professional staff—and that this could injure the country unless the administration were to have the benefit of specific contacts with the industry.

We personally believe it is a healthy sign not only for the industry but also the country that on vital matters of such stature as the health of the nation's leading source of energy, key industry people should have access to top government officials. This would certainly include the President on matters of such urgency. . . . We hope oilmen will go as far and as high as they can go in telling the industry's story.[31]

The industry had gone both far and high before the final task force's meeting on December 15, 1969. This last meeting was the first one attended by Attorney General Mitchell, whose Justice Department had theretofore been represented by its strongly antiquota Antitrust Division. Mitchell made no mention of the Antitrust Division's opposition. Instead, he is reported to have urged the task force to think about the jobs that might be lost in the Southwest, to remember where the administration's friends were, and not to "put the President in a box."[32]

After Mitchell had delivered his message, the task force reached its final decision to recommend that tariffs replace quotas. Behind this firm decision, the Mitchell plea and the extraordinary Congressional pressures took a toll. Only Chairman George Shultz ultimately adhered to a position close to staff recommendations that the tariff should be adopted with the specifically stated goal of being lowered from $1.45 per barrel to $1 per barrel over a three- to five-year period. The rest of the majority were content to recommend the conversion to a $1.45 tariff and further study.

In addition, Secretary of State William Rogers urged that the conversion not be undertaken until State had had further discussions with foreign nations.* Secretary of Defense Melvin Laird also recommended further discussions with affected nations, but only after the conversion to tariffs. The significance of these two afterthoughts was to become clear when the report was finally made public in February, 1970.

Before then the report had other hurdles to clear. Most of these were generated by the Interior and Commerce Departments, which precipitated a cloudburst of leaks once they had been outvoted. In anticipation

---

* Rogers and Hickel were the only task-force members with distinct previous convictions on oil-import controls. As Eisenhower's Attorney General, Rogers had urged the original task force not to regulate imports with a restrictive quota system.

of an unfavorable document, oil-oriented Senators and Representatives from fourteen states took turns throughout December in berating the task force's staff as a group of "theoretical economists" ill equipped to assess either oil practicalities or the national security.* Two members of the majority, Laird and Office of Emergency Preparedness director George Lincoln, were rumored to be having second thoughts. If both defected, the minority would become the majority. The gain of either one would have substantially strengthened the credibility of Hickel and Stans on the several national security and foreign affairs judgments in which they were going against the considered opinions of the heads of the nation's foreign-affairs and defense agencies.

The majority held, but only after Laird resisted last-minute pressures from Senator John Stennis (D.-Mississippi), chairman of the Senate Armed Services Committee. By mid-February, 1970, printing had been completed, and the White House was ready to release the report, which it had been studying in draft form for several weeks. On the day chosen for the release, Secretary Shultz was making a speech on the West Coast and Staff Director Areeda was teaching a class at Harvard Law School. Peter Flanigan conducted the press briefing, the transcript of which makes very clear why Areeda and Shultz concurred in the White House's judgment that they should stay away.

At 10 A.M. on February 20, the newsmen at the White House were handed the 400-page report, thirty pages of summary documents, and a two-page Presidential statement. Nixon's statement noted that the Cabinet Task Force had reached unanimity on some points on which he would take immediate action.

First, he would set up an Oil Policy Committee to advise its chairman, Director Lincoln of the Office of Emergency Preparedness, in providing "the policy direction, coordination, and surveillance of the program," whose "day to day administrative functions will continue to be performed by the Oil Import Administration of the Department of

* The following *Congressional Record* insert by Senator Gale McGee (D.-Wyoming) from an oilman's speech is typical:

"Secretary of Labor George Shultz picked a Harvard professor to head the study group. He in turn picked other professors and even students to work on the report. To the best of my knowledge, not one of the members has any experience in the oil industry or even business experience. . . .

"The only way to stop this screwball approach is contact with the President and legislators from both political parties. . . .

"The effective letter writers are anyone—individuals, businessmen, state and county officials, and particularly teachers."[33]

the Interior." Secretary Shultz was replaced on the new committee by Attorney General Mitchell.

Second, because "a unique degree of security can be afforded by moving toward an integrated North American energy market," the President directed the State Department to continue its negotiations with Canada and Mexico. He did not assert that State had ever considered discontinuing these discussions.

Third, noting that the Secretaries of State and Defense had recommended consultations with foreign nations, he directed that such consultations be completed before further action was taken on the report's substance.

Fourth, he noted that committees in both houses of Congress had scheduled hearings on the report. Sure that "much additional valuable information will result . . . I direct the Oil Policy Committee to carefully review all such information."

That was it. Eleven months, twenty-five man-years, 10,000 pages of submissions, a total cost not less than $4 million, the first real analysis ever made of oil-import problems, a 400-plus-page report that all but called the quota system a $5-billion-a-year ripoff, and the President responded by creating a committee to study the issue further.

The reporters were given forty-seven minutes to digest the 432 pages they had been handed. Then Flanigan appeared. The befuddled press never laid a glove on him, although one or two reporters clearly sensed that the eleven-month study was to be followed by more studies, and one even picked up the Mitchell-Shultz switch. The only time that Flanigan was cornered, he escaped by making explicit the lie implicit in Nixon's statement, namely that a majority of the task force (Hickel, Stans, Rogers, and Laird) opposed any change until "after consultation with other affected nations as recommended by the Secretary of State and the Secretary of Defense." While Rogers's separate statement can support such a reading, Laird's is directly contradictory. He wrote that he "strongly recommends that the economic and security implications inherent in the proposed program be brought to the attention of our allies and affected nations at the earliest possible moment, *after approval*" (emphasis added).[34]

The following exchange capsulized the White House response.

Q: Is it correct to assume, then, from the tenor of the President's statement . . . that we are going to retain the present quota system as it now stands for a while?

MR. FLANIGAN: That is correct.

Q: For how long?

MR. FLANIGAN: That is what is recommended by this study.

Q: By the minority?

MR. FLANIGAN: No, it is recommended by the Secretary of Defense and the Secretary of State, who are included in the majority.

Two other actions by Flanigan give some further insight into the approach that the White House took to the task force's report.

In January he called Dr. Hammer to ask what Occidental really wanted from the oil-import program. Hammer's response is not available; possibly, in view of the Libyan turmoil, he himself was no longer sure. If Hammer did have a wish, he didn't get it, at least not in the context of oil-import controls. The significance of Flanigan's call was that it confirmed a White House decision to implement the Hickel-Stans approach to oil-import inequities—buy off the powerful complainants and isolate the consumer.

Flanigan's second act was more flagrant. Relaxing with the staff of the task force at a get-together after the completion of their work, he offered them a few words of consolation. He and the President, he told them, thought that their criticisms of the program were basically correct but that the appointment of such a task force on so sensitive a subject had been a terrible political mistake. The President's highest priority was to gain Republican control of the Senate in 1970, and the staff would simply have to understand that Presidential acceptance of their ideas would devastate George Bush's chances to capture the Texas Senate seat then held by liberal Democrat Ralph Yarborough, who was clearly in trouble in both primary and general elections that year. He closed by noting prophetically that reports like theirs often lay dormant for a while and that they might see their work become national policy in a few years.

The actual embalming of the task force's report was to take another six months. During that time Flanigan was involved in another of the several subterranean diversions that were to lead Senator Thomas Eagleton (D.-Missouri) to describe him as "the possessor of the scuttling feet that are heard, faintly, retreating in the wake of yet another White House ordered cave-in to some giant corporation."[35]*

* The episodes that Eagleton had in mind were the torpedoing of the task-force report, the ITT antitrust settlement, White House–orchestrated capitulations by the Environmental Protection Agency in face of pressure from Anaconda Copper Company and Armco Steel, and a Postal Service bond issue underwritten under allegedly

In this case the cave-in was by the Treasury Department, and the corporation was Union Oil. The focal point was a 67,000-ton tanker, the *Sansinena*, registered in Liberia, owned by Barracuda Tanker Corporation (an offshoot of Dillon, Read & Company) and chartered to Union Oil (whom Dillon, Read served as investment bankers).

Because the *Sansinena* was of foreign registry, she was prohibited by the Jones Act from carrying cargoes between U.S. ports. Anxious to use the vessel to bring oil from southern Alaska to California, Union sought a waiver. The Defense Department refused to certify that any military need justified such a waiver, but on March 8, 1970, despite the availability of several U.S.-flag tankers, the Secretary of the Treasury granted the *Sansinena* the first waiver in the history of the statute. The waiver had the instant effect of increasing the vessel's value from $4.5 million to $11 million.

The next day Maryland Senator Joseph Tydings, urged on by the several thousand shipyard employees in his state, attacked the waiver. His speeches over the next two days disclosed that the president and managing director of the Barracuda Tanker Corporation (which was really no more than a drawer in a Bermuda filing cabinet) was, until April of 1969, none other than Peter Flanigan. Upon joining the White House staff, Flanigan had resigned this position and placed his 308 shares of Barracuda stock in a blind trust managed by his father, Horace, a director of Union Oil.

The day after the first Tydings attack, the waiver was suspended as precipitately as it had been granted. Five months later it was revoked. Flanigan denied any involvement and said that he couldn't have profited personally since the vessel was on a long-term fixed-rate charter to Union Oil and since the president of Barracuda, to spare him any embarrassment, had purchased the 308 shares from his father at a price which did not reflect the possible waiver. No definite link between Flanigan and the waiver was ever proven, but the episode flared again two months later when an official at the Maritime Administration contradicted Flanigan's assertion that he "did not discuss the [waiver] application with any government official."[36] Thus reminded, Flanigan contended that he had been calling on behalf of the Cabinet Task Force to inquire as to the general rules covering vessels like the

---

peculiar circumstances by Flanigan's former employers, the investment banking firm of Dillon, Read & Company.

Sansinena, which he said he had mentioned only by way of illustration and without knowing about the waiver application.

Though profitable enough, Flanigan's Barracuda Tanker Corporation has had some bad luck. It owned only three ships. The *Lake Palourde* has served Union Oil relatively uneventfully, but even the *Sansinena's* career was quiet compared to the briefer life of the third sister, the most notorious oil tanker in history, the *Torrey Canyon.*

With Flanigan temporarily pinned down by hostile fire, others were available to shovel earth on the task force's casket. Nixon himself, with that easy familiarity with first spadefuls that only eight years as Vice-President and seven major political campaigns could have conveyed, cast the first clod, and mightily. Eighteen days after he had received this exhaustive report recommending that oil imports be liberalized and that Canada, our most secure foreign source, be the beneficiary of a specific hemispheric preference, the President slashed Canadian imports into the Midwest by 155,000 barrels per day (27 percent). He said that he had acted on the recommendation of his newly formed Oil Policy Committee, on which Mitchell had replaced Shultz. The committee had not yet met.

Nixon justified the cutback on the ground that eastern Canada was entirely dependent on foreign oil while western Canada produced a surplus and exported it to the United States. In the event that eastern Canadian supplies were cut off, the region could have been supplied only from the United States or, after construction of the necessary pipelines, western Canada. Thus maintenance of some surplus production in western Canada was a legitimate security concern for the Midwestern United States. In the months preceding the Nixon cutback, Canadian exports had increased dramatically above the ceiling set by an informal and secret binational agreement, and Nixon's action did no more than cut Canada back to levels closer to but still slightly above that agreement.

Had the cutback been followed by a good-faith effort to reach agreement on hemispheric energy policy, it could not have been questioned, but serious efforts toward such cooperation were never made. Instead, Canadians were left to puzzle over the U.S. President telling them to conserve their oil for national-security reasons even as he followed a policy in his own country that some were to label "Drain America First." Senator Proxmire suggested that Nixon was motivated in large part by a less noble concern than national security:

Every barrel of Canadian oil that comes in subtracts from the amount of oil that can be allocated under the 12.2 percent limitation on oil imports. This means that every barrel of Canadian oil that comes in costs the holders of import tickets about $1.50. Doing some rough arithmetic, by multiplying $1.50 times the number of barrels now available for import allocations because of President Nixon's cutback on Canadian oil, we arrive at a windfall to the big oil companies of about $85 million a year.[37]*

Proxmire suggested another motive, too. In that election year of 1970, an exceptionally large group of liberal (radiclib, some called them) Senators, most of whom were later to appear on the White House enemies list, were running for reelection against carefully chosen administration spokesmen. Proxmire himself was among the targets, and there may have been a tinge of self-preservative instinct behind his suggestion that Nixon was seeking financial tigers for his party's tanks, a suggestion made more explicitly by his legislative assistant, Martin Lobel, who said during a televised debate on oil-import controls that Nixon "in effect said to the fat cats in the oil industry—Look, fill 'er up. Fill up the Republican coffers or we may take away some of your subsidies."[38]†

The task-force report remained in limbo through the summer of 1970. In June, Nixon adopted the Hickel-Stans recommendation that the East Coast terminal operators be given 40,000 barrels per day in heating-oil allocations, precisely the type of Johnson-administration-special-deal solution that the task-force majority had warned against. A few of the terminal operators promptly began to urge New England politicians against pushing for tariffs. Their warning that tariffs, whatever their taxpayer benefit, might actually boost prices if set too high was valid enough, but they had also to admit that their new 40,000 barrels per day was not enough to enable them to cut prices. Instead,

* Proxmire's calculations are a little too exuberant. Canadian oil was roughly fifty cents per barrel cheaper than U.S. oil. Since that much would have gone to importers had the President not acted, his action was worth only a dollar per barrel to them as a group, a benefit of $55 million per year, not all of which went to "the big oil companies."

† Lobel, generally recognized as one of the two or three most knowledgeable Congressional aides on oil matters, eventually decided to turn professional. With him into private law practice went Alan Novins, who had shaped Senator McIntyre's oil investigations, and John Lamont, the Justice Department attorney who had been removed from task-force matters after Justice's antiquota position paper. Their first client was an independent oil marketer seeking a special quota, which they obtained.

they could offer only price stability while they banked the $18-million annual value of the tickets.

The true meaning of the grants to the terminal operators, unperceived at the time, was that Occidental, like Monks, was dead at Machiasport. The White House had taken the cheapest ($18 million) way out. Stewart Udall must have smiled. So did Governor Curtis when he learned that Peter Flanigan had followed this grant by telling a group of terminal operators that they could count on even smoother dealings with the White House in the future if they could find ways to unseat troublemakers like Curtis in November.

Throughout the summer, Congressional sniping over the report went on. Friendly committees bolstered it; hostile ones attacked it. Assistant Secretary of Defense Barry Shillito told a hostile House committee that the armed forces had access to all the oil that they needed regardless of the quota system. Lest such testimony lead anyone to rash conclusions, the powerful House Ways and Means Committee, chaired by quota devotee Wilbur Mills of Arkansas, proposed legislation that would have required the President to regulate oil imports by quota only. The Washington *Post* carried a July 17 story stating flatly that Nixon had asked Mills for such legislation in order to get the pressure for tariffs off of him. White House press secretary Ron Ziegler denied the story, saying that the President "wanted to retain flexibility in the matter."[39]

The pro-quota forces were also strengthened by events abroad that seemed to confirm the dubious reliability of foreign oil. A pipeline carrying oil to the Mediterranean was cut by a Syrian bulldozer during "repairs," and the repairs of that repair proceeded glacially. At the same time, the new Libyan regime imposed significant production cutbacks as part of Qaddafi's first effort to increase his nation's tax take. These two events, coupled with Egypt's continuing refusal to open the Suez Canal, resulted in a major increase in tanker traffic around Africa and a spectacular rise in spot tanker rates.* As a result, the cost of Middle Eastern crude oil delivered to the U.S. East Coast temporarily rose above the cost of domestic oil.

This apparent anomaly emboldened critics of the Cabinet Task Force to proclaim the good fortune of the Northeast in not being

---

* Spot tanker rates govern the 15 percent of tankers not operating under long-term charters.

dependent on foreign oil, in effect an assertion that the region had, by paying a dollar per barrel too much for ten years, been spared paying twenty-five cents too much for six months. Foreseeing similar situations, the task force had remarked that "the possibility of paying a monopoly price in the future is not usually a persuasive reason for paying an enhanced price now."[40]

Confronted by these increased prices, task-force staff director Philip Areeda shrugged them off, remarking that higher foreign prices simply reduced the size of the tariff necessary to protect domestic production and that no protection at all was necessary when foreign prices were above domestic prices. To his astonishment, the oil trade press began to run articles to the effect that he had repented of the task-force report and no longer favored tariffs or the reduction of U.S. oil prices.

Coupling Areeda's alleged recanting with the increased oil prices, *New York Times* reporter William Smith led off a July 26 story with "If an industry could have a facial expression, the United States oil industry would be wearing a bittersweet smile"—that of one whose ignored warnings had proven all too well founded. Despite or perhaps because of several extraordinary inaccuracies, the story made a big hit with industry spokesmen, who were more accustomed to being attacked in *Times* editorials than commended on its financial pages. It even attained a dubious immortality by being reprinted in the *Congressional Record* four times in a three-day span—at the requests of Senators Hansen and John Tower (R.-Texas) and Representatives Omar Burleson (Texas) and Rogers Morton (Maryland, then Republican national chairman, now Secretary of the Interior).[41]

Whether because of international developments, because of growing industry restiveness, or just because George Bush had fallen behind in Texas, Nixon decided in mid-August of 1970 that the time had come to abandon the pretense that he was still evaluating the tariff proposal. As prelude, his reconstituted Oil Policy Committee recommended that he cease even considering the tariff plan—an extraordinary recommendation, particularly since it had been arrived at on the basis of discussion described by Chairman Lincoln as "now and then, casually"[42] without benefit of any staff working papers or advance notice to committee members.

Word of Nixon's decision was transmitted to selected Congressmen by Peter Flanigan. Bush was allowed to announce it in Texas, where he added that his faith in Nixon's oil policies "has been partially restored"—partially, obviously, because there still had to be a need for a Senator Bush to push for "less control, more incentive to drill, more realistic pricing policies. I pledge to keep hanging in there and to keep fighting for more government understanding of what makes this risky business work."[43]

The oil industry's reaction was generally ecstatic, as exemplified by *Oil Daily* columnist Keith Fanshier in a piece entitled "Big News, Good News":

> This could be the first big break for the petroleum industry in years in its relations with government and public, after a long period of one adverse development after another.
>
> The decision is a clear victory for common sense and good judgment in high official levels where these qualities often have not prevailed in petroleum industry affairs. The administration accordingly is to be commended. Also the public is to be congratulated for its good fortune—for this decision should rate high for the public good, as well as that of the industry. It is a resounding example of how what is good for one is usually good for the other.
>
> Both the nation and this industry have been going through crucial, dangerous times, and we are continuing to do so. . . . These are fateful days for all. . . . So it is especially well that there will be a cessation in the misguided attempt to saddle such a monstrosity of import regulation upon demand for and supply of this nation's principal source of the energy it must have to maintain its life and its security.
>
> It is a rule of life and logic in conditions of threatened or actual crisis, as in much of the U.S. fuel and energy situation today, to avoid complicating or worsening factors, especially in untried ways such as often appeal to the radical, theoretical or academic mind.
>
> The petroleum industry ought to accept this news not as justification for relaxing its vigilance in defending its own and the nation's best interests, but in the knowledge that its determined fight has probably been instrumental in helping kill off and prevent a fatal error of national policy.[44]

New Englanders and their allies in the Southeast, the Great Lakes region, and the Pacific Northwest expressed reactions between dismay and disgust, but for the most part their rhetoric was stale. The outcome had been foreseen, the grant to the terminal operators had taken its toll, and attention was beginning to waver. It had, after all, been twenty-six months since the first Machiasport announcement and seventeen months since President Nixon had promised a group of New England

Republican Senators action on New England's oil problems "before the snow flies next winter."

Governor Rockefeller, still ambiguous, maintained silence, but Mayor John Lindsay of New York attacked the decision as contributing to the threat of an "energy crisis," a relatively new phrase that industry spokesmen had only begun to use a few months earlier as part of a concerted campaign either to make the public realize its true stake in oil exploration and production, or, as some would have had it, to make the public realize just whom it depended on and just what could happen if it messed around too much. After all, anyone with a tiger in his tank was at least figuratively on the beast's back, and a Middle Eastern proverb said that dismounting under such circumstances was risky.

Mayor Lindsay's choice of the phrase "energy crisis" was regarded in some quarters as a usurpation. *The Oil Daily* headlined his warning, "NY MAYOR BEATS DRUMS OF FEAR."[45]

There is far more to the fate of the task-force report than campaign contributions in the 1970 elections. Nixon's action was especially conspicuous in that he rejected a clearly presented and superior alternative, but neither Johnson nor Kennedy nor Eisenhower had considered alternatives at all. The quota system's perseverance had profound roots in the politics of national security and the politics of politics.

Regarding the politics of national security, some striking parallels exist between the road to the energy crisis and the road to Vietnam. Consider the following, from Daniel Ellsberg's essay entitled "The Quagmire Myth and the Stalemate Machine."

THE STALEMATE MACHINE: A SCHEMATIC SUMMARY

A. Presidential Decision Rules in Crisis

Rule 1—Do not lose South Vietnam to Communist control—or appear likely to do so—before the next election

Rule 2—Do not, unless essential to satisfy Rule 1
 a) bomb South Vietnam or Laos
 b) bomb North Vietnam
 c) commit U.S. combat troops to Vietnam
 d) (items d-j, like a-c, are various military actions not popular with most Americans)

Rule 3—Do choose actions that will
 a) (items a-d are efforts either to win or to appear to be trying to win)[46]

Ellsberg's Presidential decision-making framework suggests that the overwhelming tendency of electoral politics to override reasoned security analysis will tend to produce national-security fiascos that will have to be blamed on superhuman complexities (the Vietnam-as-Quagmire Myth=the Energy Crisis) or scapegoats (Russians=Arabs, or peace marchers=ecologists).

By way of illustration, the following is a substitution of oil-import for Vietnam War considerations in Ellsberg's Stalemate Machine. As long as the reelection element dominates Rule 1, the end result cannot change, and the framework remains valid from one Presidency to the next.

Rule 1.   Do not harm the economic well-being of the domestic oil industry or the oil-producing states—or appear likely to do so—before the next election.

Rule 2.   Do not, unless essential to satisfy Rule 1:

a) ignore specific consumer hardships, such as those of New England or the petrochemical industry

b) retard the efficiency of the domestic industry by choking back production from efficient wells, discouraging new exploration, or retarding deep-water port development

c) ignore national-security benefits of such energy alternatives as oil shale, synthetic fuels, or extensive storage

d) spite secure Western Hemisphere allies

e) retard air-pollution-control efforts by limiting access to low-sulfur oil

f) retard regional economic development

g) interject the government into the regulation or the planning of national oil production and supply

h) permit actual shortages

i) appear to favor the oil industry at the expense of the general public

Rule 3.   Do choose actions that will:

a) minimize the risk of disruption of the existing domestic industry by malcontent regions or industries

b) if this risk is significant without resort to certain actions prohibited by Rule 2, break Rule 2 to the extent necessary to reduce the risk to a very low level

c) using any action not prohibited by Rule 2, promote oil-industry prosperity, favoring, where inconspicuously possible, particular friends

> d) avoid appearing to threaten industry well-being, even if the action in question might actually confer long-run benefits on the industry and the nation.

Ellsberg's description of the consequences of the machine fitted oil policy as smoothly as Vietnam, with only the most essential of adjustments for context and clarity. The italicized portions of the following are Ellsberg's exact words on Vietnam:

B. Consequences for U.S. Policy

Viewed from inside, resultant policies reflecting the above rules show certain discrepancies when compared to internal predictions, recommendations, and stated aims (as well as to public statements) giving policy the internal appearance of being purposefully dedicated to preserving a stalemate.

1. *Because of the short term focus of Rule 1:*
   a) *chosen policies appear—and are almost exclusively oriented to short term considerations, neglecting or trading off very large differences in predicted long-run costs, risks, benefits, and probability of success in pursuit of small reductions in short term risk (i.e. risk of violating Rule 1).*
   b) *chosen programs are predicted internally to be inadequate—or at best, "long shots" in the long run* to achieve petroleum self-sufficiency or even to maintain existing import levels (*in contrast to public statements about them, and to some recommended but rejected policies*).
   c) *actual policies chosen emphasize predominantly* industrial—*rather than* governmental *means, aims, considerations, and executive responsibility.*
2. *To compensate for avoidance of "constrained (Rule 2) instruments," the chosen policy relies heavily upon measures inadequate to a truly active pursuit of Rule 1.*
3. *For reasons reflecting both Rules 1 and 2:*
   a) *In communications to Congress and the Public, the Administration*
      1) *expresses optimism (exceeding internal estimates at the time of decision) on both the short and the long-term prospects of actual programs.*
      2) *conceals (if necessary, misleading or lying about) indications of possible inadequacy of current programs,* * including*

---

* The exception is, of course, the Cabinet Task Force report, which was to the Mandatory Oil Import Program what the Pentagon Papers were to the Vietnam War. Because of the method of preparation, the report could not have been kept secret, and, indeed, Areeda is reported to have demanded and received assurances of public

    (a) *pessimistic estimates or appraisals*

    (b) *internal recommendations for more extreme actions*

    (c) *planning activity for much greater effort or more extreme actions.*

  3) *describes the strategic stakes for the U.S. in maintaining* a flourishing domestic oil industry *in the most impressive and grave terms (whether or not currently affirmed by intelligence analysis).*

  4) *conceals (lying, or misleading as necessary) the full extent of programs actually decided upon (as well as of follow up programs expected to be approved), instead giving the impression that fully scheduled build-ups are resulting from sequential, marginal, contingent, ad hoc decisions.*[47]

In short, the dictates of reelection (or impending impeachment) lead to decisions that are known from the outset to be inadequate to attain the goals claimed for them. The resulting stalemates, when they begin to pinch, must be fobbed off as "quagmires," "crises," or "challenges," which are in Ellsberg's disbelieving words "tragedies without villains, crimes without criminals, lies without liars, a process of immaculate deception,"[48]—a cycle that only a President freed either by character or by popularity from obsessions about continuing in office can break by choosing some combination of his favorite Rule 2 alternatives.

Four Presidents, including Eisenhower even after he could no longer be reelected, decided not to relieve the American consumer of a burden that came to cost an annual $104 per family. Daniel Patrick Moynihan, a counselor on other matters to three of the four, has been said to believe that problems should not be solved by government until the constituency of the solutions is larger than that of the problem, i.e., that "it is a procedural error to anticipate the squeaking wheel."[49] This is as fair an explanation as any for the persistence of the Mandatory Oil Import Program. The theory is bottomed on a postulate of political economics holding that limited resources should only be spent in response to the most urgently articulated demands. Otherwise inefficiencies and misallocations set in. Politicians attempting to guess the shape of next year's evils will be wrong, will wrestle with problems that might never have matured, and by their solutions will create more problems.

Put more crudely, there is little political gain in solving a problem either before it materializes or before it is widely felt. Those hurt by im-

---

release before accepting his job. A truer indication of administration attitudes is the aforementioned statement by Flanigan that the task force was a mistake.

port controls did not see the issue as one that would dictate either their votes or their contributions. Many of those benefiting from quotas, including thousands of oil-field workers, saw the issue in just those terms, and Texas and California (the first and third largest oil producing states) have always been critical sources of votes and money.

In his book *The American Condition*, Richard Goodwin, like Moynihan an adviser to Presidents Kennedy and Johnson, offers another analysis of governmental behavior under which rejection of the Task Force Report was inevitable. To Goodwin, the public interest does not exist apart from coalitions of private interests. In a series of passages that would have been appropriate to the oil policy bulletin boards in Stewart Udall's Interior Department, Goodwin quotes James Madison's warning that "It is vain to say that enlightened statesmen will be able to adjust these clashing interests, and render them all subservient to the public good," and then asserts, not approvingly, that

> government is society's past . . . [The political state's] function is to reconcile the private interests established by society and to sustain the existing distribution of economic power . . .
>
> Government undertakes to heal social afflictions only when they are problems of administration, that is when solution is possible without upsetting the existing social process or, more particularly, the dominant relationships of society. It cannot act effectively if the source of discontent is fundamental, residing in the design of society . . .
>
> The true province of politics is the administration of existing interests—to remedy defects, mitigate abuses, and to reconcile competing claims. The form of the reconciliation must be consistent with the relative power of the interests being asserted.

In short, the opponents of oil import quotas could never have made an effective case by the standards of Ellsberg, Moynihan, or Goodwin without at least the support of an oil consuming public alert to its own interests. Neither the Nixon administration nor its predecessors could have been expected to make the case for oil import reform as long as public opinion was fairly reflected in the results of a poll commissioned by "The Advocates," a noncommercial television program. The nationwide interview poll of 1,000 people two months after the completion of the task-force report put this question:

> Congress now places limits on the amount of foreign oil that can be imported into the U.S. This helps maintain our domestic oil supply, but it keeps the price of gasoline and other fuels higher than they would

otherwise be. Would you be for or against Congress eliminating all limitations on the importing of foreign oil?

The poll was biased by the failure to include an alternative between quotas and abolition, but the margin was still startling. Fifty-one percent favored continued restrictions; 29 percent favored abolition; 20 percent had no opinion.[50]

Whatever the explanation for continued Presidential refusals to adopt oil-import policies designed to do their nation more good than harm, the policies and their results have not been accidental. People who know very little of energy policy know that, and many are no more receptive to the preaching that their discomfort or impoverishment is a necessary by-product of the smooth functioning of larger economic and industrial imperatives than a rabbit might be to the knowledge that his brief pain was an unavoidable and foreseen consequence of the stew of some global benefactor.

The certainty that the present is no accident has served both reformers and demagogues. The state of mind that it can induce where the energy industries are concerned shows up exceptionally clearly in a vivid commingling of paranoia and insight in the head of Enzian, a fictional Southwest African wandering through the bombed-out ruins of an I. G. Farben oil refinery in Thomas Pynchon's *Gravity's Rainbow*. As seems to have happened to many observers of oil rigs and policies, there breaks over Enzian "what seems to him an extraordinary understanding." The ex-refinery that surrounds him

> *is not a ruin at all. It is in perfect working order* . . . modified, precisely, *deliberately* by bombing that was never hostile, but part of a plan both sides—*"sides?"*—had always agreed on. . . .
> But . . . if what the I.G. built on this site were not at *all* the final shape of it, but only an arrangement of fetishes, come-ons to call down special tools in the form of 8th AF bombers *yes* the "Allied" planes all would have been, ultimately, IG-built, by way of Director Krupp, through his English interlocks—the bombing was the exact industrial process of conversion, each release of energy placed exactly in space and time, each shockwave plotted in advance to bring *precisely tonight's wreck* into being. . . . If it is in working order, what is it meant to do? The engineers who built it as a refinery never knew there were any further steps to be taken. Their design was "finalized," and they could forget it.
> It means this War was never political at all, the politics was all theatre, all just to keep the people distracted . . . secretly, it was being dictated

> instead by the needs of technology . . . by a conspiracy between human
> beings and techniques, by something that needed the energy burst of
> war, crying "Money be damned, the very life of [insert name of Nation]
> is at stake," but meaning, most likely, *dawn is nearly here, I need my
> night's blood, my funding, funding, ahhh more, more* . . . The real
> crises were crises of allocation and priority, not among firms—it was
> only staged to look that way—but among the different Technologies,
> Plastics, Electronics, Aircraft, and their needs which are understood only
> by the ruling elite. . . . Go ahead, capitalize the T on technology, deify
> it if it'll make you feel less responsible—but it puts you in with the
> neutered, brother, in with the eunuchs keeping the harem of our stolen
> Earth for the numb and joyless hardons of human sultans, human elite
> with no right at all to be where they are . . .[51]

Throughout this dawning, Enzian is troubled by a common paranoid
itch, the feeling that he may be using the right key on the wrong door,
that he may be right about the existence of a ciphered ruin but that it
isn't this one, is instead elsewhere in Hamburg, in another city, another
country.

It's an interesting thought. Supposing this book is only a distraction,
that these particular events have no order, that you should be looking
elsewhere for the cryptogrammic ruin. Perhaps in Vietnam, as Charles
Reich optimistically asserted, using again the image of a dawning,
when he wrote, "The whole edifice of the Corporate State is built on
tranquilizers and sleeping pills; it should not have done the one thing
that might have shaken the sleeper awake."[52]

When one starts thinking this way, it becomes increasingly difficult
to separate the dawn from the dream. Watergate, for example, could so
easily be a mere lightening of the malign sleigh. More pertinently, supposing the relevant nonrefinery isn't at Machiasport but is (or is also)
eleven miles from Grand Valley, Colorado, where Chris Welles
describes

> a huddle of dirty corrugated metal buildings behind a chain-link fence.
> On one of the buildings a fading sign announces: Union Oil Company
> of California. Standing on a plateau overlooking the buildings is a
> silvery structure of pipes and girders that shines brightly in the sun. The
> structure is only a frame, though, for most of the intricate inner
> machinery . . . has long since been torn down and sold for scrap. A
> few dozen black oil barrels lie in neat rows, and weeds poke through the
> shale strewn ground. In a building an elderly watchman sits at a dusty
> desk, his eye on an electric wall clock. A few sheep graze nearby.

"Essentially," says Walter Barnet, who heads Union Oil's shale-re-search efforts, "the facility is on a standby basis."[53]

The engineers who built it as a refinery never knew that there were any further steps to be taken. Their design was finalized, and they could forget it. In 1958 they proclaimed their project "a technical suc-cess [capable of producing an oil] superior in refining value to most of the world's crude oils,"[54] whereupon Union's board of directors closed it down. What the engineers had unknowingly designed was a machine which served as part of the leverage necessary to persuade Gulf Oil to supply crude to fill Union's perennial crude oil deficit on favorable terms. Gulf had an immense supply of Kuwait crude at the time and was very cool to the development of shale oil.

In supplying Union, and also Atlantic Richfield, Gulf quieted some of the ardor of two crude-poor companies for new sources, but this was largely a by-product of perfectly logical economic behavior. Another by-product was the creation of real animosity among oil-shale pro-ponents against something that they called the Oil Import Conspiracy, which "reportedly had the objective of suppressing the development of United States petroleum reserves so that foreign oil will continue to have a ready market in the United States."[55] The Conspiracy was fic-tion, but its roots also fed the anxiety which sped Colorado's Governor Love to Portland to oppose the Machiasport refinery. Love and Gover-nor Curtis were therefore divided at a time when they might have had much to gain from an energy policy that subsidized development of Colorado's shale resource at least to a point at which it provided a sufficient reserve to permit some reliance on cheaper imports through Maine's deep water. Instead, of course, Union abandoned shale and relied on offshore sources, one of which was to become notorious as Platform A in the Santa Barbara channel and another of which was a supertanker carrying that Kuwait crude when it—yes, the *Torrey Canyon* again—took its fated shortcut onto the Seven Stones Reef.

Pynchon continues, plowing for Ellsberg's seeds:

> We have to look for power sources here, and distribution networks we were never taught, routes of power our teachers never imagined, or were encouraged to avoid . . . we have to find meters whose scales are un-known in the world, drawing our own schematics, getting feedback, making connections, reducing the error, trying to learn the real function . . . zeroing in on what incalculable plot? Up here, on the surface, coaltars, hydrogenation, synthesis were always phony, dummy functions

to hide the real, *the planetary mission* yes perhaps centuries in the un-
rolling. . . .

Well, this is stimulant talk here, yes Enzian's been stuffing down Nazi
surplus Pervitins these days like popcorn at the movies, and by now the
bulk of the refinery . . . is behind them, and Enzian is on into some
other paranoid terror.[56]

One joker remains in the deck. Although neither its critics nor its
pallbearers knew this at the funeral, the task force (itself serving functions unsuspected by its hardworking drones) had made two serious
miscalculations. Its report drastically underestimated both the rate of
increase of U.S. demand, and the likelihood of the producing nations'
forming an effective cartel.

One example will suffice to suggest the magnitude of the task force's
error in projecting demand. From a 1968 U.S. demand of 13.1 million
barrels per day, the task force foresaw a 1975 demand for 16.4 million
barrels per day *if the price of oil fell from $3.30 per barrel to $2 per
barrel.* At $3.30 the 1975 projection was 16.1 million barrels per day.
Comparable figures for 1980 were 19.3 million barrels per day at $2
or 18.6 million barrels at $3.30. In fact, the price soon rose above
$3.30, tending to reduce demand. However, the 1975 projections at
$2 per barrel were exceeded in 1972 at $3.50 per barrel. The growth
rate was double that foreseen by the task force, and the 1980 projections, even with energy conservation, seem likely to be exceeded no
later than the end of 1977.

The rising prices encouraged unforeseen U.S. production, but the
staggering increases in demand were such that imports increased from
19 percent of U.S. consumption in 1968 to 28.3 percent in 1972, a
jump greater than that foreseen by the task force even for 1980. The
bulk of the increase in imports had to come from the Middle East.

The task force's error (which was no greater than that of the oil
companies themselves)* was attributable to a variety of factors. The
most important appear to have been the failure of nuclear generation
and natural-gas supplies to live up to expectations, the enacting of air-
pollution restrictions which resulted in the construction of less efficient
automobile engines, and the unacceptability of coal as a power-plant
fuel in urban areas.

---

* The task force's 1980 demand forecast of 18.6 million barrels per day was based
on such estimates as Mobil's 17.7 million barrels per day; the Interior Department's
18.8; and Esso's 19.3. Demand in 1980 now seems likely to exceed 21 million barrels
per day.

The second forgettable prediction read: "We do not predict a substantial price rise in world markets over the foreseeable future. . . . The exporting countries might form an effective cartel that would charge us a monopoly price. But that seems unlikely. . . . The landed price of foreign crude by 1980 may well decline, and will, in any event, not experience a substantial increase."[57]

By mid-1971 the Organization of Petroleum Exporting Countries (OPEC) was a very effective cartel. By early 1974 the f.o.b. price of typical Middle Eastern crude had increased more than 700 percent from the 1970 figure of $1.40 per barrel. Like the other, this error cannot be dismissed as the misfiring of academicians in over their heads. It was signed by the Secretary of Defense, the Secretary of State, and the Director of the Office of Emergency Preparedness.

These errors in forecasting demand and price were to lend aid and comfort to those who had opposed the tariff plan, with the argument running "We told you so. Now aren't you glad that imports were not liberalized?" While Dr. Hammer had ample reason to thank his extraordinary stars that he didn't spend 1973 trying to cut 10 percent off of New England heating-oil prices with Libyan oil, consumers generally owe no such gratitude. They are no better off in terms of security than they would have been if a tariff plan coupled with emergency planning had been implemented immediately, and they are several billion dollars poorer.

Eye-catching though the task force's errors were, they detracted very little from the validity of the recommendations they inspired. The task force itself was careful to say of its "no cartel" prediction: "If this estimate turns out to be wrong, a substantial increase in the price of foreign oil would tend to reduce . . . the [discouraging] domestic production-exploration effects that would otherwise attend the relaxation or abandonment of import restrictions."[58]

This prediction was accurate. The increase in foreign-oil prices has meant that increased imports have not harmed domestic production, which remained consistent with task-force predictions.* In short, the possibility of an effective cartel was never a sound argument for preferring quotas over tariffs.

The underestimation of demand has also proven irrelevant to the validity of the tariff recommendation. The unanticipated 1972 surge in demand coupled with Presidential refusal to make even the mini-

---

* This consistency could not continue, because task-force predictions assumed that North Slope oil would become available during 1973.

mum necessary adjustments to the quota system in an election year dealt a death blow to the quota system in the winter of 1973. Of these events, more later. For the moment, it is enough to note that when the quota system finally fell apart, when President Nixon was unexpectedly confronted by a day of reckoning that his best projections had indicated was in store for his successor, when the nation was at last face to face with a real danger of overdependence on insecure sources of supply and needed a program capable of responding quickly to true national-security needs, what did the President do? Tighten controls to reduce dependence? Give away more import-quota "incentives" to needy sectors of the industry?

Hell, no. He scrapped the quota system and instituted a tariff system. In saying farewell to this fourteen-year program with its more than $30 billion in consumer costs, he struck a note closer on his scale of grieving for fallen public servants to the Agnevian ("entitled to the presumption of innocence") than to the Haldemanic-Ehrlichmanic ("two of the finest public servants I have ever known"). On April 18, 1973, President Nixon said that the Mandatory Oil Import Program

. . . encouraged the development of our domestic petroleum industry in the interest of national security.

Today . . . the Mandatory Oil Import Program is of virtually no benefit any longer. Instead, it has the very real potential of aggravating our supply problems, and it denies us the flexibility we need to deal quickly and efficiently with our import requirements. General dissatisfaction with the program and the apparent need for change has led to uncertainty. Under these circumstances, there can be little long-range investment planning for new drilling and refinery construction.

Thus the petroleum shortages which had in 1970 been used to justify rejecting tariffs in favor of quotas came in 1973 to justify rejecting quotas in favor of tariffs. The President did not discuss the paradox.

9: More Winter, 1970

One generation passeth away, and another generation cometh: but the earth abideth for ever.

The sun also ariseth, and the sun goeth down, and hasteth to his place where he arose.

The wind goeth toward the south, and turneth about unto the north; it whirleth about continually, and the wind returneth again according to his circuits.

All rivers run into the sea; yet the sea is not full: unto the place from whence the rivers come, thither they return again. . . .

The thing that hath been, it is that which shall be; and that which is done is that which shall be done: and there is no new thing under the sun.
Ecclesiastes 1:4–7, 9

When we try to pick out anything by itself, we find it hitched to everything else in the universe.
John Muir, 1910[1]

The first law of ecology: Everything is connected to everything else.
Barry Commoner, *The Closing Circle*

Like other sorts of paranoia, it is nothing less than the onset, the leading edge, of the discovery that *everything is connected*, everything in the Creation, a secondary illumination—not yet blindingly One, but at least connected, and perhaps a route In for those who are held at the edge.
Thomas Pynchon, *Gravity's Rainbow*

MOST OF THE COMPANIES probing Maine's oil-import potential necessarily spent the last half of 1969 contemplatively. None could make a serious move until the completion of the Cabinet Task Force report. Occidental broke the calm briefly with its move on Perry but was largely preoccupied with developments in Libya and Venezuela. Atlantic Richfield, having put its swamp purchase behind it, was proceeding with in-depth feasibility studies of the economics of a Machias Bay refinery and the technical and environmental suitability of Stone Island as a supertanker terminal. On behalf of Atlantic World Port,

Bob Monks had retained the prestigious Arthur D. Little consulting firm to analyze the economics of his proposed refinery. Only King Resources was moving fast, on a trajectory that was to flash briefly across the Maine sky en route to oblivion over the horizon.

The rapid rise of the King Resources Company had begun in Denver some three years earlier, when John King had hit upon his concept of providing tax shelters to average investors through oil-drilling funds. The average investor paid some above-average management fees to the King-owned management companies. They in turn paid a variety of service and management fees to King Resources, to which they also made interest-free loans.

One of the King-owned management companies, the Denver Corporation, was

> headed by Dr. Edward Annis, ex-president of the American Medical Association, and the man who led the battle against John F. Kennedy's Medicare program. . . . Dr. Annis prepared drilling-fund propaganda to be beamed especially at doctors, whose average income topped $32,000 nationally in 1969, but who tend to "lack adequate knowledge of investments," as King publicity noted.[2]

King Resources' successes attracted the attention of Investors Overseas Services (IOS), a gigantic mutual fund complex headquartered in Switzerland and run by former Philadelphia social worker Bernie Cornfeld. Cornfeld's fantasy-fulfilling career as the billionaire suavely shedding his Nehru jacket just off camera at the edge of a *Playboy* centerfold has been chronicled elsewhere.[3] Its only relevance here is that during 1968 and 1969 (after King and IOS president Edward Cowett had been introduced to each other by a shrewd Washington attorney with a croupier's eye for paying combinations—the same Mike Feldman who was simultaneously brokering Occidental's stormy approach to New England) IOS invested heavily first in King Resources stock, then its bonds, then its oil-exploration ventures. By late 1969, IOS was King Resources' largest customer.

Cornfeld and King got along, and Cornfeld suggested an arrangement whereby King Resources would join IOS in mineral-resource-development ventures in the several underdeveloped countries that were imposing reinvestment requirements in order to halt the balance-of-payments drain caused by local participation in IOS funds. The most dramatic of these turned out to be King's "Midbar" plunge, in which John and Bernie, with Israeli permission, teamed up to find oil in exposed international waters off the coast of territory seized by Israel from Egypt in the 1967 war.

Israel could not protect the rig, so the well was capped. The venture was exposed when King tried to slip a second drilling unit around Africa and into the Gulf of Suez. A group of Arab saboteurs tried to blow it up on the Ivory Coast. Their effort exposed Midbar, and other American oil companies, fearing Arab retaliation against their holdings, persuaded the State Department to persuade King to abandon the project, with a loss of some $7 million.

Midbar notwithstanding, the King-Cornfeld Natural Resources account in IOS's Fund of Funds did handsomely for a while. King collected his usual unusual fees, while IOS had an account full of speculative resource investments whose vague and volatile values were well suited to managers who liked to take percentages of changes in value. The account went into South African diamonds and Canadian Arctic oil properties. The King-Cornfeld skies had no horizons, but then the market went sour.

Throughout the last quarter of 1969, IOS entities were forced to sell their stocks to meet the redemption demands of their mutual-fund customers. As the end of the year approached, Cornfeld was faced with the fact that his annual report was not going to show either the growth or the growth potential on which his sales force depended. Too many prime stock holdings had been converted to cash in order to meet the redemptions. To offset this bad news, Cornfeld hit upon a plan to stimulate growth from one of IOS's nonstock investments, the mineral exploration rights to fifty percent of 22 million acres of the Canadian Arctic which the Natural Resources account in IOS's Fund of Funds held jointly with King Resources. This one-half interest was carried on IOS books at roughly the one dollar-per-acre price for which King had sold it to IOS earlier in the year, a price which had already produced a windfall for King at IOS's expense. Because the land had not been explored, a valuation based on actual or potential discoveries was impossible. However, the oil discoveries in the Alaskan Arctic earlier in the year inspired Cornfeld to salt his mine.

His plan had an appealing simplicity. The only possible measure of the value of the land was the price that a purchaser was willing to pay. In the waning days of 1969, Cornfeld persuaded King, with a promise of greater drilling outlays in 1970, to find purchasers for a 3/64 interest in the exploration rights at what seemed to be fifteen dollars per acre. King actually sold 6/64 of the package, but 3/64 didn't count, for the purchaser turned out to be none other than John King in two new guises.

Cornfeld then revalued the Fund of Funds acres from one dollar per acre to about fifteen dollars per acre. On one half of a 22-million-acre tract, this transaction provided a gain to the Fund of Funds of some $156 million on paper. After some adjustments, IOS decided that the Fund of Funds holding had actually gone up by eleven dollars per acre, or $119 million. To reward itself for achieving this benefit to FOF investors, IOS took $9.7 million out of FOF for itself. This was the only cash transaction in the entire sequence, and it provided 95 percent of IOS's 1969 profit. The willingness of the auditors (Arthur Andersen & Co., who happened to be auditors for both IOS and King Resources) to accept this transaction had drawn the veiled scorn of one set of commentators[4] and the outright denunciation of another.[5]

No one can have believed that the ruse could go undetected for long, and it didn't. In all probability, King and Cornfeld, who exemplified the type that John Kenneth Galbraith was to christen "geniuses of the rising market," simply assumed or dared not doubt that the market would turn back up in the new year. Annual reports would not be due for a couple of months and by then, if IOS had recovered its footing, it might even have been able to survive a disallowing of the 1969 gain.

In fact, the market did not turn around. Redemptions continued almost unabated, and sales were virtually nonexistent. The sales force, once the pride of the IOS organization, quit in droves. Confidence was not improved by the initial hesitancy of the auditors to sign the annual report on the ground that they needed more information about the Canadian Arctic transaction. The first quarter of 1970 produced an IOS operating loss of $5 million. Many members of the IOS board of directors felt that Cornfeld had to go. John King decided to succeed him.

This decision was a mixture of ambition and prudence. King was a man of considerable ego. His company had withstood the market decline respectably. He may well have felt that control of the world's largest mutual fund was a logical next step. In addition, there are reports that he was encouraged by IOS president Edward Cowett, who had lost faith in Cornfeld. In any case, IOS was a large shareholder and customer of King Resources, and the companies were entwined in a series of mutually supporting transactions. If IOS collapsed, it might well take King Resources with it.

To acquire sufficient IOS stock to back his bid for control, King took several extraordinary steps. He borrowed extensively from King Resources without obtaining the approval of his board of directors. He also borrowed on the basis of stock that he was not legally free to sell. By the time he arrived in Geneva in May, 1969, to make his bid for IOS, he had either to succeed or be ruined. Against this background, Donny McNamara was running King's Atlantic Division, consisting primarily of the proposed Portland harbor supertanker port and the disputed offshore exploration permits.

McNamara's problem was that both of the ventures had long natural lead times, compounded by a need for permits that various governments were showing no inclination to grant. Because the offshore exploration was hopelessly stymied by litigation pitting every state on the Eastern Seaboard against the federal government, his only prospect for an early income-producing property in Maine was his plan to hook the Long Island deep water onto the Portland-Montreal pipeline, thereby affording to Canada the supertanker transportation savings which the oil-import program denied to the United States. The pollution risk would remain in the United States. This arrangement was perfectly legal.

It was not, however, acceptable to the pipeline's ultimate owners, the Canadian divisions and New York headquarters of six large oil companies. Those of the owner companies primarily using oil from Venezuela, where shallow waters and the shorter run precluded supertankers, had no particular incentive to change. The whole operation was profitable enough for the other companies to have little incentive to push their partners. McNamara realized that he needed an agreement with just one of the six to force the others to go along. As he sought this wedge, his plan ran into more vocal and better financed environmental opposition than any that had developed over Machias Bay. Although even this opposition was not a serious menace, McNamara had to deal with it.

In a series of hearings throughout the summer and fall of 1969, he won the approval of the Portland planning board, the Portland city council, and the Portland board of harbor commissioners. He also successfully fended off a lawsuit and a petition seeking a referendum on the city council's rezoning decision. These were no mean feats, since he could give no real idea of what he was proposing other than suggestions of a supertanker pier and an increase in the Portland tax base.

Both King Resources and its Portland opponents received outside assistance from sources not disclosed at the time. First, the city of Portland was asked to withhold its rezoning pending federal study. The request came from Russell Train, a highly respected conservationist whom Nixon had appointed Under Secretary of the Interior Department to offset widespread conservationist distrust of Hickel. Portland ignored this request because of fear of delay, thus saving Train considerable trouble. After his statement the Under Secretary had been reprimanded by Peter Flanigan, who told him that King, who had been a reported contributor of $42,500 in 1968 and is said to have boasted of giving Nixon ten times more, was not to be harassed by suggestions of further study of his proposal.

The second paladin was also no stranger to Maine's oil problems. McNamara's primary environmental opposition had come from a group called Citizens Who Care, headed by Harold Hackett, a Bates College biology professor. Hackett's statements occasionally contained startling insights into oil-industry operations. Asked about them, he admitted that they came from "a man named Jack Evans."

Evans had become aroused by King Resources' frequent attacks on Occidental's project, an understandable reaction, since the venture's success meant several million dollars to him. Precluded by his agreement with Occidental from any direct involvement, he had made subterranean contact with Citizens Who Care and had fought a rear-guard action through Harold Hackett, whose biological training apparently inclined him toward symbiosis when the environment so dictated.

While McNamara was being embraced in Portland but held at arm's length by the major Canadian oil firms, Atlantic Richfield and Atlantic World Port were wrapping up their feasibility studies against two very different backgrounds.

Atlantic Richfield's attention was focused almost exclusively on Alaska. In September the strike on the North Slope had led to the largest oil-leasing auction in U.S. history. When the bidding was over, $900 million, enough to run Maine state government for four years or to give Alaska an income of more than $50 million a year, had been invested in North Slope leases. The largest bid had been $28,233 per acre for rights to 2560 acres.

Massive capital investments in pipelines and tankers as well as leases were made in the belief that the oil could begin to move to the West Coast during 1973. Simultaneously, Esso spent $40 million to send the 115,000-ton tanker *Manhattan* from New York to the Alaskan North Slope, fulfilling 80 percent of the centuries-old explorer's dream of a Northwest Passage rainbowed to the Pacific Ocean across the top of Canada.*

Although the *Manhattan* refused what must have been a tempting invitation to call at Machias Bay to emphasize the possibility of a Maine refinery running on U.S. crude oil, the voyage's apparent success inspired reminders that both King Resources and Atlantic Richfield might build in Maine regardless of import controls if their Arctic holdings panned out. Indeed, Atlantic Richfield's pitch to businessmen in the Pacific Northwest during this period was that if they hoped to refine Alaskan oil, they should support the import controls that would guarantee it a worthwhile market. Copies of these speeches were mailed to Maine as well.

Actually, the *Manhattan*'s success was illusory. Although the ship got there and back (with a black eye in the form of a hole which, had the vessel been full of oil, would have been a sizable spill), the voyage failed for three reasons. First, its $40-million cost was 33 percent above expectations and suggested that icebreaking tankers could not deliver oil to the U.S. mainland at rates competitive with most pipeline-tanker routes (perhaps even including a pipeline across Panama connecting Pacific to Atlantic tanker routes). Second, the tanker's experience did not solve the problem of building an Arctic supertanker port several miles offshore in water which was at times covered by the ice pack. Third, the voyage prompted an environmental awakening (it is always easier to have an environmental awakening when the traffic is going somewhere else) on the part of the Canadian government. Studies suggested that a massive spill in freezing waters would be long-lasting and impossible to clean up, and could even, by absorbing heat from

* Earlier Northwest Passages also began in Maine. The Maine novelist Kenneth Roberts opened *Northwest Passage*, his 1937 saga of the pre-Revolutionary struggles of Robert Rogers's Rangers in northern New England and southern Quebec, with words revived in the Maine press at the news of the *Manhattan* voyage: "The Northwest Passage, in the imagination of all free people, is a shortcut to fame, fortune and romance, a hidden route to Golcönda and the mystic East. . . . Who shall say [that those who seek it] are not happier in their own way than wiser, duller folk who sit at home, venturing nothing, deriding the seekers for that fabled thoroughfare —that panacea for all the afflictions of a humdrum world."

sunlight, melt sufficient ice to affect the level of the oceans. The aroused Canadians claimed jurisdiction over the Northwest Passage and threatened to prevent, limit, or tax its use. Esso waited a respectable time and declared the voyage a failure.

Even as the fate of the *Manhattan* was undermining one basis for a Maine refinery, two federal defenses of other public interests were further diminishing Atlantic Richfield's interest. First, the Interior Department held up the granting of permits for the Alaskan pipeline in order to study environmental objections. Atlantic Richfield, with millions of dollars frozen into North Slope development, could not consider a major East Coast expansion without assurance that it would have income from Alaska. Second, the Justice Department, disturbed by increasing concentration in the energy industries, filed a suit in the last hours of the Johnson administration ("One of the Democrats' going-away presents,"[6] an Arco official was to call it) seeking to enjoin Atlantic Richfield's merger with Sinclair. A preliminary injunction was issued, and the company had to agree to spin off to British Petroleum all Sinclair service stations, marketing outlets, and pipeline interests in sixteen Eastern states plus 200,000 barrels per day of refinery capacity. The arrangement saved the merger, but it reduced the company's need for new refinery capacity since its existing refineries could supply its remaining markets adequately.

Very little of this background was understood in Maine when, in January, 1970, Atlantic Richfield released its engineering-feasibility study for a Machias Bay supertanker terminal. The study confirmed the feasibility of such a terminal but pointed out two problem areas. First, Stone Island was essentially unprotected from the southwest. In the event of exceptionally high seas from that direction, offloading would have to be discontinued until the seas abated. As long as this precaution was taken, the $75-million breakwater that King Resources said made Machias Bay unfeasible would not be necessary. Second, fog too would occasionally force the closing of the port, particularly during the summer. These two reservations aside, the study concluded that Machiasport could become an excellent but not foolproof supertanker port for $30 million. Thus it was that two years after the site had been chosen, careful study confirmed the 1967 intuitions of Jack Evans, Ron Green, and Don Nicoll.

Unlike Atlantic Richfield, Atlantic World Port's study was not constrained by concern over company interests in Alaskan leases, Middle Eastern concessions, or existing East Coast markets. The company's only assets were several thousand dollars' worth of options on the Machiasport Peninsula coupled with the energy, imagination, and wealth of Bob Monks. On that basis, Monks's consultants at the Arthur D. Little Company were willing to say that Machias Bay was a good site for a terminal and a refinery, to estimate the types and costs of necessary pollution-control measures, and to analyze the costs of Iranian and Alaskan oil delivered to Machias Bay. The study concluded that a refinery on Machias Bay was economically feasible if it received an import allocation and that Machias Bay was as viable a supertanker port as any location in Maine. The study hedged on the breakwater, saying that if one was necessary it would cost $86 million and alter the viability of the entire project. This hedging was the product of some last-minute gymnastics occasioned by the Atlantic Richfield study. The Arthur D. Little Company had concluded that a breakwater was necessary before the Harris study said that it was not. Since the Little consultants had done no independent hydrographic work, they hastily qualified their conclusion.

Arthur D. Little was not asked for and did not volunteer any assessment of its client's chances of actually building a refinery. Such an assessment would have had to conclude that Monks didn't have one chance in twenty of pulling off the Atlantic World Port plan but that he had a fifty-fifty chance of assuring, either by design or by misstep, that no one else would be able to build a refinery either.

Since Maine public opinion would have no effect on the federal and industry forces opposed to any grant of import permits to market-rocking newcomers, Monks's hold on Maine audiences did little to increase Atlantic World Port's minuscule chances of success. On the other hand, public opinion would probably decide whether or not Maine would accept a refinery. For this reason, the highly visible and undeciphered Monks, controller of key land options, oilman with an environmental conscience, probing as much for a political opening as for an economic one, as prepared to impede as to promote a Machias Bay refinery, ticked like a bomb among sets of plans as volatile as the hydrocarbons they involved.

Already halfway to his decision to challenge Senator Smith in the Republican primary two years later, Monks had frequent speaking engagements up and down the coast in which he took environmental positions highly critical of past oil-industry performance. These beliefs were sincerely held, but their reception was becoming increasingly complicated by his political intentions.

Monks paid careful court to Maine business columnists and editorialists and was rewarded by frequent and generally favorable media attention. The coverage of the Atlantic World Port study was more than double that of Atlantic Richfield's release of its own report, something of a disproportion in view of the fact that Atlantic Richfield had had more than $2 billion in sales in 1969 while Atlantic World Port had had none.

The fuzziness was compounded by the continuing inability of several Maine reporters and much of their audience to keep the companies distinct in their own minds. Maine was one of the few states in which Atlantic Richfield did no business, and the company therefore had what pollsters call a low recognition factor. Because the titles of both companies began with the name of the pertinent ocean, many who should have known better believed that they were in some way affiliated.

With Atlantic World Port, Atlantic Richfield, King Resources, and Occidental all proclaiming their eagerness to break ground as soon as the imminent Cabinet Task Force report laid down the rules, the Maine legislature convened in special session in January, 1970, to consider the most advanced oil-pollution control and industrial-siting legislation in the United States. Given Maine's notorious bias against local zoning or state planning and given also the state's dubious efforts to control air and water pollution from the paper industry, the legislation's prospects appeared dim, but the appearance was misleading.

In terms of conventional development technique, Machiasport had been around too long. Developers' rules of thumb were those of any invader. Plan in secret. Identify and communicate with potential welcomers. Let them impugn opposition motives. Proclaim friendship and benefit. Move fast. Appear invincible. Avoid stalemates.

The imbroglio over oil-import controls had violated the last rule. Machiasport refiners had been stalemated for a year, and by 1970 their opponents had formed new alliances. Conservationists had had time to develop mailing lists and raise money. Lobstermen had at last understood not only that oil development would impair their fishing grounds but that neither patriotism nor progress demanded that they support it. Santa Barbara had aroused those whose incomes depended on tourism. The summer residents, many of them having been given the *Maine Times* for Christmas, had come and gone, unanimous in their articulate if sometimes counterproductive prophecies of pollution, political corruption, and urban industrial desolation. ("We live there. Believe us," they said. To which Governor Curtis replied, "It's wonderful to see all those people who made so much money polluting the hell out of everywhere else taking an interest in keeping Maine clean. Maybe now they'll do something about the sewage pipes that have made us close so many clam flats every summer.")

Even the White House had become interested in the Maine environment. Chappaquiddick had elevated Senator Muskie, and polls showed him running close to the President, in no small part because of his status as an environmental pathfinder. Presidential aides with nothing better to do prepared questions about oil and sugar beets for use by friendly reporters, and the White House decided, in Nixon speechwriter Patrick Buchanan's later phrase, "to turn the dogs loose on Ecology Ed." The most convenient canines were the newer and more militant environmentalists, who had little sympathy with the compromise legislation that Muskie could claim to have passed in the 1960s and who were infuriated both by the Vahlsing episode and by Muskie's support of a Maine oil refinery. At the suggestion of the Republican national committee, Maine Republicans undertook to provide ammunition.[7] During the 1970 state legislative session Republicans ordered a $75,000 investigation of the sugar-beet refinery. The Republican state committee subsequently passed a resolution stating that the Machiasport oil refinery was neither needed nor desired by the people of Washington County and calling on the state's political leadership to stop promoting it. This resolution made a nice book end to the unanimous participation of these same Republicans a year earlier in a legislative resolution urging the Secretary of Commerce to grant the Machiasport trade zone in order that the badly needed oil refinery might be built without further delay.

Although the investigation of Vahlsing found nothing, the legislative resolution and the *Congressional Record* inserts that it spawned sank in. In early 1970 a Nader study group on air pollution climaxed a devastating chapter (arrived at independently of White House handouts) on Muskie's role in the national air-pollution fiasco with a facile implication that the worst for Maine was yet to come in that the Senator had ardently supported plans to build "a huge petrochemical complex near the beautiful, unspoiled Machiasport Harbor."[8]

These several forces succeeded in raising serious doubts about oil development. The doubts were not dominant, but they offset Maine's traditional development-at-any-price bias. Between the extremes, a clear consensus could still favor oil development under the "strict controls" which the governor's Machiasport Conservation and Planning Committee had been preparing for eighteen months.

The conservation subcommittee had completed most of its work five months earlier, in October, 1969. By that time, Gardiner Means's prodigious initial gleanings had been sifted into standards to govern permissible refinery discharges, to regulate the transfer of oil between ship and shore, and to require the maintenance of adequate standby equipment to contain, clean up, or unload oil from a stricken tanker. The subcommittee recognized that the risk of a tanker disaster could never be eliminated and that spilled oil could not be completely contained or cleaned up. However, an oil spill was clearly like a house fire. Caught at its start, its potential for damage could be sharply reduced; allowed to spread unchecked for a short time, it would always cause loss. All major tanker spills had been made worse by slow reactions and bungled cleanup efforts. Trained personnel, adequate equipment, and early notification were the difference between minor spillage and the *Torrey Canyon* disaster, but the maintenance of such equipment against the remote contingency of a major accident would be expensive. The final issue faced by the subcommittee was how this preparedness was to be paid for.

There were only three alternatives worth serious consideration. First, the state could provide the equipment and the personnel. Second, the companies could be required to maintain equipment and personnel at their own expense. Third, the state could maintain the equipment and personnel with funds raised by a special levy against the transferring companies.

The first alternative would have charged Maine taxpayers with the costs of preventing and controlling spillage of oil that was largely destined for Montreal. The second invited rampant duplication and the loss of valuable time in the event of a spill for which no company would take immediate responsibility. The third alternative, a fund based on an assessment against companies transferring oil, put the costs where they belonged while leaving the control and use of the equipment in hands whose sole responsibility would be to keep oil out of the water.

Ultimately, the full Conservation and Planning Committee was to recommend the establishment of just such a fund, to be sustained by payments of one cent per barrel of oil transferred between ship and shore in Maine waters. Under such a fee, the proposed Occidental refinery would have paid $2.2 million per year, Atlantic Richfield $730,000, the Portland-Montreal pipeline $1.5 million.* The pipeline alone would have combined with existing Maine traffic to build a $10-million fund in six years. With Occidental, such a fund could have been built in the third year. The levy could have been cut off at $10 million and refilled by a prorata annual assessment. The cost would have been roughly $.00024 per gallon transferred, or roughly thirty-six cents per year to each Maine and Montreal heating-oil consumer.

The fund was not limited to maintaining a standby cleanup force and the payment of cleanup costs. It was to support research into the prevention and control of oil spills, with special emphasis on such Maine problems as oil in cold water and oil's impact on lobsters. It could also purchase insurance against damage above its ceiling. It could even reimburse individuals damaged by oil spills, the amount to be determined by arbitration in the event of dispute. After claims had been settled, the fund could sue the spilling company to recover the amount disbursed. This measure would relieve fishermen of the burdens and delays of proceeding individually against a major oil company. Instead, those who had lost income would recover quickly while the burden of lengthy litigation would fall on a fund fully capable of matching an oil company's expenditures for legal talent and expert witnesses. In the event that the fund was unable to identify the spilling company or failed for some other reason to recover its expenditure, its losses would in any case be replaced through the working of the transfer fee so that the costs even of a mystery spill would ultimately be borne by the oil industry and its customers rather than by shore-front property owners or by fishermen.

Upon releasing the report of his Conservation and Planning Committee in October, 1969, Governor Curtis singled the fund out for special attention, remarking that it would be "unique in state legislation today and will, if enacted, assure that the oil industry in Maine pays its own way." Because the oil industry shared his appraisal but not his enthusiasm, he realized that he would need allies in the Republican-controlled legislature.

During the 1969 legislative session, conservationists had mustered sufficient strength to persuade the legislature to appoint a special com-

* The refinery figure equals one cent times twice the refinery capacity (because the oil is shipped in and out). The pipeline's oil only goes one way.

mittee to study the environmental problems associated with "the coastal conveyance of petroleum." Like most state legislatures, Maine's was not staffed to confront many of the growing complexities of state government, oil-pollution control among them. The committee had funds enough for a few hearings and the hiring of a law student to do research. The legislators themselves had other jobs occupying most of their attention. The committee could not possibly have prepared adequate legislation for the 1970 session, but its product would probably be given a higher priority than anything coming out of the Democratic governor's office, particularly since the committee was chaired by the house majority leader, Harrison Richardson, one of the governor's sharpest Republican critics.

A University of Maine football star who had attended the University of California Law School and had practiced in Chicago before realizing that he preferred Maine, Richardson was a popular and liberal Republican with a record of proven environmental concern. He was conceded by Democrats to be a potentially formidable candidate for higher office if he could ever get a nomination from the dominant conservative wing of his party, with whom his ideas and his outspokenness kept him in constant disfavor. Oil-pollution control was a perfect issue for him. It was of immense and nonpartisan concern. It suited the personal outlook that had led him to tell a questioner asking what he would do if paper mills made good their threats to leave the state, "I'll wave goodbye from the Kittery Bridge." And some of the same conservatives who could see only money in the pea-green waters of Maine's paper-mill rivers weren't happy about the threat that oil posed to their control over Maine affairs.

Because competing bills would have invited the enactment of the weaker or the defeat of both, cooperation between the governor and the house majority leader was essential. Curtis offered Richardson the complete work product of the Conservation and Planning Committee. Richardson accepted and ultimately persuaded his committee to report out the recommendations intact. He used the last of his appropriation to put Frank Chapman, a leading Augusta lobbyist and attorney, to work on the side of the angels in drawing up the actual legislation. This was prudent. Not only did Chapman produce a solid bill, he was also able to sell it to some conservative legislators suspicious of Richardson and deaf to the young immigrants on the governor's staff whose hair sometimes obscured their collars.

The bill preserved the fund concept intact. It also gave the state a power to license all terminal operators and therefore to impose all of the specific safeguards recommended by the Conservation and Planning Committee. Because the state already had control over air and water discharges, it was in a position to precondition refinery licenses on compliance with the recommended air and water standards. In addition, Chapman came up with a variant of his own.

Chapman's concern was that states seeking to control oil spillage were often thwarted by the impossibility of obtaining jurisdiction over the vessel responsible for spills. As a practical matter, a ship pumping its bilges in the night would probably be beyond state jurisdiction in the morning. Any vessel escaping state jurisdiction after a spill automatically would move into the realms of international and admiralty law, in which state governments would have little standing and would have to rely on their national government. Further complications would arise from the balkanization of assets to which oil and tanker companies resorted both for tax purposes and so that no plaintiff could seize more than a fraction of their assets. Even that fraction was further hidden by the Limitation of Liability Act. That act, a relic of a pre-petroleum era of American concern for its infant merchant marine, permitted a shipowner to limit his liability to the value of the ship after the accident.

To Maine, with its international boundary, the *Torrey Canyon* accident was a constant reminder of the consequences of these several factors. The *Torrey Canyon* was American-built, Japanese-enlarged, registered in Liberia, owned out of a Bermuda filing cabinet by a company put together by a New York investment banking firm for a California oil corporation. Carrying British-controlled Kuwait crude oil and an Italian master and crew, she went aground in international waters, was bombed by British planes, and discharged oil onto British and French beaches, doing upwards of $10 million worth of damage. She had been insured by companies in the United States and Great Britain and was claimed for salvage by a Dutch corporation. The official Liberian investigation was conducted in Italy by a board consisting exclusively of Americans. The defendants in subsequent legal proceedings sought to limit their liability to the post-accident value of the vessel, one fifty-dollar lifeboat, but the British government was able to attach her sister ship (the *Lake Palourde*, not the *Sansinena*) in Singapore while the French did the same in Rotterdam. Ultimately, Union Oil paid $7.2 million to Britain and France.

Neither Richardson nor Governor Curtis felt that the U.S. government could be counted on to pursue a major oil company through such a thicket. The governor's solution had been to pay the damages from the fund, thereby laying the loss generally on the oil industry rather than on the state or its individual citizens. Frank Chapman went further.

He suggested that Maine terminal operators be made liable to the fund for damage from tankers bound to and from their terminals. Under this theory, the terminal to which the *Torrey Canyon* had been bound would have had to pay the damage to Great Britain regardless of the elusiveness of the sister ships and regardless of the Limitation of Liability Act, which applied only to the shipowners. Although the terminal owner would rarely have control over the tanker's behavior at sea, such a measure was less Draconian than it seemed. It had precedent in workmen's compensation legislation, which often imposed the costs of an industrial accident on an employer regardless of his fault simply because he could more easily insure himself against such accidents. The same logic justified making the terminal owners liable for oil spills, for they were more able than property owners and fishermen to protect themselves either through insurance or by a requirement that tankers using their facilities sign contracts indemnifying them against any costs arising from pollution damage. Such a contract, by giving one link in the industry chain a real interest in seeing spill costs paid, would put the full weight of private contract law, insurance-company resources, and such less formal measures as tanker black-listing on the side of the state instead of against it.

Responding to Governor Curtis's request for comments, Bob Monks called the proposed legislation "an excellent job." The rest of the oil industry was less enthusiastic. Andy Nixon and I, attending a conference on oil-spill control in New York City in mid-December, 1969, were asked to meet with representatives of the tanker and terminal divisions of half a dozen oil companies. For two hours, we were told repeatedly that the oil industry was fully prepared to be responsible for cleaning up its spillage, but not on our terms.

What the industry preferred was a program of self-regulation ("After all, nobody wants to spill oil"). They conceded that a state-managed cleanup and indemnification fund "might have some merit," but urged that such a fund be small and supervised by a board which included industry representatives. Parts of the law providing for unlimited liability and an irrebuttable presumption that a ship spilling oil had been negligent were "alien doctrine,"* and Maine should undertake further studies before seeking to impose sweeping revisions in an area of law that had traditionally been left to Congress or to international agreement. Terminal-operator liability was simply unthinkable and might result in all of the companies' refusing to do business in Maine.

Most of the issues raised at the New York meeting reflected disagreement as to who should bear the risk of a spill for which no company could be made to take financial responsibility. The industry representatives pointed with some pride to the recently concluded Tanker Owners Voluntary Agreement Concerning Liability for Oil Pollution (TOVALOP), in which the industry undertook to insure itself up to the lesser of $10 million or $100 per ton to pay to clean up oil spills. TOVALOP was a vast improvement over existing laws and agreements, but it did not cover damages to third parties such as a lobsterman whose pound was poisoned or a motel owner with a useless beach. Under existing law, the burden of such losses fell predominantly on the victim. The Maine legislation placed it on the spilling vessel, the terminal to which it was bound, or, if the first two were for any reason unreachable, on the industry as a whole.

Even without TOVALOP, the issue of state deference to federal action was a serious one, but not one that we could take seriously at the New York meeting. Oil pollution from vessels was obviously best dealt with at national and international levels, but both U.S. and international efforts had been feeble. Senator Muskie was pushing stronger legislation, but the oil and shipping industries had opposed it because, among other reasons, oil pollution was basically a local problem, best left to state governments. One of the industry representatives who urged Maine to await federal legislation had been among those asking Muskie to temper his federal efforts in order to protect state rights.

Throughout the meeting, one individual sat at the far end of the table glowering at both of us. Discussion of the fee and fund arrangement seemed particularly to upset him. Whenever the subject arose, he would shake his head in clear anger and snicker an unpleasantry to

---

* The law normally required that a party claiming to have been damaged by an oil spill prove that the spill had resulted from negligence. Since the damaged party rarely knew the precise cause of the spill, such proof was difficult. The effect of the Maine law was to say that since spillage without negligence was unlikely, negligence need not be proven as a precondition to a damage recovery.

those nearest him. Finally his indignation overwhelmed him, and he offered us insight into one oilman's image of state employees.

"Shit," he began. "You know damn well what this fund is all about. It's much bigger than it has to be so that the governor can get all his friends on the payroll. It won't matter what you pay them anyway. After a few months of everybody drinking coffee together at the terminals, they won't even be sure who they're working for." Although pressed, he wouldn't elaborate.

Rebuffed at every attempt to weaken the measure during the drafting stage, the oil industry retained one of the largest lobbying forces in Maine history to greet the legislature when it convened in ⸏pecial session* in January, 1970. Conscious that out-of-state lobbyists would inevitably be counterproductive (though Mobil did go as far away as Massachusetts), the oil companies instead relied on Maine lobbyists who usually represented paper companies. The poisonous state of Maine's major rivers was testament to their past environmental effectiveness.

King Resources retained no fewer than five representatives, including a Democratic former speaker of the Maine House of Representatives and a Republican state chairman. They were allied with representatives of other companies and of the Maine Petroleum Association, the Portland-Montreal Pipeline, the Bangor and Aroostook Railroad, and two paper companies. Even the cities of Portland and Bangor were against the bills—Portland because it wanted King Resources, Bangor because it feared that an increase in the price of jet fuel at its growing airport would cause international flights to refuel elsewhere. Some large oil companies were not represented by name, but they were watching and paying.

Opposing this lobbying force were the governor's office plus Harry Richardson and his subcommittee. They were joined by a loose coalition of some thirty-five liberal and fishing-community legislators and by the first two environmental lobbyists in Maine history.

The lobbyists were hired by the Coastal Resources Action Committee (CRAC) which had been organized by Horace "Hoddy" Hildreth, the son of a former Maine governor and U.S. ambassador to Pakistan. The

* The Maine legislature, in one of its several continuing tributes to an era when people expected less of their governments, meets in regular session only in odd-numbered years. In even-numbered years it holds a regular special session.

Hildreth family was very much a part of Maine's establishment. Hoddy had been a lobbyist for the International Paper Company and had served two terms in the state senate. In 1968 he had won the Republican nomination to oppose Peter Kyros for Maine's First District Congressional seat. In the campaign's closing days he had charged that Democrats had made a political football out of the badly needed Machiasport oil refinery and had conjectured that as a Republican he would be better able than Kyros to pressure the front-running Nixon to cough up the refinery.

Defeated by a substantial margin, he became a private attorney, free to express his essentially anti-oil instincts. Because lobbying could not be tax-exempt, he and several like-minded Maine people and summer residents endowed CRAC separately from Maine's deductible natural-resource organizations. CRAC's first act was to retain Hildreth to lobby Republican legislators for conservation; its second was to hire Harold Pachios to lobby Democrats.

Pachios's Democratic credentials were impeccable. He had worked for Senator Muskie in the early 1960s and had moved on to the Johnson White House staff, where he eventually became a deputy press secretary under Bill Moyers. With his services in that capacity no longer in demand after the Nixon inauguration, he returned to Maine to practice law early in 1969 and had no trouble resuming old Democratic friendships.

His credentials as an environmental lobbyist were less apparent. When Muskie's administrative assistant learned of the assignment he chortled, "Jesus Christ! The only time Hal Pachios ever went outdoors in Washington was to call a taxi." But, as Pachios was to demonstrate, a natural lobbyist can learn conservation principles much more effectively than a natural conservationist can learn to lobby. This may be because conservation is based on learnable scientific principles, but politics is, in Norman Mailer's words, "not an art of principles but of timing . . . which makes the moves of athletes look heavy."[9] Good lobbyists are born with timing. They can learn the principles.

The returning legislators were greeted by a letter from Governor Curtis cautioning them that "oil industry decisions are being made by and about the State of Maine which will affect our future as profoundly as similar pulp, paper, and power company decisions have affected our past and present," and concluded that failure to pass the two bills would be to say "to all future industry and to our own citizens that we do not care very much about the surroundings in which we will hereafter have to live." Richardson abandoned a plan to summon the mayor of Santa Barbara to Augusta on two days' notice, but he did provide sufficient pictorial proof of the ineffectiveness of oil-spill-control techniques to startle legislators of the "this-is-the-nation-that-put-a-man-on-the-moon" persuasion.

The legislative hearings on the bills produced massive and spontaneous citizen support, including an exceptional turnout by the normally undemonstrative people of Washington County. The only opposition came from the fourteen lobbyists. Even *The New York Times* took notice, urging the bills onward with an editorial suggesting that Maine live up to its state motto, "Dirigo" (I lead). *The Times, Newsweek,* and *Time* all sent reporters who were astonished by the casual contact between lobbyists and legislators and began to search eagerly for potential scandal. The search was unavailing but did prompt several defenses of "our fine lobbyists" by veteran legislators. *Newsweek*'s Chuck Roberts was particularly surprised to learn that lobbyists for the Portland pipeline and King Resources had been permitted to present their own draft bills at an executive session of the legislature's Natural Resources Committee. These drafts, while much weaker than the legislation itself, would still have given Maine the most stringent oil controls in the country.

Roberts also mentioned that he had heard stories of "booze and broads" available at Augusta motels for negative voters. If there was any truth to them, eighty-three-year-old Harry Williams passed some of the wildest nights of his life during the special session, for his was to be the only vote cast against the oil-handling bill. The senate passed the measure on a voice vote. The total in the house was 134–1. Williams, a former chairman of the legislature's Natural Resources Committee, explained that he voted against the half-cent-per-barrel tax and the $4-million fund* because he didn't want to raise the price of heating oil.

The overwhelming final margin was both anticlimactic and misleading. Several legislators willing to vote against the measure chose not to do so when its passage became certain, and some forty members of the

---

* The tax had been reduced from a penny per barrel and the fund from $10 million after Frank Chapman had devised his provision making terminal operators liable for spills from tankers bound for their facilities. Because this measure almost eliminated the possibility of the fund's being bankrupted by unrecoverable costs, the state seemed to have less need for the full $10 million. Furthermore, the lower fee meant that Maine customers would pay less to the fund before the new refineries came along to help fill it up.

house missed the vote. Nevertheless, the result clearly showed an environmentally backward state turning sharply on some of the very men who had kept it that way. The environmental clout of existing industry was not transferable to a potential newcomer who had not yet made hostages of employees or municipal tax bases.

As the actual vote approached, the lobbyists were reduced to lobbying each other and to exchanging derogatory references to "Richardson's Supreme Court," their term for the three attorneys and two laymen on whom Richardson relied in resisting compromise and rejecting allegations of unconstitutionality. Gerald Amero, a lobbyist for the Portland-Montreal pipeline, denounced the 134–1 rout as "a clear case of hysteria taking over," a view which *Newsweek* noted did not differ far from Richardson's own: "As long as we had the word antipollution on my bill, I think we could have printed it on toilet paper and got it passed."[10]

The law giving Maine a veto power over large industrial and commercial developments passed almost as easily. Again seeing the need for bipartisanship, Governor Curtis had entrusted it to the sponsorship of Republican Representative Paris Snow, elected from the Aroostook County town of Caribou, who saw the bill as necessary "to protect the people from their own overeagerness."[11] Its only difficult moment came when conservationists concerned about municipal opposition proposed an exemption for any town with a zoning ordinance. Snow rejected the suggestion, for he saw it as an invitation to hasty local zoning, and he and Richardson were more confident than the conservationists that they had the votes. The bill eventually passed by a 2–1 margin, and Maine, in its 150th year, became the first state with the power to reject an environmentally unsatisfactory development.

The law's only blemish was an exemption for power-company transmission lines which had been attached at the last minute by Senator Richard Berry, chairman of the Natural Resources Committee. In private life Senator Berry was the owner of the growing Rangely Power Company, and his solicitude for transmission lines was the lesser of two capers during the special session. The greater, a bill which would have imposed a thirteen-month moratorium on petroleum refineries, became a textbook demonstration of the manipulability of environmentalism.

Although most conservationists had supported the other two bills, only the moratorium would have stopped oil development in its tracks. The oil-handling and siting laws provided for detailed case-by-case scrutiny and rigorous enforcement, but they also forced those opposing oil to take on would-be refiners one at a time. Rather than face years of recurring alarms in the night, conservationists preferred a law that shut the door absolutely. Lawyers among them saw some constitutional problems in making oil refining as much a criminal activity as prostitution or robbery, but others felt that the protection of Maine's coast justified so drastic a prohibition.

Senator Berry wasn't concerned with constitutional arguments in the moratorium he eventually put together. As a legislator, he was continuing faithfully to represent the strong environmentalism of his wealthy Cape Elizabeth district except insofar as it might inconvenience the electric-power industry. Furthermore, attacks on oil distracted from existing environmental abuses in Maine and helped to perpetuate the existing economic leaders. He knew that Governor Curtis opposed any moratorium as superfluous in light of the other two bills and any permanent ban as economically unwise.

Berry devised a moratorium on refineries and aluminum smelters, but not on terminals or power plants. The bill would have been no obstacle to King Resources or Central Maine Power but would have halted Occidental. It was congenial to Berry's beliefs, his business, and his politics.

Conservation groups backed it fervently, and its presence may have served a function that some legislators called "ridge running"—that is, it presented a ripe target on the skyline and drew fire from some favoring oil while making them more willing to compromise in favor of the other two bills. Once those bills had passed, this middle group committed to strictly controlled development fell away from the moratorium.

At that point, Senator Berry was advised by an assistant attorney general that the moratorium would be unconstitutional unless it included both the large terminals of the King Resources variety and major power plants. Berry replied that such a change would offend King Resources and "step on too many toes." The following day at a news conference, he attacked the governor, who, he said, was opposing the moratorium out of a desire to help King Resources. Later in the day he told a governor's aide, whom he apparently mistook for an assistant attorney general, that his real interest in the moratorium was to get it on the governor's desk and force a veto, which conservationists presumably would not forgive in the gubernatorial election nine months later.

Unaware of their champion's other motives, conservationists pressed for a moratorium in some form. The bill passed the senate, but during the house debate Richardson questioned both its purpose and its constitutionality. He bolstered his argument by noting that the chairman of the Environmental Improvement Commission, one of the state's most respected environmental voices, felt that his commission no longer needed the moratorium to protect the coast. A Portland representative who had supported both the siting and oil-handling laws noted that the state had had an unofficial moratorium on development for fifty years and that he opposed making a law out of it. The bill was defeated 86–51 on its first reading.

Senator Berry rushed from the gallery to the attorney general's office in order to quell the constitutional doubt raised by Richardson. Attorney General James Erwin, the certain Republican nominee to face Curtis in November, obliged with an instant twelve-line opinion that the bill was constitutional. He made no analysis and simply ignored his assistant's recent opinion to the contrary. Berry raced his new weapon back to the house, where it was read into the record before the final vote. The bill then received seven fewer votes than before.

Despite a final plea from King Resources that he veto the other two bills, Curtis signed them at a tripartisan ceremony involving Richardson (his former political enemy), Robert Fuller (an assistant and subsequently a campaign manager to Attorney General Erwin and Paris Snow.) *The New York Times, Time,* and *Newsweek* all took approving note.

I found myself less than exultant. Eighteen months of work on legislation had been vindicated; the Cabinet Task Force report was known to be favorable; several companies seemed ready to build. Maine at last had procedures for controlling development—procedures that Maine citizens could trust to yield results no worse than those they would have consciously chosen. The governor's guiding principle of carefully controlled economic growth had been strongly affirmed against attacks from both sides. We had our mandate, and a refinery seemed certain.

Still, firm mandates take on lives of their own, obsessing those who have worked hardest for them. The Tonkin Gulf resolution came to mind as daily headlines announced the flaming eruption of a Standard of California oil well in the Gulf of Mexico and smaller but sizable tanker spills in Florida, Massachusetts, and Nova Scotia. I wondered then whether the two laws would remain sources of pride or whether I would one day regard their consequences with the remorse of Senator Fulbright or the zest of Walt Whitman Rostow.

On the day that the oil-handling law took effect, its enforcement was enjoined pending the outcome of two suits filed by ten major oil companies and the Portland-Montreal pipeline. These suits alleged that the law violated a dozen provisions of the Maine and United States constitutions. The *Maine Times*, feeling that such formidable resources (annual revenues nearly a hundred times those of Maine) were likely to prevail, urged the state to prohibit all oil refineries until the suit had been finally decided.

The litigation lasted three years and took on added luster by involving several then unknown Watergate luminaries. This process commenced when Governor Curtis and Attorney General Erwin agreed to seek outside counsel to help Erwin's undermanned staff defend the law. Assistant Attorney General Stephen Murray and I were assigned to go for help. We eventually agreed upon a list of five names for final consideration. One of these was a public-interest lawyer who often worked on litigation for Ralph Nader. Three years later he was to become known for playing Milk Fund tapes at cocktail parties, but at the time he was just Bill Dobrovir, in practice by himself, and he agreed that he didn't have the office backup to take on a case of this size.

A second possibility was the Boston law firm of Hale and Doerr, where we had been told to seek out a first-rate litigator named James St. Clair. We never got that far, for one of St. Clair's partners sometimes represented one of the plaintiff oil companies and the firm felt that it would be a conflict of interest for it to defend the Maine law.

Among the remaining three, we decided on Roberts Owen, a partner in the Washington law firm of Covington and Burling. The decision was made after a day spent watching Owen presenting an environmental case under rugged circumstances. He was urging a U.S. District Court judge to enjoin the efforts of the Department of Transportation to construct another bridge into the District of Columbia. Owen's problem was with the judge, who seemed singularly unsympathetic to environmental issues. He eventually ruled against Owen and was reversed on appeal. Several years have passed since then, and I realize now that the judge was not necessarily hostile to the environment. It's just that he was a traditionalist who rarely ruled against the government, who was in fact so notoriously proprosecutor that in those days, before he became *Time*'s Man of the Year, he was known to Washington's criminal bar as "Maximum John" Sirica.

Shortly after the enactment of the Maine law, an Esso tanker went aground in Florida's Tampa Bay and put 10,000 gallons of heavy industrial oil on the beaches around St. Petersburg. Like many oil spills, this one was as pleasing to conservationists as it was dismaying to oilmen. The fouled beaches were in the district of Congressman William Cramer, who was at that moment championing the industry-administration oil-pollution legislation in the House-Senate conference against the tougher Muskie bill. Infuriated by the ineffectiveness of the cleanup efforts, Cramer broke a two-year deadlock by switching his support to the Muskie version, which then became law.

The Tampa Bay spill activated some odd enzymes in the local political environment. Cramer's own behavior was in part dictated by the race the White House had urged him to make for the U.S. Senate, but his belated awakening did him no good. A miscalculation in the Justice Department removed G. Harrold Carswell from the Court of Appeals without giving him anything else to do, so he ran against Cramer in the G.O.P. primary. He lost, but he so weakened his foe that Democrat Lawton Chiles defeated him easily.

The Tampa Bay spill may also have found its way into the gills of Florida's lieutenant governor, for he, two aides, and two photographers rocketed into Augusta a few days later in a small jet searching for that tough law they'd just heard about. He chatted for twenty minutes with Governor Curtis and Andy Nixon and then flew on to Portland to talk with Harry Richardson before heading down home.

Florida passed an approximate copy of the law, and right away a third state official started acting strangely. This time it was the attorney general, who decided to defend his new law all the way to the Supreme Court by himself.* Doubtlessly just as happy not to have Covington and Burling to worry about in the other suit, the Maine plaintiffs slowed the proceedings to await the results in Florida. They won the first round as the District Court ruled that the law sought to extend state power into the admiralty jurisdiction reserved to the federal government by the Constitution.

---

* This is apparently a popular way to handle big cases in Florida. Its pitfalls are told in Anthony Lewis's *Gideon's Trumpet*, the story of the case of *Gideon* v. *Wainwright*, in which a court-appointed lawyer named Abe Fortas bested Florida's overmatched attorney general and persuaded the Supreme Court that defendants in all criminal cases have a constitutional right to an attorney.

Florida appealed, and while that case (known as *Askew* v. *American Waterways Operators, Inc.*) was pending before the Supreme Court, the Maine case was finally argued before the Maine Supreme Court. The argument took place two years after the suit had first been filed, and Maine attorneys had, making full allowance for the difficulties of a ten-plaintiff case on a difficult set of issues, become impatient with the pace being set by the oil companies. Nevertheless, it was they who had to request one final extension, for Bob Owen's wife was expecting a baby on the day of argument. The request was denied by the oil companies. One of their attorneys, Fred Scribner, was also general counsel to the Republican National Committee, and he too had a problem with a medical dimension.

The nomination of Richard Kleindienst to be Attorney General had come before the Senate two months earlier, and with it had come the fertile humus now known as the ITT case. Kleindienst had been confirmed, and the ITT lobbyist Dita Beard had gone to ground in a Denver hospital, gruesomely pursued by most of the Senate Judiciary Committee and by a strange-voiced White House consultant often named Howard Hunt, whose lopsided red wig must have shown, if only he had looked closely into a mirror, that his misgivings over Yalta, the Rosenbergs, the fall of Chiang, and the rise of Fidel were somehow playing him false.

One legacy of the ITT furor was the Republican decision to move their convention from San Diego to Miami. The decision meant endless June headaches for the general counsel to the Republican National Committee, for it was not clear that President Nixon could be validly renominated except at the originally chosen convention site. Faced with so busy a June, Scribner did not want to delay the May argument further. When the Attorney General's office explained Bob Owen's problem, he replied jovially, "Tell him that modern medicine will take care of everything."

As it turned out, modern medicine did indeed take care of everything. The birth went smoothly, and doctors were found to certify that Ms. Beard's heart had been seized by something so much stronger than remorse that she could testify no more. The argument was held as scheduled, and within a year the U.S. Supreme Court overruled the District Court, thereby sustaining the Florida law and vindicating the Attorney General. The Maine Supreme Court then upheld the Maine law, and the U.S. Supreme Court refused to upset that decision. The Canadian government used the Maine law as a model for a similar cleanup fund of its own, and an international treaty embodying the same principles of private citizen protection had been ratified or acceded to by seven nations by October, 1974.

The crucial decision had been the U.S. Supreme Court's holding in the Florida case. Writing for a unanimous court, Justice William Douglas said that

> To rule as the District Court has done is to allow federal admiralty jurisdiction to swallow most of the police power of the states over oil spillage—an insidious form of pollution of vast concern to every coastal city or port and to all the estuaries on which the life of the ocean and the lives of the coastal people are greatly dependent.[12]

Justice Douglas spun much of his reasoning around Section 1161 (0) of Senator Muskie's federal oil-pollution law. That section gave to states a power to set standards stricter than the federal law if they so desired. It had been drafted by Muskie aide Eliot Cutler and inserted by the Senator with the Maine law and the U.S. Supreme Court in mind. Seeing it as the centerpiece in Douglas's opinion must have given Cutler something of a boost among his classmates at the Georgetown Law School, where he was in his first year when the decision came down.

The eventual vindication of the Maine law meant that the state could use the fund to pay the Covington and Burling legal fees. Since the fund came from the tax on the oil companies, the cost of their delays was ultimately billed back to them, a small amount by their standards, but large enough to give Bob and Kathy Owen some pleasure in the knowledge that it was not covered by Blue Cross.

10: Spring and Summer, 1970

In *Civilization and Its Discontents,* Sigmund Freud identified a tragic paradox in human history: that material progress requires the repression of the instinctual life . . . people become more disciplined . . . the simpler joys of "acting out," of immediate gratification and violent expression are lost—and so are the simpler evils of infant mortality, hunger, disease, shortened life span and the like. . . . Economic progress will require that [low-income people] surrender some of the pleasures as well as all of the horrors, of being poor.

Michael Harrington, Toward a Democratic Left

The blacks are for it. The reason the developers don't want the plant is that they are afraid of losing their cheap help. . . . I'm tired of fish. Give me some meat. . . . If BASF pollutes the sea, I'll buy my oysters from Maine.

Reactions of low-income South Carolinians[1] to a
proposed petrochemical plant adjacent to the
resort and fishing communities at Hilton Head
and Port Royal Sound

As A RIVER, beginning at some hillside spring or bog of lake, flows seaward, each merging freshet deepens or widens or speeds it. At first, any tributary makes a visible difference as the main waterway takes on new volumes and importances, but eventually only streams of consequence in their own right or those containing special effluents can cause meaningful change. Finally, before the main river becomes part of another or of the sea, only the largest of tributaries can produce the slightest of deflections. Tributaries that would have mattered earlier mean little near the end. This story is at that point now, for although some submerged currents are going to surface with surprising virulence, little of new importance will be added. Now, early 1970, is the last good moment to inventory the aquatic life, for during the forthcoming combats in Maine's littoral zone, both double counting and oversight would be likely in the mud, and, as Cyril Connolly put it, any large river "is always splitting up into arms that re-unite. Islanded between the arms, the inhabitants argue for a lifetime as to which is the main river."[2]

In mid-February, 1970, the international developments of greatest significance to Maine's oil dilemma were the Libyan coup and the imminent collapse of Investors Overseas Services. The Libyans were about to embark on their first test of strength with their oil-company tenants. The very oil which Occidental had proposed to bring to Maine in supertankers was to alter patterns of world oil commerce even more profoundly by being held in the Libyan ground.

IOS was doomed, and with it King Resources. Long Island dangled like the potential centerpiece of a winning canasta hand. Its pairings were not to materialize, and, at the game's end, it was useful only to reduce the size of the loss.

In Washington, the Cabinet Task Force had made its decisions and President Nixon had made his. His oil blockade would continue until his nation could no longer supply itself. Only then would he negotiate, and the truce on import restraints would have to include the Alaskan pipeline, new oil refineries and supertanker ports, higher prices, lower environmental standards, and oil exploration off the New England coast.

Maine, its environmental laws at last in place, was a host with table set but no guests. Occidental kept its options at Perry, but the refinery idea was like an athlete past his prime. It could no longer carry the company (whose stock had fallen from fifty dollars on the day of the announcement of the company's interest in Machiasport to twenty-five dollars in early 1970 and would go below ten dollars later), and it was trade bait.

Atlantic Richfield was mired in Alaska, where its capital investment was not producing the cash flow to support an East Coast marketing surge. The Justice Department had undercut the Sinclair merger, the *Manhattan* had flopped, and Nixon was clinging to rigid oil-import controls. As long as the verdict on the *Manhattan* was uncertain, the Trans-Alaska Pipeline had seemed antithetic to Atlantic Richfield's building in Maine, but after the tanker had failed, the company's expansion anywhere depended on approval of the pipeline. Until that happened, Atlantic Richfield was in a holding pattern over Maine.

Shaheen had finally put everything together in Newfoundland. With the $10 million that he had been able to raise and with his extraordinary Canadian concessions, he was able to attract the $178 million he needed to build his 100,000-barrel-per-day refinery. But his staff still had some payless paydays ahead, and creditors kept haling him into court. A money shortage was to compel him to mothball a plan to help his friend the President by starting a conservative New York afternoon newspaper to undercut the liberal *Post*, and a shortage of something forced him to back away from a shadowy Boston-area refinery proposal, leaving a puzzled but eager Saugus town manager peering into the vapors and telling the press, "They're a rather large corporation, and I'm sure they know what they're doing."[3]

As its more substantial competitors went backstage, Atlantic World Port made more than enough noise to cover their retreat. Through sheer availability, Monks had maintained the most visible presence of any oil developer except Donny McNamara. The fact that he was unheard of in the oil industry did not prevent Maine from treating him as a major in his own right.

In late 1969 he had concluded that his road to the U.S. Senate lay over Margaret Chase Smith rather than Ted Kennedy, and he had consequently transferred his legal residence to the Sprague family compound in Cape Elizabeth. One of his first acts upon assuming Maine citizenship was to set up a dummy florist association to send a handsome and well-publicized bouquet of roses to Senator Smith on her seventy-third birthday. His polls had shown him that her support had dropped off among people who realized that she would pass eighty during her next term.

Because Monks saw Atlantic World Port as much in political as in industrial terms, Nixon's continued oil blockade did not paralyze him as it did his competitors. Indeed, it was a godsend, for it preserved an equilibrium in which he needed neither to put up nor shut up. He could remain indefinitely the would-be developer with a heart, the man who put the regional economy above his own and the environment above all. His position was that if a clean refinery could not be built, he would use his land control to see that no refinery was built. If a clean refinery could be built, he would build it. Had Atlantic Richfield or Occidental been in a position to break ground, Maine would have exercised its options on his options, and his position would have collapsed. As long as events elsewhere stymied the real companies, he had the stage to himself, and the stage was expanding.

The dual furor over Machiasport and Maine's environmental legislation had rekindled the interest of the national media in the easternmost county. *Newsweek*, *Time*, and *The New York Times* were followed by *Business Week*, the St. Louis *Post-Dispatch*, the Washington *Post*, and

The Wall Street Journal. Machiasport Selectman Hammond Flynn, lobsterman Millard Urqhart, and journalist Marc Nault were repeatedly reported to favor a clean refinery and the jobs it would bring. Monks was given equal billing with Occidental and Atlantic Richfield. Finally, NBC-TV, preparing its first environmental special to coincide with the nation's first Earth Day, took notice.

Needing twenty minutes on the oil debate in Maine, NBC was able to persuade the Downeast Improvement Association and the town of Machiasport to put on a special meeting to debate the issue. The meeting again demonstrated the power of a television camera to inspire events that would not otherwise have happened. The Sierra Club, the Downeast Improvement Association, and the Maine Lobstermen's Association leafleted Washington County with a message urging people to come and make their views known on nationwide TV. Several hundred responded. Neighbor disputed neighbor, and NBC got footage for its first environmental hour, a juxtapositioning of Machiasport against Gary, Indiana, and a jetport in the Everglades.

Bob Monks was the only refiner to appear at the Machias show, although Atlantic Richfield's Lou Ream was interviewed in New York. Monks announced that he would sponsor a Machias Bay area referendum on oil development.* If the vote favored oil, he would proceed as a developer. If oil were defeated, he would deny his land to any company. Economically, the ploy was risky, but politically, in the short run at least, it was both brilliant and foolproof. As Monks himself put it later, "It [the outcome] really didn't matter to me." Whatever the result, he could hardly be criticized for letting people determine their own destinies. Nevertheless, one suspicious questioner asked whether there was any truth to the rumor that he was planning to campaign against Mrs. Smith in the primary then fifteen months away. Monks replied, "I never make any plans more than six months in advance, and as far as I know, Mrs. Smith is planning to keep her seat until 1972."[4]

---

* Before the passage of the site-approval law, the Natural Resources Council had proposed legislation subjecting any heavy industrial development to local referendum approval. A more well-meaning expression of the Maine conservationist death wish would be hard to find. Referenda are political contests. They can be bought and/or propagandized, as was a 1973 Maine referendum in which a public power authority was defeated by a 3–2 margin after having been favored 3–2 in midsummer polls. The dramatic turnaround was largely attributable to a skillful and expensive television and newspaper campaign waged by a power company–financed committee. Maine's major power companies had aggregate 1969 sales of less than $125 million; Occidental's were $1.7 billion; the Natural Resources Council was perennially broke.

The Atlantic World Port referendum was politically unique, something out of Mark Twain rather than Theodore White. Monks, who could campaign, didn't care; Occidental, Atlantic Richfield, and Governor Curtis, all of whom cared very much, couldn't campaign. Each took the position that the outcome would be advisory to Monks alone, without legal weight, and that they would not be bound by it, but each knew that the establishment of one oil refinery in an area that had just voted against another would probably be impossible.

Monks conducted a gloriously evenhanded campaign. He freely conceded the possibility of spillage and the damage that might occur. At one point he even suggested that lobstermen put out of work by the refinery could always find jobs cleaning up the inevitable oil spills. To allay fears based on unfamiliarity, he flew a group of eight Machias-area residents to the Virgin Islands to view the Hess refinery which had been made possible by import permits that Stewart Udall had conditioned on environmental performance. Making an unusual mistake for an aspiring politician, Monks neglected to "advance" the trip. Armed guards turned his group away at the refinery gates, and they were forced to assess the environmental impact from a hilltop half a mile away. Monks's explanation that Hess didn't want him competing for quotas or markets is more believable than Hess's own assertion that he was protecting "highly sophisticated, unpatentable" pollution-control equipment.[5] The quota system, like the Maine environment, had no more vehement defenders than those who had just gotten their piece of it. Despite this setback, most of the travelers were favorably impressed. A *Maine Times* reporter went so far as to concede that Atlantic World Port seemed to be "the best of a bad thing."

Against so apparently diffident a proponent, the refinery opponents were able to take the offensive. They almost destroyed themselves at the outset in a frantic meeting at the Reverend Dorchester's house, during which one overwrought Downeast Improvement Association member announced himself ready to lay down his life under a bulldozer blade, to sabotage refinery construction, and to put torpedo tubes in lobster boats. This zealot gave way to John Garber, a Columbia University professor, who asserted that, much as he loved Washington County for its *"Lebensraum"* and sorry as he was that he couldn't afford to give up his tenure to come up and help out full time, he thought he could arrange for two busloads of Columbia students to come for the referendum campaign. This suggestion was supported by

a young woman* who had recently liberated herself from her husband
and then from the embryonic women's movement to form *"Environment!"*, then even from New York to carry *"Environment!"* with her
throughout a three-month sojourn in Washington County. Neither she
nor Garber understood Washington County well enough to see that if
two busloads of Columbia students had worked in Machiasport to reelect President Nixon, they might have driven the county to vote for
Shirley Chisholm. Fortunately, this suggestion also fell well short of
consensus, and the campaign was waged more conventionally.

The Natural Resources Council commissioned a brochure refuting
the more exuberant prorefinery claims and concluding that what was
left wasn't worth the risk. A group from the Machias Bay area visited
the site of Nova Scotia's February spill and reported a scene of wild-
life devastation compounded by oil clinging stubbornly to the rocks,
shoreline, and boat hulls.†

Local harbormasters and lobstermen measured the exposed Stone
Island terminal site by the standards of their small vessels and concluded that it was "an open roadstead" at which pitching tankers would
inevitably lose oil through broken hoses. Refinery supporters replied
that no one would try to offload a supertanker in bad weather, but the
real question was whether weather bad enough to trouble the stability
of a 300,000-ton ship was frequent enough to create strong demurrage
pressures against the normal practice of riding storms out at sea. These
pressures had driven the captain of the *Torrey Canyon* to attempt his

---

* Here granted anonymity, wherever she is, in return for what I assume was the
complimentary intent of her admonition that I should "get out of Maine. Go back to
work for Nader. Quit fronting for the oil industry. People believe you who would
never believe them." It's a perspective she unknowingly shared with a lobbyist for
one of Maine's less savory oil suitors, who put it, "Why don't you just go back to
Nader and quit trying to fool people that you're anything but a goddamn preservationist?"

† The devastation may have been exaggerated. A subsequent Canadian government
report noted that "the bottom life was unaffected by the spill. Consequently the lobster
season opened on schedule and the catch has been normal. The herring catch has
been above normal." Clamming was closed down for a time and some 7000 birds and
a few seals were killed. Nevertheless, the lasting effect of the spill on the bay was
found "not significant." Cleanup costs were another matter—the study estimated them
to have been $3.1 million.

The report concluded, in refreshingly blunt language, that while oil spillage could
in large part be prevented, oil spills could no more be eliminated than "spills in one's
own kitchen. But if spills in a kitchen were as frequent as spills in the oil industry,
our homes would be pigsties."

last shortcut, and many in Maine felt that a prolonged storm or fog bank would make even the best-intentioned company take risks.

The refinery won, 1391 to 1159. Thirty-nine percent of the electorate voted, a respectable referendum turnout. The margin of victory would have been much greater if the women in the lobstering communities of Jonesport and Beals Island, knowing that their husbands would be at sea, had not harangued Monks into permitting liberal absentee eligibility rules. The absentee vote rolled in 357–68 against Atlantic World Port, and the vote from the two lobstering towns was even more lopsided. Beals Island's final 179–1 total must have elicited whistles of admiration in the sepulchral pounds where Boss Tweed once stored disembodied voters until the price was right.

Some unintended nonelectoral mischief was done. Irked by the clamor of the opponents, refinery proponents formed a group called People for Progress, which printed up bumper stickers to counter those of the Downeast Improvement Association. Intercommunity animosities developed, and old ones were revived. Monks found himself involved in arguments about school districts and an unbuilt Beals Island–Jonesport bridge that had been causing trouble for fifteen years.

He survived, though, and was acclaimed the winner. With added luster and credibility, he moved on to new interviews and speaking engagements, very much the man to see about oil in the Machias Bay area. His hand strengthened by the vote, he requested that Maine decide whether or not it wanted his options. With no refiners definitely available, the state let its claim lapse. Thus in July, 1970, Monks finally gained sole control of the land with which he had outbluffed Armand Hammer for two years.

The best assessment of the referendum was Monks's own: "I don't consider that the results of this election had a winner or a loser." Like many election winners before him, Monks couldn't fulfill the expectations he had created. The losers didn't lose; the winners didn't win. The best evidence that neither side forgave him is that Senator Smith took all eleven towns by a cumulative margin of more than 2–1 in her primary election victory over him fourteen months later.

Donny McNamara, who really wanted to build something, wasn't fooling around with referendums. Muskie's oil-pollution law and Maine's new siting and oil-handling laws each imposed new license requirements on top of the fistful of Portland permits that he had already acquired.

Making the best of his new burdens, McNamara acknowledged that the laws were "probably something our industry deserved."[6] He spoke of plans to seek a grant from the oil-pollution fund to enable King Resources to install a truly modern pollution-detection system in Casco Bay. The system consisted of two pollution-monitoring buoys capable of analyzing and describing any pollution that they encountered. The buoys were to have been based on

> an integrated and miniaturized chemical instrumental-analysis detector which combines micro gas-liquid chromatography, pyrochromatography, and mass spectroscopy . . . to be based upon existing technology developed by the National Aeronautics and Space Administration for its forthcoming "Viking" Project (sampling of soil on the planet Mars).

McNamara's Martian connection came from the fact that few companies played the astronaut-employee game more enthusiastically than King Resources. Frank Borman was a director of the parent company. Walter Schirra headed a subsidiary, in which capacity he spoke idealistically of his work as "human, compassionate, exciting. . . . That's what it's all about. The people here. The ideas . . . One of John's basic philosophies that drew me in is that whenever you develop something in a country, you pump monies and know-how back in . . . bootstrap a country as I would say it."[7]

The astronauts exuded technological frontiersmanship and were excellent door openers. McNamara used a "Me and Wally" pitch on one occasion to get an appointment with Curtis, on another to get on an Earth Day panel being run by the chairman of the Environmental Improvement Commission. Schirra was detained from both at the last minute, but McNamara was able to keep the engagements.

Development of the proposed buoy system would have required $1.2 million and twenty-two months, at the end of which King Resources would have been free to sell the system to the highest bidder. No one in Maine government was capable of translating and fully evaluating the proposal. One skeptic observed that the company wanted "to send a buoy out to do a man's job." Another suggested that Maine not buy the system without a performance clause giving the state a right, in case of failure, to put McNamara and Schirra out in the buoys with litmus paper, a year's supply of sandwiches, and a walkie-talkie.

The first hearing on the King proposal was held by the Army Corps of Engineers in Portland just three days after the Atlantic World Port referendum and six days before Earth Day. The Corps's approval would have been a formality a year earlier, but by April, 1970, the National Environmental Policy Act required an environmental-impact statement. Furthermore, Senator Muskie's Water Quality Act (signed into law just two weeks earlier by President Nixon in a ceremony to which Ecology Ed was not invited) required Maine's Environmental Improvement Commission to certify that the project posed no threat to Maine's water-quality standards.

The Corps didn't have the slightest idea how to discharge its new responsibilities. The public hearing consisted of nothing more than the unsworn, uncross-examined speeches of some fifty consecutive witnesses. King's application stated no more than an intent to rebuild the existing pier and to use the existing storage facilities. McNamara stated explicitly, "We have no active plans to build a refinery."[8] The examining board did not question this, despite other testimony that McNamara, in a debate with Harold Pachios two days earlier, had stated that King Resources had considered a refinery in the general Portland area. Asked where, he had replied, "That's our business."[9]

In fact, King Resources was involved in negotiations with the National Iranian Oil Company regarding a joint-venture refinery in the Portland area. McNamara hoped to get approvals from the state and the Corps on a minimum project consisting of the existing storage facility, and then to expand it either into a refinery or major storage terminal tied to the Montreal pipeline. Because the minimum project offered little economic benefit, he kept offering veiled hints that King Resources had something more in mind. These hints got him support from those interested in jobs, taxes, or growth, but they offered conservationists continuing ammunition with which to challenge the veracity of his reticent applications.

A month after the inconclusive Corps of Engineers hearing, the King controversy came to a head at the Environmental Improvement Commission's first site-approval hearing. Although protesting that the Long Island terminal existed before the site law, McNamara went ahead with the hearing, which was necessary in any case for his certification under Muskie's Water Quality Act. Once again he mentioned neither the National Iranian Oil Company nor the Montreal pipeline.

His application was attacked on several grounds. Portland's coastal suburbs wanted no part of the risks of a supertanker terminal that paid taxes only to the central city. Harold Pachios, representing several environmental groups opposed to the terminal, noted that the project actually gave Casco Bay a triple exposure to spillage because the oil would go from a tanker to the terminal, from the terminal to the barge, and from the barge to the shore. Since the King plan was indefinite as to future expansion, Horace Hildreth drew considerable applause merely by asking, "Who knows what King Resources is really up to?"[10]

Hildreth's question was being asked at the same time by many people who had never heard of Casco Bay, for while McNamara faced the Maine environmental commission, John King was making his bid to take over Bernie Cornfeld's Investors Overseas Services.

Armed with a sizable block of IOS stock, acquired in large part with money raised against King Resources credit without the approval of the directors, King hoped to convince the IOS board that he could rescue the company and then to use his and their stock to vote Cornfeld out entirely. As a sign of his good faith and confidence, King offered to make a $40-million loan to IOS. Eight of these millions were a loan from the state of Ohio to King Resources. The loan was one of several dubious transactions by the Ohio state treasurer that were shortly to mortify the state Republican Party. Like several other unwitting loans by Ohio taxpayers to beautiful losers, their generosity to King Resources was illegal because it was for two years despite a statutory 270-day ceiling on such transactions.

A series of nasty shocks awaited King. IOS president Edward Cowett, who had prompted him to attempt the take-over, had lost the confidence of the IOS board and was useless to him. This left King without clear control, and he had to come to disadvantageous terms with Cornfeld. Their uneasy truce collapsed when the U.S. Securities and Exchange Commission ruled that if King Resources took over IOS, it would have to stop selling securities in the United States. Not even Maurice Stans, whom King had cultivated with hunting trips and campaign contributions, dared intervene actively on behalf of so highly publicized a dollar outflow.*

---

* Stans's later adventures with IOS are better known. The company floundered leaderless in King's wake for a while before falling under the controls of financier Robert Vesco, who milked it enthusiastically. Perhaps because Vesco avoided publicity, perhaps because he employed Nixon kinfolk instead of astronauts, perhaps because the 1972 campaign was at hand, his contributions earned him more attention than

King salvaged little from the wreckage. He remained outwardly ebullient and even served jauntily as President Nixon's special ambassador to Japan's Expo '70 World Trade Fair, but his company's stock plummeted and was no longer adequate collateral for his loans. Banks that tried to sell the stock discovered that some of it contained restrictions making it unmarketable. This increased both their concern and their demands for further collateral. King was asked to resign from the board of the First National Bank of Denver. His own board of directors refused to ratify his efforts to gain control of IOS. Ultimately, the outside directors resigned and explained their resignations to the Securities and Exchange Commission. In September they were replaced on the board of directors by the company division managers, including Donny McNamara, who had been through some rough times of his own.

McNamara had emerged from his May hearings confident of quick approvals. The colonel who had presided at the Corps of Engineers hearing had told him that he could expect Corps approval in mid-June. A member of the Environmental Improvement Commission who favored his terminal told him that the EIC would vote approval at their June 14 meeting, an indiscretion which merely reinforced the confidence that had been born in McNamara when EIC chairman Donaldson Koons had made a speech to the effect that Portland was, all things considered, a better place for oil than Machias Bay.

The EIC did not act at the June 14 meeting, but those present were able to tell from the discussion that King Resources was unlikely to get its permit. The Corps of Engineers could not act ahead of the EIC. The company was in turmoil, its chairman in desperate need of income. McNamara, learning that his permit was in jeopardy, began to play more roughly.

He had concluded that his most serious opponent on the commission was Curtis Hutchins, chairman of the board of the Dead River Company, who was in the oil business himself and who had been involved with Monks in the Machiasport land acquisitions. In addition, Andy Nixon, a known proponent of a Machiasport refinery, had recently left

---

King got, although apparently no more success. For their parts in these and related events, Maurice Stans and John Mitchell have been tried for influence peddling and perjury, and acquitted. Vesco is under indictment, living in Costa Rica. King is currently the subject of a criminal investigation. Cornfeld has done time in a Swiss jail.

the Department of Economic Development to join Dead River, and he frequently represented Hutchins at EIC meetings.

Convinced that Hutchins was opposing them for competitive reasons, King Resources agents caused letters to be written to the Portland *Press Herald* impugning both Hutchins and Nixon for conflicts of interest. Hutchins, who often did disqualify himself when oil matters came before the commission, responded that he had participated in the King Resources hearing because the proposal involved only industrial oil, a commodity that Dead River did not usually handle. McNamara also gave circulation to the slumbering fact that a company of which Hutchins had been an active director was under Interstate Commerce Commission investigation, and he announced that the EIC delay had forced King Resources to release a tanker full of oil from, of all places, Russia that had been ready for delivery in August.

None of this softened Hutchins discernibly. On July 2 the commission voted 6–3 against the proposed terminal on the ground that it posed an unacceptable risk to the Casco Bay islands, "a uniquely valuable recreational asset." At the same time, the commission also refused to make the required certification to the Corps of Engineers. McNamara was particularly disturbed that Chairman Koons, whom he had considered a safe vote on the basis of his speech on the virtues of Portland as an oil port, was unwilling to accept the triple-transfer risk.

Far from disqualifying himself, Curtis Hutchins inserted an explanation of his vote in the record of the commission deliberations. Perhaps he had McNamara's conflict-of-interest charges in mind when he quoted from a Supreme Court decision to the effect that undesirable development could consist of a "right thing in the wrong place—like a pig in the parlor instead of the barnyard."[11]

McNamara filed an immediate appeal, but the damage had been done. The National Iranian Oil Company, startled anyway by events in Geneva, backed away. The Portland pipeline lost all interest in him. Pressures from Denver mounted. On July 17 McNamara hoisted a signal flag soon to become common to corporations in simultaneous economic and environmental distress. He instructed his Atlantic Division subordinates as follows:

> There are to be absolutely no more hirings or commitments to hire unless you have received written permission from me.
>
> I would like to weed out the three least productive employees on the

Island. Before they are given any notice, however, I want one of us to talk with each individually so that they understand our cutting back is a function of political "fact finding" by the Maine EIC so that they in their own way can register their objections with the elected officials in their legislature.

The summer of 1970 passed in legal maneuvering as King Resources had to go to the Maine Supreme Court to appeal the site-approval decision and to the Superior Court to appeal the certification denial. With autumn came a shortage of industrial fuel oil and a close Maine gubernatorial election. Both extended mirages of new opportunity before McNamara's parched eyes.

The industrial-oil shortage was worldwide in character, but McNamara argued that Maine could safeguard its position by filling Long Island with the fuel. All that was necessary was for the governor to persuade his Environmental Commission to reverse itself or suspend its ruling. If he didn't and Maine ran out of oil before the election, people would know whom to blame.

The proposal had two flaws. First, Maine already had unfilled storage tanks, and the suggestion that a worldwide industrial-oil shortage could have been met through additional storage was in some ways equivalent to suggesting that a penniless man would be richer if he carried a second wallet. Second, the governor had no power to issue temporary permits, and he would not pressure the commission to do so.

As his proposal was being rejected, McNamara was added to the King board of directors and became more clearly aware of the desperation of both his company's position and his own. As an in-house director, he was expected to ratify several transfers of funds and stock between the various King companies, transfers that were designed to relieve John King of personal liability for the IOS disaster. This was the same demand that had driven the outside directors to resign after their insurers had canceled the company's policy protecting directors from stockholder suits.

McNamara decided that he could wait no longer for income from Long Island. His court appeal was nearly four months old, and he wanted a decision. Furthermore, he had a tanker of oil on the way to Portland and no place to put it. Against the advice of his attorney, he concluded that he could compel a decision from the Maine Supreme Court by offloading oil at his terminal. His logic was that of a man who, feeling he has been kept waiting too long for a badly needed driver's license, decides to force the issue by running a few red lights.

On a Saturday night ten days before the gubernatorial election, Assistant Attorney General Stephen Murray received a call from a Long Island member of Citizens Who Care. The caller said that a tanker was offloading at the King Resources pier. At 1:30 A.M. Murray's third phone call persuaded pajama-clad Supreme Court Justice Sidney Wernick to issue an injunction against the transfer operation. Murray then roused a local sheriff's deputy and a Coast Guard launch to serve the injunction. At 3 A.M. he called McNamara to tell him that he had just obtained a court order halting the offloading. As Murray remembers it (McNamara does not), McNamara called him a "triple asshole," threatened to have him fired, to sue him for all he was worth, and to call the governor later in the morning to offer him full support against Murray's boss in the election.

The call was never made, and McNamara must have realized that the imminent election would not paralyze the government. The following day King Resources attorney Robert Schwartz went before Judge Wernick and argued that the oil had to be offloaded or it would congeal in the tanks and sink the ship. When Wernick was openly skeptical, Schwartz replied that he was no expert and was just saying what his client told him. Unamused and perhaps influenced by reports that the escapade had led to a small spill, Wernick continued the temporary injunction, and King Resources began to accumulate $5500 per day in demurrage fees. Schwartz subsequently called Murray to thank him, saying, "Now maybe my client will listen to me."

Seeing an opportunity to rid Maine of McNamara, a *Maine Times* reporter called the episode to the attention of *Time*. A *Time* reporter called Denver and was told that McNamara had resigned. Maine conservationists had their first scalp, or so they believed. Actually, McNamara had resigned before trying to run the blockade. Alone among the inside directors he had been prudent enough to refuse to endorse King's proposed intercompany transfers and had submitted a detailed letter of resignation on October 20, six days before running the Long Island blockade. The resignation was effective November 4, and the offloading had just been a final crapshoot.

On November 19 the Maine Supreme Court overruled the EIC's denial of the King Resources application. The court held that the World War II facility fell within the law's exemption for facilities in existence prior to January, 1970. Two days later the EIC gave King a temporary license to use the existing pier. It was the 1964 Olympic finish all over; McNamara could once again have written, "My chance was needless, but there had been no way of knowing."

Conservationists were unrepentant. They were no more prone than oilmen to scrutinize their victories for bothersome ironies. Even Mc-Namara landed on his feet, writing a racy and successful novel entitled *The Money Maker* about the rise and fall of Jason Steele, a Houston entrepreneur who builds an empire on oil-drilling partnerships packaged to extend tax breaks to the average investor. Steele is ruined by his attempt to take over World Equities Ltd., a Geneva-based offshore mutual fund complex run by one Manny Kellerman, but before the fall he and Kellerman become multimillionaires on the basis of mutual-fund manipulations, tax avoidance, and natural-resource ventures off Israel and in the Canadian Arctic. Kellerman's ultimate tribute to a Steele plan to create a world stock exchange on an artificial island in the mid-Atlantic is "Christ Almighty, I like it. Jason, ya got big balls."[12]

McNamara's Maine experience peeps out of the novel on occasion. At one point Steele loses a key board of directors' decision by one unexpected vote. The vote that lets him down belongs to David Coons, who is then forced from the board when Steele has him compromisingly photographed with Steele's sister-in-law. The book ends with Steele's trial for larceny, mail fraud, and embezzling. The trial has been shifted from Houston to Portland, Maine, because of prejudicial pretrial publicity. As he awaits the proceedings (which he ultimately short-circuits by fleeing in a rented plane from whose subsequent wreckage both he and the survival gear are missing), Steele in Maine is described as follows:

> The bright glare of the March morning hit him as he stepped from his hotel and brought sharp pain between his eyes. Jason hurriedly put on his sunglasses. It was a beautiful day, the kind of weather that had been the joy of his youth. Winter was not yet off the field, for there were still sullen gray heaps of snow in the deep shadows of the buildings, and an occasional blast of cold from the north cut through his light topcoat. But it was a day that spoke of spring, with an occasional puff of the south wind. It took Jason back to the days of fishing with his father. . . .
>
> Often he idly window shopped along the way and observed people around him and he sometimes found himself wondering if these Maine

people, with their conspicuously slower way of doing things, didn't
have the right answer after all.[13]

Contemporaneously with Monks and McNamara, a third figure was
to hang ten atop the pipeline of the oil issue in Maine in 1970. More
agile than the other two and less committed to building a refinery,
Senator Muskie alone was able to dismount without wiping out.

Machiasport had become a continuing thorn in the side of the Senator's flourishing Presidential campaign. Much of his national support
came from people who appreciated his early environmental leadership
and who had little comprehension of the economy that lay behind the
coastline they idealized. Finding each week's news laced with fresh
spills and knowing of Maine's fogs and tides and rocks, they were
quick to rebuke Muskie for considering a Maine refinery. Their rebuke
was sharpened by sporadic newspaper columns pointing out that Hammer-Vahlsing tie and the mess on the Prestile Stream.

To increase public understanding of Maine's dilemma and his own,
Muskie conceived of a series of public hearings on "the relationship of
economic development to environmental quality." The hearings were
to have been held by his Air and Water Pollution Subcommittee at the
several sites around the nation that were enmeshed in controversies
over the desirability of new industry. The first two hearings were set
for Machiasport and Hilton Head, South Carolina.

Although such hearings would have been unlikely to produce legislation, their educational and research value would have been considerable. Unfortunately, only the Machias hearing was ever held. Hilton
Head vanished in Carolinian indignation when Muskie's staff announced the hearing before notifying anyone in the state. With
Muskie's time at a premium and the other Senators having less cause
than he to spend days on the road, subsequent sessions were never
scheduled.

The Machias hearing was an extraordinary show. Armand Hammer
testified for Occidental, Lou Ream and a team of five for Atlantic
Richfield, Bob Monks for Atlantic World Port. The Sierra Club was
represented, as were the National Audubon Society, the National Resources Council, the Maine Lobstermen's Association, the Downeast
Improvement Association, and Keep Oil Out. Some local residents and
officials testified on either side, each supporting the goals of the other
but proposing to attain them on different terms. Thus those favoring
oil wanted it only with "the strictest of controls," while those opposed

expressed a commitment to clean-industry alternatives, particularly aquaculture.

Both Occidental and Atlantic Richfield were testifying with their eyes very much on other horizons. Occidental's problem was in Libya, where President Qaddafi was moving toward the first real producer-industry confrontation since Iran's Premier Mossadegh had nationalized the Iranian oilfields in 1951, only to be ousted two years later by a worldwide oil company boycott and CIA intervention.

Qaddafi avoided Mossadegh's error. Instead of taking on the entire industry, he confronted Occidental, the company most heavily dependent on Libya, with a 30 percent cutback. Suddenly in need of help from those companies that had been hostile to the Machiasport quota request, Hammer stripped his testimony of its former rhetoric vilifying the pricing practices and political power of the domestic oil industry. Instead it was devoted largely to pollution control, Campobello, and the Doctor's desire to minister to the sickly Washington County economy. His coyness on the subject of prices got him into environmental trouble briefly. Asked by Senator Muskie whether he could give New England any hope for reduced oil costs, Hammer parried, "Well, you had a Boston tea party once. You may have a Boston oil party."[14]

Hammer was equally coy about Perry. He had wanted to use the hearings to announce his preference for this Monks-free site and had even gone to the expense of having the Frederic R. Harris company do a quick and frivolous survey of Perry and conclude that it was roughly equal to Machias Bay. Yeoman efforts by Occidental economist John Buckley and attorney John Zentay convinced him that any admission of Occidental's role in the Perry land grab should not come in the form of a preelection boast before a volcanic ecologist. He ultimately contented himself with reiteration of public relations consultant George Bevel's "several alternative locations have been offered to us."[15]

For very different reasons, Atlantic Richfield was suffering a fate in Alaska just as dire as Occidental's in Libya. With the failure of the *Manhattan*, the development of the company's North Slope holdings depended entirely on the Trans-Alaska Pipeline, whose construction Walter Hickel had announced on Earth Day he was ready to authorize. The line had promptly run afoul of court injunctions obtained by environmental and Alaskan native and Eskimo groups. Hickel himself was on his way out ("with an arrow in my heart rather than a bullet in my back") as a result of his dissent on the invasion of Cambodia coupled with industrial discontent over his unanticipated environmental concern.

Atlantic Richfield was as prepared as Occidental to pay any price to those who held it hostage. The company's concern with Arctic cleanliness approached the fanatical. It maintained continuing liaison with native and Eskimo associations and lobbied in support of their land claims. Its executives took on heavy speaking schedules, and Robert Anderson even maintained his poise when doused with a can of motor oil before a conference of collegiate newspaper editors ("Esso, I see," he is reported to have observed while taking off his coat to continue the discussion).

None of it helped. Despite embittered Alaskan lobbying, the Interior Department came up with conditions faster than the pipeline consortium could meet them. No one was reassured when the first roadway to Prudhoe Bay, built by the state in defiance of basic permafrost engineering, melted into an impassable slough even as Hickel's successor governor, knowing that the road had overrun its budget and been completed behind schedule, thoughtfully named it the Walter J. Hickel Highway. It has not been used since.

Atlantic Richfield had oil-industry headaches other than Alaska. The 1969 tax-reform surge* had cut the depletion allowance to 22 percent. Delays in nuclear power-plant construction and natural-gas production were beginning to place unexpected demands on petroleum. Just ahead lay a struggle with the automotive industry over just who was going to do what about the several poisons coming out of the internal-combustion engine. Because their Machias Bay hopes were still vaguely alive and because Senator Muskie stood a good chance of becoming President in 1973, Atlantic Richfield attended the hearing, but Ream's presentation, like Hammer's, seemed preoccupied and lacked the urgency of a man with bulldozers idling outside.

Neither Bob Monks, the local officials, the state officials, nor the conservationists said anything new, though each found ways to say it better. The only new testimony came from Dr. Max Blumer of the Woods Hole Oceanographic Institute and from Anthony Mazzocchi,

---

* An oil-reform surge which did not go as far as it might have. One reform that failed was Senator McIntyre's effort to subject the King Resources type of drilling funds to regulation by the Securities and Exchange Commission. During the preparation of this bill, McIntyre aide Alan Novins, whose project it was, was called by King, who mentioned that his company "needs bright young men" whom it sometimes paid as much as $50,000 per year.

legislative director for the Oil, Chemical and Atomic Workers International Union.

Dr. Blumer's testimony was based on his continuing observations of an oil spill at West Falmouth, Massachusetts, a year earlier. His conclusions were devastating to those who believed that oil-spill damage could be confined to the surface. Toxic fractions of the spilled oil, including carcinogens, had spread throughout the water column and had persisted for more than a year on the bottom, where the oil devastated shellfish populations and impeded their reproductive ability. Blumer calculated that a well-run oil port would spill one one-hundredth of 1 percent (.01%) of the oil handled. He asserted that a 300,000-barrel-per-day port would lose thirty barrels (1260 gallons) per day, or more every eight months than the total of the West Falmouth spill. In view of this apparently inevitable rate of spillage, Blumer concluded that "the presence of an oil port and of refineries is incompatible with the maintenance of an unpolluted environment."[16]

However valid Blumer's conclusion, the numbers that underlay it were wrong in two respects. First, he neglected to consider that oil entering a refinery at 300,000 barrels per day must leave at roughly the same rate. Thus the actual port traffic and spillage would double his estimate. Second, the harbor from which he had derived his .01 percent figure was Milford Haven, England. Unfortunately, he had chosen Milford Haven's worst year and had then inadvertently incorporated a decimal error from the spillage reports. The result was an exaggeration of the spillage risk by 100 times. Without the two errors, Blumer's probable daily spillage at a well-run 300,000 barrel-per-day refinery became about three-fifths of a barrel (twenty-five gallons), or thirty-one tons per year, a substantial but much less spectacular amount.

Following almost immediately after Blumer, Mazzocchi gave oil proponents further pause. Two Maine labor leaders had testified in unqualified support of refinery construction, but Mazzocchi suggested that refineries were unhealthy places to work. Conceding that they could enhance an economy, he warned against a situation familiar in Maine's mill towns—"cases where one large company enters an economically depressed area and soon becomes the dominant political and financial force. Many company towns were and still are notorious for their spoiled land and ruined health of the workers."[17]

He warned also that refinery workers receive exceptional exposure to carbon monoxide, hydrogen sulphide, sulfur dioxide, hydrochloric acid, hydrofluoric acid, and asbestos, plus risks of gradual poisoning from lead, nickel, and benzene. Furthermore, exceptionally high levels of emphysema and heart disease prevail among refinery workers. Mazzocchi was to some extent seeking to assure his union an opportunity to help the potential workers "retain the dignity of their labor and the quality of their health," but his testimony gave added credibility to some environmental concerns and suggested unpursued opportunities for environmentalist–labor union rapport.

Muskie's personal high point of the two-day hearing came during the testimony of Ossie Beal, president of the Maine Lobstermen's Association. Beal had argued that Curtis and Muskie, in their single-minded pursuit of oil, had neglected clean alternative industries. Muskie replied:

> I think it is time we had some frank talk about this business of what is possible in the way of clean industry. . . . What kinds of clean industry are there? We have explored them all. . . . The committees and economic development groups have been formed in the county, real efforts have been made over the years. A small branch of the Hathaway Company went into Eastport, and another little textile mill or yarn mill somewhere else. Little bits and snatches of little industries that have come, stayed a while, and disappeared, but none of the economic miracles that Washington County has been praying for and dreaming of and pressing those of us in public service to find in some way, legislative or otherwise.
>
> Nobody really, in the 16 years that have passed since I first went to Beals Island, has found one of these so-called clean industries for Washington County or any other part of the coastal counties which are depressed economically. You know that, I know that.
>
> I can understand, as I say, your opposition to the oil. But I don't understand, frankly, why you should be critical of efforts to get economic growth and industry in this county. This has been the one urgent message I have gotten from Washington County people all these years.
>
> But this is the first real possibility in terms of a boost to the economy and jobs that has come along. I wish it were a clean industry. But you have got to take a good look at this one before you say no to it—because nothing else is around the corner.
>
> We can talk about aquaculture, and harvesting the sea for $2 billion a year. I have to see that supported, and you people down here in the county look at things with a pretty stark sense of reality. You are not going to let people pull the wool over your eyes about astronomical figures like that without asking them what the basis is. The fishing industry along the Maine coast has never approached $2 billion at best.

Now we are going to suddenly believe, because of doubts about the oil industry, that we are going to find a $2 billion fishing industry . . . in the oceans off the Maine coast, available to provide the jobs that are needed. You know [that] is sort of whistling in the dark.

I have not been coming to Washington County to try to fool you into thinking that if you say "no" to this, I can reach into my pocket and find another economic opportunity for Washington County. That just isn't in the cards.[18]

At the end of two days, the hearings had documented the nature of the choice that the county would face if national oil-import policy changed—a choice that seemed from the semantics to be between the reverent destructiveness of the oil developers and the destructive reverence of their opponents. Bereft of legislative purpose, the hearings could do little more, but this achievement alone would have been a significant service to a county too rarely involved in the discussions of its future.

The other purpose of the hearings, to get Muskie out of the White House–orchestrated conservationist crossfire, was achieved six weeks later when the Senator announced that, as a result of testimony at the hearings, he could not support oil development in Maine until the industry's ability to prevent and clean up spills had transcended platitudes and bales of straw. This announcement, coming a month before the 1970 election, probably helped the Senator achieve his 60–40 re-election and boosted his Presidential stock, but it very nearly ended Governor Curtis's political career.

Curtis was involved in a very close race with the Attorney General James Erwin. As in most gubernatorial elections, state spending and taxation were the dominant issues, but oil, economic development, the environment, and gun control* were also important. Although his office had worked hard in support of the trade-zone application, Erwin had eighteen months later declared himself opposed to oil at Machiasport because "they haven't shown me any benefits." He had not made clear how he would implement his opposition or whether it extended to areas

* Gun control is not an issue in most Maine elections, for few serious politicians dare endorse it. In the wake of the 1968 King and Kennedy assassinations, Curtis had proposed mild controls to the 1969 legislative session. He was bombarded with even more abusive mail than he received for proposing an income tax. Several hundred hunters overwhelmed the legislative hearings. Andy Nixon tells of being served lunch on the day of the hearing by a waitress wearing pro-gun buttons across her chest like bandoliers. Asked why she felt so strongly, she replied, "If they take away our guns, they'll be coming up from Harlem." The legislative vote against the measure was unanimous.

other than Machiasport, but his position had the political strength that stems from simplicity.

Curtis had favored any oil development that could satisfy the Environmental Improvement Commission, a position which did not satisfy those who felt strongly on either side. Conservationists and fishermen understandably preferred the apparent security of the Erwin negative, while those who had supported oil for the twenty-six months since the Vermont announcement were wondering where it was. Many oil supporters also felt, in view of the King Resources rejection and the strict legislation, that Curtis had sold out to the conservationists.

Muskie's actual statement was "If I had to vote today on a refinery I would vote no. We don't have the technology to protect us."[19] He later elaborated: "If industry can make oil compatible with the Maine environment, if they can develop a technology to deal with the threat of oil spills, then we should invite them to Maine. This has been the Governor's attitude . . . and it has also been my attitude. Maine should write the terms on which oil can come to Machiasport."[20]

Despite the elaboration, the statement was properly seen as a diminution of his former enthusiasm for oil and, less properly, as a near endorsement of the Erwin oil position. One of Maine's largest television and radio networks editorialized:

> Republican candidate James Erwin has taken a firm stand against an oil refinery in Maine. Both Muskie and Erwin have exercised judgement and courage to oppose oil in Maine during a political campaign. Each of them deserves high praise for making their decision known.
>
> Democratic Governor Curtis, who has been the strongest and most persistent advocate of locating an oil refinery in Maine, has not made his position clear in recent months. Once the champion of all development, the Governor now senses a rising tide of concern and opposition to a refinery in Maine. It may be that Governor Curtis will hedge his political bets even further and tentatively side with Senator Muskie. . . .
>
> Throughout all of this, it should be evident that Governor Curtis in particular has not been consistent. On the one hand, he has pandered to the conservationists, and on the other hand he has pushed for an aluminum plant and an oil refinery.[21]

Curtis was able to offset some of this sentiment by pointing to his role in the preparation of the siting and oil-handling laws. He was further aided when Stewart Udall, by then the author of a weekly syndicated environmental column, named him and Republicans Francis

Sargent of Massachusetts and Daniel Evans of Washington as the country's three environmentally strongest governors.

Governor Curtis ultimately won the election by some 700 votes out of 320,000. He was clearly damaged by the oil issue, for the coastal communities in Washington County, many of which he had carried in 1966, voted solidly for Erwin. Only Machiasport was constant. Curtis had taken it by 153–104 in 1966, and he won it 130–94 in 1970. The 13 percent decline in votes cast prevailed throughout the county. It was attributable in equal parts to outmigration and apathy.

11: Late 1970–Early 1971

Let me tell you about the very rich. . . . They possess and enjoy early, and it does something to them, makes them soft where we are hard, and cynical where we are trustful, in a way that, unless you were born rich, it is very difficult to understand.

F. Scott Fitzgerald, "The Rich Boy"

Anson Hunter's central trait, in the story, is the sense of superiority that he feeds by captivating others. It makes him willing to help or destroy others, almost in the same gesture.

Malcolm Cowley, preface to "The Rich Boy"

I had written a novel about rich people to find out why they seemed to me as dangerous as wild boars and pythons.

Rebecca West[1]

I've been rich and I've been poor, and believe me, rich is better.

Tallulah Bankhead[2]

U.S. OIL-IMPORT POLICY suffered a series of minor strokes in 1970. The afflictions took the form of sudden shortages and higher prices in industrial fuel and asphalt. Compared to subsequent strokes, these were mild ones, without lasting paralysis. Consequently, the root causes escaped detection once the symptoms had receded.

The asphalt shortage resulted from nothing more complex than a growing demand coupled with the efforts of U.S. refiners to maximize production of more profitable products. The Cabinet Task Force had pointed out that asphalt controls were unjustified by any national-security consideration. President Nixon had retained them anyway, but when real shortages occurred, he reversed himself. New England then solved its asphalt problems with purchases from Canada, which, despite never having had any import controls, enjoyed lower prices and a surplus.

The explanations for the industrial-fuel shortage were more complex. This was the one petroleum product entirely exempted from East Coast import limitations, and its sudden scarcity and increased prices seemed to some to confirm the unwisdom of relying on foreign oil. They reasoned that an assured supply at five dollars per barrel was preferable to a less secure supply that fluctuated between two and four dollars per barrel.

Some of the causes of the shortages were of limited duration. These included the Libyan production cutbacks, the Syrian refusal to permit repair of the pipeline ruptured by a bulldozer, the tanker shortage resulting from the need to take more oil around South Africa, and disappointments in the development of natural gas and nuclear power. Other causes were enduring. These were increasing worldwide demand, the unacceptability of high-sulfur coal or oil in urban industrial areas, and improved refining technology that enabled refiners to concentrate on heating oil and gasoline.

The Mandatory Oil Import Program had compounded these trends in an ironic but perfectly foreseeable way. By permitting imports only of industrial oil, it had forced refiners making that product to build outside the United States in order to get access to the prohibited crude oil. This was the senseless result that either a tariff system or Maine's trade-zone plan would have avoided. Once the refineries were built abroad, they became vulnerable to whatever taxes or export limitations the host nations chose to impose, and the United States, New England in particular, lost the chance to build refineries suited to particular national or regional needs.

Even within Interior these events were viewed with alarm, and Ralph Snyder, deputy administrator of the Oil Import Administration, devised a complex program to offer further special quota incentives to the makers of low-sulfur oil. Occidental was interested, for its low-sulfur Libyan crude oil would give it a clear edge under any "special incentive" program. Snyder pushed his plan into the Oil Policy Committee, where it was buried.

As the fears of shortage deepened, the New England governors decided to try again to present their regional plight directly to the President. The obstacles to this course were not so widely known in those days, and the governors began what was to be a six-month effort with a September 19, 1970, telegram reading:

> New England faces a serious fuel crisis. Communities, school districts, hospitals, and industries throughout New England have been unsuccessful in obtaining minimum supplies to heat their facilities through the winter. We six governors feel that the interests of citizens in our states are being ignored. Only you have the statutory authority to solve this problem. . . . We are convinced that a personal meeting with you is

absolutely necessary to state the urgency of New England's needs and develop a program required to meet our needs. We request a meeting as soon as possible since the problem is deepening. We will be prepared to meet with you anywhere, anytime at your convenience.

The White House replied promptly:

It will not be possible for the President to meet with you due to his European trip. However, he has asked that you meet with Dr. Paul McCracken and General George Lincoln to discuss the matter of fuel oil in New England.

Hugh W. Sloan, Jr.
Staff Assistant to the President

The President had settled on a more innovative way to deal with the New England situation. On September 29 he announced that he was permitting an extra 105,000 barrels per day of home heating oil to be imported to the East Coast, an amount that he was confident would solve any problems relating to that fuel and, since home heating oil could be blended with industrial oil, a contribution to the industrial problem as well.

"PROGRESS AT LAST," exulted New England newspaper headlines, but they were wrong. It was a fraud, a triumph of press agentry over substance. The 105,000 barrels per day included no new oil. The first 40,000 barrels per day was an extension of the same grant that the President had made to the terminal operators in June in order to lay the groundwork for his August rejection of the task-force report. The second 40,000 barrels per day was a requirement that all the tickets under this grant be used within three months instead of the previously allowed six-month period. The grant thus became 80,000 barrels per day for three months instead of 40,000 barrels per day for six. It also forced the terminal operators into the market during the winter, when prices were highest. The last 25,000 barrels per day was merely the continuance of certain special allocations that had been renewed annually since 1959. The announcement concluded with the assurance that, with prices rising, the free market would solve any remaining problems.

Governor Curtis, less restrained than Special Prosecutor Leon Jaworski was to be in the face of similar Presidential magnanimity, called the announcement "another reshuffling of the same unsatisfactory deck of cards" and "an insult to the intelligence of New Englanders." The New England Governors' Conference, milder in deference to its three

Republican members, said that the actions "will not meet the needs of our region" and again requested a meeting with the President. This time the response was a telephone call from an assistant to Hugh Sloan telling them that the President would be unable to attend their December 4 session in Boston but again offering McCracken, Lincoln, or Chuck Colson. It was at about this time that Flanigan told a group of terminal operators that their lot would improve if Erwin were to defeat Curtis.

In early October, General Lincoln evinced skepticism as to whether New England faced real shortages. Governor Curtis's reply was prophetic:

> Industrial oil prices have increased extraordinarily in the last six months. Suppliers . . . are not taking on any new customers. They are making no commitments as to price escalations. . . .
>
> The price increases, coupled with supply shortage, are clear evidence of scarcity of supply which is either real or artificially imposed by the oil industry. In either case, action by the national administration is clearly required. . . .
>
> I cannot overemphasize the disillusionment and alarm which New Englanders feel at the failure of this administration and its predecessors to respond to this problem on anything more than a stopgap basis. For two years we have warned that the Oil Import Program threatened us with being the first victims in cases of shortages and price squeezes. That is what has happened now, and I cannot find a knowledgeable home owner or businessman who is not already feeling the pinch. Neither they nor I see any prospect of long-term relief in any measure taken to date.
>
> I appreciate your recent efforts in talking to oil companies about New England's supply problems, and we will cooperate in every possible way with the Regional Fuel and Energy Board. However, I must point out that this is the fifth board or commission on oil problems which has been created since 1968, and the only concrete recommendations to emerge were immediately shelved. It is past time that these groups stopped studying the victims and started taking a serious look at the causes. The theme of the McCracken Report, that we should pay more and, if that doesn't work, consume less, is not satisfactory as long as this country is needlessly excluding available Western Hemisphere oil.

On December 4, the governors again telegraphed the President: "On two previous occasions we have requested meetings with you to discuss the fuel oil shortage in New England. . . . We again emphasize our desire to meet with you."

Hugh Sloan's assistant responded with a call to Chip Stockford, executive secretary to the Governors' Conference, expressing puzzlement at this latest request, since the New England problem had been solved in September. As a result of this call, Curtis, as chairman of the Governors' Conference, wrote to Nixon:

> On three recent occasions the New England Governors have requested a meeting with you to discuss the continuing hardship worked on our region by national oil policy. Each time we stated our willingness to meet with you at any time and place convenient to you. The first time we were told that conflicts in your schedule would prevent such a meeting. The second time we were told that you could not meet with us on December 4 in Boston. The third time we were told that your staff was "somewhat confused" by our request in light of recent developments. I will clarify that request.
>
> Residual fuel prices in New England have more than doubled in the last nine months. Home heating oil prices have increased by about 2 cents per gallon and are likely to go higher. Gasoline prices are up more than one cent per gallon since Gulf Oil increased its crude oil prices by 25 cents per barrel. . . .
>
> We do not seek to meet with you to achieve immediate rollback of all recent price increases, for we recognize that they result in part from forces beyond your control. We do feel, however, that the present oil import program will confront New England with the possibility of annual September crises for oil products, and this prospect is not tolerable.
>
> Some time ago, the former Chairman of the Board of the Standard Oil Company of New Jersey came away from a meeting with you expressing pleasure that you understood the oil industry's problems. We are seeking a meeting in order to establish a similar understanding of the problems of the New England oil consumer and the ways in which we feel that these problems might be alleviated.

The day after this letter was sent, Governor Sargent of Massachusetts received a letter from the President with blind copies to the other five governors:

Dear Governor Sargent:

I appreciate the concern you and your fellow Governors express for the fuel supply and fuel price situation in New England.

My concern over these matters does, of course, extend across the entire country. I explicitly set forth my views and some guidelines on our inflationary situation in my December 4 speech.

Upon receiving your telegram, I asked the Joint Board on Fuel Supply and Fuel Transport, which I established on September 29, to provide me with an up-to-date report on the fuel situation in New England. . . .

After reading the enclosed report, which I have asked be made available to the public, you may wish to meet with Dr. McCracken and General Lincoln to discuss any questions you have. If, after seeing them, you still feel we should have a meeting, please let me know.

The report said:

The problem of the possibility of a fuel shortage was foreseen last summer. The President moved to take forehanded action with an administration study which resulted in the measures announced . . . on September 29. . . . One of these actions was the establishment of a joint board of heads of federal agencies to keep the fuel situation continuously under review and to coordinate needed actions. . . . The report yesterday from that Board states that inquiries to the offices of all governors in New England have not resulted in a report of any specific fuel shortage. The expressions of concern are about price.

An unprogrammed interruption such as a rail strike or a long spell of very cold weather may generate problems. But under normal conditions, fuel supply for New England will be adequate this winter. Every New England governor has taken prudent action to deal with any fuel emergency.

The price rise has been major indeed, occasioned not only by being subject to the world price, but also by a recent increase in demand resulting in part from our environmental programs which we all support. . . .

As to prices, the reported price of No. 2 heating oil in New England is substantially the same as in New York and Chicago. The New England spot price of low sulphur residual oil is also substantially lower than in Chicago, and about the same or lower than on the West Coast. It does not appear that the New England situation is a special case.

This exchange was too much for Chip Stockford. He wrote to Sloan that he regretted that he had not earlier informed him

loudly, sarcastically, and emphatically of my personal opinion concerning the rude, cavalier and unprofessional manner the White House staff has treated the six New England Governors on the fuel oil issue. I can not comprehend how insensitive you must be to believe that six Governors do not resent your brushing aside their request to meet with the President on an issue of vital concern to the consumers and economy of their region. The first telegram of the Governors was answered by you on behalf of the President, while at that very time, the press was reporting of the President's daily meetings with citizens to accept paintings and converse on trivial matters. After 2½ months, the Governors are still waiting a response to their second telegram of September 30, requesting a meeting with the President.

I frankly question whether the Governors' desire to meet with the President has been discussed with him.

Unfazed, Sloan responded:

Dear Mr. Stockford

I am enclosing a copy of the President's letter of December 17 to Governor Sargent. I trust this will clarify the situation for you and correct some of the misconceptions you are apparently laboring under.

A year later, a former secretary of Sloan's, surprised at a Curtis aide's annoyance over the President's refusal, said, "But we circulated that to everyone who handles those things—Chapin, Haldeman, Ehrlichman, Colson, Flanigan—not one of them thought the President should meet with the Governors. If he did, he'd have had to meet with everyone with an oil problem."

Governor Curtis concluded the correspondence through clenched teeth:

Thank you for the blind copy of your letter to Governor Sargent and for the repetition of your offer that we meet with Dr. McCracken and General Lincoln. The New England Governors have no objection to such a meeting, but Governor Sargent and I have each met previously with General Lincoln. In addition, I have met with Arthur Burns, George Shultz, Peter Flanigan, and Hendrik Houthakker* to discuss the Oil Import Program. For reasons set forth in my letter of December 17, the results of these meetings and other contacts do not seem to reflect a full appreciation of New England's problem.

The latest report by the Joint Board on Fuel Supply and Fuel Transport continues this insensitivity. We fully agree that our own efforts, coupled with those of your Board and the New England congressional delegation, have averted, for the moment, the probability of oil runouts under normal conditions this winter. We reiterate our concern in the following areas:

First, your report confuses prices with cost. As your Task Force pointed out, with prices not dissimilar to those in the rest of the country, the per capita cost in New England is more than $35 while the average cost nationally is $26. In Northern New England, where winter is most severe, the annual cost is more than $41 per person. Thus it is

* Dr. Houthakker was a member of the President's Council of Economic Advisers.

not enough to say that New England's prices are in line with those in other regions. Furthermore, even if we were not at a regional disadvantage, we would see no reason why we or your administration should remain complacent about a program which your own Task Force says is costing every American $26 per year in this period of intense inflation while failing to achieve its statutory objectives.

Secondly, the report of your Board suggests that we have adequate supplies unless problems are generated by "a rail strike or a long spell of very cold weather." It occurs to us that this is a confession of the bankruptcy of present Federal oil policy. The Oil Import Program, for which we are paying $5 billion per year, is supposed to assure us of security of supply in the event of a major war, never mind an exceptionally cold winter.

Thirdly, we recognize the unlikelihood of a rollback of most of the recent price increases. The major oil companies do not usually operate that way, and your recent actions regarding federal offshore production and Canadian imports,* commendable first steps though they are, do not seem to have shaken them. However, we believe that even present price levels will not protect the New England consumer against the annual price hikes which are inevitable as long as fuel contracts must be negotiated from crisis to crisis, a situation which the Oil Import Program exacerbates by reducing East Coast refinery capacity.

The correspondence ended there. The governors turned their attention to challenging the constitutionality of the oil-import program on the ground, uncovered by a member of the Cabinet Task Force staff, that a relatively obscure section of the Constitution† prohibited the imposition of different quota systems on the East and West Coasts. Because of difficulties in preparation (some of the inequities such as the industrial-oil exemption and the terminal-operator quota actually favored New England), the suit was not filed for fifteen months, and had not been decided when the President mooted it by abandoning the quota system in April, 1973.

In the interim, the governors finally gave up on a Machiasport refinery. They continued to press for more of the only type of relief that the President was willing to give—import permits to the terminal operators. The industry would accept these quotas as the price of New

* The President had ordered slight increases in Canadian imports and in oil production on federal lands in the Gulf of Mexico.

† Article I, Section 9, provides in part that "No preference shall be given by any Regulation of Commerce or Revenue to the Ports of one State over those of another." Section 8 requires that ". . . Duties, Imports and Excises shall be uniform throughout the United States."

England acquiescence, and many New Englanders were willing to accept them because they exported the environmental problems. However, they also exported refinery jobs, capital investment, and control over a vital link in the petroleum-supply chain. As Professor Adelman has elegantly dismissed other aspects of U.S. oil policy at this time, "we now live with the consequences."

Along with the President's indications that oil imports would not be significantly liberalized, Senator Muskie's statement against oil in Maine had been a minor but last straw for both Occidental and Atlantic Richfield. Without prospective tenants, the governors were unwilling to take the environmental heat, and attention shifted to the havoc wrought by two of Machiasport's humblest eddies: the refinery-building efforts of Northeast Petroleum Industries in Rhode Island and Maine Clean Fuels, formerly Fuel Desulphurization, Inc., in Maine.

Northeast had not been part of Jack Evans's never-was consortium, but it had joined the independent marketers in their efforts to come to terms with Occidental. When those efforts failed, Northeast president John Kaneb branched out in search of finished-product quotas and his own refinery site. Willing to settle for moderately deep water and unwilling to enter the turmoil in Maine, he chose a tract of land owned by Northeast in Tiverton, Rhode Island, a picturesque former fishing village and a suburb to Fall River, Massachusetts. To guide the refinery through the permit process, he hired John Buckley, released by Occidental when the company pulled back from its Washington County plans.

Buckley had learned a lot during his Maine campaign. Upon joining Northeast, he supervised the preparation of a tasteful twenty-four-page brochure to introduce the refinery to the town. Placed in every mailbox in Tiverton in August, 1970, the brochure was a reasonably straightforward appraisal of the benefits of a modern refinery. It avoided overstating the jobs and taxes, and it acknowledged environmental problems. Northeast proposed to create a Citizens' Advisory Committee to advise the company of community concerns, and, reminiscent of Occidental's marine resources fund, it also offered to endow a Narragansett Bay Foundation for oceanographic research to the tune of an initial $500,000 to be followed by $100,000 per year. Only once did the brochure overreach itself. That was when it noted that the refinery would discharge only carbon dioxide and water into the air and added that these were "the chief ingredients, incidentally, of soda pop."

The brochure did not mention Northeast's brief effort to enlist Stewart Udall as an environmental consultant. Udall had refused the job upon being told that the site he would be asked to defend had already been chosen. "This kind of work is meaningless," he said, "unless we have a chance to help choose the site. I'd have been glad to help them pick the best site for their plant and then to defend it, but I didn't want to defend a choice that I wasn't sure had been made on environmental grounds in the first place."

Tiverton's initial response to the proposal was overwhelmingly favorable, but a small group of residents incorporated an opposing entity called Save Our Community (SOC). SOC raised money and hired a lawyer to oppose Northeast's request that the town rezone the refinery site from residential to industrial. Despite this opposition, the early hearings went well for Northeast. Kaneb and Buckley made effective witnesses. They established that the refinery would discharge only half as much sulfur as nearby Brown University. They promised to screen off their plant with a buffer of evergreens. Kaneb offered a Homeowners Guarantee Agreement under which Northeast would either buy any house adjacent to the refinery for its fair market value any time in the next fifteen years or would make an outright gift of 15 percent of the appraised value to the owner as protection against any decline in property value. Any homeowner who wanted to take up these options only had to promise not to oppose the refinery, a clause which looked so much like blackmail that Northeast dropped it.

SOC's lawyer cross-examined Kaneb for four painfully dull hours, alienating many with his apparent repetitiveness but establishing that Northeast was new to the refinery business and had no real idea where its oil was coming from. When SOC presented its own witnesses, the uncertainties planted during the cross-examination began to bloom, nourished in part by the general anti-oil company sentiment that Kaneb and Buckley had helped to stir up to aid Occidental in its struggle for import permits. A retired refinery engineer questioned the wisdom of putting a refinery in a residential area. An economist testified that a refinery would not necessarily lower property taxes. A planner warned that the community would change in unforeseeable ways. The president of Tiverton High's senior class put the environment ahead of the refinery.

The intervenors were also helped by three of those fortuitous oil spills that conservationists have learned to anticipate with gleeful horror in any proceeding lasting more than two months. First, part of an

Esso refinery in New Jersey blew up, injuring workers and horrifying Northeast's prospective neighbors. Then, as a mosquito before the eye may look like a jumbo jet in the middle distance, a cracked valve on a tank at Northeast's Tiverton terminal spread fifty gallons of home heating oil in a thin film over some six miles of Sakonnet River shoreline during the same week that two colliding tankers liberated 2.5 million gallons of crude oil under the Golden Gate Bridge. Northeast reacted to the Esso explosion by shifting its proposal to 300 newly acquired acres in an area already zoned for industry. As Buckley put it, "When that refinery in Jersey exploded, that was it for me. I knew we had to get rid of that residential site."[3] Far from soothing Tiverton, Northeast's retreat encouraged the opponents. A group of theretofore neutral fishermen asserted, "We can blockade Northeast and we will. What do you think they will do when there is a line of half-drunken fishermen blocking their terminal gates?"[4]

Twenty-five hundred of Tiverton's 12,500 people signed a petition of opposition. The town council (shipping clerk, lawyer, businessman, fisherman, unemployed industrial engineer, accountant, and used-car salesman) rejected the residential area without waiting to hear the rebuttal evidence that Northeast was entitled to present. Then, to Northeast's astonishment, they voted 4–2 at a tumultuous postmidnight session not to consider the alternative industrial site at all. Northeast did not appeal. Instead Kaneb sought to pair up with a major company to build the refinery in the Canadian Maritime Provinces. Uncertainties in Canadian and U.S. oil policy chilled that venture, and Northeast, despite John Buckley's five years of ghostwritten attacks on the arrogance of the oil states, undertook to build the refinery unopposed in Louisiana.

While Northeast rose and fell in Tiverton, another of Machiasport's children churned bays on Maine's western and central coastlines. The would-be refiner this time was Fuel Desulphurization, Inc., a firm fresh from an abrupt rejection at Riverhead, New York, and seeking to build a 200,000-barrel-per-day plant in Maine.

Like the Hess Refinery in the Virgin Islands and the Puerto Rican petrochemical complex, Fuel Desulphurization was the offspring of one of those socially benign seat-of-the-pants exemptions with which Stewart Udall had bought time for the quota system. Beginning in 1967, the Secretary had liberalized importation of low-sulfur industrial oil to power plants on the West Coast. In 1968 Consolidated Edison of New York demanded similar treatment.

Passage of the Clean Air Act of 1967 had created Con Ed's urgent demand for more low-sulfur fuel, and several businessmen saw this demand as their entrée to oil refining. Eager to get an allocation before Udall left office, Fuel Desulphurization president David Scoll decided to help the administrative process out a bit. Ralph Nader's air-pollution task force described his efforts as follows:

> He began drafting his own proposed regulations, designed, of course, to suit the needs of his corporation. When questioned about this by the Task Force, Scoll described his view of the administrative process: "they tinker with what you give them and ask if you can live with it. If you can't, they tinker some more."
>
> On May 28, 1968, the Interior Department published three proposed rules, most of which were inspired by Scoll's draft. When asked about the regulations by the Task Force, Scoll snapped, "I wrote them!" In our second conversation, he backtracked somewhat: "no, I just helped out a little." Robert Nunn, of Batzell and Nunn [representing Supermarine, a second would-be refiner], also remarked, "I wrote them." But as a jaded observer of the oil scene remarked, "They'll all tell you that."[5]

Semper paratus, the oil industry once again launched its coastal patrol, warning that air-pollution control was fine in its place but that it had no role in a program designed solely to protect the national security. *The Oil and Gas Journal* reacted to the proposal in words that might as easily have been written by Ralph Nader: "Strong pressures, economic and political, always exist to use any legal advantage that can be found. . . . The Interior Department is not always able to resist such pressures. . . . It appears obvious that Interior is no longer in control of the Oil Import Program."[6]

In the final fortnight of the Johnson administration, despite the opposition of the President, to whom he was no longer speaking, Udall announced grants of import allocations conditioned upon the production of the low-sulfur industrial fuel necessary to reduce air pollution in urban areas on the U.S. East Coast.* The grants went to Fuel Desulphurization, Inc., and two other newly formed companies. The permits were not for crude oil, but they allowed the importation of high-sulfur foreign industrial oil to be desulfurized and/or blended in the

* See page 115.

United States. Home heating oil and gasoline emerging from the desulfurization process would not be subject to import controls.

The allocations in their final form were acceptable to the industry, for they permitted little new oil and seemed to offer little hope of a profitable operation. The economics of the allocations were so dubious that two of the three recipients never seriously tried to use them. Fuel Desulphurization, Inc. was to spend well over a million dollars in proving that the other two were right.

FDI began its corporate odyssey at Riverhead on the eastern end of New York's Long Island. There President Scoll announced plans to construct a 160,000-barrel-per-day, $150-million desulfurization complex, producing 100,000 barrels per day of low-sulfur fuel and 60,000 barrels per day of gasoline and jet fuel. All that he needed from Riverhead was the rezoning of his potato-field site from agricultural to industrial use.

Unfortunately for Scoll, the 7585 citizens of Riverhead were unwilling to risk exposure to the 200 tons of sulfur which FDI would be removing each day from the atmosphere of 12 million metropolitan New Yorkers. Following long petitions and short hearings, the town planning board voted 3–0 against recommending the rezoning. Two other members abstained because they had already signed the petitions. Not waiting for formal action by the town board, Scoll withdrew his application, commenting that FDI appeared to have fallen victim to "a paradox of pollution."[7] Donald Denis, a Riverhead architect who had organized a group called "It Stinks" to fight the refinery, said that Scoll was the victim of a fallacy, not a paradox. Noting that the air was already clean in Riverhead, he observed, "We all look out for our own interests."[8]

Conservationists warmed by this vision of an oil-industry comeuppance at the hands of sturdy Long Islanders defending their beachfronts might reflect on the dismal absence of process that attended Scoll's ejection in the context of certain covenants that residents of Levittown, Long Island, used (until the Supreme Court forbade their enforcement) to exclude others who, though useful as energy sources, posed an undocumented but strongly felt threat to local property values and life styles. Those covenants read in part: "No dwelling shall be used or occupied by members of other than the Caucasian race (except for domestic servants)."

Foreseeing the unhappy ending to his Riverhead foray, Scoll had already approached Maine's Department of Economic Development, where he received a misleadingly warm welcome. Despite, or perhaps because of, its frequent knife and pillow fights with the *Maine Times,* DED continued to feel that its mission was to bring jobs and prosperity to Maine and that it should be judged in those terms. Commissioner James Keefe was sincerely proud that he had adopted a theme of "Development Through Conservation" and resentful that no one remembered the very substantial role that Andy Nixon, his special assistant, had played in the creation of the site and oil-handling laws. Because the site law vested a veto power in the Environmental Improvement Commission, DED felt more strongly than ever that its departmental mission was promotional rather than selective. The Environmental Improvement Commission was the agency assigned to guard against mistakes.

These priorities led DED to regard its environmentalist detractors as an elite and selfish threat. Since the critics were no less convinced of the sacredness of their own priorities, they tended to dimiss the development personnel as political hacks and industrial lackeys. Upon approaching Maine, Scoll was so delighted by DED's enthusiastic welcome that he made the mistake, reasonable enough in the late 1960s but fatal by 1970, of placing FDI's future in Maine solely in the hands of the development agency.

The mistake was a surprising one for Scoll to have made. He was a New York admiralty lawyer of some repute, and his creation of an oil company out of an air-pollution problem won him the admiration of Stewart Udall, who for a time regarded him as the man most likely to put together a successful Maine refinery proposal. His name appears on the letterhead of the International Salmon Foundation, a group dedicated to reviving the Atlantic salmon sport fishery, and also of the National Committee for an Effective Congress, a fund-raising group for liberal Congressional candidates of both parties through which Scoll became acquainted with Stewart Udall during the latter's career in the House of Representatives. Those familiar with his angling and reformist political pursuits describe him as absolutely sincere about them and good company too. They feel that he has some blind spots about the conflicts.

The smoothness with which Scoll moved through the Washington oil-policymaking maze also earned him the admiration if not the approval of the Nader air-pollution task force, but it was the wrong smoothness for Maine in 1970. Indeed, his entire Maine career was to illustrate the incompetence of a shrewd 1960s promoter-industrialist to cope with the environmental demands of the 1970s. In this failing both he and his DED supporters confirmed behaviorial psychologist B. F. Skinner's insight, here taken far out of context, that "If a person can no longer take credit or be admired for what he does, then he seems to suffer a loss of dignity or worth, and behavior previously reinforced by credit or admiration will undergo extinction. Extinction often leads to aggressive attack."[9]

Scoll's initial choice of site was South Portland, Maine's most industrialized city. Because his permits were good only for Western Hemisphere oil, South Portland's relatively shallow water did not deny him supertanker savings. The waterfront was the terminus for the Portland-Montreal pipeline, through which nearly 500,000 barrels of crude oil passed daily. Portland Harbor was extensively polluted already, and the South Portland government had a record of particular friendliness toward new industry. DED assured Scoll that his company would be welcome, and some members of the Environmental Improvement Commission made indiscreet statements that they hoped approval of a Portland area refinery would relieve the pressure for oil development elsewhere. Scoll incorporated an FDI subsidiary entitled Maine Clean Fuels and plunged ahead with Riverhead North.

To his astonishment, South Portland was no more enthusiastic than Riverhead had been. The city's industry was primarily light manufacturing along with oil storage for the pipeline. The area had a relatively low unemployment rate and air much cleaner than nearby Westbrook, on which a Scott Paper Company mill flopped a noxious 5000 tons of sulfur dioxide and particulate matter per year.

Surplus "It Stinks" buttons were sent up from Riverhead to be recycled on South Portland lapels. Several thousand residents signed petitions of opposition. Scoll encountered extraordinary difficulty in acquiring two key pieces of land, one owned by the Maine Central Railroad (whose chairman was trying to make Scoll and McNamara bid against each other), the other owned by a Mr. Wainwright who leaned for advice very heavily on his friend Bob Monks.

Seeking to allay the growing local uneasiness, Scoll urged South Portland to ask the National Air Pollution Control Administration whether or not his project would pollute the air. South Portland did, but Scoll's Washington technique for once played him false. The city's letter somehow wound up in an unexpected office, and the reply said that the proposed pollution-control system fell well short of the capabilities of modern technology and might actually degrade the atmosphere. The South Portland City Council then denied the Maine Clean Fuels request for a zoning change on the questionable ground that the refinery would inevitably be a fire hazard. The Environmental Improvement Commission refused to consider a project in a town which had already rejected it. And so, in September, 1970, Scoll withdrew his application, folded up his charts, consulted his supporters at the DED, and headed with apparently undiminished confidence for Sears Island at the head of Penobscot Bay, an area which he had previously dismissed as being too far from his markets and which Jack Evans had rejected in 1967 as "a waterway that is difficult and full of underwater hazards . . . not the place for a refinery under any conditions."

Sears Island is scarcely an island at all. It is connected to the town of Searsport at low tide and protrudes about a mile into Penobscot Bay. Searsport itself was once a home of Maine ship captains (captains of 10 percent of the nation's merchant shipping are said to have lived there in 1885), but it has since become the moderately industrialized site of a sizable oil terminal and a chemical manufacturing plant. It would have been as logical a site as any for an oil port if the lower end of Penobscot Bay, where the tanker approaches were narrowest and most difficult, had not been Maine's leading nesting ground for summer residents.

Within a twenty-mile radius of Sears Island lay Acadia National Park and the towns of Maine's Gold Coast—Bar Harbor, Seal Harbor, Vinalhaven, North Haven, Dark Harbor, Southwest Harbor, the Cranberry Isles, Great Spruce Head Island, Isleboro, Castine, and Camden. The area was a veritable Everglades to several migratory species united by increasing devotion to the terrain they saw in winter daydreams of sailing, tennis, fishing, and summer romances—daydreams formed behind doors locked against urban dirt, crime, and noise.

When Scoll approached the newly reelected Governor Curtis to explain his plan, the governor said only that he thought Maine Clean Fuels was underestimating the resistance it would meet. Excluded by Maine's new site law from his formerly active role in the placing of refineries, Curtis suggested that the company should look farther Down East. Scoll rejected the suggestion as too expensive. His Sears Island plan seems to have sprung from his South Portland rejection as Nixon's nomination of G. Harrold Carswell to the Supreme Court flowed from the Senate's refusal to confirm Clement Haynesworth. Having been denied his plausible first choice on somewhat spurious grounds and having been consoled and encouraged by his true-believer associates at the Department of Economic Development, Scoll concluded that his opponents could not muster the strength to thwart him again. He therefore filled his own criteria with a disregard for the concerns of his opposition, which suggested that he was prepared to bask in their regret at having denied him his first choice. Like the Carswell nomination, the Sears Island proposal reinvigorated the opposition and was rejected even more embarrassingly than its predecessor.

Scoll announced his plans for Sears Island in January, 1971, just as Kaneb and Buckley crashed in Tiverton. His application began: "The purpose of this project is to implement the Federal Clean Air Act of 1967, as amended, by making available to consumers of fuel oil in Maine, and elsewhere in New England, a large volume of low sulphur oil." On the day the application was filed, the Department of Economic Development announced plans to make the oil refinery part of a Penobscot Marine Industrial Park to include a container port and a shipyard.

The year-round residents of lower Penobscot Bay voiced strong disapproval of the refinery at a series of public meetings, and the summer community went berserk. A latter-day Paul Revere lit his lanterns with a mimeographed notice, mailed nationwide, implying that Maine Clean Fuels, aided by the governor and other high state officials, was seeking to ram the application through without so much as an EIC hearing. He urged letters of protest to the governor, Senators Smith* and Muskie, Representative Hathaway, EIC Chairman Koons, and state representative Marie Wood. He inspired at least 300 letters with 1,500 carbon copies.

An extraordinarily powerful network sprang from this and other mailings. No fewer than 1200 letters deluged the governor's office.† They ran 100 to 1 against the refinery, and the strength they represented is clear in the following excerpt from a letter from W. B. Murphy, chairman of the board of Campbell Soup, to J. Hallowell

---

* Senator Smith's low-BTU response was: "The proposers of an oil refinery on the coast of Maine from the very beginning have chosen Senator Muskie as their champion and have excluded me from any participation. This is completely agreeable with me. Consequently, your appeal should be to Senator Muskie, rather than to me."

† The next most explosive issues of Curtis's term had been gun control and the state income tax, which did not together generate 500 letters.

Vaughn, whose family once owned twenty miles along the Kennebec River:

> I sent copies of my letter to Douglas Dillon, former Secretary of the Treasury, who has a home on Isleboro and to Mr. Albert Nickerson, former Chairman of Mobil Oil Corporation, who has a home on an island off Tenants Harbor. Today at the A.T.&T. meeting I shall deliver "Island Advantages" and the Bangor *News* clipping to Douglas Dillon on the chance that he has not seen it.*

More than half the letters came from outside of Maine, mostly from Boston and New York but with occasional notes from Omaha, Oklahoma City, Paris, Lisbon, Puerto Rico, and the Canal Zone. Among those moved to write were IBM board chairman Thomas Watson, naval historian Samuel Eliot Morison, pianist Lorin Hollander, Mitchell Goodman (codefendant in the trial of Dr. Benjamin Spock), and Mrs. Archibald Cox.

Mostly written in longhand on monogrammed or corporate letterhead stationery, these letters demanded, cajoled, pleaded, flattered, and reasoned, in the name of integrity, ecology, history, tourism, the New Politics, the North Atlantic fishery, and generations unborn, that the governor personally oppose and veto the Maine Clean Fuels refinery. About 25 percent of the letters also urged that he fire Commissioner Keefe, who had been reported to have told an anti-oil audience in Camden that Maine law required him to promote new industry and that public sentiment "makes no difference to me," at which *Maine Times* editor John Cole abandoned mere journalism to roar from the rear of the room, "I won't stand here and let you lie to these people."[10]

The flavor of the letters to Curtis is reflected in the following excerpts:

> Washington, D.C.—We, the summer residents of Maine do not want an oil refinery on Sears Island or anyplace else on the coast of Maine.

---

* Murphy's concern for Maine's environment seems to have been confined to Penobscot Bay. He was a director of the International Paper Company, which had two mills on the Androscoggin River, designated by federal officials as one of the country's ten most polluted. His Campbell Soup Company had been unable to locate a plant in Maine a year earlier because it could not find an adequate supply of clean water.

Douglas Dillon, Peter Flanigan's senior partner at Dillon, Read & Co., wrote to Governor Curtis that "It would be a pity if you were to go down in history as the one who permitted the rape of Penobscot Bay." Although he did not support Maine Clean Fuels, Curtis replied that "the coast is too much the privileged domain of a wealthy few."

Why are you and Senator Muskie so interested in oil? Why not some other industry?

This question is asked me by many permanent residents. They need industry, heaven knows, and they are troubled that their elected officers should emphasize an industry obviously unsuitable for the State of Maine.

P.S. I own 2 houses, 20+ acres and 500 feet of waterfront and I spend a good deal of money on Deer Isle.

Oklahoma City—Please don't take the chance of ruining Penobscot Bay with an oil refinery near Searsport. My father's family, the Thurlows, helped settle the Deer Isle area, and I hope that my children can enjoy the beauty their ancestors passed to them.

Besides, you can always get oil from Oklahoma—but Oklahoma has no way of providing a beautiful rugged coastline.

Princeton, N.J.—We are Maine summer residents, Maine taxpayers and Maine lovers. Who ARE you going to listen to. I hope you examine your reasons for listening in the light of human existence and not material profit.

Gorham, Maine—My home, 8 rooms, very little insulation heats for $300 a year. I can't imagine additional oil activity lowering the price of oil more than 20%. This I'll gladly pay to keep our coast as free as possible from oil. I have an idea most of our residents feel the same way.

Omaha, Nebraska—For the most stupid stance of 1971 by a state department head anywhere, I nominate James O'Keefe. Yes, Mr. O'Keefe's pigheadedness on the Sears Island oil port issue was duly recorded in the midwestern press . . .

I am enclosing $1.00 cash to initiate an outmigration fund for unwanted public servants who outrage public sensibilities on ecologically sensitive issues. Travel to chosen destination may be sweetened by detour (and layover) to areas that have experienced the type of disaster Mr. O'Keefe invites.

Middletown, Connecticut— . . . the letter [alerting summer residents to the oil project] has been sent to Peter Boynton who owns—or alas, I must say owned—St. Helena Island off Stonington. "Owned" because Mr. Boynton died suddenly in Honolulu last January 12. . . .

Mr. Boynton's novel deals with the sort of thing at stake here . . . the novel *Stone Island* will (when it appears: I am putting it in order for publication) be further witness for our side, a side which must win but which, he often thought, had increasingly less chance of doing so in a country run by grotesque greed and blindness to what makes the world fit for human dwelling.

The sea and the air of Maine were sacred to Peter as they are to so many others.* . . . I urge you in his name to do your best to oppose this refinery. . . . If I can be of any further help, let me know.

Arthur S. Wensinger
Chairman, Department of German Language and Literature
Wesleyan University

East Vassalboro, Maine—My feeling is that the coast of Maine is no longer for the natives but for the tourists. I know that I could not possibly stay in most of the motels or eat in the restaurants as the prices are geared for the well to do, not the average working man.

Also the shoreline is being taken over by the outsiders more and more every year. I cannot begin to recall how many times I have been told to get out and stay out, or have run into a keep out sign, when all I was trying to do was take pictures or show my children places where I used to climb rocks or play when I was a child and was visiting my aunt who lives in Friendship.

No, Governor, unless something is done, the coast of Maine as I knew it will never be again for the people of Maine but for the rich out of stater. So therefore, I find that in order to get the most for my money and feel welcome I will have to either go roughing it or go into New Brunswick or Quebec Canada in order to get the most for my hard earned dollars.

Bluehill, Maine—I am writeing you in regard to oil refinery at Searsport. i am in favor of it as we got to put men to work as you know we cant tax people unless we make jobs. the most of the people who are against are people who are well of or people who just come here summers some of those summer people run full page add in our news papers and pay for them out of there own pocket. . . . as you know any thing like manufacture comeing in here the people never gets to vote on it. it always been taken care of behind closed doors we will never have Government for the people by the people untill we have law to forse people to vote in election. there is no reason for people not voteing unless sickness or out of state and that no reason as they could get absent T ballots . . . when less then half of the people voteing age vote the other magority is getting a raw deal. one way would be to do

* *Stone Island* was eventually published and favorably reviewed. It was a serious work, but when it went into paperback, it too became a vehicle for the exploitation of a Maine coastal stereotype. The cover showed a naked woman from behind, her lower half immersed in unlikely tranquility in the 60° Maine ocean. Three men gaze out to sea from distant ledges. The back cover proclaims, "To the rocky coast of Maine, where men are raw and elemental, comes a woman—lonely and obsessed with sex . . . retreating from the frustrations of the real world into the womblike peace of a small coastal town . . ."

it is to make it a must to vote to get any State surfices welfare included must show they voted in last election. i am 70 years young and i always found time to vote. . . . it makes anyone sick to go to Town meeting and see the Chamber of Commerce the Doctors all lined up against the poor people who are not there to vote. the poor people think it loss of time to try to out vote socity. i think thes names who are against oil should be looked over closely as they are getting grammerschool children to sign up against oil refinery comeing to Searsport i cant say they are going to send them in but i would guess they are as i was talking to one of the boys who signed it and he said the names would be sent in. i asked him why he signed it. he said he would not work in oil refinery so i asked him what he was going to do if there was no other work he is 12 or 13 years old i think people is getting pretty low to use the kids for this kind of business. when there parents are very poor people. if this letter does not make any sciense to you put it in wast basket and forget i ever wrote to you.

Unable to answer the letters individually, Curtis resorted to a form letter which he eventually converted into a statement opening the EIC hearing on the Maine Clean Fuels application. Although he still wanted a refinery complex in Maine, the governor was convinced that Scoll was in the wrong place and could not get approval. Two and a half years had passed since he had testified fervently on behalf of Occidental at a Foreign Trade Zones Board hearing at which the environment had scarcely been mentioned, and his Sears Island statement was a fair measure of how far he and the nation had come:

This hearing will be the first clear cut test of Maine's ability to analyze and regulate heavy industry under the Site Approval Law. The task before the Environmental Improvement Commission is to reconcile the incalculable recreational and fishery value of Searsport and the Penobscot Bay area with the undeniable economic and energy benefits which the Maine Clean Fuels application offers to Maine and New England. If such a reconciliation is not possible at this time, the application must be rejected, for the premise of the Site Approval Law is that Maine will not sacrifice present jobs or quality of life for future development. Most American industry, including the oil industry, has taken significant steps toward environmental self control in the last decade, but to locate on Penobscot Bay an oil company will have to show that it is capable of matching or exceeding the very best environmental efforts which have been made elsewhere.

Many people have overlooked the significance of the fact that this hearing is being held at all. Maine was the first state in the nation to provide a state-level approval process for major industries, and we are still one of a handful of states which have such a process. In short, we have rejected claims on the one hand that any industry is so hopelessly dangerous that we should ban it outright forever and on the other hand that all industry is automatically beneficial and should be granted whatever sacrifices it demands of us.

This hearing is the first step in a case by case process through which Maine will make clear the terms on which our future industrial development will take place. This case by case method is not so heroic, not so grandiose, not so totalitarian, as the extremists on either side would like, but it is more impartial, more thorough, and more fair. It reflects the goal for the settling of difficult questions, even in times of strong and sincere feeling, that is set forth in the Constitution of the United States and the State of Maine, namely due process of law and the realization that the way in which a decision is made is frequently as important a safeguard of our way of life as the decision itself.

I have received more than a thousand letters urging me to take a position, to exert a so-called moral leadership with regard to this application. I feel that the time for moral leadership was in the preparation, support, and passage of the Site Approval Law and in pledging, as I do again now, to veto any effort to weaken it . . .

We are not talking now about the abstract aspects of poverty or pollution. Discussion, letters, petitions, and speeches which assert that the one evil is worse than the other are exercises which have no place in the specific case before the EIC. Maine government has decreed that the Commission must find that there will be "no adverse effect on existing uses." Those who would make this hearing a popularity contest should think carefully about whether a series of public relations contests involving America's most powerful industry offers Maine a better guarantee of environmental integrity than this strict standard applied fairly.

I think not, and in rejecting mere popularity as a yardstick for judging this application, I am defending Maine's legal process with the same determination with which I expect this Commission to safeguard the Maine environment.

The statement was generally well received, but many conservationists found it "unspecific," "unsatisfactory," "disingenuous," or "equivocable." Mitchell Goodman, himself only recently acquitted in the Spock trial because of a continuing national concern for due process of law, responded to the governor's sentiments with, "The case against oil is perfectly clear. Do you mean you do not see it or do not believe it. What you say here is simply evasive."

In response to Goodman's and several similar letters, Curtis developed a second form answer:

> I apparently am unable to make clear to you that you are better off having this issue decided under rules of law by the Environmental Improvement Commission than you would be in having it decided as a political popularity contest. Let me point out again that if I were to take the course you suggest today, you would have no right to appeal from the actions of a subsequent Governor who took the opposite course in response to, let us say, the appeal of a power company executive that he permit such a refinery in order to meet the need for cheaper fuel.
>
> Perhaps I can best illustrate my position by pointing out to you the nearly universal dismay which all lawyers felt when President Nixon proclaimed Charles Manson to be guilty before the end of his trial. There is no doubt that the President was expressing a consensus of public opinion and was exercising what you would call moral leadership. Nevertheless, he was disregarding the concept of due process of law in precisely the same manner that you are now urging upon me.
>
> If we were not protected by the site approval law, my position would perhaps be different. I am, however, more than tired of the would be heroes on both sides of the environment-development question and am entirely satisfied to proceed on a case by case basis, relying upon our strict law and the expertise of the EIC.

Pestilential though it may have seemed to individual members, the Maine Clean Fuels application was a godsend to the Coastal Resources Action Committee. CRAC's lobbying successes and bankruptcy-aided victory over King Resources were behind it, and the organization was again in need. When the proposed Penobscot Bay refinery was announced, a $40,000 war chest rolled in in a matter of days.

The mere suggestion of a Penobscot Bay refinery would have been enough, but CRAC had plenty of help. The legislature, simmering over a series of collisions with Jim Keefe, was goaded by the commissioner's alleged refusal to heed public sentiment into passing a resolution advising all state agencies "to forthwith halt any promotion of or material assistance to any business activity involving the drilling for or refining of oil or oil products." Noting that the resolution did not override his statutory mandate, Keefe replied, "We don't plan any changes in the department's policy."[11] At this, Senator Richard Berry reintroduced his moratorium with a statement predicting that it would be vetoed. John Cole demanded to know why, if DED felt obliged to promote all comers, it had refused aid to the producers of a made-in-Maine film on the ground that it would be X-rated.*

Bob Monks, struggling to avoid his own ten-month-old referendum mandate to build a Machias Bay refinery, came out against Scoll's proposal. Senator Muskie reaffirmed his preelection opposition, prompting Scoll to accuse him of being out of touch with unspecified recent developments in clean-up technology. Muskie and the architect-inventor R. Buckminster Fuller, another Penobscot Bay island owner, traded exhortative poems about the wonders of tidal power and the dangers of oil on the Op Ed page of *The New York Times*. Not content with the ambiguities of poetry, the Boston *Globe* editorialized:

> No more wicked, cruel, greedy, foolish, misguided, shortsighted, taste-less and generally disreputable proposal has come to public attention in recent years than the plan to build a refinery on Sears Island. . . .
>
> But one cannot help thinking that one clear unequivocal word from Senator Muskie, who just might be President some day, would block the Sears Island refinery for years to come. It is within the Senator's power to say that word or leave it unsaid.[12]

At times CRAC's greatest ally seemed to be Scoll himself. Although his salmon-fisherman-in-waders gait had long since become more familiar in Augusta corridors than the stride of any other aspiring refiner, he still shared his predecessor suitors' ability to impose personal import quotas on Maine realities. He made little allowance for the extreme public concern with oil and none at all for Maine's being a small, homogeneous state in which people compared notes.

To consumers, Maine Clean Fuels suggested that its 1975 refinery output would precisely match Maine's oil needs, enabling the refinery to supply the state. The company was correct in saying that its oil output would roughly equal Maine's 1975 oil demand, but the equation

---

* The Sears Island controversy was more than enough to bring the *Maine Times*–DED relationship to its lowest point, but matters weren't helped any by DED's simultaneous "Me." campaign.

Maine's state abbreviation had been Me. for 150 years, but in 1970 an advertising agency retained to help DED promote the state suggested that the abbreviation could be the basis of a catchy publicity campaign. Soon signs saying things like "Ski Me.," "Lover Come Back to Me.," and "God Bless Me.," adorned magazines and Boston billboards. Some found this offensive. The *Maine Times*, enraged anyway by a DED snowmobile ad extolling the Maine woods as a snowmobile "Heaven, Miles of wilderness where you can go like Hell," suggested that the basic message of the campaign was "Screw Me." Others found it appealing. The National Association of State Development Agencies gave it a first prize among the promotions of the fifty states.

did not extend to the product mix. Scoll's import permits required that he concentrate heavily on low-sulfur industrial oil, a product that most Maine mills weren't required to burn and that Maine cars couldn't use.

To labor groups, he sometimes overestimated the percentage of refinery workers that could have come from Maine.

To conservationists, he promised that his use of larger tankers would actually reduce the number of tankers plying Penobscot Bay each year. His promise was true as far as it went, but it did not mention that Maine Clean Fuels would also be sextupling the number of barges.

In the most unusual confrontation spawned by oil's brush with the Maine coast, he even visited Peggy (Mrs. David) Rockefeller, whose in-laws owned several houses in the Bar Harbor area, in New York City, arriving unannounced with a mutual friend to try to convince her that his plan had merit. The commingling of histories inherent in this visit is as striking as the nerve required to have undertaken it.

To understand the commingling, picture a ladder of aspiring refinery owners. On the lowest rung is Scoll, who is seeking a piece of his first refinery. On the next step, owning a piece of one, stands Jack Evans, who would like to start his second. Next, having broken ground on his second, comes John Shaheen, his eye on global significance. Above him, a significant newcomer to the world petroleum market, Dr. Armand Hammer works like Harry Sinclair in the 1920s to shed his maverick status in order that he may join Atlantic Richfield's Robert Anderson, who now runs Sinclair's former company, in inner circles and philanthropies. From there Anderson can see the feet of the top man on the ladder, John D. Rockefeller, before whose granddaughter-in-law stands David Scoll. They are in the comfortably immense living room on the second floor of the Rockefellers' mid-Manhattan residence, surrounded by articles purchased in part by the inheritance from the most successful oil refiner in history. Scoll attempts to convince her that his proposed construction of the manufacturing unit that they have in common is very much in the public interest and will do her no harm. She, although aware that the Standard Oil trust was the father of the revenues that had helped to create Acadia National Park, offers him only coffee.

Back in Maine, more fissures in Scoll's structure appeared at a Searsport meeting organized by a Maine Clean Fuels realtor to enable the company to state its case. To discourage opposition, the organizer had limited the attendance to Searsport residents and had called in several municipal police officers and county deputy sheriffs. In an apparent effort to assure favorable footage for a CBS camera crew lured from New York, no rebuttals from the floor were permitted, and while the audience was permitted to ask questions, it was told that the questions might not be answered. The following description of the give-and-take is from the *Maine Times* of February 26, 1971:

> In his introductory remarks, Scoll said it was "thanks to the genius of Senator Edmund Muskie" that the Clean Air Act had created a demand for the low sulphur oil products the refinery would produce. Asked later if he would explain his estimate of the Muskie genius in relation to the Senator's announced opposition to the oil refinery, Scoll said, "No, I will not."
>
> Asked a question on the general topic of oil spills, Scoll replied snappishly, "You shouldn't worry so much about oil spills. We are going to be right here, in this community, right on the job." Later, in answer to a question about the connection between Maine Clean Fuels and the Ashland Oil Company, Scoll replied, "We have a handshake agreement with Ashland that they will run the refinery once it is built. We don't much want to stay around to run refineries."
>
> Asked about the so-called Decca controlled electronic navigation system, Scoll said it is the most failsafe ship guidance system yet developed and would assure the residents of Penobscot Bay that oil tanker accidents would not occur. A bit later, in answer to another question, Scoll said, "The use of the Decca system for ship guidance is not legal in the United States."
>
> Asked if his firm had made any study of the effects on marine life of dredging in Penobscot Bay, Scoll said, "No, we haven't sampled one bit of that bottom." Yet his firm's application to Environmental Improvement Commission included plans for a 2,000-yard channel and a large ship turn-around area to be dredged.
>
> Asked who would be liable in case of an oil spill in the bay, Scoll said, "Don't worry about that. We'll assume liability for all oil spills from any vessel, foreign or otherwise." Yet, instructions to company officers in Clean Fuels' application read: "oil spills can generate complex technical, legal, and public relations problems for the company. . . . No statements shall be made . . . concerning liability for a spill or its legal consequences."
>
> Asked by Leroy Stoddard, Jr., of Bucksport: "Is technology infallible?" Scoll refused to answer, although in his introductory remarks he had said, "All you boys and girls who are worried will get your chance to ask about tankers." When Stoddard rephrased his question to ask "What can you do if a tanker goes aground and starts spilling all over

the Maine coast?" Scoll turned away from his microphone and nodded to moderator Fallon, who, in turn, nodded to a police sergeant who sent two deputies down to remove young Stoddard from his place at the question microphone.

Asked if the refinery would be non-polluting, Scoll said, "Yes, it will be the cleanest refinery in the world." Later, he said he had no refinery experience, and that no refinery like the one his firm plans has ever been built anywhere.

It was nearly 11 pm and about a third of the audience had already left, some looking a bit confused, when moderator Fallon said: "Some of the newspapers want us to end this so they can make their deadlines. Personally, I don't give a damn if they make their deadlines or not, but I think we've kept Mr. Scoll here about long enough."*

Deeply resentful of what he felt were entirely unprincipled attacks on him by the *Maine Times* and by Cole in particular, Scoll paused on his way out of the Searsport meeting and, as Cole remembers it, said, "We're not worried about you; we know who's paying your bills."

The *Maine Times* was not John Cole's only vehicle for challenging Maine Clean Fuels. During 1970 he had formed The Allagash Group (TAG), a "mini think tank" designed to focus Maine's intellectual resources on Maine development problems. Funded largely by Bob Monks, who was preparing for his role in Maine public life by enrolling as a student at the John F. Kennedy School of Government in Boston, TAG retained three graduate students in the Kennedy School's Public Policy Program to evaluate the refinery.

Their report, which received extensive coverage in the *Maine Times*, concluded that the refinery would result in a net loss of $948,000 in wages to residents of the Penobscot Bay area and that "the most attractive employment development strategy available to the state is a program to increase poultry production and to establish production of modular housing."

CRAC used the contributions that flowed in after Scoll's Searsport meeting to hire Harold Pachios to intervene in the site-review proceeding before the Environmental Improvement Commission. Superficially, Scoll and Pachios were well-matched antagonists, for Pachios's stocky

---

* Scoll vehemently disputes parts of this account. He says that the *Maine Times*, strongly biased against him, slanted the general tone of the meeting. Specifically, he points out that the Decca navigational system, while not certified for use in the U.S., guided tankers into some Canadian ports and through the crowded lanes of Rotterdam and England's Thames River.

build and politically intuitive manner made him at times appear a twenty-five-year-younger version of his opponent. Ironically, among the many respects in which they differed was that Scoll had been a salmon and trout fisherman for most of his life, while Pachios, fresh from ten years in Washington, was just taking up tennis and sailing in his first real participation in outdoor recreation since leaving Maine.

To strengthen his case going into the hearing, Scoll decided to add the national-security lure to his tackle box. Relying on his excellent ties to President Nixon's Oil Policy Committee, he prepared a letter for Governor Curtis to send to the committee's chairman, General Lincoln. The letter asked the Oil Policy chairman whether he thought "national security, and particularly the security of fuel oil supplies for the State and the neighboring states, should influence the decision of this State."

Scoll's request that Governor Curtis send such a letter was in itself unusual. Viewed against the Nader group's analysis of his governmental-relations technique and coupled with his ill-fated effort to extract an endorsement from the National Air Pollution Control Administration, the request suggested that perhaps Scoll was not leaving his peripheral ploys to the same Providence to which Maine's site approval law required that he entrust his central ones—that, in short, this champion of renewed Congressional effectiveness had somehow made sure that the reply would indeed say that a heavy-fuel refinery in Maine would be in the national interest.

Curtis sent the letter, but only after slipping in a question on whether the promised price reductions were very likely. Unfazed, General Lincoln responded that price cuts could not be predicted, but that domestic refineries would be more secure than those abroad and that the best refinery for New England would be one making home heating and low-sulfur industrial-fuel oils while deemphasizing gasoline. Lincoln's response was perfectly tailored to Scoll's plant, but Scoll hadn't been in Maine long enough to appreciate the peculiarity of Lincoln's telling Curtis exactly what Curtis had been saying in vain to the federal government for three years about the Occidental proposal. Exasperated, the governor sat on the reply until after the EIC hearings closed before forwarding it without press attention to the commission to treat as it wished.

By that time, nothing Lincoln could say would have helped Maine Clean Fuels. Scoll's application had irked the commission at the outset, for his pollution-control exhibits consisted largely of unverified advertisements from trade journals. Then, despite repeated warnings that the

commission was interested solely in environmental impacts, Maine
Clean Fuels witnesses spent much of the first day outlining possible
employment and energy benefits. Eventually Chairman Koons ruled
this testimony out of order, thereby infuriating several labor-union
representatives who were waiting to testify.

Scoll's refinery economics, relevant because environmental controls
represented an added cost which only an adequately financed firm
could afford, were also unstable. His principal backer, the Ashland Oil
Company, insisted on remaining well in the background, partly out of
fear that its products might face a conservationist boycott. Ashland
would vouchsafe no more than a willingness to negotiate with Scoll if
his project was approved. The banking firm of Kuhn, Loeb & Company
took the same position on financing. Their reticence left Scoll in an
impossible position, which accounted for many of the mistakes that his
opponents seized on. Not only was he overextended personally, but he
had also to promise large expenditures for complex technologies without any apparent capital or experience. This situation invited what
Scoll later described as "efforts to make us look like cheap, stinking
promoters."

Maine Clean Fuels was also buffeted by forces beyond Maine. The
inevitable oil spill this time took the form of a leak of several hundred
gallons of fuel from an Air Force tank in Searsport. Thousands of
bushels of clams were killed, and Maine's Department of Sea and Shore
Fisheries estimated the marine-resource loss at about a million dollars.

Meanwhile, the EIC staff had become concerned about an apparent
inconsistency between Scoll's application (which contemplated crude
oil) and his oil-import permits, which were good only for high-sulfur
industrial oil. A letter of inquiry brought a reply from the Interior
Department that Scoll's entire plan was illegal, in violation of his permits. Furious, Scoll pointed out that Interior was using inconsistent
definitions of crude oil in different import regulations and added that
General Lincoln had assured him that his permits would be amended.
Privately he added that the official who had sent the letter "lunched
with a Texas Company [Texaco] lobbyist weekly, and they don't want
to compete with me in New England." He was also annoyed that
Interior had neither called him nor sent an advance copy of its letter.

The defects in the Maine Clean Fuels case might have been fatal by
themselves, but CRAC had prepared an extensive case of its own. Bor-
rowing both ideas and witnesses from the conservationists' victory at
Tiverton, they established that some refineries stink, some tankers spill,

and most spills kill. Much of their case rested on a form of guilt by association, but the Penobscot Bay mystique and Maine Clean Fuels' lack of either expertise or a track record of its own made it effective. For variety, CRAC witnesses also alleged that the fresh-water requirements of the refinery exceeded the known available supply and that Maine Clean Fuels' refinery diagram showed a facility that would have overhung Sears Island by 100 feet to the south.

In July, 1971, the EIC found that the Maine Clean Fuels project posed an unacceptable risk to everything from scenery to navigation to the fishing industry. The vote was 6–3. Scoll felt that the commission had acted arbitrarily in the absence of any guiding land use plan and had treated him unprofessionally and with bias. He alleged, "They used any stigma to beat a dogma." He suspected that he had been rejected because the cleanliness of his refinery would embarrass the paper mills and the state agency that had tolerated them. Rejecting the advice of its attorneys, Maine Clean Fuels appealed the decision.

Two years later the Maine Supreme Court removed any shadow of doubt over the constitutionality of the Site Approval Law by rejecting the appeal unanimously. By then Scoll and his shy sponsors were long gone from the stage which they had borrowed from better-known actors, but his "paradox of pollution" lingered on. The shortage of low sulfur fuel that he, Hammer, and many others had predicted was a reality, to be met through a crash energy conservation program and dirtier air. The crash conservation program would increase unemployment. The dirtier air would increase the several forms of cancer, emphysema, bronchitis, heart disease, and property damage that have been conclusively linked to reductions in air quality.

To the victors went the spoils. Only a few corners of Penobscot Bay are less than pure—one harbor because of chicken guts from a Belfast processing plant and several miles of clam flats closed off in the summer because the sewage levels are high enough to cause hepatitis. Visitors to Acadia National Park can still enjoy the view from Cadillac Mountain without interference from aluminum smelters or oil refineries. No one of them contributes much to the growing problem of topsoil attrition near the wooded paths, reportedly attributable to the millions of footsteps of summertime tourists.

These paths on Cadillac Mountain were part of the $4-million gift of land and money made to the National Park Service by John D. Rockefeller, Jr., as his share of the several private acquisitions and donations which saved the mountain from lumbering operations. Many of the trees were subsequently lost in a 1947 fire. They have been replaced by hardwoods which lend an agreeable variety to the park, particularly in autumn.

The fire also destroyed 100,000 mice and their complete cancer histories at the Jackson Memorial Laboratory, since rebuilt at the same spot because the island is free from instrument-agitating earth tremors and because

> the whole atmosphere of the place is remotely quiet and serene, so that technicians suffer few distractions and little pressure and can give their undivided attention to their work. A large percent of the staff is local, the sons and daughters of Maine fishermen and farmers.[13]

Gone also with the fire were most of the island's great estates, those eroding peninsulas of a life style already doomed by the income tax and servant shortages. Although *Le Figaro* speculated to Parisians that the fire had been set by Maine peasants fed up with feudal oppression, the better evidence is that the year-round residents were more tolerant of summer folks' cravings for pastoral surroundings. They had, after all, acquiesced for some years in a state law, lobbied by summer residents, barring automobiles from Mount Desert Island, and they went on electing a fence viewer and a hog reeve long past the time when anyone remembered their duties.

The estates had been built in the half century following the social "discovery" of the island in 1844 by Thomas Cole, a cofounder of the naturalistic Hudson River school of painting. Cole's enthusiasm spread so rapidly that steamboat- and railroad-borne visitors elevated Bar Harbor to Newport status among summer travelers. The life style thus spawned has been chronicled in novels such as F. Marion Crawford's *Maidens Call It Love in Idleness* and in more straightforward accounts such as the following two from Stephen Birmingham's *Our Crowd* and Louise Dickinson Rich's *The Coast of Maine:*

> June and July were spent at Seabright [New Jersey]. There, on the last Thursday of July, the Schiff family had an early supper and boarded their private car—usually one of E. H. Harriman's cars of the Union Pacific—parents, children, nurses, governess, maids, and at least sixty pieces of luggage, many of them trunks. The car was presided over by Madison, the Schiffs' chef, and a helper. Sometimes a second private car was needed. The family would travel overnight to Ellsworth, Maine, then disembark and board a boat to Bar Harbor. The horses, meanwhile,

were traveling, along with grooms, tack and equipment, by boat from New Jersey. . . .

They stayed in Bar Harbor exactly a month. Then in September, the whole process reversed itself, and everyone went back to Seabright for another month.*[14]

One of the great houses had a dining table that sank through the floor into the kitchen below between courses, to rise again with the next course beautifully served; but often there was no fresh meat to fill the Limoges plates, because of primitive refrigeration and lack of adequate transportation, and the water in the lovely crystal goblets was pumped from a well of questionable purity.

They went on long walks and collected flowers and shells, and even the emptiest-headed debutante knew the proper Latin names. They espoused Nature and observed the stars and kept records of the flight of birds. They gave elaborate parties to the same people they entertained back in New York or Boston or Philadelphia, and then they built little cabins hidden deep in the woods where they could retire to escape their social obligations and think about Life and write their memoirs. They were rather sweet.

The sweetest of all were Dr. Robert Derby of New York and Colonel Albert Stickney of Boston. Every year, starting in 1871, they used to row a little wherry or light skiff from the Union Boat Club in Boston to Roberts Wharf in Bar Harbor. The expedition took weeks. It's a long way, hundreds of miles. During the early laps of their journey, they could go ashore at fashionable resorts and stay at good hotels over night; but as they progressed farther and farther up the coast, they had to stop at farmhouses and lobster shacks and lighthouses. . . .

No one knew exactly when they would arrive, of course, but the local grapevine carried word of their slow approach. As soon as the bulletin came that they had passed the little island of Thrumcap, the entire summer population went down to Roberts Wharf and gave them a big welcome. It was one of the Events of the Season. . . .

Another phase of the antipathy to change was the Great Automobile War. The automobile represented speed and noise and restlessness, and the summer people had come to Bar Harbor in the first place to escape all this. They were not going to have their peace and leisure destroyed

* Jacob Schiff, about whose family this paragraph was written, died in 1920, and his family stopped going to Bar Harbor a few years later. He might, nevertheless, have been struck by one facet of the Scoll situation fifty years later. Schiff had, primarily through astute railroad financing, been responsible for elevating the firm of Kuhn, Loeb & Company to the preeminent position among New York banking houses from which it had offered to bankroll David Scoll if he got his environmental approvals.

without a struggle. Therefore they passed a law forbidding the introduction of cars to the island. It wasn't easy. Some of the native islanders
depended on summer people for a prosperity the like of which they'd
never had before and the scions of the rich had been brought up to
respect the wishes of their elders, so long after cars were common on
the mainland, Mt. Desert was still horse-drawn.

Finally, however, a patient died because his doctor, who could have
saved him had he owned a car, was unable to reach him in time to
administer aid. This affair aroused so much feeling that the law banning
automobiles was revoked in 1913, and now there are hundreds of cars
all over Mt. Desert.[15]

Many summer residents had always taken a strong interest in the
well-being of their communities. Gardiner Means's Styrofoam rowboat
factory reflected an exceptional level of commitment, but substantial
donations to local schools, hospitals, churches, and historical societies
were frequent. In an effort to harmonize their concern for preservation
with their respect for the local tax base, a group of the summer residents led by Mrs. David Rockefeller had formed the Maine Coast
Heritage Trust to encourage the granting of scenic easements (essentially a veto over unsuitable development) on the property of many
who sympathized with conservation but wanted to hang on to the land
itself.

Although opposed to the Maine Clean Fuels refinery, the Rockefellers felt increasingly uncomfortable with frequent suggestions in the
Maine press that they were seeking to preserve the Maine coast as their
private playground. While the Maine Clean Fuels case was pending
before the EIC, David Rockefeller, chairman of the board of the Chase
Manhattan Bank, offered to be joint host in New York with Governor
Curtis at a luncheon for Maine summer residents who were in positions
to help Maine develop in ways consistent with a clean environment.
Although skeptical of the willingness of the summer people to go much
beyond saving Penobscot Bay, Curtis was impressed by the economic
potential of such a group, and he agreed to the meeting.

Rockefeller proved his good intentions by assembling a group of
executives that would have made Maurice Stans's mouth water. Their
companies controlled assets worth more than the state of Maine and
everything in it. Governor Curtis made a presentation which tightroped
between an elaboration of Maine's economic needs and implicit extor-
tion. He reminded his audience, "The question before this group, therefore, is whether you wish to play the guiding and constructive role in

our development of which you are capable or whether you are willing to have it take place entirely according to the economic dictates of a very needy state."

Following a lengthy discussion of Maine's disadvantages (mostly transportation costs) and future options (stress tourism, offer more tax incentives), Rockefeller closed the meeting with a suggestion of follow-up sessions. Only one such session was held. It was poorly attended and, in the opinion of people from both sides, a waste of time. The tendency in Maine was to say that the summer residents' interest had faded with Scoll's rejection, but the summer people could reply that they had responded to any requests that Maine had made of them and could point instead to the failure of the state to establish a meaningful apparatus to evaluate proposals and sustain interest. The Maine Coast Heritage Trust has thrived and by mid-1974 had generated seventy-three easements covering forty entire islands, twenty-five parts of islands, and six thousand shorefront acres, but the involvement of the summer community in Maine's economic development has not increased.

While Maine Clean Fuels convulsed coastal Maine, the Libyan ripple spread throughout the Middle East. Occidental's capitulation in late 1970 to the Libyan tax demands which Qaddafi had reinforced by ordering production cutbacks was quickly followed by similar agreements with other companies producing in Libya.

What happened next is described by Professor Adelman in *Foreign Policy:*

> The Persian Gulf producing countries then demanded and received the same increase whereupon Libya, which had not rescinded the cutbacks, demanded a further increase, and the Persian Gulf countries followed suit. Finally, agreements were signed at Tehran in February 1971, increasing tax royalty payments at the Persian Gulf as of June 1971 by almost 46 cents per barrel, and rising to about 66 cents in 1975. North African and Nigerian increases were larger. In Venezuela the previous 1966 agreement was disregarded and higher taxes were simply legislated. . . .
>
> The multinational companies producing oil were amenable to these tax increases because, as was openly said on the morrow of Tehran, they used the occasion to increase their margins and return on investment in both crude and products. In Great Britain the object was stated: to cover the tax increase "and leave some over," and the February 1971

tax increase was matched by a product price increase perhaps half again as great. The best summary of the results was by a well known financial analyst, Kenneth E. Hill, who called the agreements "truly an unexpected boon for the worldwide industry."

Mr. Hill rightly emphasized product price increases, but arm's length crude prices also increased by more than tax increases. When the producing countries made fresh demands later in 1971, an American investment advisory service (United Business Services) remarked that tax increases were actually favorable to oil company profits. And 1971 was easily the best year for company profits since 1963. . . .

The price pattern is set for the 1970's. From time to time, either in pursuance or in violation of the Tehran-Tripoli agreements, the tax is increased, whereupon prices increase as much or more, but then tend to erode as the companies compete very slowly at the crude level, and less slowly at the products level. Thus prices increase in steps, yet at any given moment there is usually a buyer's market, i.e., more is available than is demanded at the price, which is under downward pressure.

The companies' margin will therefore wax and wane, but they benefit by the new order. . . . As a group, they can profit by a higher tax through raising prices in concert, for the higher tax is that clear signal to which they respond without communication. . . . The then head of Shell, Sir David Barran, spoke of a "marriage" of companies and producing governments. Most precise of all was Sir Eric Drake, the chairman of BP, who called the companies a "tax collecting agency," for both producing and consuming country governments.[16]

As Adelman went on to note, many of the consuming nations, particularly the United States, had an interest in higher oil prices. The rising world price lessened both the need for and the embarrassment of protecting the cultivated inefficiencies of the domestic industry. Higher oil prices also tended to rescue commitments to coal and nuclear power that were appearing as bad judgment when measured against cheap foreign oil. Furthermore, higher world prices would actually help the United States, which had significant oil production of its own, in competing against goods manufactured in Western Europe, Japan, and the many underdeveloped nations that depended almost entirely on OPEC oil. Lastly, acquiescence in higher prices enabled the United States to buy popularity in Arab nations, using, for the most part, someone else's money.

The events of September, 1970–February, 1971, seemed to reveal continuing ineptness in U.S. oil policy. In Adelman's view:

The most important player in the game is the American State Department. This agency is deplorably poorly informed in mineral resource economics, the oil industry, the history of oil crises and the participation therein of the Arabs with whom it is obsessed; in fact, State cannot even give an accurate account of its own recent doings. . . .

Without active support from the United States, OPEC might not have achieved much. When the first Libyan cutbacks were decreed, the United States could have easily convened the oil companies to work out an insurance scheme whereby any single company forced to shut down would have had crude oil supplied by the others. . . . Had that been done, all companies might have been shut down and the Libyans would have lost all production income. It would have been helpful but not necessary to freeze its deposits abroad. The OPEC nations were unprepared for conflict. Their unity would have been severely tested and probably destroyed. The revenue losses of Libya would have been gains to all other producing nations, and all would have realized the danger of trying to pressure the consumer countries. Any Libyan division or brigade commander could consider how he and friends might gain several billions of dollars a year, and other billions deposited abroad, by issuing the right marching orders.

Failure to oppose does not necessarily imply that the United States favored the result. But there was unambiguous action shortly thereafter. A month after the November agreements with Libya, a special OPEC meeting in Caracas first resolved on "concrete and simultaneous action," but this had not been explained or translated into a threat of a cutoff as late as January 13, nor by January 16, when the companies submitted their proposals for higher and escalating taxes.

Then came the turning point: the United States convened a meeting in Paris of the Organization for Economic Cooperation and Development (who account for most oil consumption) on January 20. There is no public record of the meeting, but—as will become clear below—there is no doubt that the American representatives and the oil companies assured the other governments that if they offered no resistance to higher oil prices they could at least count on five years' secure supply at stable or only slightly rising prices.

The OECD meeting could have kept silent, thereby keeping the OPEC nations guessing, and moderating their demands for fear of counteraction. Or they might have told the press they were sure the OPEC nations were too mature and statesmanlike to do anything drastic, because after all the OECD nations had some drastic options open to them . . . but why inflame opinion by talking about those things? Instead an OECD spokesman praised the companies' offer, and declined to estimate its cost to the consuming countries. He stated that the meeting had not discussed "contingency arrangements for coping with an oil shortage." This was an advance capitulation. The OPEC nations now had a signal to go full speed ahead because there would be no resistance.

Before January 20, an open threat by the OPEC nations would not have been credible, in view of the previous failure of even mild attempts at production regulation in 1965 and 1966. But after the capitulation threats were credible and were made often. . . . They culminated in a resolution passed on February 7 by nine OPEC members . . . providing for an embargo after two weeks if their demands were not met. The Iranian Finance Minister, chief of the producing nations' team, said: "There is no question of negotiations or resuming negotiations. It's just the acceptance of our terms." The companies were resigned to this, but wanted assurances that what they accepted would not be changed for five years.

The United States had been active in the meantime. Our Under Secretary of State* arrived in Tehran January 17, publicly stating his government's interest in "stable and predictable" prices, which in context meant higher prices. He told the Shah of Iran the damage that would be done to Europe and Japan if oil supplies were cut off. Perhaps this is why the Shah soon thereafter made the first threat of a cutoff of supply. It is hard to imagine a more effective incitement to extreme action than to hear that this will do one's opponents great damage.

Resistance to the OPEC demands would have shattered the nascent cartel. As late as January 24, the Shah told the press: "If the oil producing countries suffer even the slightest defeat, it would be the death-knell for OPEC, and from then on the countries would no longer have the courage to get together."

When the Tehran agreement was announced, another State Depart-

---

* John Irwin, brother-in-law to IBM's Thomas Watson and himself an occasional visitor to Penobscot Bay.

While Adelman saw Irwin's actions as designed to encourage higher oil prices, Senator Henry Bellmon of Oklahoma denounced the Under Secretary for opposite reasons. Seeing that higher world oil prices would lessen the oil import menace to his state, Bellmon told the Senate on February 9 that Irwin's presence was an "unprecedented and unholy involvement of our government in a heavy-handed act of neocolonialism. . . . Reports are that Mr. Irwin and his team are working hand in glove with the officers of the big international oil companies to force OPEC to sell their single resource for bargain basement prices. . . . Our government should assist OPEC to sell oil at good prices . . . so that these nations can become economically strong and independent, and so that the energy subsidy Japan and the industrial nations of Western Europe have enjoyed can be ended."

ment special press conference hailed it, referring many times to "stability" and "durability." They "expected the previously turbulent international oil situation to calm down following the new agreement." They must have really believed this! Otherwise they would not have claimed credit for Mr. Irwin . . . or induced President Nixon's office to announce that he too was pleased.[17]

Neither the companies nor the producing governments took the agreements seriously. They have been trampled in the name of devaluation adjustments, participation, nationalization, and embargo.* For a while the State Department continued to speak of stability, then it turned to warning of embargo and scarcity, which Adelman viewed, to his later regret, as unlikely at best† and self-defeating at worst. Further nationalization by Libya in the midsummer of 1973 drove President Nixon to warn Qaddafi to "remember what happened to Mossadegh," a warning roughly equivalent to suggesting to Huey Newton that he remember the fate of Nat Turner.

The State Department did not accept Professor Adelman's analysis. Clearly stung, James Akins‡ responded, in a *Foreign Affairs* article subtitled "This Time the Wolf Is Here," that

> Oil experts, economists and government officials who have attempted in recent years to predict future demand and prices for oil have had only marginally better success than those who foretell the advent of earthquakes or the second coming of the Messiah. . . .
>
> The threat to use oil as a political weapon must be taken seriously. The vulnerability of the advanced countries is too great and too plainly evident—and is about to extend to the United States. . . .
>
> After an arduous round of discussions [in 1970] the international companies operating in Libya yielded one by one. It seemed at the time and still does that they had little choice. Libya had $2 billion in currency reserves; its demands were not unreasonable; its officials could

---

* The companies have offered little resistance and do not feel that they could have. Thornton Bradshaw told a "Dick Cavett Show" audience of an Atlantic Richfield negotiator reporting back to his board of directors after one session and being congratulated on "holding them to their terms."

† "An Arab boycott will hurt only the Arabs and soon collapse. . . . 'There just can't be [quoting a former OPEC Secretary General] an effective selective embargo.' "[18]

‡ Then director of State's Office of Fuels and Energy and on detail to the White House; in 1968 and 1969 a leading opponent within the federal government of Occidental's efforts at Machiasport; in 1973 posted as U.S. ambassador to Saudi Arabia.

not be corrupted [one wonders how he knew] or convinced; and, most important, Libyan oil could not be made up elsewhere. . . .*

Libya's currency reserves could keep the government at current expenditures and import levels for four years. . . . [The assumption that these reserves would be blocked by all the European and Central banks was not likely to be realized.] We in the State Department had no doubt whatever . . . that the Europeans would have made their own deals with the Libyans . . . and that the Anglo-Saxon oil companies' sojourn in Libya would have ended. As for the possibility of using force, . . . suffice it that it was never for a moment considered. . . .

Hindsight considerations as to how that threat might have been countered seem to me quite unrealistic, and the charge that the State Department by inaction was to blame for creating a new monster is, in simple terms, nonsense. . . .

It has been suggested that American representatives virtually invited the threat of cut-off and thus built up OPEC's bargaining position, specifically through statements at a meeting of OECD in Paris on January 20, 1971. . . . By January 20, the threats had already been made;† thereafter, on American representations, they were modified. As for the thought that the OPEC countries need to be told how damaging a withholding could be, this seems to me to belong to a bygone view of the capacity of leaders in less-developed countries.[19]

Akins's article is actually a stronger indictment of U.S. oil policy (though not of the State Department) than Adelman's. If the United States were as vulnerable to OPEC action as he suggests, the failure of the government to have pursued alternative conventional and new energy sources, standby storage, energy conservation, and emergency rationing plans is folly of a much higher level than if Adelman is right in saying that OPEC was able to coalesce with such dramatic effectiveness largely because of the incompetence and/or connivance of the State Department. Under either view, if precautionary measures had been taken during the 1960s, U.S. imports could have been safely and gradually increased, and the country's new leverage in the world market, wisely used, might have undermined OPEC solidarity, deterred the 1973 embargo, and maintained lower prices.

---

* One must assume that Akins refers here to the 1970 tanker shortage. There was no absolute oil shortage or any probability of production cutbacks by other OPEC nations. Individual companies, especially Occidental, were dependent on Libya, but the world as a whole was not.

† Akins is at best disingenuous here. Adelman is clearly referring to a chain of U.S. conduct throughout 1970 culminating in the January 20 meeting.

While Akins's political realism overshadowed Adelman's economic verities after 1971, the immense gap between the price and cost of OPEC oil, a gap which at the end of 1973 was being divided 70–30 between governments and companies, loomed over either analysis. The turbulence in oil prices was such that no one could confidently assert that he knew exactly which forces were gravity and which were wind, or whether oil prices have risen like feathers or like smoke.

Nevertheless, the two men seemed in general agreement that oil-company ownership of (as distinguished from concessions to seek and produce) OPEC oil could and should be eliminated, in order to end the role of the companies as tax collectors. They agreed also that consuming nations should but probably wouldn't seek to exert their combined market power against OPEC, and that the United States had some reasonable options available to reduce the Arab (if not the OPEC) threat to its national security (if not its per capita consumption) over the next five years. One could even see, reading optimistically, a recognition by Akins that the U.S. failure to have had a meaningful domestic energy policy was troublesome.

Since Akins is In and Adelman Out, it would be reassuring to believe that he had expressed such a view in the Oval Office, but his 1973 posting as ambassador to Saudi Arabia suggests the contrary, or at least that he wasn't making himself heard. Perhaps he was just being diplomatic. Perhaps he never got in. Or perhaps he perceived there, right there, between the Sony and the shredder, the career-stifling silhouettes of Peter Flanigan and the Stalemate Machine.

12: 1971–1974

What happened here was the gradual habituation of the people little by little to being governed by surprise; to receiving decisions deliberated in secret; to believing that the situation was so complicated that the Government had to act on information which the people could not understand or so dangerous that, even if the people could understand it, it could not be released because of national security. And their sense of identification with Hitler, their trust in him made it easier to widen this gap, and to reassure those who would otherwise have worried about it.

This separation of government from the people . . . took place so gradually and so insensibly, each step disguised (perhaps not even intentionally) as a temporary emergency measure or associated with true patriotic allegiance or with real social purposes. And all the crises and reforms . . . so occupied the people that they did not see the slow motion underneath, of the whole process of the Government growing remoter and remoter.

Milton Mayer, They Thought They Were Free[1]

In all, fourteen tons of fireworks—more than ten thousand pieces—were set off from the bridge. It lasted a solid hour. . . . Rockets went off hundreds at a time and were seen as far away as Montclair, New Jersey. . . .

Hundreds of thousands of people were watching—probably the biggest crowd ever gathered in New York until that time [1883]. . . . On one big excursion steamer, ablaze with lights, a calliope was shrieking out "America." Bands were playing on board other boats.

Rockets were going up all over New York meantime—and in Brooklyn. From the middle of the bridge now came great thunderclap reports as zinc balls, fired from mortars, burst five hundred feet up, fairly illuminating the two cities like sustained lightning.

And finally, at nine, as the display on the bridge ended with one incredible barrage, five hundred rockets fired all at once, every whistle and horn on the river joined in. . . .

It had been announced in advance that the bridge would be thrown open to the public at the stroke of midnight and that anyone might cross upon payment of one cent. . . . People poured across the bridge through the entire night and were still coming with the first light in the sky. . . .

In another time and in what would seem another world, when two young men were walking on the moon, a very old woman on Long Island would tell reporters that the public excitement over the feat was not so much compared to what she had seen "on the day they opened the Brooklyn Bridge."

David McCullough, *The Great Bridge*[2]

Government can do things for you only in proportion to its ability to do things to you.

James Madison

THE MEASURES influencing energy supply have long lead times. Complete planning and implementation for any particular year take at least ten years; the events of 1974 began to take shape while Jack Evans first tentatively stalked the coast of Maine. The reactions to 1974 will not have their full impacts until 1984.

Any given year between now and 1984 is the board for a chess game —our energy supply against energy scarcity. Few pieces have yet moved on the 1984 and later boards; a broad range of imaginative and conventional measures is still available to keep supply equal to demand. Carelessness gives away the queens and castles of solar, tidal, wind, and fusion energy first. They are gone from all of the pre-1984 boards.* Such bishops and knights as acceleration of nuclear power plants (breeder or conventional, dangerous or safe) and radical changes in home and transportation construction are gone from the pre-1980 boards. The knights and pawns of new conventional sources, new drilling, new pipelines, new refineries, and new storage facilities have been taken from the pre-1978 boards, on which remain only such pawns as foreign-policy alterations, rationing (by coupon or price), slapdash energy-conservation schemes, and suspension of various measures enacted to protect not just our environment but our health. These pawns pit principle against expediency, conservationists against consumers, and comfort against carcinogens. They are the types of options that a losing chess player faces, and a Bobby Fischer could only advise that we resign ourselves to learning, as we muddle through the next few years, the basic lesson that we cannot, as individuals or as a nation, depend for essential uses on energy sources whose terms for delivery

---

* Note that this is a national game. Individuals and communities in parts of the country have already begun to use the sun, the wind, common sense and their own solid waste as energy sources.

we cannot predict. This is all that most people know of basic energy policy, and it is all that they need to know.

During 1970 and the first half of 1971, conservationists showed an exclusionary strength that a White Citizens Council would have envied. Litigation tied the Trans-Alaska Pipeline in a bowknot. Badische Anilin & Soda-Fabrik Aktiengesellschaft (BASF) was driven from a planned petrochemical complex at Hilton Head, South Carolina, by a coalition of conservationists and fishermen backed by real-estate developers. John Kaneb was repulsed at Tiverton. David Scoll took called strikes at Riverhead and South Portland before going down swinging at Searsport. Oregon's governor asked people not to move to Oregon, and Delaware attracted national attention with a law banning heavy industry from the state's entire 160-mile shoreline.

The Delaware law attracted considerable attention in Maine. It had been strongly supported by Delaware's Governor Russell Peterson, whom Maine conservationists promptly offered to Governor Curtis as an example of true moral leadership. Curtis replied by pointing out that Maine's coastline, twenty times longer than Delaware's and far less densely cottaged, could support more and different uses. Noting that Delaware already had a petrochemical plant and a low unemployment rate, he suggested that Maine's case-by-case review procedure was more consistent than Delaware's prohibition with the interests of a nation that expected to rely heavily on refined oil.

One group opposing the Delaware law seemed from Maine to be appallingly inconsistent. This was the federal oil-policy establishment, principally the same Commerce and Interior Departments that had been deaf to the arguments in favor of a deep-water oil port on Machias Bay. The national security, they had said, required that Maine not import large volumes of foreign oil. And yet there they were in Delaware, sounding for all the world like Ken Curtis and Armand Hammer, admonishing Governor Peterson to remember that the national security, the balance of payments, the revitalization of American shipping, economic development, pollution control, and a growing demand for foreign oil all dictated that East Coast states not ban deep-water ports, at least not in Delaware.

There was only one difference between Delaware's proposed port and Maine's. In Delaware a consortium of established major oil companies wanted to offload supertankers at a floating mooring in Delaware Bay. The oil would then be piped to refineries in New Jersey and sold by established companies under established pricing practices. All of Maine's would-be refiners except Atlantic Richfield were mavericks, planning to upset the quota system and cut prices. They were opposed by the same companies that wanted the terminal in Delaware Bay, and those companies were the ventriloquists to solemn federal declarations that deep-water terminals could be treason in Maine, where they were wanted, and patriotic in Delaware, where they were not.

Later in 1971, after the Delaware law had been passed and Occidental had given up at Machiasport, federal officials sought to place some of the blame for the incipient New England oil squeezes on conservationists. To this end, Andrew Gibson, chief of the Federal Maritime Administration, and Interior Secretary Rogers Morton both indicated that New Englanders had no one but their own conservationists to blame for bottlenecks in oil transportation and refining. Since Gibson's agency, though it had supported the Occidental plan, was part of the Commerce Department, Governor Curtis saw Maine people accused of having blocked construction of New England refineries by the two federal departments that were still sitting on Machiasport applications. He replied:

> In the last 24 hours, the Secretary of the Interior and a high Commerce Department official have accused Maine conservationists of harming the New England economy by denying oil refineries permission to locate in Maine and forcing them to go to Canada. These accusations are inaccurate and self-serving attempts to rewrite history by the officials who are in fact responsible for exporting oil refineries to Canada and the Caribbean through their handling of the Oil Import Program. . . .
>
> We have put up with the high priced consequences of this discredited subsidy to the oil industry for long enough . . . now that its friends among the major oil companies are showing an interest in Maine, this administration seeks to blame conservationists for its past discriminatory policies.
>
> As Governor of Maine, I want to assure Secretary Morton and Mr. Gibson that Maine's environmental standards are high because Maine people want them that way. They will remain every bit as high because they have support not only from conservationists but from fishermen, from businessmen involved in the tourist trade, and from all Maine citizens who prize our present relatively clean environment. If a responsible oil company able to meet those standards, to provide employment

for Maine workers, and perhaps to provide price relief from the Oil Import Program comes along, it will be welcome.

Despite Curtis's reply, the myth of the omnipotent New England conservationist was off and running. To Southwesterners, especially those who read *The Oil Daily*, Northeastern energy policies had been to Southwestern oil what the grasshopper's frivolous summers had been to the ant's stockpiling for winter. With some justification, the South-westerners blamed the consuming states for low natural-gas prices; with much less reason, the consuming states were accused of opposing drilling off the Atlantic coast* and of unreasonable attitudes toward air pollution, new refineries, superports, oil prices, tax incentives, and the Trans-Alaska Pipeline.

A Houston *Chronicle* editorial wondered "why the waters off Mas-sachusetts should be any more sacred than the waters off Texas and Louisiana."[3] American Petroleum Institute president Frank Ikard, who had done as much as any one man between 1968 and 1970 to keep refineries out of Maine, told a graduating class at a New Hampshire college that New England did not have enough refineries. He ascribed this to "a misunderstanding about the nature of modern refineries."[4] Russell Long, Machiasport's leading senatorial opponent in 1969, told a 1973 Senate hearing of his pride that Louisiana "was the first state in the Nation to create an agency to promote and develop a superport and at its own expense to undertake detailed legal, engineering, eco-nomic, and environmental studies."[5]

Long's colleague J. Bennett Johnston was even worse. He asserted that Louisiana was "not only the first state to recognize the great things that a superport can bring to both the State and to the Nation, but also the first to recognize the great dangers that superports present environ-mentally. I think that the thrust of Louisiana's legislation, as opposed to the other states, has been to recognize that environmental possibil-ity, and to cope with it."[6]

Several Southern governors were sharply indignant over New Eng-land's unwillingness to build the very deep-water facilities that several of their immediate predecessors had testified against in 1968, and popular support for the commercial underpinnings of the Republic was further corroded by the blossoming of Southwestern bumper stick-

---

* The federal government had not moved to lease these acres until 1971 in order to protect existing producers, and ownership of the sea bed remained in doubt.

ers reading (deletions theirs), "Let the Yankee b-st-rds freeze in the dark."

While federal officials sought to blame conservationists for triumphs they had never achieved, environmental groups did score significant victories in Congress and in state legislatures with the passage of more stringent air and water standards. These standards tended to increase demand for oil over coal and for desulfurized or Libyan oil in particular.

Largely because of oil-import controls (even the Tiverton and Sears Island refineries would have been illegal without special arrangements) and better tax breaks, but partly to avoid conservationist opposition, refineries to meet the new demand were built or expanded in eastern Canada and the Caribbean, where they could not become part of a U.S. contingency-planning system or be subjected to emergency storage requirements, neither of which in any case existed.

The Canadians, more committed than the United States to involving the government in rural economic development, offered extraordinary tax and grant incentives to heavy industries willing to locate in eastern Canada. Because the Maritime Provinces were neither populous nor wealthy, they could not provide markets for the products of these industries, which in large part had to be exported to and financed from the eastern United States.

Environmental resistance in Canada was slight. The Maritime Provinces had long had unemployment rates well above Maine's and had not enacted any laws around which conservationist opposition could crystallize.* The provincial governments had actively encouraged the clustering of heavy industry in a few areas, leaving extensive stretches of coast free of development. The resulting refinery construction in Canada galvanized Maine's oil advocates just as the Delaware moratorium had stimulated conservationists. It seemed to provide a nearby example of progressive behavior to which Maine's controversial and unsatisfying course could be contrasted. Rallying around the theory that Canadian development was as threatening to Maine shores as Maine development but much less profitable, proponents of oil development in Washington County were able to persuade a legislative

---

* The most important Canadian oil-pollution law was the per-barrel oil-handling charge patterned closely after Maine's 1970 law. The fee mollified the fishing industry, did not impede development, and is largely passed on to American consumers.

committee to undertake an examination of the feasibility of oil development at Eastport.

The hand behind the Eastport investigation belonged to the Metropolitan Petroleum Company, a subdivision of the Pittston Company, a major coal producer to whom Metropolitan was a small but important beachhead in the market of a competing fuel. Metropolitan had acquired land on the Eastport waterfront in 1965, in hopes of setting up a terminal to break the C. H. Sprague monopoly in the eastern Maine market.* Because the land happened to be on protected deepwater, reachable by a difficult deep-water channel, Metropolitan tried to promote it as a deep-water refinery site—first to Occidental, then to Northeast Petroleum, then to Scoll. Each rejected the site because of the difficulty of the approach, the limited land available at Eastport's island location, and corporate preferences for other sites. Early in 1970 Metropolitan decided to try to build its own Eastport refinery. Aside from the difficulty of the supertanker approaches, the town had much in its favor, particularly for a company with Pittston's experience in manipulating the hardship-engendered eagerness of eastern Appalachia.†

The Eastport region, unlike Machias forty miles to the southwest, had been briefly settled by the French as early as the sixteenth century. The King of France granted a patent running from Nova Scotia to New York, and the King of England, several years later, granted similar patents running from New York to Nova Scotia. The waters teemed with fish, and Catholic Europe, unafraid of depending on the New World for its then thrice-weekly soul food, set up outposts from Newfoundland southward. Weather and wars eventually drove the French from the region, but Moose Island (which was to become Eastport) did not become a firm piece of the United States or part of Maine until the 1818 conclusion of negotiations provided for in the treaty ending the War of 1812.

Throughout the nineteenth century, Eastport prospered as a fishing and canning center. Its cannery row contained twenty plants in 1900, but the peak had been even earlier. According to a local history com-

* See page 24.
† Pittston had amassed a distinctive coal-mine safety record of $20 million in fines, none paid. It was also a Pittston slag dam, built without the required state permit, that killed 127 people on Buffalo Creek, West Virginia, when it collapsed because of heavy seasonal rains in 1971.

piled in 1888, "If one were called upon to point out the period when the social and intellectual life of the place had been at its best . . . I think he would select the years of the thirties, about half a century ago."[7] Outmigration and the decline of the fishery eroded the town. Over a seventy-year span, its population fell by 60 percent, and by 1970 only two canneries still operated at all.

The town emits more of a sense of decline than others in Washington County. The streets and houses carpet two hills on the edge of Passamaquoddy Bay. Some homes are still well maintained. Many have regal views, but dozens of impressive frames are now betrayed by some combination of sagging sills, sloping porches, peeling paint, missing panes, and boarded doors and windows. Junked cars crop up in unlikely back yards, and small shanties with big antennas encircle the more prosperous areas.

The town has a Southern Gothic quality. Faulkner's "A Rose for Emily" would not be mislocated there. The defendant in a recent murder trial was accused of shooting the lover of his daughter, whose bed he also shared. Long-haired out-of-state settlers have learned that arson is a form of communication in the Eastport area. An erratic former bodyguard of Tennessee Williams implied that Metropolitan agents threatened to communicate with him in the same way unless he sold his land. He also claimed to have been pinned for hours in a phone booth by the front bumper of a car operated by the aforementioned murder victim, whom he suspected of being connected with Metropolitan.

The only road into Eastport was still marked in mid-1974 by a sign advertising an August, 1972, "PUBLIC AUCTION—30 homes as low as $2000. 16 land parcels as low as $300—All overlooking beautiful Quoddy Bay." The houses and land parcels are in Quoddy Village, jerry-built in haste to house the workers for the tidal power project from which President Roosevelt retreated in 1936. Roosevelt's retreat implanted the same cynicism in Eastport that federal delays of the Trans-Alaska Pipeline spawned more recently in Alaska, and the same energy crisis that eventually midwifed the pipeline has revived discussion of the power dams. The dams of the tidal power project would block tanker access to Eastport once and for all. Maine's Commissioner of Sea and Shore Fisheries is unperturbed by the ecological impact of the dams, for he feels that the reduction in tidal scouring action could make Passamaquoddy Bay a superlative site for aquacultural experimentation.

The legislative resolution creating the Eastport refinery-study committee came into being by mistake. It passed the Maine lower house under the shepherding of the speaker, who was later to become a Pittston lobbyist. The president of the senate, no friend either to oil or the house speaker, left to Senator Berry, the champion of earlier oil moratoria, the task of killing the resolution in the senate. Berry passed it instead.

No harm was done. The committee held two meetings and discovered that tricky currents and fogs obscured political as well as nautical hazards where oil was concerned and that navigation could more safely be left to the Environmental Improvement Commission. The legislative committee arranged for Metropolitan to come forth at its third meeting and announce plans to apply for site approval within ninety days. Upon receipt of this news, the committee went into executive session and voted that, since the matter was now before the EIC, the legislature should play no further role and the committee should recess indefinitely. Metropolitan did not apply in 90 days, nor 180, nor 270, nor 360, nor 450. Pittston headquarters, apparently exasperated by the fact that the land had lain unused for seven years, eventually brought in a new team which managed to file the application some 540 days after the dissolution of the legislative study group.

The eighteen-month interval between the announcement and the filing saw the coming and going of Maine's most bizarre refinery proposal. A group calling itself THT Associates suggested a terminal on a Passamaquoddy Indian reservation adjacent to Eastport on Moose Island. The terminal would have been linked to a refinery on a second Passamaquoddy Reservation by a forty-mile pipeline. The logic seems to have been that the Indians, impoverished even by Washington County standards, would welcome the refinery and that liberal conservationists would be less likely to oppose a project sought by representatives of another of their causes.

More exact assessments of motives are impossible. No one from THT Associates granted an interview in Maine. Their address was a one-man office in Boston, and that man wasn't talking. An improbable local speculation was that the project was a hoax, perpetrated for murky reasons by the Passamaquoddies' federally funded attorney, one Thomas H. Tureen, whose initials had to be altered to fit the rumor. Passamaquoddy leader John Stevens is sure that he was offered a $20,000-per-year job at the refinery by a man calling himself David Scoll, but the noted salmon fisherman is vehement in denying this (on the basis, among others, that "that whole Eastport area is just too unsafe for the big tankers"). His name is not on the few documents that the Passamaquoddies still have.

American coastal history is replete with natives looking wonderingly to sea at the arrival of ships bigger than any they had ever seen, ships bringing new opportunities, new baubles, new addictions. Satisfying though it would be to think that ninety-six (of five hundred registered) voting Passamaquoddies had Manhattan, the Cherokees, and the Seminoles in mind when they overwhelmingly rejected THT, John Stevens says it was "just common sense. We didn't know much about them."

The Metropolitan and THT episodes raised the specter of a continuing and expensive game of refinery hopscotch over the length of the coast, and they cast doubt on the wisdom if not the fairness of the case-by-case approach mandated by the site-approval law. Few doubted that this approach would produce an equitable result, but many wanted to short-cut the exhausting and uncertain processes exposed by Maine Clean Fuels. An impatience, stemming in some people from a desire to rush the future, in others from simple nervousness, revived demands both for a moratorium and for environmental relaxation.

Even the Environmental Improvement commissioners were uneasy over the prospect of a prolonged series of refinery battles. The commission's members could not live on esprit de corps alone, and its full-time staff could not enforce the laws against existing pollution if they had to drop everything for semiannual refinery hearings. In August, 1971, Donaldson Koons and Curtis Hutchins jointly urged the governor to appoint a task force to review the state's experience under the site law and to see whether it could recommend more efficient ways to cope with oil.

As with the original Conservation and Planning Committee, Curtis used Lyndon Johnson's let-us-reason-together approach. His Task Force on Energy, Heavy Industry, and the Maine Coast mixed bankers with lobstermen, power- and paper-company executives with environmentalists, labor leaders with summer residents, and legislators with planners. For the chairmanship, Curtis was able to get Joseph Fisher, president of Resources for the Future, a former mayor of Arlington, Virginia, and a man with twenty years of experience in researching and mediating resource policy disputes. Fisher had been raised in the Washington County town of Cherryfield and still spent two weeks each summer in the area. Maine's pull on him, as on Gardiner Means, was strong enough to outweigh the hardship of journeying monthly from Washington to his unpaid chairmanship, to which he brought the advantages of an informed outsider without the albatross of a previous public stand.

The task force worked through the first eight months of 1972, ultimately attaining a remarkable degree of consensus. It did no independent research, relying instead on basic data that had accumulated in Maine since 1968. The homework done by its individual members varied, but most of them did not move far from their preconceived positions. Fisher functioned like a modern fishing trawler, netting, processing, and freezing consensus wherever he could find it. Only occasionally did he also chum the water.

The areas of basic disagreement were surprisingly small. The conservationists did not oppose oil refineries, but they felt that the terminal facilities should be limited to Portland harbor, from which the refined oil could move to southern New England by pipeline instead of by tanker or barge. Even John Cole, retained to present the case for excluding all new heavy industry, felt that no harm would come from one or two carefully chosen and regulated heavy-industry zones.

Most of those favoring refinery development did not insist on open hunting over the length of the coast, so the task force reached early agreement that

> Properly controlled heavy industry at a limited number of sites would add a desirable balance to Maine's economic base and job opportunities and would not threaten the growth of the nonindustrial and light industrial activities which will continue to predominate on the coast. Uncontrolled recreational growth poses at least as much of an environmental threat to most of the coast as controlled heavy industry. The exclusion of heavy industry generally and oil refining in particular from the entire coast is neither necessary nor wise. . . . The establishment of heavy industry zones is feasible, and . . . offers the best opportunity for Maine citizens to realize in a balanced way the potential benefits of their entire coast.
>
> Continuation of the case-by-case site review method . . . is a satisfactory defense against disastrous land use mistakes [but] it provides no assurance that the best industrial sites from a public interest standpoint will be the ones actually developed. [It] inserts an unsettling element of uncertainty into the efforts of industry, conservationists, and the general public to enjoy the coastal resources of the entire state.[8]

Once this area of unanimous agreement had been established, specific recommendations proved harder to secure. Several of those who favored limiting oil to preselected zones wanted as many as three such zones. Conservationists, fearful of the considerable increase in coastal traffic inevitable from any Washington County refinery, were adamant that they would accept only Portland. Motions to recommend Machias Bay and Eastport were defeated (Machias by 10–8 and Eastport by 13–5), and compromises on nonoil industrial zones were reached.

As the report was ready to go to press, a Texaco tanker gashed its hull on a ledge in Portland harbor and lost 100,000 gallons of industrial fuel at the peak of the summer tourist season. The company and the Coast Guard were both slow to respond, and Maine's vaunted oil-handling law was still locked up in the three-and-a-half-year lawsuit that had been filed on the day the law took effect. The oil spread among the Casco Bay islands and onto boat hulls and beaches. The task force tempered its Portland oil recommendation by stating that it applied only if the state had effective spill-prevention and cleanup capabilities of its own.

The report finally recommended that future coastal heavy-industrial development be confined to two zones, one at Portland and one on Machias Bay. Only the Portland zone would be eligible for oil development and then only after EIC approval of specific projects. The responsibility for developing and managing the zones would be lodged in a special authority responsible for maximizing the job, tax, and product benefits to the state.

Aside from the two zones and limited exemptions for power plants and mining operations,

> The remainder of the coast—on [the] order of 98 percent of the total coastline—would not be eligible for heavy industry. We see great advantage in making this crystal clear. What are hopes to the industrial developers, threats to the environmentalists, euphoric or nightmarish dreams to local residents, and titillations to everyone in the state about big industry anywhere, anytime on the coast should be laid to rest once and for all. Heavy industry, with the few exceptions already noted, is to be located in one or the other of two zones of limited extent and with careful internal controls, as outlined previously, and that's the end of it.
>
> This overwhelmingly large remainder of the coast, in our view, should be protected and used for residences, parks, outdoor recreation, un-

developed scenic areas, summer homes, and the like. Also under existing and improved regulations, some of this very large remainder can be used for further development of coastal towns, and for light industry such as boat building, canneries, aquaculture, marinas, wood products manufacturing, and similar activities. In the main, these activities should probably be congregated in a relatively few places in or near towns. . . .[9]

Fundamentally, our preferred future is not characterized by extremism in which one set of values or point of view is allowed to dominate. Economic advancement and security for Maine people over the coming few decades require, we think, some new industrial development, including heavy industry, to provide jobs and income. . . . As noted earlier, the Maine coast over the last two centuries has seen spectacular and less spectacular development come and go. Its inhabitants have learned that the essential properties and characteristics of their coast must be conserved and not jeopardized in any serious or long lasting way simply to gain a quick return. Therefore, in the future we prefer, the scenery, the amenities, the charm of the coast have to be safeguarded.[10]

Governor Curtis received the report warmly and submitted legislation that would have codified its principal recommendations. Although he supported the legislation, Curtis was preoccupied by property-tax reform and government-reorganization measures. He did not push this legislation as hard as he had the industrial-siting and oil-handling laws three years earlier, and it ultimately was defeated by three groups.

First, Pittston lobbied against it, fearing that it would lessen its prospects for approval at Eastport.* Second, some groups in Portland opposed it because it enhanced the chances of a Portland refinery. Third, the task-force coalition itself, once outside the meeting room, fell apart, with the developers looking longingly at a smorgasbord of deep-water sites and the environmentalists hoping again for a moratorium. Harry Richardson, favoring a continuation of the case-by-case approach and cranking up a 1974 gubernatorial campaign that would need support in both Portland and Eastport, dealt the task force's report one of the unkindest blows, calling the heavy-industry zones a "pin the tail on the donkey approach" to economic development.

* In fact, the bill would have permitted pending applications like Pittston's to be passed on by the Environmental Improvement Commission, which the legislature, in a realistic moment, had renamed the Board of Environmental Protection (BEP). Pittston believed, with justification, that the company's Eastport prospects would nevertheless suffer if the legislature had recently ruled Eastport off limits to all future refiners.

Curiously, the Machias Bay area was not heard from during the debate on the bill. At least a few people must have been puzzled that, after four years of telling them of the wonders of their deep-water port, the state was considering moving the crap game elsewhere. Noted for their laconic sense, the people of Washington County can hardly have been satisfied with the explanation that only Portland was close enough to southern New England to support the environmentally preferable pipeline to Boston. The geography had not, after all, changed much in four years.

Perhaps they no longer cared. Shaheen had been gone for four years, Occidental for two. Atlantic Richfield still renewed its options but had made no public statements for eighteen months. Atlantic World Port no longer existed. Bob Monks, concerned over the impact his oil association might have on his senatorial prospects, had dissolved the company twenty months after his referendum victory. He turned the land options over to The Allagash Group, a nonprofit research operation run by John Cole, which thus became charged with finding the most economically and environmentally beneficial use for the tip of the Machiasport Peninsula plus Stone Island.

Since the options could not have been exercised for less than a million dollars and were of questionable use for anything except an oil terminal or the existing residences, The Allagash Group (annual budget $15,000) was stumped. Cole appointed an advisory group which had no better luck. This group was approached by a man interested in buying Stone Island. He was L. M. C. (Alphabet) Smith, a wealthy part-time raiser of organic beef cattle in the central coastal town of Freeport. Smith, a wealthy Philadelphian, had attended the Rockefeller-Curtis meeting. He had in the past purchased coastal land for parks and held it until the state was able to raise enough money to buy it from him at cost, and he was strongly opposed to oil in Maine. He saw Stone Island as the key to oil development in Machias Bay, and, unaware of Atlantic Richfield's single-point-mooring alternative, he wanted to buy it. His offer was rejected by the advisory group because two members, Machias resident Marc Nault and marine scientist Ed Myers, could see no benefit to the Machias Bay area from the sale. Eventually, however, the Stone Island option lapsed, and Smith bought the property from its real owner. Determined to keep oil out of Machias Bay, he gave the island on which Jack Evans's vision had nested with the ospreys to the Nature Conservancy, to be preserved in its natural state. The Allagash Group let the options to the rest of the peninsula lapse, and control of the land has reverted to those from whom Monks scrambled to buy it in late 1968.

Maine's failure to implement the report of Governor Curtis's task force raises again some of the questions surrounding President Nixon's dismissal of the work of his Cabinet Task Force on Oil Import Controls. Again the problem seems to have been one of constituency. Ideas do not roll uphill on their own. Their ability to prevail is directly proportional to the continuing force behind them. The most careful analysis delivered to an executive not fully committed to it must acquire a separate constituency or it will be of only slightly more lasting importance than a clever letter to the editor.

Nevertheless, these interdisciplinary analyses, putting projections and models together with hopes and fears to show what the consequences of "solutions" really are, seem the only possible foundation to enlightened public action. This is a sadly stale insight. Volumes as solid as Eugene Rostow's *A National Policy for the Oil Industry* (1948), as heavy as the *Report of the President's Materials Policy Commission* (1954), as infuriating as *The Politics of Oil* (1961), as urgent as *Night Comes to the Cumberlands* (1962), and as sober as *Natural Resources for U.S. Growth* (1964) are just a few sticks in a logjam of pleas to the U.S. government to make some effort, in the field of resource policy alone, to understand the consequences of its inactions.

Lately the same urgings have been more ecological but only a little more successful. Quoting Winston Churchill's 1943 plea for a precise rebuilding of the bombed British House of Commons ("We shape our buildings and afterwards our buildings shape us"),[11] René Dubos culled from a 1968 review of man's biological, intellectual, social, philosophical, and psychological history a warning that

> We may hope eventually to develop techniques for predicting or recognizing early the objectionable consequences of social and technological innovations so as to minimize their effect, but this kind of piecemeal social engineering will be no substitute for a philosophy of the whole environment, formulated in the light of human aspirations and needs.[12]

In the same year, Paul Ehrlich warned in *The Population Bomb* that neither natural resources nor the environment nor man's ability to grow food could withstand continuing unchecked population growth. Within the next four years *The Closing Circle, The Limits to Growth,*

Future Shock, and *Beyond Freedom and Dignity* sold several million copies warning that man's relations with himself and his world might be fatally out of kilter. These books advocated solutions involving behavior modification, education, the humanization of technology and technologists, population control, income redistribution, an end to economic growth, and the rebirth of a sense of human community. Even the optimists, such as the authors of *The Retreat from Riches, The Greening of America,* and *The Doomsday Syndrome,* acknowledged basic environmental and economic flaws. Their optimism sprang from a faith that technologies and/or consciousnesses appropriate to specific and general problems could be made to emerge without coerced social or economic modifications.

These books might have been so many Cabinet Task Force reports for all the effect that they have had on national-resource policies. Like the report on oil-import controls, they created Rule 2 constituencies, groups whose concerns were not to be disregarded unless necessary to satisfy the ultimate Rule 1, reelection. Taken together, their analyses, careful quilts of recycled time, have reached fewer than half as many people as a gasoline commercial during the Super Bowl, a comparison that tends to confirm Rebecca West's 1949 observation that

> The crucial political argument of our time will not be carried on in books, it will be lived. Perhaps the debate may continue for decades, for centuries, during which the West and the East may flag and fade. . . . But in the end the obscure millions must establish a truth by discovering what is necessary for them.[13]

Comprehensive planning has never been a dominant political issue, and many of President Nixon's 1972 supporters were future-shocked members of Consciousness I, trapped in a closing-circle belief that freedom and dignity were inconsistent with planning, or at least with a society that revealed its planning.

Neither oil nor energy nor resource policy nor ecology was seriously discussed during the 1972 campaign. The oil industry had been increasingly critical of the President's failure to take energy policy seriously and had begun to warn of shortages unless the government expanded offshore exploration, permitted the Alaskan pipeline and deep-water ports, and accepted higher oil and gas prices. Nevertheless, John Connally reassembled the Democrats for Nixon wagon train that Texas Governor Allan Shivers had put together for Eisenhower in 1952, when President Truman and Adlai Stevenson betrayed a reluctance to turn the tidelands over to the states for leasing. Oilmen contributed avidly and sometimes illegally to the Committee to Reelect the President, and Minor Jamieson, an independent oil-company spokesman who had been critical of the Nixon administration, confessed in the October 31, 1972, issue of *The National Journal* that "I don't know anybody in the oil business that's for McGovern."*

What had been an argument of some profundity over the national-security implications of increased oil imports degenerated into a trivial pinball game. The balls of domestic demand rolled inexorably over domestic supplies throughout 1971 and 1972. Whenever they got close to the inevitable hole of import liberalization, the administration worked the flippers of ad hoc permits, thereby keeping Northeastern terminal operators and consumers happy without appearing to undermine the 12.2 percent ceiling, which was in fact ignored. The balls then clanked another precarious and costly course past the bumpers of diminishing domestic surplus, rising prices, and industry sullenness.

The President had no defenses stronger than the ad hoc flippers and the ineffectual body english of the Council of Economic Advisers' blandishments to the oil industry and the state prorationing boards. Anything more might have tilted away the 1972 support that was flashing up on the scoreboard at a gratifying pace. Machiasport, the Cabinet Task Force, Walter Hickel, the 1970 industrial-oil squeeze, and the 1971–72 home heating-oil problems followed one another between the flippers into the oubliette. On the tally board the bells stopped ringing, the lights stopped blinking, and the running totals summed to their verdict—a bonus game, four more years.

Like a lot of other energy consumers, the machine barely made it through the winter of 1972–73. In 1970, 1971, and 1972, the President had increased imports east of the Rocky Mountains by an extra 100,000 barrels per day, for a total increase of some 30 percent (300,000 barrels per day). In March, 1972, he added another 230,000 barrels per day, and in September he threw in another 160,000. To assuage the worries of the domestic producers, these changes were always an-

---

* There was at least one—Occidental's Dorman Commons, who was McGovern's California finance chairman.

Not many lobstermen favored McGovern either. One of the most vocal opponents of a Machias Bay refinery, lobsterman Jasper Cates, wrote in a July 21, 1972, letter to the Bangor *Daily News*, that McGovern and other Democrats harbored a "guilt complex" because they had lacked "the guts to destroy the North Vietnam invaders and end the war. The war could have been ended quickly by turning North Vietnam into a smoking gravel pit."

nounced as temporary, to be reviewed from year to year. This can't have made much difference to the producers, who were pumping at 100 percent of capacity for the first time in their lives, but it did deny the recipient companies the assurance of permanent supply that they would have needed to build new refineries.

In October, 1972, Peter Flanigan rejected energy conservation as an alternative, telling *The National Journal,* "We're certainly not going to ask everybody to heat their homes at 68 degrees." As federal officials continued to career from interview to meeting, embracing ecology while denouncing ecologists, the nation was treated to an insufficiently noticed example of the governmental tactic known as "blaming the victim."

The real reason for the need for increased imports had little to do with refinery shortages. It was instead the sudden home heating-oil scarcity, caused in part by the blending of home heating oil with industrial fuel to meet sulfur standards, in part by the shortages of natural gas, and in part by the imposition of the Phase I price freeze when home heating oil was priced low relative to gasoline. Oil Policy Committee Chairman Lincoln, having accepted oil-company assurances that the 1972–73 winter was well taken care of, was reported to be "hopping mad" as he became the nation's first ex-energy czar.

In February, 1973, with reelection and Vietnam behind him, Nixon met the shortage by suspending the quota system for the rest of the winter and creating a White House Energy Council consisting of George Shultz, Henry Kissinger, and John Ehrlichman. The White House hired Charles Dibona to staff the new office and prepare a Presidential energy message outlining a program to avert future shortages. The message, twice delayed, came out in mid-April. It abolished the Mandatory Oil Import Program and announced a new research effort and new incentives to stimulate U.S. energy production. Along with nuclear power, the research effort emphasized oil shale and coal gasification, the realms that President Eisenhower had abandoned to the inattention of private enterprise at the suggestion of the National Petroleum Council twenty years earlier.*

Among the incentives was a tariff plan for foreign oil that was designed to give less expensive oil to new refineries while protecting domestic production and refining from foreign competition. Even without the subsequent increase in world oil prices, the protection was greater than necessary, as were the incentives, but most remarkable of

* See page 201.

all was the fact that in time of crisis the President turned to the very tariff framework he had rejected as too risky thirty months previously.

Several refinery projects and expansions, including Pittston's at Eastport, were announced immediately, and the newly appointed Oil Policy Committee chairman William Simon was quick to credit them to the new Nixon plan. He did not mention that several of them faced environmental opposition or that, as the administration pushed so hard for the construction of new refineries, it had opposed Congressional appropriation of coastal planning funds that could have been used to make sure that they were well sited and therefore less controversial.

There is little to be gained from a review of the postquota import policies. The year 1973 passed in federal fiasco, and oil was no exception. When Governor Jimmy Carter of Georgia sought to tell the 1973 National Governors' Conference of the difficulty he had encountered in trying even to find someone in Washington with whom he could discuss energy matters, he was rebuked by Governor Jack Williams of Arizona. Williams, who as a radio broadcaster had enthusiastically described to his Southwestern audience the ground-breaking for the Glen Canyon Dam, said that the nation should be more positive, that "We've done great things in our history, made much beauty available to all. Just look at our golf courses. . . ."

The Arab embargo proved only that the United States could stave off hardship for a while by reducing waste. Some people were quick to point out that Occidental's Machiasport refinery running on imported oil would have been a liability during the embargo, but this argument assumed that the refinery would have been built as part of a special deal, without overall reform of import policy. It ignored the fact that prudent import reform, combining adequate protection for domestic producers with storage requirements and advance allocation plans, might have prevented or nullified the embargo. Even a special deal at Machiasport would have been no worse than the policy of drift that had actually been followed. That policy left the East Coast heavily dependent on foreign oil refined in Canada and the Caribbean by refineries that were embargoed just as firmly by the Arabs as Occidental would have been if it had been permitted to make its investment in the United States.

After General Lincoln's departure, energy policy passed through the hands of Peter Flanigan, William Simon, Charles Dibona, John Love, back to Simon again, and on to John Sawhill followed by Rogers Morton. Another year was lost to any but the most immediate considerations, but a jump from fiasco to brilliance would hardly have been noticed in 1974. The consequences of inaction in 1973 will not be strongly felt before 1976, at which time 1973 will appear even more frivolous than the Portland foreign-trade-zone hearing does today.

That hearing—a three-day monument to the proposition that government itself is an unnatural resource, available for damming, drilling, and draining by whoever has the maps—looms over present U.S. oil policy like a haunted house. It is rarely visited now, but some people, seeking to appear brave or wise, pretend to have been there. They whisper tales of ferocious and greedy conservationists backed by phalanxes of headless politicians and moaning consumers. It seems more accurate to think of it as a waxworks, in which one may re-examine the following:

—The quota system, now retired, its thirteen-year costs somewhere between $30 billion and $50 billion, not counting the consequences of its having drained U.S. oil wells first while distracting attention from the measures and expenditures that might have brought real security. Its principles, such as they are, still underlie U.S. oil policy, which is now a cornerstone of Project Independence.

—The deceased: N. Norman Engleberg, Reddington Fiske, and Hale Boggs. Each personified, for those three days, lasting elements in national energy problems.

—Gary Merrill, Boggs's unemployed supporting actor, is working again. He is Dr. Kildare's senior physician figure. In May, 1974, the *Maine Times* announced that he was running for President in 1976.

—Jack Evans has become something of a revisionist himself. His Hawaiian refinery, which required a trade zone but no quota, has, in his words, "made so much money that it's embarrassing." In October, 1974, it was given the first annual Blue Sky Award by the American Lung Association of Hawaii for its "extra efforts and accomplishments" in controlling air pollution.

Evans spent 1973 and 1974 working hard to surmount environmental opposition to a refinery in Virginia, which he called the Mid-Atlantic Clean Energy Center before splitting it into the Hampton Roads Energy Company and the Security Marine Terminal Company. Virginia's governor had insisted on the split so that the terminal could serve other users.

Evans came to regard the New England plight with disinterested exasperation, blaming it on the federal oil-import program because it precluded refinery construction, on New England political leaders for their willingness to settle for finished-product tickets to the independent terminal operators, and, in one bizarre instance, on New England conservationists for stopping the Machiasport project. In a January, 1973, letter out of the blue to the Portland *Press Herald* and the Bangor *Daily News* he asserted,

> I then developed a plan to locate a large refinery complex in Machias, but as time passed it became apparent to me that I did not possess the necessary financial resources to successfully combat the attacks of uninformed conservationists most of whom spent only a few weeks a year in Maine, but who had ample funds to generate opposition.

Evans, a prolific and sometimes impetuous letter writer, has since corrected himself on this point, but Bob Monks and Armand Hammer must have smiled, though not as broadly as Harold Hackett, Evans's former environmental ally against King Resources.

—Armand Hammer no longer thinks much about Maine. His cultural and entrepreneurial "coups" in the Soviet Union have been much in the headlines, but they have not kept his Libyan-imperiled Occidental stock above 12. High Soviet officials have been reported to hope that he will be the next U.S. ambassador to Russia, but he had 1974 troubles with both the Securities and Exchange Commission and the Internal Revenue Service. Early in 1974 *Business Week* reported that the company had attractive assets but that Hammer had a serious credibility gap which was causing investors to shy away from Occidental until he retired.

Perhaps just as painful was an earlier Washington *Post* story suggesting that Hammer's personal art collection consisted of second-rate paintings by first-rate painters and served in part as a tax dodge. The IRS agreed, for in 1974 it charged Hammer with overvaluing his charitable donations, including many works of art, by several million dollars.

The Foster Wheeler engineers who designed Occidental's Machiasport refinery did not realize that they were really diagramming a sacrificial piece in global gambit. By giving it up, Hammer solidified his status as a reliable member of the oil community and as a friend of the Nixon administration. Foster Wheeler may not have minded much, for their familiarity with Maine helped them get the contract to design the proposed Pittston refinery at Eastport.

Hammer's Maine ally Fred Vahlsing was less resilient. He eventually defaulted on the payments on his beet refinery, saddling the state with its debts. He kept trying to regain control, but early in 1974 his potato plant had further pollution problems and on May 20 the Portland *Evening Express*, once a supporter of his ventures, editorialized that it was time for him to leave Maine, that he had for too long "taken advantage of Maine's hospitality, our generosity, our friendship, our money, our laws, and our good name."

Once he had made peace with the Nixon administration, Hammer was able for a time to fly off to the Middle East accompanied by John Connally, who apparently saw nothing wrong with representing his clients and his President on the same visit to heads of state. Hammer's changed relationship to the White House must have owed at least a little to a cash contribution of $46,000 made just before the 1972 requirements for reporting campaign donations took effect and to Tim Babcock's having furnished $14,000 to Fred LaRue for use in the White House's first Watergate defense fund. Babcock, a former Montana governor and Occidental employee, considered and reconsidered a 1972 return to Montana to seek a seat in the U.S. Senate.

—The New England independent marketers may have thought they had the last chuckle on Hammer when the White House chose to give them token but lucrative finished-product quotas rather than give Occidental its request for a major Machiasport allocation. However, they were to have only two years to enjoy their table scraps. By early 1973 they were confronted by the perennial independents' nightmare, a prolonged supply squeeze. The opportunities for quick, lucrative maneuvers in the spot markets dried up, and the more agile of the Machiasport survivors sought their own refineries or firm ties to major companies.

Northeast Petroleum, despite having picked up John Buckley on waivers from Occidental, was rejected in Rhode Island and turned its attention to Louisiana. There it joined with the Ingram Corporation to form the Energy Corporation of Louisiana (ECOL) to plan a 200,000-barrel-per-day refinery on the Mississippi River northwest of New Orleans. The refinery's profitability depended on its ability to secure a substantial allocation of cheap ($6.50 per barrel) domestic crude from the Federal Energy Office to offset the high ($11 per barrel) cost of Northeast's foreign sources. This was a difficult problem, and the last time I talked to John Buckley he, George Bevel, and John Zentay were pondering it in Zentay's Washington office, where they had first met six years earlier to seek a way to get an allocation of cheap ($1.75 per barrel) foreign crude for Occidental to offset the prohibitive ($3.50 per barrel) cost of domestic crude to a potential New England refiner. They were also working on the guest list for the ECOL groundbreaking, a list that was to include Representative Lindy Boggs, Hale's wife and successor.

Another of the independents, the Gibbs Oil Company, kept its refinery plan closer to home. Gibbs executive Herb Sostek had been present at the creation of the heating-oil component of what had begun as Evans's industrial-oil plan. Excluded from Hammer's plans, Gibbs had kept its eye on the concept of an independent refinery at Machiasport long past the time when the other New England independents had lost interest. By the time the 1973 shortages forced the company to make a move, the Governor's Task Force report recommending a Portland area site had come out.

Sostek had himself thought that a pipeline to Boston, with its reduction in tanker traffic, might reduce environmental problems and resistance. He hired two former antagonists, Donny McNamara and Harold Pachios, to advise him. In September, 1974, Gibbs Oil, in partnership with the Northern Illinois Natural Gas Company, Burmah Tankers Ltd. (a subsidiary of the very substantial Burmah Oil Company), and promoter Lovett Peters, filed an application with Maine's Board of Environmental Protection for a 250,000-barrel-per-day refinery in southern Maine. Neither the Natural Resources Council nor the Coastal Resources Action Committee opposed the project, but a local group called Friends of Intelligent Land Use (FOIL) challenged the proposal in court even before the state hearings could begin.

—Bob Monks, the most independent independent, was out of the oil business well before the shortages struck. After unloading his Machias Bay albatross on John Cole's Allagash Group he ran a strong campaign against Margaret Chase Smith. He reported expenditures of $300,000 (a Maine primary record), but if expenditures not covered by reporting requirements are included, he spent half a million dollars.

Monks created an organization called Aid for Industrial Development and Expansion (AIDE) to help bring clean new industry to Maine. John Cole was among the trustees. AIDE played a well-publicized role in attracting two modular housing plants, but its obvious political dimension alienated potential support and eventually forced its creator off its board.

He also founded an organization called Senior Power to help "senior citizens" with their problems. Senior Power answered its widely advertised telephone number with a cheerful "Monks General Offices." Upon being told that one caller was responding to an advertisement requesting views on a pending electric rate increase, Senior Power thanked her for telling them how she felt. "But what are you going to do about it?" she asked.

"Oh, we're just gathering opinions."

"But aren't you going to do anything? I'm calling long distance."

"Well, you could try Combat [a consumer protection group]. I understand they're intervening in the case."

A mid-campaign article in *The Bowdoin College Orient* concluded: "Before his talk . . . Monks said of Governor Sargent that 'he's a lot like Curtis, nice but not very smart. But a real nice guy!' At Bowdoin, Robert Monks came across as a real nice guy but not entirely convincing."

Curtis sent the paragraph to Sargent with a note reading, "Dear Frank, Who's your friend?"

Mrs. Smith hardly stirred, returning from Washington only on weekends in order to maintain her record of extraordinary attendance at roll-call votes. Her opponent never mentioned her age; she never mentioned his name. He outspent her by 50 to 1; she outpolled him by 2 to 1 despite a flurry of Monks-released polls labeling the contest too close to call.

After the primary election, Monks paid a congratulatory call on his opponent, telling her that at least he had assured her victory in November, an apparent suggestion that the primary results would remove any doubts about her continuing vitality. Instead, enough of Monks's supporters voted Democratic in November to give Congressman Hathaway a 52–48 victory in the general election.

Monks's own career survived. A 33 percent showing was actually respectable in a primary against so formidable an incumbent. He emerged with a statewide image that he sought briefly to translate into the governorship in a 1974 primary against Jim Erwin and Harry Richardson (Curtis could not succeed himself). Despite polls that he said showed him ahead, Monks ultimately withdrew "in the interest of party unity." Erwin won the primary by a narrow margin and promptly endorsed the Pittston refinery, his firm 1970 stand against oil forgotten among the shortages of 1974.

In July, 1974, Governor Curtis astonished many by naming Monks to head Maine's newly created Office of Energy Resources. Monks immediately undertook a program of developing and investigating Maine's indigenous energy resources, from chicken manure to the Passamaquoddy Bay tides. In defense of the latter he came out against the Pittston refinery, whose tanker approach to Eastport would be shut off by the tidal power project. Despite his stated intention to remain non-political, rumors persist that he has his eye on Senator Muskie in 1976 or Senator Hathaway in 1978.

One sidelight of the Monks-Smith primary was the fascination that Monks held for *Maine Times* editor John Cole. It may initially have been rooted in Cole's dislike for Mrs. Smith, but it quickly took on a more active dimension. Not only did Cole take the Machias options off Monks's hands and support AIDE, but he boosted the candidate constantly, even referring in an otherwise lucid *Harper's Magazine* piece on Maine's new directions to the vision in "Bob Monks's blue entrepreneurial eyes."[14]

The Cole-Monks relationship was a source of some concern to others at the *Maine Times* who felt that the paper might be compromised by its editor's partisanship. Cole saw the matter differently. To him, the Monks-Smith primary was a clash between a style that he admired and much that he detested in Maine. As he put it in another context, "I am a pushover for style, and any person who possesses it will be forgiven much by me."[15]

Monks had style, but Mrs. Smith's support came mostly from what Cole called "the gray people . . . dour middle-management types. . . . They drive pickup trucks with a rifle slung across the rear window . . . [wearing] Day-Glo orange hunting caps . . . steel-rim glasses . . . short hair . . . and uniformly devoid of sexuality." Cole felt that these gray people threatened Maine's finer values much as Faulkner's Snopeses gnawed at Mississippi's. To combat them, he seemed willing to glorify Monks, to hope that Monks would conform himself to an idealized portrait.

In this, as in much else, Cole has been Maine's closest thing to David Brower, of whom Environmental Protection Agency administrator Russell Train once said, "He makes it easy for the rest of us to be reasonable. Somebody has to be a little extreme. Dave is a little hairy at times, but you do need somebody riding out there in front."[16] Cole had indeed been out in front. As early as October, 1970, he had called for more emphasis on energy from "the sun, the wind, and the tides" on the ground that U.S. security was being menaced by overdependence not on the Arabs but on its own oil companies.

Like Brower, Cole has been known to put more emphasis on the feel of a story than on its detailed accuracy, and like Cole, Brower has on occasion sought to create a man who wasn't there. In *Encounters with the Archdruid,* author John McPhee describes a conversation on Georgia's undeveloped Cumberland Island. Brower is talking to real estate developer Charles Fraser whose Hilton Head development he had admired. The words are those that Cole seemed to be saying to Monks, and Fraser's reply is no less parallel:

> "You, Charles Fraser, have got to persuade the whole God-damned movement of realtors to have a different kind of responsibility to man than they have. . . . I have seen evidence of what you can do. . . . Now make others do it. The system must be used to reform the system."
> When Brower finished, Fraser said nothing and sipped his wine.[17]

Cumberland Island was an appropriate site for this encounter, for Monks's wife is a descendant of the island's Carnegie owners. When Fraser's proposed development of a part of the island generated so much opposition that he turned his land over to the National Park Service, the Interior Department undertook to acquire the entire island as a National Seashore preserve. The Monkses, unable to come to terms with the federal government, left responsibility for the transfer of their share in the hands of a Georgia lawyer, who attempted to set a price for the land based on quick sales of small parcels.

When Georgia Governor Jimmy Carter learned of the advertisements, he accused Monks of "seeking to mislead gullible buyers . . . to artificially create a development price on undeveloped land."[18] The charges were front page in Maine. The Monkses flew to Georgia, met with Carter, and agreed to take the land off the market. Carter wrote a pleasant letter acknowledging the withdrawal and regretting the unpleasantness. Monks released the letter as a retraction of the charges, which so annoyed Carter that he attacked Monks again. Monks left the matter there.

As the Monkses fought to hold on to Cumberland Island, they did not notice a past acquaintance of theirs seeking to move into a somewhat less exclusive neighborhood across the straits in the paper-mill-dominated town of Brunswick. There David Scoll, his old quota permits miraculously converted into a fee-free allocation under the new import program, sought to build a desulfurization plant to help the Brunswick Pulp and Paper Company to comply with state and federal air-pollution requirements. Faced with rejection by Georgia authorities, he was last seen headed for Pascagoula, Mississippi. He has said that the Mississippi environmental board is much stricter and more professional than the Maine agency and is less likely to reject his refinery out of a fear that its cleanliness would emphasize the poor job of law enforcement being done on the state's present polluters.

On the way to Pascagoula, Scoll paused to form the American League of Anglers, the country's first organized nationwide sport fishermen's lobby. With a roster of outstanding names in sports, entertainment, and government, the ALA made brief headlines by presenting a flyrod to retiring Senator George Aiken of Vermont to kick off its fight for cleaner fresh and salt water.

—Maine Lobstermen's Association president Ossie Beal has remained a staunch opponent of oil development on Maine's coast, but even for him the threat has brought tangible benefits. He became a widely quoted and interviewed man. One of the interviews went so well that he married the writer, an out-of-state free-lancer. There are some in Washington County who feel that local sympathy for his first wife, whom he left for the writer, cost him the 1972 campaign for a legislative seat that Bob Monks helped to convince him to undertake.

—John Shaheen completed his Come-by-Chance refinery in 1974, three years behind schedule but at a peak of the U.S. energy crisis. A slight breakdown in the final timetable brought 1500 guests to the refinery dedication on the *Queen Elizabeth II* some four months before the plant could begin operation. Still, dedications do not necessarily accompany openings any more than press releases accompany ground-breakings. Shaheen has a going refinery at an opportune moment, and he has announced unconsummated plans for at least two more. Critics suggest that he has been lucky, but admirers credit energy and foresight. President Nixon told Prime Minister Pierre Trudeau that his former client was "the world's greatest salesman," in response to which Shaheen opined that Nixon was "the greatest strategic lawyer I have ever known. When he is talking about the second stage of an operation, you know that he's already thinking out the sixth stage."[19]

Putting his money where his mouthpiece was, Shaheen contributed more than $100,000 to the 1972 Nixon campaign, but his apparently bright future suddenly darkened late in 1973, when Canada imposed severe export limitations on its refineries in response to domestic shortages of its own and to Arab threats of cutbacks proportional to any shipments to the United States. The Canadian restrictions did not immediately apply to Shaheen, for his refinery was not in operation. Nevertheless, Shaheen Company president Homer White hastened to offer the oil to Canada. "If rape is inevitable," he enthused, "relax and enjoy it."[20]

The Shaheen and other Canadian export cutbacks could alter the trend toward supplying U.S. energy markets from plants located in Canada. The same refineries built in the United States could be required to adapt their storage capacity to the security of their sources and might therefore be of some use in deterring or minimizing future embargoes. This cornerstone of Project Independence was what Jack Evans, Governor Curtis, Senator Muskie, and Armand Hammer had been called unpatriotic and irresponsible for suggesting in 1968.

—Atlantic Richfield periodically renews its Machias area options, but the company's attention is very much on Alaska. It has also been a leader in efforts to produce oil from Canadian tar sands and, to a lesser extent, Colorado oil shale. Arco was the first major oil company to urge the repeal of the depletion allowance, but Maine is very much on a back burner.

Whatever the company eventually does in Maine will be done under new leadership. Lou Ream, the executive vice-president who oversaw the company's Machiasport involvement, retired early in 1973 to grow varietal wine grapes and start an experimental school on a 6000-acre ranch in California.

Andy Nixon and I, having considered him the most open and cooperative of the top-ranking executives with whom Maine dealt, were sorry to see him go. He's probably better off though, for the nation (undeterred by Maine's avant-garde 1859 Temperance Act) has already experimented and come to terms with its inability to shake its dependence on the liquid from which he will derive his future income.

—Atlantic Richfield's former Washington counsel, Tom Matthews, still handles oil matters, though rarely for Arco. Matthews, that most ingenious of challengers to Occidental and to Norman Engleberg's dignitaries at the 1968 hearings, called me in December, 1974. He had, it seemed, been retained by Occidental to help resist a takeover bid by Standard of Indiana. The merger would be the largest in U.S. history, and Matthews was anxious to get a copy of this book. He needed the book because one of his lines of defense was to be that Occidental's efforts at Machiasport had shown the company to be an aggressively competitive force, a force which should not be allowed to disappear into one of the same major oil companies that had resisted its every innovation six years earlier.

—John King remains the subject of an apparently endless series of investigations arising from the King Resources bankruptcy. He put his own assets, among others, in the hands of his wife and son, who give him an allowance and contribute heavily to congenial Colorado Republicans.

King has begun to fulfill the prophecy implicit in the cryptic plane crash with which Donny McNamara ended *The Money Maker*. He announced in March, 1974, that he would run for the U.S. Senate from Colorado as an independent. His campaign was premised on the belief that the people were ready to elect a man who could admit and learn from his mistakes.

Although Don McNamara's racing odyssey, *White Sails and Black Clouds*, begins on a compatible note ("One learns far more from defeats than from victories"), the former Olympian was not at King's winches for the political cruise. *The Money Maker* made more than money in Denver, and anyway, McNamara's prudent refusal to ratify his skipper's manipulations during his brief tenure as a King Resources director in late 1970 drew far less admiration from John King than it did from the local U.S. Attorney. McNamara was the only director who resisted and the only one to avoid subsequent investigation for criminal and civil wrongdoing. In February, 1974, he was subpoenaed to appear before a grand jury investigating criminal wrongdoing by his erstwhile colleagues during their efforts to provide tax shelters to the masses. The testimony required him to interrupt work on his second novel, this one about drug smuggling and international oil tankers.

I last saw Don McNamara over a beer in a New York City bar at the bottom of the thirty-story glass building where he had come to work for one of the nation's largest tanker brokers. His sailing races had continued to reflect both the talent and the impetuosity that had spun him through Casco Bay four years earlier. A recent issue of *Yacht Racing* had contained the following:

> Then, however, the human element asserted itself. In a day race, sailed in Narragansett Bay because of a strong southwesterly wind off shore, although she was well in the lead, *Cascade* failed to observe the only government mark mentioned in the course instructions as having to be observed.

When later notified of the error, owner Milgram withdrew *Cascade*. Skipper Don McNamara, however, withdrew the withdrawal and elected to fight the issue on semantic grounds in a hearing. He lost his argument, and *Cascade* lost the series lead.

The latest America's Cup races had just concluded, but McNamara had had no part in them. His last America's Cup participation had been in 1962, when a dispute with his cohelmsman and the owners had resulted in his dismissal from the *Nefertiti* on the eve of her disastrous performance in the final trials to select the Cup defender.

McNamara waxed both skeptical and ironic in discussing the environmental plaudits that the Gibbs Company and Harold Pachios had been gathering for a plan not so different from the one that John King's ruin had taken out of his hands in 1970. As the light ebbed out of the nondescript afternoon, my concentration drifted with it, away from his discussion of "worldscale" tanker rates and "the Rotterdam netback." I thought instead of a story I had first heard at the age of fourteen during a summer vacation in Massachusetts in 1956, the last year before oil import controls were presidentially imposed. The story was about a 5.5 metre yacht named *Quixotic*, built by Don McNamara and others with tax deductible financing obtained as a result of a yacht builder's loophole known as "the Olympic vehicle." *Quixotic* had gone into the last two races of that summer's pre-Olympic trials needing only to finish next-to-last in either race to secure the right to represent the U.S. at the Olympics in Australia.

In the first of the two races, *Quixotic* was disqualified for a foul committed while inexplicably scrapping for an unnecessary third place finish. The helmsman committing the foul had been Ted Hood, who was six years later to replace McNamara at *Nefertiti*'s helm and twelve years after that to steer *Courageous* to her successful 1974 defense of the America's Cup. The helmsman who was fouled had been Pierre duPont IV, a Harvard contemporary of McNamara and Bob Monks and later a Delaware congressman. In 1971, duPont helped to push through his state's ban on coastal refineries to the dismay of his petrochemical family. A year before that, he had called Bob Monks to inquire about the availability of the Machias Bay options for the very type of petrochemical development that he later aided in legislating out of Delaware.

Halfway through the last race, *Quixotic* stood second when a halyard shackle suddenly opened and the mainsail fell to the deck. As McNamara told it in *White Sails and Black Clouds:*

There wasn't a word said. I jumped on deck, grabbed the spinnaker halyard, and in a few seconds was three-quarters of the way aloft, hand over hand, but there I ran out of things to grab . . . *Quix* without sail was wallowing something fierce in the tide-driven chop. The whip aloft was wild. I started to shinny. To preserve the new aluminum mast, we had coated the mast with clear epoxy. It was our downfall, for the mast was slippery as a greased pole. There was only the sharp rod rigging to grab, yet I kept trying and got cut to ribbons. I got within a foot and no farther. There the halyard dangled, a foot away, as my sweaty, bleeding hands slipped slowly . . . It was thus that *Quixotic,* the American boat of her day, didn't get to Melbourne.

In the words of a Leonard Cohen song, "If I've got to remember, that's a fine memory."

—John Love, who had testified in Portland in 1968 against the Maine proposal, resigned the governorship of Colorado in June, 1973, to become the Nixon administration's "energy czar" (the phrase is theirs, which is curious, since the oil industry had frequently mocked Harold Ickes for acting like an "oil czar" under President Roosevelt). His early political career was reportedly financed in part by John King, but the jump to Washington was, according to the same report,[21] engineered by Peter Flanigan's brother Bobby, a former Colorado Republican state chairman.

Had Love known energy policy well, he would have had a difficult time. Had he known the subject moderately well, he would not have taken the job. The summer of 1973 was simply not the time to seek on-the-job training at that level on that subject. Staffing problems, Presidential inaccessibility, bureaucratic and Congressional sniping, and a personal tendency to defer decisions all contributed to his resignation after six months on the job (and to that of his deputy, Charles Dibona, who promptly took over the No. 2 job at the American Petroleum Institute). Love was also doomed in large part by the 1968–69 inactions in favor of which he had testified in Maine. This irony did not escape him any more than he escaped it. *The National Journal* of October 10, 1973 (five years less one day from his Portland appearance), quotes him as saying, "With hindsight, I wish devoutly that there were a refinery at Machiasport."

Despite Love's experience, a Federal Energy Agency now exists. William Simon, Love's successor at its helm, got off to a bad start. At a December 14, 1973, hearing in Hartford, Connecticut, he repeatedly asserted that "Machiasport was killed by conservationists." Finally an aide to Governor Philip Noel of Rhode Island mentioned that he understood that Machiasport refineries had been prevented by oil-import limitations. "No, no," Simon said. "That's not right. It was environmentalists. Ask these guys [pointing toward a group of oil-industry representatives]. They'll tell you the score."[22]

—Andy Nixon left state government in March, 1970, to become a special assistant to Curtis Hutchins at the Dead River Company. Maine's oil policies lost some coherency, but Dead River's oil business thrived. Nixon was named president and chief executive officer of the company in the fall of 1973 at the age of thirty-four.

Governor Curtis named him to replace Hutchins on Maine's Board of Environmental Protection in 1972. This didn't work out, for Nixon felt that since Pittston would inevitably be either a competitor or a supplier at Eastport, he had to disqualify himself from consideration of their application. Seeing that the pressure of the work and continuing conflicts over oil would reduce his usefulness to the board, Nixon resigned in December, 1973, but the hearings were too far along for Curtis to name a replacement. Spurred on by telegrams of support from William Simon, by the energy crisis, and by the illness and eventual death of a staunch conservationist member of the BEP, Pittston was within reach of approval by a single vote by September, 1974.

—Maine's renowned individualists are having to learn to coexist with substantial numbers of urban refugees, who come as professional people, subsistence farmers, craftsmen, non-nuclear families, and dropouts. Like the rest of us, the native Mainers may have begun to wonder whether when they say, "Help! Oil!" they are uttering an appeal ("Help! Police!") or a warning ("Help! Fire!"). They may be better able than most to weather an energy crisis, but the accompanying expansions of governmental power will not go down easily.

The following is from three speakers on the losing side of a 1973 debate in the same Maine legislature that must now come to grips with energy interrelationships. The issue was the mandatory wearing of blaze orange clothing by deer hunters.

> This fluorescent material is suitable for a sportsman, a jolly boy, but a man that has to work it is not suitable for. . . . Many of those were in one holers that were shot, some were upstairs in bed shot, some were in a restaurant shot and these are considered hunting fatalities. . . .

If the warden sees a young lady in the woods and she had a fluorescent dress, it says it must be visible from all sides. He can ask her to remove that dress and he can remove it to find out if it is the same color underneath . . .

My own father was shot and killed while hunting. . . . But this is taking away from us all our rights. This is just putting the foot in the door. . . . Back when my father was shot and killed, we just had horses. It was 20 miles to the nearest hospital. Today you have ambulances that can get you there within 20 minutes or less. We can save lives today we could not save then.

—No women testified at the trade-zone hearings, and women have not been much involved in the energy industries or in energy policy-making. Most of the politically active women in Maine have opposed oil refineries, but on no uniquely feminist ground.* There are fewer pipefitters and property taxpayers among them, and some have more of the unsalaried time that environmentalism demands. Their energy perspectives derive from different machines and different days, and it has been argued that men are more subject to "the male defect, which is lunacy: they are so obsessed by public affairs that they see the world as by moonlight, which shows the outline of every object but not the details indicative of their natures."[23] I sometimes wonder what a feminine energy policy would consist of, but it is not mine to devise.

—We live in an old house, built around 1818, just before the Missouri Compromise made Maine a state. It is heated by fireplaces, by an oil furnace, and, in two newer rooms, by electricity. Between the house and the barn several apple trees, still blossoming but aged beyond redeeming, are collapsing into firewood with a heating-oil equivalent of about 150 gallons per tree.

In one corner of the barn lie the last remnants of a long-discontinued coal heap. Above, among swallows' nests in the sagging rafters, brackets hold a thirty-foot steering oar that has probably been there more than fifty years, almost certainly put away while Armand Hammer was in Lenin's Russia by two men who did not realize that they would never lift it down.

---

* There were two women on Governor Curtis's coastal task force. One, representing low-income people, was prevented by the combined demands of child care and an inflexible employer from participating. The other, representing the League of Women Voters, participated as a conservationist with no special energy background. Her contributions were accepted as femininely environmental by those who agreed with her and dismissed as environmentally feminine by those who did not.

The dining room is still dominated by the mantel of a huge cooking fireplace long since torn out to make room for indoor plumbing and an entire bathroom. We sometimes think about moving the bathroom and replacing the chimney, a decision that until recently would have involved only economics, convenience, and aesthetics, but that seems today to have taken on moral and civic dimensions.

The house and fireplace were built just beyond the midpoint between the present and the year that the first two hundred French settlers spent a frigid winter on a Passamaquoddy Bay island near Eastport, plagued by too little food and too much weather, getting by on community, French equivalents to "Rock of Ages," and aspirations toward a prosperous society of fairly allocated liberty. Their star-crossed failure is part of the history of Acadia, the French community in eastern Canada forcibly scattered and deported by the British in the name of imperial security, leaving little in Maine beyond the name of the present national park.

Most of the Acadians were taken to Louisiana, there to be sold with the land as "Cajuns" to the United States in 1803, in order to finance Napoleon's armies. Their great great grandchildren were to benefit from some of the continent's richest oil strikes and to form a key Catholic bloc in the occasionally narrow reelections of Hale Boggs. Neither they nor the descendants of their more somber Pilgrim rivals, whom their forefathers and the Indians had burned out of Maine as late as 1700, seem to have maintained either the ancestral fervor for institutions no less just than human nature itself or the accompanying commitments to the covenant, to democracy, and to education—commitments forged from firsthand knowledge that governmental pursuit of more personal ends is rooted in a totalitarian impulse.

Epilogue

And all is done as I have told.

William Blake, "The Mental Traveller"

WHEN I BEGAN to write this book in mid-1971, I thought that readers would be as startled as I by oil-policymaking in Washington, especially in the White House. The implications were, I then thought, so extraordinary that my greatest difficulty would be to remain credible while telling an incredible story.

Like those who believed in the oil-import program, I was guarding against the opposite of the approaching reality. While I was writing, others were unraveling ITT, the milk fund, the corporate contributions, Agnew, and Watergate. Much that had seemed inferential and serious became indictable and pardoned. At this writing, several trials are still before us, but the former President has grudgingly made many voices public. It is now clear that those who in 1971 walked and looked like ducks were quacking like ducks as well.

We are not likely ever to hear the tapes of the Nixon oil discussions, but who can doubt their contents? How scandalous would they have to be to surprise? More scandalous certainly than the persistent Washington rumor that a subcommittee of the Senate Foreign Relations Committee has in its files a document describing an Occidental effort to persuade and subsidize the CIA to undermine Qaddafi in Libya as it was then doing to President Salvador Allende in Chile.

More scandalous also than a September 21, 1974, *Business Week* article about Armand Hammer's contributions via Tim Babcock to the 1972 Nixon campaign. According to this piece, Leon Jaworski joined those who wondered at Hammer's remarkable three-year rise in the esteem of a vindictive administration whose original Vice-President had been bruised by the Occidental-inspired 1969 leak of the Midlands, Texas, campaign promise.

The gist of the *Business Week* story was that Hammer's reported 1972 contribution of $46,000 was a bit of an understatement. It seems that Tim Babcock, along with four other Montanans, may have contributed another $54,000. The other four testified that Babcock, shades of Harry Sinclair, loaned them their shares of the contribution. Unlike

Sinclair, however, Babcock didn't have the money at the time, which is why Jaworski came to suspect that the funds originated with Hammer or Occidental.

Dr. Hammer once again summoned Louis Nizer to his side. As a *Business Week* source described the Jaworski investigation, it "comes down to Hammer's word against that of Babcock," which was why Nizer "hired a private investigating firm to probe Babcock's financial affairs . . . to get as much on the former employee as possible to weaken his argument."

Even the $100,000 total Hammer-Babcock effort doesn't seem to have satisfied the CREEP greed. A postelection list of "individuals to be solicited for further contributions" targeted the Doctor for $250,000. The initials of the man assigned to extract this sum were MHS—Maurice H. Stans.

We can only assume that when Stans made his contact, Maine's trade-zone application, still pending on the ex-Commerce Secretary's desk, was discussed with smiles, if at all.

One must remember Stans's role in the Machiasport stalemate to appreciate fully the blow that struck the Pittston Company on September 20, 1974. On that date Chairman Russell Peterson of the Council on Environmental Quality wrote to Alexander Butterfield, Administrator of the Federal Aviation Administration, that the FAA's proposed release of the Eastport Municipal Airport to the town of Eastport for conveyance to Pittston Company "may result in substantially different environmental effects and must, under NEPA, be preceded by the preparation of an impact statement."

Since Maine Attorney General Jon Lund had already ruled that Maine could not issue a permit to an applicant that did not control the land necessary for its project, Peterson's letter stopped all consideration of the Pittston venture 18 months after the application had been filed. The Lund opinion said, in effect, that Pittston must await completion of a federal review process comparing Eastport to other ports, oil to other energy sources, and tanker routes to the dams of the Passamaquoddy tidal power project. Even if the project survives this review, it must obtain tanker passage permits from a Canadian government whose former environmental minister was quoted in the *Maine Times* as saying, "We're going to do everything short of sending gunboats to prevent an Eastport refinery."

Treasury Secretary William Simon, shrugging off any appearances of impropriety arising from a relative's role as a consultant to the project,* has remained faithful to the refinery. Peterson's letter was sent out in the face of vehement objections from Simon and his aides to the effect that the refinery was essential to the regional and national security even though it planned to run on Middle Eastern crude oil and would preempt the only conceivable tidal power site on the U.S. East Coast.

Governor Curtis was personally opposed to the Pittston project because he felt that Eastport was inferior to Machias Bay and Portland as a deep-water port. Despite his concern, he took no active role in leading the opposition, for he felt, in this case as with Maine Clean Fuels, that he should not intrude his personal preference on the Environmental Improvement Commission deliberations. Furthermore, he expected the commission to reject the project.

Curtis's willingness to trust due process of law was shaken when three probable anti-Pittston votes on the commission were eliminated by a resignation, a disqualification, and a death. Taking no chances on due process of law, a Pittston realtor who also served on the Maine Executive Council took an active role in persuading the Council to delay confirmation of new appointees to the board until the proceedings had progressed past a point at which they could participate. Thus the ten-member board appeared to be split 4–3 in Pittston's favor when Peterson wrote to Butterfield.

On the day that the Peterson letter set back the Pittston Company, the Gibbs Company, through a consortium called the New England Energy Corporation, filed its application for a terminal in Portland to serve a southern Maine refinery. The refinery was to supply southern New England by pipeline rather than small tanker or barge. Despite local opposition, Maine's leading environmental groups were cautiously favorable toward the project. If it solved the usual problems of land, oil, and money, it seemed likely to enjoy a relatively smooth environmental path.

There was a certain symmetry to the possibility that Gibbs vice-president Herb Sostek might be on the dais at Maine's first refinery groundbreaking. Sostek was present at the April, 1968, creation of the first

* Simon's relationship to Pittston consultant William Stott was inadvertently disclosed by the energy czar himself. On several occasions he mentioned to oil industry visitors that those in Maine who resented his interference in the state hearings would be really upset if they knew that he had a close relative involved in the project. Suffice it to say that his office was less secure than he thought.

Machiasport consortium. He watched in horrified fascination at the wondrous first and only meeting of that consortium with Occidental in New York in September, 1968. With the agility, opportunism, and resiliency necessary to survival in the tightening petroleum spot markets, he clung like a mongoose to Hammer's back as the Doctor tried to use and then lose the New England independent marketers over the next two years. When Occidental's attention wavered in 1970, Sostek and the Gibbs Company reverted to the concept of a Maine refinery consortium.

Neither Sostek nor Gibbs Company president Henry Gibbs was an instinctive environmentalist. Their willingness to accept the more costly but environmentally preferable pipeline system was their perception of the entry fee necessary to a Maine refinery. It was comparable to Occidental's $7.2-million Marine Resources Fund, or even to Dr. Hammer's having wrapped his successful 1966 bid for Libyan concessions in a ribbon dyed the color of Libya's flag. As Esso board chairman Michael Haider implied in his "We can play by any rules at all" statement, corporations perform like most suitors in tailoring their bids to the present level of self-respect in the relevant state.

The Gibbs refinery would, of course, do nothing for or to Washington County. The Pittston stalemate and the rise in oil prices revived discussion of the Passamaquoddy tidal power project, although executives of Maine power companies assert that the immense chain of dams will remain unfeasible "while there's still a ceiling on the national debt." In any case, the project would have to be restudied in the Pittston environmental impact statement as one of the alternatives to the Federal Aviation Administration's release of the Eastport Airport to a proposed oil refinery.

The stalemate engendered by that review lasted some fifteen weeks. In January, 1975, the Maine environmental commission reconsidered the suspension of its hearings and resumed its consideration of the Pittston application.

At the final hearing, a month later, a commission consultant testified that Eastport would be "the toughest oil port in the world," and the commission rejected the port proposal. Regardless of possible modifications or court appeals, the continuing Canadian opposition appeared to doom the project.

Simultaneously with Pittston's revival, the Gibbs consortium crumbled as a key member, the Burmah Oil Company, pulled out in the face of financial difficulties and uncertainties over U.S. oil-import policies.

The consortium then requested that its environmental hearings be recessed until May 1, 1975, while its remaining members regrouped.

Thus, as the Maine oil refinery question moved into its eighth year, its ninth and tenth proposals, and its fourth and fifth sites, the President of the United States was proposing new barriers to oil imports, barriers that could only pave the way for domestic oil-price increases while imposing special hardships on New England's economy and consumers. With cheap foreign oil an apparent anachronism, suggestions by refinery proponents that they could alleviate these hardships were nonsense, but so were the claims of their opponents that the refineries would clearly be a net economic loss to the state. Maine's own self-respect and standards appeared to have declined somewhat from the 1970–71 peak that David Scoll had found insurmountable, but it remained to be seen whether Maine's standards mattered much.

Meanwhile life in Washington County continues much as it was before the county's deep harbors called it to national attention. The major federal presence in 1974 has been the Internal Revenue Service, which has been rigorously auditing the lobster fishermen, denying them all but the most carefully documented business-expense deductions. The contrast to the IRS's supine acceptance of the Nixon returns has not gone unremarked.

The economic forces that ruled the county in 1968 have not been disturbed. A state official charged in August, 1974, that conditions in the county's migrant blueberry-picker camps were inferior to the quarters of most farm animals and "a disgrace to this state." Maine's largest blueberry grower, State Senator J. Hollis Wyman (R.-Milbridge), chairman of the powerful legislative committee on taxation, replied, according to the Portland *Press Herald:*

> These people think that just because we don't provide the migrants with flush toilets or running water for three or four weeks that it's a terrible imposition. The workers don't complain. . . .
>
> The strange part of it is that if you look at these pickers you might think they should have flush toilets, running water and all those other things. Yet you have people who go camping and stay in tents and sleep in sleeping bags, and they don't have these things.

The plight of the small landowner has not improved much either. As one of them wrote in an open letter to Governor Curtis, published in the Bangor *Daily News,*

> The house we live in and the land around it have been in my family for over a hundred years. They have been handed down from my great

grandfather's time, from generation to generation. I have farmed the land, raised two fine sons on it, kept livestock on it, and cut pulpwood from it.

As you know, times have changed. It isn't very easy to make a living in Washington County today. But I am not complaining. I enjoy making a living from my own land and from the mudflats nearby. If only given a chance, I can support my wife and her mother, who lives with us. (My two sons have married.) Mostly I dig clams for a living. In winter, when ice shuts off the mudflats, I can scrape by selling a few cords of pulpwood from my land, though there isn't much good wood left. I take firewood from my land, and that helps me get by the winter. We get food from the garden I raise in summer.

But now I believe the Town of Milbridge is trying to drive me off the land we depend on. They think they can get more tax money if the land is sold to real estate people and developed. I have already had to sell off several pieces of my land because I couldn't pay the higher taxes the town imposed on me. But this didn't help me at all. They just keep raising the tax on the rest of my land because they said when the land I sold was developed it raised the value of my land nearby. . . .

One assessor said if I tore down that old house of mine, the land would be worth even more. I don't think they should talk to a man like that.

I have been to the County Commissioners about this, and they recommend that the town reduce my taxes, but the assessors say no. I have tried to get a Pine Tree Association lawyer, but they never call me back. I would be willing to pay a lawyer.

I am not trying to get out of paying my fair share of taxes. I want to pay my taxes, and I would be happy if they would just cut my present taxes in half. But there are a lot of poor people like my wife and me who are being treated unfairly so as to drive us off the land. I don't think the towns should be that greedy for tax money.

My wife and I want to stay on our land. We couldn't live if we were cooped up on an acre or two. Where would we get our firewood? Where would we grow our fresh vegetables? We don't want to sell to developers. But I guess the town feels it would be more economical to put us on welfare with some of the money they'll get from taxes after the land is developed.

Governor Curtis, can you take a few moments out to help a man and a woman who are willing to help themselves if they are only given half a chance?

Respectfully yours,
(s) Clarence Bagley

Among the inexplicable interconnections in Thomas Pynchon's *Gravity's Rainbow* is the reappearance of a mouth organ which falls from a pocket into a 1930s Boston dancehall toilet to be flushed away and found by its owner half a dozen years and 560 pages later beside a Central European mountain stream toward the end of World War II. Such unlikely recurrences seem random at first, but they come in time to suggest a pattern and then even a design. They invite insatiable inferences of cosmic harmonies or conspiracies, inferences that create legions of ill-equipped special prosecutors who will keep businessmen and public officials up against the wall for some time to come.

I had not intended to invoke these recurrences again at this point, but then, after I thought this book completed, I read Hunter Thompson's *Fear and Loathing on the Campaign Trail '72*. At the very end, relaxed and unprepared for Jack Evans's Yuletide exhortations to fellow summer residents of Consciousness I, I found the following:

> Later, when the big rain started, I got heavily into the gin and read the Sunday papers. On page 39 of *California Living* magazine I found a hand-lettered ad from the McDonald's Hamburger Corporation, one of Nixon's big contributors in the '72 presidential campaign:
>
> PRESS ON, it said. NOTHING IN THE WORLD CAN TAKE THE PLACE OF PERSISTENCE. TALENT WILL NOT: NOTHING IS MORE COMMON THAN UN-SUCCESSFUL MEN WITH TALENT. GENIUS WILL NOT: UNREWARDED GENIUS IS ALMOST A PROVERB. EDUCATION ALONE WILL NOT: THE WORLD IS FULL OF EDUCATED DERELICTS. PERSISTENCE AND DETERMINATION ALONE ARE OMNIPOTENT.
>
> I read it several times before I grasped the full meaning. Then, when it came to me, I called Mankiewicz immediately.
>
> "Keep your own counsel," he said. "Don't draw any conclusions from anything you see or hear."

An understandable reaction, but terrible advice. Dr. Thompson did well to reject it.

Acknowledgments

The foregoing story is as factually accurate and as true as I could make it. Nevertheless, three areas of distortion have resulted from my own involvement.

First, I have had access to a small amount of material that I have not been free to disclose. Fortunately, this material is more entertaining than significant, my own favorite example being an episode in which an oil expert prepared perceptive position papers and speeches for opponents during their campaigns for seats in the U.S. Senate. I have felt free to use anything that an enterprising journalist could have uncovered. Because Governor Curtis ran a singularly open administration, this standard has been unrestrictive and sometimes self-serving. I have justified the inclusion of several items on the ground that Andy Nixon or I would have told them to anyone who had asked.

Second, I found no graceful way of handling my own sporadic appearances. To avoid the distraction of sudden first-person pronouns, I have kept these appearances to a minimum. Norman Mailer may have been able to write of himself as Aquarius with a straight face, but, having been born in late July, I have preferred not to appear as Cancer. I was, nevertheless, deeply involved in these events after early 1969, and, to the extent that misjudgments or foolishness are attributable to anonymous "governor's aides," I was at least among them.

Third, this book does not do justice to the impact that Kenneth Curtis has had on state government in Maine. A subordinate fulsomely praising his chief is almost automatically unreliable, and I have shied so far away from the Jack Valenti ("I sleep better each night just knowing that Lyndon Johnson is my President") syndrome that I have understated the Governor's role in shaping Maine's response to the forces that whirled around it. Fortunately, another aide has been less reticent, and Kermit Lipez's *Kenneth Curtis of Maine* (Brunswick, Maine: Harpswell Press, 1974) is a balanced portrait of a man who governed affirmatively, without fear, without neurosis, during a time when the national models behaved very differently. He did not as governor have a chance to attend the refinery groundbreaking that he hoped to see in Maine, but he can be sure that, if it comes, it will be on sounder terms because he circumscribed his hopes with judgment.

Other Maine friendships qualifying as disclosable assets for purposes of this book include Andy Nixon, Gardiner Means, Marc Nault, Donaldson

369

Koons, John Cole, Joseph Fisher (who in 1974 became a Virginia Congressman by upsetting 22-year incumbent Joel Broyhill), Harry Richardson, Steve Murray, Horace Hildreth, and Harold Pachios.

Others who have been especially generous with time and information are David Anderson, George Bevel, John Buckley, Walter Corey, Howard Goldenfarb, Sam Hill, Robert Howe, Christopher Hutchins, John Lamont, Ed Langlois, John Lichtblau, Marty Lobel, Thomas Matthews, Robert McLaughlin, Don Nicoll, Alan Novins, Joe Onek, Mrs. Peggy Rockefeller, Herb Sostek, Chip Stockford, Stewart Udall, and John Zentay.

I owe a particular debt to four who were generally candid, with no guarantees of immunity, about events that did not always flatter them. These are Jack Evans, Don McNamara, Bob Monks, and David Scoll.

I am also indebted in a different way to those who have contributed patience or at least tolerance while this book fractured more schedules and deadlines than the Penn Central. Gerry Dick kept impeccable records without which much of the book would have been unwritable. Nancy Marple and Debby Allard typed and retyped; colleagues at the Maine Public Utilities Commission adjusted to eccentric borrowings of time; Larry Freundlich at Harper's Magazine Press was unwaveringly supportive; Arthur and Laura have put up with a distracted father for most of their lives; Kathy coped perceptively.

Source Notes

1: HEADWATERS

1. David Brower, quoted in John McPhee's *Encounters with the Archdruid* (New York: Farrar, Straus and Giroux, 1971), p. 80.
2. I am indebted to Mrs. Evelyn Carroll of Machiasport for access to her very useful paper on the history of Machiasport, prepared for the town government as part of its bicentennial celebration in 1963.
3. Quoted in Marion Jaques Smith, *A History of Maine: From Wilderness to Statehood* (Portland: Falmouth Publishing House, 1949), p. 292.
4. Louise Dickinson Rich, *The Coast of Maine* (New York: Thomas Y. Crowell Company, 1956), p. 276.
5. Some of the 1948–1959 barriers to foreign-oil imports are discussed in Maurice Adelman's *The World Petroleum Market* (Baltimore and London: Johns Hopkins University Press, 1972), pp. 139–59. Dr. Adelman also discusses and rejects theories of import restraint based on intercompany collusion.
6. Christopher Tugendhat, *Oil: The Biggest Business* (New York: G. P. Putnam's Sons, 1968), p. 156.

2: 1961–1968

1. Tugendhat, *Oil: The Biggest Business*, p. 233. Hunt himself disclaimed knowledge of this caper, attributing it to "a subordinate."
2. Richard O'Connor, *The Oil Barons* (Boston: Little, Brown & Co., 1971), pp. 318–19. Also Ed Kilman and Theon Wright, *Hugh Roy Cullen* (Englewood Cliffs, N.J.: Prentice-Hall, 1954), pp. 297–98.
3. Robert Engler, *The Politics of Oil* (Chicago: University of Chicago Press, 1961), pp. 263–64. This is only one of many incidents of oil money influencing political campaigns and governmental decisions that Engler thoroughly documents in this vast and often appalling study.
4. The Archbold letters are discussed in Allan Nevins's *John D. Rockefeller* (New York: Charles Scribner's Sons, 1940), pp. 499–515 and 593–94.
5. *The Wall Street Journal*, October 30, 1962, p. 2. The Kennedy-Kerr pact is discussed in Adelman's *The World Petroleum Market*, on p. 242.
6. Kenneth O'Donnell, "LBJ and the Kennedys," *Life* magazine, vol. 69, no. 6, p. 52.
7. The historically high costs and prices of electricity in New England are documented in William Shipman, *An Inquiry into the High Cost of*

Electricity in New England (Middletown, Conn.: Wesleyan University Press, 1962) and the New England Regional Commission, "A Study of the Electric Power Situation in New England," 1970.

8. Allan T. Demaree, "Our Crazy, Costly Life with Oil Quotas," *Fortune* magazine, vol. 79, no. 7, June, 1969, p. 182.

9. *Ibid.*, p. 106. The narrowness of his escape seems to have made a considerable impression on Secretary Udall. Discussing oil shale policy, he said, "The Interior Secretaryship is the most high-risk, dangerous, perilous job in the Cabinet. Just by signing a piece of paper, you can give away the resources of the nation . . . I can tell you, I'm goddamned relieved I got out of there without going to jail." Quoted in Chris Welles's *The Elusive Bonanza: The Story of Oil Shale* (New York: E. P. Dutton & Co., 1970), p. 132.

10. Frederick Lewis Allen, *Only Yesterday* (New York: Harper & Brothers, 1931), pp. 154–55.

11. *Ibid.*, p. 155.

12. *The Wall Street Journal*, February 8, 1972, p. 1.

13. Paul E. Steiger, "Who Is Armand Hammer," *Los Angeles Times Magazine*, November 9, 1969.

3: SUMMER, 1968

1. Quoted in O'Connor, *The Oil Barons*, p. 30.

2. *Ibid.*, p. 59.

3. *Independent Petroleum Monthly*, August, 1968, p. 52.

4. Letter from A. W. Tarkington to the Secretaries of Commerce and the Interior, September 9, 1968.

5. Quoted by Harriet Henry and David Halperin in *Maine Law Affecting Marine Resources* (Portland: University of Maine Law School, 1970), vol. 3, p. 419.

6. Charles Reich, *The Greening of America* (New York: Random House, 1970), p. 23.

7. *Ibid.*, p. 38.

8. *Ibid.*, p. 39.

9. Joseph L. Blotner and Frederick L. Gwynn, eds., *Faulkner in the University* (Charlottesville: University Press of Virginia, 1958), p. 277.

10. Harry M. Caudill, *Night Comes to the Cumberlands* (Boston: Atlantic Monthly Press/Little, Brown, 1963), p. 394.

11. Portland *Press Herald*, October 4, 1974.

4: OCTOBER, 1968

1. Quoted in O'Connor, *The Oil Barons*, pp. 121–22.

2. *Oil Weekly*, November 19, 1934. Quoted in O'Connor, *The Oil Barons*, pp. 312–13.

3. U.S. Department of Commerce, "Official Report of Proceedings before the Foreign Trade Zones Board, Court House, Portland, Maine, October 10–12, 1968," pp. 14–17.
4. *Ibid.*, p. 37.
5. *Ibid.*, pp. 40–41.
6. *Ibid.*, pp. 45–47.
7. *Ibid.*, pp. 63–67. (The pagination of the transcript is unreliable. The Boggs testimony actually spans some twenty-five pages, but many of them are unnumbered.)
8. While this quotation fairly summarizes the thrust of Dr. Adelman's Portland testimony, it is actually from his testimony before a Senate subcommittee five months later (U.S., Congress, Senate, Subcommittee on Antitrust and Monopoly, *The Petroleum Industry*, 91st Congress, 1st Session, March 11, 1969, p. 7).
9. This account is taken from the speech that Boggs made in the House of Representatives the following Monday (U.S., Congress, House, *Congressional Record*, 90th Congress, 2nd Session, October 14, 1968, pp. H10007–H10022). Because Boggs's staff took full advantage of the right of Congressmen to edit their remarks, the *Congressional Record* version is easier to follow than the press conference transcript.
10. Transcript of the Portland-Machiasport trade-zone hearings, pp. 370–71.
11. *Ibid.*, vol. 3, pp. 509–11.
12. David Nevin, *Muskie of Maine* (New York: Random House, 1972), p. 206.
13. Transcript of the Portland-Machiasport trade-zone hearings, vol. 4, p. 601.
14. The story of Agnew's meeting in Midland first appeared in the March 21, 1969, "Washington Merry-Go-Round" column co-authored by Jack Anderson and the late Drew Pearson. Agnew admitted the meeting but denied that Machiasport was discussed. A story in *Newsday*, March 10, 1974, claimed to have confirmed the story separately through Jack Bradford, president of the Midland Petroleum Club. Bradford told *Newsday*, "Nixon got a ton of money out of us out here."

5: NOVEMBER, 1968–JANUARY, 1969

1. Quoted in *Sports Illustrated*, July 22, 1974, p. 22.
2. Joseph C. Goulden, *The Superlawyers* (New York: Weybright and Talley, 1972), p. 161.
3. *The New York Times*, November 21, 1968, p. 67.
4. Portland (Maine) *Press Herald*, November 23, 1968.
5. *Dallas Morning News*, November 24, 1968, p. 26A.

6. Walter J. Hickel, *Who Owns America?* (Englewood Cliffs, N.J.: Prentice-Hall, Inc., 1971), p. 5. Secretary Hickel's book was published some months before Ms. Beard made her more famous mistake.

7. *Ibid.*, p. 6.

8. U.S., Congress, Senate, Subcommittee on Small Business, *Handling of the Foreign Trade Zone Application of the State of Maine by the Department of Commerce* (unpublished) 91st Congress, 1st Session, March 14, 1969, pp. 301, 303.

9. Statement of Senator Edward Kennedy, prepared for delivery at the December 19, 1968, session of the hearings cited in Note 8, above. Senator Kennedy was called from the hearing "to accompany Mrs. Robert F. Kennedy and his new niece to their home," and the transcript has a blank at page 60 for his statement to be included in the never-completed printed record. The statement was put out in press-release form by the Senator's office.

10. *Montreal Gazette,* January 10, 1969.

11. *Kennebec Journal,* January 20, 1969, p. 1.

12. The story of the Johnson meeting and subsequent phone calls is told by Hickel in *Who Owns America?*, pp. 16–17.

6: SPRING, 1969

1. Morton Mintz and Jerry S. Cohen, *America, Inc.* (New York: The Dial Press, 1971), Dell Edition, p. 243.

2. *Ibid.*, p. 31. The financing of the Gettysburg farm is discussed in more detail by Drew Pearson and Jack Anderson in *The Case Against Congress* (New York: Simon and Schuster, 1968), pp. 432–33. They note that the three executives tried to treat their payments as business expenses but were required by the Internal Revenue Service to report them as outright gifts, made while the recipient was President of the United States. One of the three, Cities Service chief executive W. Alton Jones, died in a plane crash on his way to visit Eisenhower in May, 1960. Pearson and Anderson could find no explanation for the $61,000 in cash and traveler's checks that Jones was carrying in his briefcase at the time.

3. Ronnie Dugger, "Oil and Politics," *The Atlantic Monthly,* vol. 224, no. 3, p. 67. Nixon's retreat from this commitment is described by Rowland Evans and Robert Novak in *Nixon in the White House: The Frustration of Power* (New York: Random House, 1971), pp. 219–23.

4. *Lewiston Daily Sun,* February 11, 1969, p. 1.

5. *Kennebec Journal,* February 22, 1969, p. 1.

6. *Washington Post,* January 31, 1971.

7. Portland *Press Herald,* February 28, 1969, p. 1.

8. *Maine Sunday Telegram*, March 2, 1969.

9. *Maine Times*, February 7, 1969.

10. Frank Graham, Jr., *Man's Dominion: The Story of Conservation in America* (New York: M. Evans and Company, 1971), pp. 163, 164.

11. Keith Roberts, *Machiasport: Oil and the Maine Coast* (Report of the Eastern New England Group of the Sierra Club, 1969), pp. 1–2.

12. Sarah Orne Jewett, *The Country of the Pointed Firs and Other Stories* (New York: Doubleday Anchor Books, 1928), pp. 9, 13.

13. Roberts, *Machiasport: Oil and the Maine Coast*, p. 30.

14. *Washington County Times*, September 11, 1969, p. 6.

15. U.S., Congress, Senate, *Congressional Record*, 91st Congress, 1st Session, November 10, 1969 (Reprint of letter from Governor Curtis to the Sierra Club, dated September 10, 1969).

16. *Ibid.*, October 8, 1969, p. S12184.

17. John J. McNamara, Jr., *White Sails, Black Clouds* (Boston: Burdette & Company, 1967), p. 145.

18. U.S., Congress, Senate, *Congressional Record*, March 12, 1969, p. S2698.

19. *Ibid.*, April 15, 1969, p. 9150.

20. *Kennebec Journal*, April 21, 1969, p. 1.

21. *Ibid.*, April 19, 1969.

22. Michael Harrington, *Toward a Democratic Left* (New York: Macmillan, 1968), p. 4.

23. U.S., Congress, Senate, Subcommittee on Antitrust and Monopoly, *Governmental Intervention in the Market Mechanism: The Petroleum Industry*, 91st Congress, 1st Session, March 12, 1969, p. 99.

24. *Ibid.*, p. 115–16.

25. *Ibid.*, April 2, 1969, pp. 304–305.

26. *Ibid.*, p. 304.

27. *Ibid.*, p. 308.

28. *Ibid.*, pp. 308–309.

29. *Ibid.*, March 26, 1969, pp. 231, 232.

30. *Ibid.*, March 25, 1969, p. 167.

31. *Ibid.*, pp. 191, 193.

32. *Ibid.*, April 2, 1969, pp. 377–78.

33. *Ibid.*, March 11, pp. 30–31.

34. *Ibid.*, p. 28.

35. Gene T. Kinney, "Hart Hurricane Wanes on Import Curbs," *The Oil and Gas Journal*, June 16, 1969, pp. 48, 50.

7: SUMMER, 1969

1. Quoted in Tugendhat, *Oil: The Biggest Business*, p. 230.

2. Quoted in Welles, *The Elusive Bonanza*, p. 56.

3. Quoted in *Fortune,* June, 1969, p. 180.
4. Quoted in *Oil: The Biggest Business,* p. 206.
5. Quoted in *Newsweek,* January 21, 1974, p. 79.
6. Quoted in John Holdren and Philip Herrera, *Energy* (San Francisco and New York: Sierra Club, 1971), pp. 244–45.
7. "The Year Oil Gets its Lumps," *Business Week,* May 17, 1969, p. 102.
8. Stephen Birmingham, *Our Crowd* (New York: Harper & Row, 1966), p. 38.
9. Transcript entitled "Press Briefing of Atlantic World Port," June 25, 1969, p. 30.
10. Daniel Jack Chasan, *Klondike '70* (New York: Praeger Publishers, 1971), p. 157.
11. Bangor *Daily News,* July 3, 1969, p. 2.
12. *Machias Valley News Observer,* November 21, 1969, p. 1.
13. Bangor *Daily News,* October 22, 1969, p. 1.
14. *Congressional Record,* September 16, 1969, p. 25657.
15. *Governmental Intervention in the Market Mechanism: The Petroleum Industry,* vol. 3, July 30, 1969, p. 1410.
16. *Ibid.,* pp. 1411, 1414–15.
17. *Ibid.,* p. 1417.
18. Willie Morris, *North Toward Home* (Boston: Houghton Mifflin, 1957), pp. 208–209, 213.
19. *Williston* (N.D.) *Daily Herald,* April 13, 1951, quoted by Robert Engler in *The Politics of Oil,* p. 11.

8: WINTER, 1970

1. Quoted in A. J. P. Taylor, *The Origins of the Second World War* (New York: Atheneum, 1966), p. 231.
2. *The Second World War: The Gathering Storm* (Boston: Houghton Mifflin Company, 1948), pp. 7, 9–10.
3. Quoted as preface to Garry Wills's *Nixon Agonistes: The Crisis of the Self-Made Man* (Boston: Houghton Mifflin, 1970).
4. Welles, *The Elusive Bonanza,* p. 225.
5. *Ibid.,* pp. 236, 237.
6. Engler, *The Politics of Oil,* p. 172.
7. *Ibid.,* pp. 132–33. Engler's source is a collection of I. G. Farben documents compiled at a 1946 Senate subcommittee hearing into the *Elimination of German Resources for War.*
8. *Ibid.,* pp. 107–108.
9. *Ibid.,* p. 191.
10. *Ibid.,* p. 196.
11. *Ibid.,* p. 277.
12. *Ibid.,* p. 431.

13. *Ibid.*, p. 197.
14. *The New York Times,* October 28, 1955, p. 6.
15. U.S., Cabinet Task Force on Oil Import Controls, *The Oil Import Question: A Report on the Relationship of Oil Imports to the National Security* (Washington, D.C.: Government Printing Office, 1970), Section 405d, p. 123.
16. *Ibid.*, Section 115, p. 8.
17. *Ibid.*, Section 116, p. 8.
18. *Ibid.*, Section 421, p. 128.
19. *Ibid.*, Section 423, p. 129. On this point, as on several others, the task force reaches conclusions similar to those of Eugene Rostow twenty-two years earlier. Rostow's *A National Policy for the Oil Industry* (New Haven: Yale University Press, 1948) predated the quota system, but on the general subject of import and other restraints he wrote, "Our system of oil law is wasteful and expensive; its consequences have no connection with its avowed purposes. It permits and strengthens monopolistic patterns of policy for an industry which, in an appropriate legal environment, might serve the community as a model of the social and economic benefits of competition. . . . If we were really serious about conserving our oil supply, we would eliminate our oil tariffs; we would use foreign oil in peace time and perhaps have a holiday in one or more areas of production, keeping the American oil extraction industry as a model plant and a standby for defense purposes; we would mix gasoline with alcohol made from grain; and we would discourage consumption by a horsepower tax and perhaps by a prohibition against using oil where coal or water power would do."
20. *Ibid.*, Section 422, p. 129.
21. *Ibid.*, Section 424 (1), p. 130.
22. *Ibid.*, Section 425, p. 131.
23. *Ibid.*, Appendix L, Section 7, p. 319.
24. *Ibid.*, Section 324, p. 8.
25. *Ibid.*, Section 307 (b and e), pp. 73, 74.
26. *Ibid.*, Section 317 (c), p. 84.
27. *Washington Star,* August 14, 1969, p. 1.
28. *Lewiston Daily Sun,* September 25, 1969, p. 1.
29. *Kennebec Journal,* November 22, 1969.
30. *Oil Daily,* November 12, 1969, p. 1.
31. As recorded in the *Congressional Record,* November 26, 1969, pp. S15109–10.
32. *St. Louis Post-Dispatch,* January 4, 1970, p. 2A.
33. *Congressional Record,* January 19, 1970, p. S93.
34. *The Oil Import Question,* Section 425 (a) (3) (e), p. 133.
35. *Congressional Record,* March 14, 1972, p. S3889.

36. *Oil Daily*, May 26, 1970.
37. *Congressional Record*, March 17, 1970, p. S3838.
38. "The Advocates," April 5, 1970, reprinted in the *Congressional Record*, April 10, 1970, p. S5569.
39. *Oil Daily*, July 20, 1970.
40. *The Oil Import Question*, Section 219, p. 35.
41. For the background to the *Times*'s story, including Smith's assertion that "Anti-oil people don't come up here badgering us to get their points of view across; the industry does. My job is to report about the industry. . . . I interview the President of Standard Oil of New Jersey; he gives me the partyline, and it is my job to quote him," see "Oily Reprints at the Times," *The Washington Monthly*, vol. 2, no. 9, November, 1970, pp. 23–28.
42. Washington *Post*, August 19, 1970.
43. *Oil Daily*, August 18, 1970.
44. *Ibid.*, August 19, 1970.
45. *Ibid.*, October 7, 1970.
46. Daniel Ellsberg, *Papers on the War* (New York: Simon and Schuster, 1972), pp. 132–33.
47. *Ibid.*, pp. 133–34.
48. *Ibid.*, p. 129.
49. Garry Wills, *Nixon Agonistes*, pp. 531–32.
50. *Oil Daily*, April 6, 1970.
51. Thomas Pynchon, *Gravity's Rainbow* (New York: Viking Press, 1973), pp. 520–21.
52. *The Greening of America*, pp. 215–16.
53. *The Elusive Bonanza*, pp. 81–82.
54. *Ibid.*, pp. 83–84.
55. *Ibid.*, pp. 521–22.
56. Thomas Pynchon, *Gravity's Rainbow*, pp. 521–22.
57. *The Oil Import Question*, Section 204, p. 20; Section 219, p. 35; Section 204 (c), p. 21.
58. *Ibid.*

9: MORE WINTER, 1970

1. Quoted in McPhee, *Encounters with the Archdruid*, p. 84.
2. Charles Raw, Bruce Page, and Godfrey Hodgson, *Do You Sincerely Want to Be Rich* (New York: Viking Press, 1971), Bantam edition, p. 383.
3. Raw et al., *Do You Sincerely Want to Be Rich*.
4. *Ibid.*, p. 401.
5. Abraham Briloff, *Unaccountable Accounting* (New York: Harper & Row, 1972), pp. 183–90.

6. *Business Week*, April 18, 1970, p. 68.
7. This strategy is discussed in the *Washington Star*, April 29, 1970, p. 8.
8. John Esposito et al., *Vanishing Air* (New York: Grossman, 1970), p. 298.
9. Norman Mailer, *St. George and the Godfather* (New York: New American Library, 1972), p. 38.
10. *Newsweek*, vol. 75, no. 7, February 16, 1970, p. 22.
11. *Kennebec Journal*, February 6, 1970.
12. *Askew* v. *American Waterways Operators, Inc.* 411 U.S. 325, at 329 (1973).

10: SPRING AND SUMMER, 1970

1. Arthur Simon, "Battle of Beaufort," *The New Republic*, vol. 162, no. 21, May 23, 1970, p. 13.
2. *The Unquiet Grave* (New York: Viking Press, 1945), p. 103.
3. *Boston Evening Globe*, March 13, 1972.
4. *Maine Times*, March 13, 1970.
5. Bangor *Daily News*, April 3, 1970, p. 1.
6. Portland *Press Herald*, February 6, 1970.
7. Raw et al., *Do You Sincerely Want to Be Rich*, p. 383.
8. U.S., Department of the Army, Corps of Engineers (New England Division), "Minutes of Public Hearing on the Application of King Resources Company for a Federal Permit to Construct a Large-Scale Oil Handling Facility in Casco Bay at Portland, Maine, on the Northwesterly Side of Long Island," Portland, April 16, 1970, p. 179.
9. Portland *Press Herald*, April 5, 1970.
10. *Ibid.*, May 23, 1970.
11. *Village of Euclid et al.* v. *Ambler Realty Company*, 272 U.S. 365, at 389 (1926).
12. John J. McNamara, *The Money Maker* (New York: Thomas Y. Crowell, Popular Library, 1972), p. 175.
13. *Ibid.*, p. 408.
14. U.S., Congress, Senate, Subcommittee on Air and Water Pollution of the Committee on Public Works, *The Relationship of Economic Development to Environmental Quality*, 91st Congress, 1st Session, Machias, September 9, 1970, p. 639.
15. *Ibid.*, p. 638.
16. *Ibid.*, September 8, 1970, p. 39.
17. *Ibid.*, p. 126.
18. *Ibid.*, pp. 147–148.
19. Portland *Press Herald*, September 29, 1970, p. 26.

20. *Ibid.*, October 24, 1970.
21. WABI-TV, WAGM-TV, WPOR radio, October 13, 1970.

11: LATE 1970–EARLY 1971

1. Rebecca West, *Black Lamb and Grey Falcon: A Journey through Yugoslavia* (New York: Viking Press, 1945), p. 1084.
2. Quoted in Peter Passell and Leonard Ross, *The Retreat from Riches: Affluence and Its Enemies* (New York: Viking Press, 1973), p. 183.
3. Roger Vaughan, "The Tempting of Tiverton," *Life*, vol. 71, no. 5, July 30, 1971, p. 55.
4. *Ibid.*, p. 57.
5. John Esposito et al., *Vanishing Air* (New York: Grossman, 1970), pp. 253–54.
6. *Ibid.*, p. 244.
7. *The New York Times*, April 1, 1971, p. 45.
8. *Ibid.*
9. B. F. Skinner, *Beyond Freedom and Dignity* (New York: Knopf, 1971), p. 212.
10. *Camden Herald*, February 18, 1971.
11. Portland *Press Herald*, February 11, 1971.
12. *Boston Globe*, February 3, 1971.
13. Rich, *The Coast of Maine*, p. 262.
14. Stephen Birmingham, *Our Crowd*, pp. 183–84. A virtually identical passage appears in Frieda Schiff Warburg's privately printed *Reminiscences of a Long Life* (New York, 1967), pp. 58–59.
15. Rich, *The Coast of Maine*, pp. 255–57.
16. Maurice Adelman, "Is the Oil Shortage Real? Oil Companies as OPEC Tax-Collectors," *Foreign Policy*, no. 9, Winter 1972–73, pp. 77–79.
17. *Ibid.*, pp. 71, 79–82.
18. *Ibid.*, p. 90.
19. James E. Akins, "The Oil Crisis: This Time the Wolf Is Here," *Foreign Affairs*, vol. 51, no. 3, April, 1973, pp. 462, 469–73.

12: 1971–1974

1. Quoted in Ellsberg, *Papers on the War*, p. 276.
2. David McCullough, *The Great Bridge* (New York: Simon and Schuster, 1972), pp. 540–42.
3. *Houston Chronicle*, December 6, 1972.
4. *Maine Sunday Telegram*, May 19, 1974, p. 2a.
5. U.S., Congress, Senate, Special Joint Subcommittee on Deepwater Ports Legislation, *Deepwater Port Act of 1973*, 93rd Congress, 1st Session, July 24, 1973, p. 206.

6. *Ibid.*

7. William Henry Kilby, comp., *Eastport and Passamaquoddy: A Collection of Historical and Biographical Sketches* (Eastport, Maine: Edward E. Shead & Co., 1888), p. 272.

8. *Energy, Heavy Industry, and the Maine Coast,* report to Governor Curtis, September, 1972, pp. 27–28.

9. *Ibid.,* p. 24.

10. *Ibid.,* p. 21.

11. René Dubos, *So Human an Animal* (New York: Charles Scribner's Sons, 1968), p. 171.

12. *Ibid.,* p. 237.

13. Rebecca West, *A Train of Powder* (New York: The Viking Press, 1955), p. 161.

14. John Cole, "Oil and Water," *Harper's Magazine,* vol. 243, no. 1458, November, 1971, p. 47.

15. *Maine Times,* November 30, 1973, p. 6.

16. John McPhee, *Encounters with the Archdruid,* p. 87.

17. *Ibid.,* p. 144.

18. Portland *Press Herald,* December 22, 1972.

19. *Toronto Globe and Mail,* August 1, 1973, p. 11.

20. *The New York Times,* December 30, 1973.

21. John Carmody, "The Energy Czar and His Crises," Washington *Post,* "Potomac" magazine section, November 11, 1973, p. 12.

22. *Providence Journal Bulletin,* December 15, 1973, p. 1.

23. Rebecca West, *Black Lamb and Grey Falcon,* p. 3.

Index

Index